Norms beyond Empire

Max Planck Studies in Global Legal History of the Iberian Worlds

Editor

Thomas Duve

The book volumes in the *Max Planck Studies in Global Legal History of the Iberian Worlds* publish research on legal history of areas which have been in contact with the Iberian empires during the early Modern and Modern period, in Europe, the Americas, Asia and Africa. Its focus is global in the sense that it is not limited to the imperial spaces as such but rather looks at the globalization of normativities within the space related to these imperial formations. It is global also in another sense: The volumes in the series pay special attention to the coexistence of a variety of normativities and their cultural translations in different places and moments, decentring classical research perspectives and opening up for different modes of normativity.

The monographs, edited volumes and text editions in the series are peer reviewed, and published in print and online.

Brill's Open Access books are discoverable through DOAB and distributed free of charge in Brill's E-Book Collections, and through OAPEN and JSTOR.

VOLUME 3

The titles published in this series are listed at *brill.com/mpiw*

Norms beyond Empire

Law-Making and Local Normativities in Iberian Asia, 1500–1800

Edited by

Manuel Bastias Saavedra

BRILL
NIJHOFF

LEIDEN | BOSTON

The Library of Congress Cataloging-in-Publication Data is available online at http://catalog.loc.gov
LC record available at http://lccn.loc.gov/2021044820

Typeface for the Latin, Greek, and Cyrillic scripts: "Brill". See and download: brill.com/brill-typeface.

ISSN 2590-3292
ISBN 978-90-04-47282-2 (hardback)
ISBN 978-90-04-47283-9 (e-book)

This book is printed on acid-free paper and produced in a sustainable manner.

Contents

Preface

In recent decades, research studies in legal history, international law, the history of empires, and global history have begun to look more closely at the relationship between law and empire. Within this, the study of empires has started to observe law more closely, through the lens of imperial law and legal pluralism, and legal historians have begun to consider the legal experience in colonial territories. These studies have moved away from previous narratives that focused on Europeans delivering civilization to the world, proposing critical and empirical readings of this process instead, highlighting the localization of law and the colonial origins of international law, as well as illustrating how much of European law was 'made in empire'. The research that articulates questions of law and empire, however, still tends to dedicate too much attention to the European experience, particularly concerning its focus on how European empires ruled their overseas territories and how European law was modified as a result of the colonial enterprise. American, Asian, and African experiences are usually not given a role other than as fields of action or objects of interest for European agents and legal scholars.

By focusing on case studies from the Iberian empires in Asia, this volume seeks to revise this narrative of law and empire by proposing a decentered perspective that places a multiplicity of normative arrangements at the center of observation. By focusing on the idea of normativity, it looks at the experiences of empire to understand how norms adapt to new conditions, how local communities navigate these changing normative orders, and how law-making was tied to diverse local histories, traditions, and practices. This approach allows integrating different orders of norms, from imperial law, canon law, and moral theology to local rituals, customs, and practices, as well as written traditions such as *Dharmaśāstra* and *Smṛti*, the *Ritsuryō*, and Confucian and Taoist philosophy. The case studies highlight these features of the relationship between law and empire by looking at China, India, Japan, and the Philippines, illustrating the ways in which the making of law in Iberian Asia drew from diverse experiences and normative knowledge beyond that of the empire to produce unique configurations of norms from place to place.

The question of law and empire also addresses the global origins of contemporary law and raises important analytical and methodological questions. Research being done from a global perspective has unsettled certain very deeply ingrained manners of conducting legal-historical research through the use of intertwined, connected, and more comparatively aware readings of national or regional legal histories. Further, the global perspective has reorganized the spatial framework of legal historiographical traditions, expanded the analytical categories of research, and strengthened non-hegemonic historical narratives. This has also led historians and legal historians to engage more deeply with how law was produced and reproduced across space and time. From this perspective, the local reproduction of norms is placed within a horizon of potentially global dimensions and highlights the coexistence and interaction of different normative orders.

The ten chapters of this volume thus restate the relationship between law and empire using this more nuanced perspective. The first chapter (Manuel Bastias Saavedra) provides an introductory study that places the historiographical discussion of law and empire within the context of Iberian imperialism in Asia. The following chapters explore normative production in China (Fupeng Li; Marina Torres Trimállez), the *Estado da Índia* (Patricia Souza de Faria; Miguel Rodrigues Lourenço; Ângela Barreto Xavier), Japan (Rômulo da Silva Ehalt; Luisa Stella de Oliveira Coutinho Silva), and the Philippines (Marya Svetlana T. Camacho; Abisai Perez Zamarripa). The volume also integrates a range of different themes of the Iberian experience in Asia ranging from the Christian mission (Coutinho Silva; Ehalt; Torres Trimállez) and Church history (Camacho; Faria; Lourenço) to the processes of empire-building (Perez; Xavier) and the influence of Western science in Asia (Li). The legal-historical topics discussed in the volume include the compilation/creation of local customs for imperial rule (Perez; Xavier), the adjustment or creation of rules and procedures to conform to local norms and societies (Faria; Lourenço; Torres Trimállez), the ways in which local conditions reshaped the practice of Catholic sacraments (Camacho; Coutinho Silva; Ehalt), and the articulation of norms with culturally diverse forms of knowledge and representations of time (Li). Finally, the chapters also illustrate the interaction between local norms and the circulation of normative knowledge, which not only involved connections between Asia and the Iberian Peninsula and Rome, but also reflected dense exchanges within Asia—Goa, Macau, Manila, Malacca—and between Asia and America.

The volume was produced under the very unique circumstances and disruptions of the global Covid pandemic. I am therefore grateful to the contributing authors for making the best out of what has been a very challenging year for everyone. The initial impulse for this volume came from the panel "The Iberian Empires and the Production of Normativities in Asia (1500–1800)", co-organized with Luisa Stella de Oliveira Coutinho Silva for the 49th Annual Meeting of the American Society for Legal History held in Boston in 2019. Ângela Barreto Xavier's contribution was presented in the "Norms and Empires Lecture Series" at the Max Planck Institute for Legal History and Legal Theory, within the context of the joint project "Glocalizing Normativities: A Global Legal History (15th–21st Centuries)". I would like to thank the participants of these events for the discussion of these papers. I would also like to thank the anonymous peer-reviewers and the colleagues of the Max Planck Institute for Legal History and Legal Theory for their detailed and insightful comments on the chapters. Melissa Aramayo was of great assistance in the formal revision of the manuscript and Christian Pogies kindly helped with the design of the charts. I also particularly appreciate Miguel Rodrigues Lourenço's help in revising the final manuscript. Finally, I would like to thank Nicole Pasakarnis for her support in the editorial process.

Manuel Bastias Saavedra
Frankfurt am Main, May 2021

Illustrations

Figures

Charts

Tables

Notes on Contributors

Bastias Saavedra, Manuel
is Researcher at the Max Planck Institute for Legal History and Legal Theory (Frankfurt am Main).

Camacho, Marya Svetlana T.
is Associate Professor at the University of Asia and the Pacific (Manila).

Coutinho Silva, Luisa Stella de Oliveira
is Researcher at the Max Planck Institute for Legal History and Legal Theory (Frankfurt am Main).

Ehalt, Rômulo da Silva
is Researcher at the Max Planck Institute for Legal History and Legal Theory (Frankfurt am Main).

Faria, Patricia Souza de
is Professor in the History Department at the Universidade Federal Rural do Rio de Janeiro (UFRRJ).

Li, Fupeng
is Associate Professor at the Law School of the China University of Political Science and Law (Beijing) and Affiliate Researcher at the Max Planck Institute for Legal History and Legal Theory (Frankfurt am Main).

Lourenço, Miguel Rodrigues
is Researcher at the Center for the Humanities (CHAM, FCSH, Universidade NOVA de Lisboa), the Center of Religious History Studies (Universidade Católica Portuguesa), and of the Cathedra of Sephardic Studies Alberto Benveniste (Universidade de Lisboa).

Perez Zamarripa, Abisai
is a PhD candidate in History and a student of Data Science and Statistics at the University of Texas at Austin.

Torres Trimállez, Marina
is Researcher in the Department of Early Modern History of the Universidad de Cantabria.

Xavier, Ângela Barreto
is Researcher at the Institute of Social Sciences (ICS) of the Universidade de Lisboa.

CHAPTER 1

Decentering Law and Empire: Law-Making, Local Normativities, and the Iberian Empires in Asia

Manuel Bastias Saavedra

1 Introduction

Although they constantly shape behavior and nudge people to act in certain ways, norms tend to be taken for granted. Taking off shoes or removing a hat when entering a sacred space are not merely the result of individual decisions made upon crossing the threshold of a temple; they are appropriate ways of acting in that specific context and they signal conformity with a norm. This can also be noticed when one does not know the appropriate behavior and so looks around for social cues: if others take off their shoes, it may perhaps be appropriate to do so too—even if we do not know why. In this sense, norms have a way of being always present yet going unnoticed; that is, until a violation exposes our normative expectations. For example, social faux pas, such as arriving underdressed to a cocktail party or overdressed to an informal gathering, only once they happen, reveal that conventions and expectations have been offended. Beyond the transitory embarrassment, the consequences of such violations are not necessarily grave. But the offence itself shows that, until then, everyone else at the gathering had been observing an implicit and intuitive norm. And besides those that are implicitly and intuitively followed, conventions, standards, commandments, rules, and laws, among innumerable others, are also norms that are—to a greater or lesser extent—institutionalized or explicitly stated.

As they tend to structure behaviors, utterances, and practices, historians have long confronted the question of whether it is possible to study norms at all. On the one hand, historical sources reveal what people said and did, but they rarely show what they believed, thought, or understood while saying and doing so. On the other hand, since norms are pervasive and are grounded in culture and experience, people do not simply act arbitrarily, instead operating by following norms and evaluating the consequences of offending them. These norms can thus be reconstructed through historical sources with careful attention to the practices.[1] This latter approach can be said to focus on *normativity*: instead of merely seeking to describe what people said and did, it uses these behaviors and utterances as ways of looking into their broader normative content. To use some examples from this volume, wearing a hat when attending mass, providing shelter to missionaries, or deciding on the date of a wedding are all actions and decisions which can be simply described as such, but they can also be described as complying with or defying explicit or implicit normative expectations. And, often, acting in a certain way or saying certain things is not as straightforward as it seems, but in fact pits interests against norms, as well as different kinds of norms against each other. Accordingly, looking at normativity means paying attention to both the factuality and the normative meanings attached to different practices, behaviors, and utterances.

The sharp distinction between norms and practices has certainly been shaped by the contemporary difference between legal norms and other kinds of norms (social, moral, religious, etc.). This difference, however, is relatively recent. Early modern European law was a complex repository of norms that not only included laws, edicts, and ordinances, but also encompassed a wide range of habits, conventions, customs, values, and moral instructions. The production of norms was not centralized in the hands of political power, and explicitly formulated *laws* were not the only norms that composed the corpus of law. Instead, law was understood to be spontaneously produced through social life; longstanding traditions, conventions, habits, and other social norms were understood to derive their validity from the mere fact that they were followed. In this sense, "the juridical sphere and that of factuality tended to merge; the dimension of 'validity' ceded to that of 'efficacy'".[2] Norms were thus not imposed on social reality, but *derived* from it. Practices, social mores, and the *status quo*—as a prevailing factual order—were, in and of themselves, considered to have a deep juridical undergirding in their quality of, ultimately, having derived from divine creation. The hypostatization of the distinctions between legal and non-legal norms, between facts and norms, and between norms and practices is a phenomenon of perhaps only the last 250 years, during which time law was reimagined as a purely normative sphere, detached from social life more generally.

The distinction between legal and non-legal norms has since created a kind of disciplinary division of labor. While anthropologists and sociologists have

---

1 In a recent debate, these positions have been argued, respectively, by Lauren Benton and Tamar Herzog in their contributions in: Owensby and Ross (eds.), *Justice in a New World: Negotiating Legal Intelligibility in British, Iberian, and Indigenous America.*

2 Grossi, *El Orden Jurídico Medieval*, 75. All translations in this chapter are mine.

focused on rituals, taboos, social roles, institutions, religious and cultural practices, *habitus*, and a wide variety of informal and non-legal norms anchored in social practices, the world of formal law became the focus of legal scholars, legal theorists, and legal historians. Social and cultural historians, for their part, have moved between these disciplinary boundaries but have not always successfully recognized the normativity of social life nor the factual dimension of the legal system. This division of labor, however, has been slowly but steadily eroded in recent decades by interdisciplinary approaches from legal sociology to legal pluralism. Recent legal-historical approaches have further moved to dissolve the distinction between legal and non-legal norms, which had become increasingly problematic as research began to favor global historical perspectives by moving toward studying normativity and the production of normative knowledge.[3] Understanding the ways in which decentralized processes of normative production occurred in different times and places is now increasingly the focus of a global legal history.[4]

This volume, as a contribution to this effort, looks at the way in which norms were constructed in the Iberian empires in Asia. The arrival of the Portuguese in Calicut in 1498 and the Castilians in Cebu in 1521 transformed the Iberian age of explorations into a decidedly global enterprise. In little more than a century, between 1415 and 1529, what had begun as a struggle between Portugal and Castile to control the islands and positions gained in West Africa and the Atlantic turned into a transoceanic competition to reach the Indies and secure control of the Spice Islands of Ternate and Tidore, on the other side of the globe. While the Portuguese quickly set about laying the foundations of their *Estado da Índia*, as the Portuguese empire in Asia came to be known,[5] Castilians would only begin to establish secure footing in the region once Andrés de Urdaneta finally discovered the return route between the Philippines and New Spain, across the Pacific, in 1565.[6] This era of long-distance voyages would inaugurate the centuries-long presence of the Iberian empires in Asia characterized by tenuous, disparate, and fragmented jurisdictions with many centers that connected settlements, goods, persons, and institutions across the Atlantic, the Pacific, and the Indian oceans.

3 Duve, "What is Global Legal History?"; Duve, "Rechtsgeschichte als Geschichte von Normativitätswissen?".

4 This is the focus of the joint project 'Glocalizing Normativities: A Global Legal History (15th–21st centuries)' carried out at the Max Planck Institute for Legal History and Legal Theory.

5 Disney, *The Portuguese in India and other Studies, 1500–1700*; Subrahmanyam, *The Portuguese Empire in Asia, 1500–1700: A Political and Economic History*; Thomaz, *De Ceuta a Timor*.

6 Gruzinski, *Las Cuatro Partes del Mundo: Historia de una Mundialización*; Spate, *The Spanish Lake*.

The complex geopolitics of the region, the articulation of secular and religious interests, and the combination of formal and informal enterprises make the expansion of the Iberian empires in Asia an excellent backdrop for the study of normative production and change. First, Portuguese and Castilians encountered well-established trade networks and competed for influence with numerous powerful empires. Though the Portuguese were quite successful in securing control of navigation and commerce in the Indian Ocean, from East Africa to the Moluccas, the presence of important competing empires, such as the Mughals, the Safavids, the Ottomans, the Ming, and the Vijayanagara, limited their territorial control to small territorial enclaves that articulated spaces of supply (Goa), strategic outposts (Malacca and Hormuz), and areas of logistic importance (Mozambique).[7] Portuguese influence in Asia also limited the Castilian presence to the islands of Luzon and the Visayas in the Philippines, which were similarly threatened by powerful empires and neighboring sultanates. Whether it was in defining the relations between imperial polities, establishing commercial treaties, organizing imperial jurisdictions, or defining the ways in which inhabitants would be ruled, these geopolitical conditions created an intense need for regulation and provoked shifts in such rules as the balance of power changed over time.

Second, evangelization was a central element of the Iberian empires and, thus, with imperial expansion came the Catholic Church. The *Padroado* and the *Patronato* placed the crowns of Portugal and Castile, respectively, in charge of the administration of ecclesiastical affairs in their territories. Bishoprics and dioceses were created across Asia throughout the 16th and 17th centuries, and spiritual centers were created with the elevation of Goa (1558) and Manila (1595) to archdioceses. With the Church also came the Inquisition. As such, the Inquisition was only established in Goa (1560), where it functioned until its final suppression in 1812. In the Philippines, the Inquisition was established in 1583, represented by a commissary but dependent on the Tribunal of the Holy Office in New Spain in Mexico City. The Philippine Inquisition was abolished in 1821, one year after the abolition of its Spanish counterpart.[8] Additionally, since the Church had jurisdiction over all Christian communities in Asia, its influence was often territorially much vaster than that of the Iberian crowns.[9] Missionaries frequently became "'first conquerors', 'pioneers', of political expansion",[10] opening spaces that would later be incorporated into royal jurisdiction, and

7 Thomaz, *De Ceuta a Timor*, 30.

8 Angeles, "The Philippine Inquisition: A Survey"; Paiva, "The Inquisition Tribunal in Goa: Why and for What Purpose?".

9 Hespanha, *Filhos da Terra: Identidades Mestiças nos Confins da Expansão Portuguesa*, 205.

10 Xavier and Olival, "O Padroado da Coroa de Portugal: Fundamentos e Práticas", 147.

also integrating populations that were otherwise never under direct control of the Iberian crowns.[11] While Japan was perhaps the most emblematic case of this latter phenomenon, Portuguese and Spanish missionaries reached Persia, the Mughal Empire, Tibet, Bhutan and inland China.[12] The presence of the Church in Asia was important for the generation of norms not only because it regulated important aspects of social and religious life both within and outside the jurisdiction of the Iberian empires, but also because it fostered dense networks of normative communication with important spiritual centers in Mexico City, Manila, Goa, and Macau—often beyond the influence of Rome, Lisbon, and Madrid.[13]

Third, while the Portuguese imperial network was reinforced in the western Indian Ocean, where the military and administrative focus of the *Estado da Índia* was placed, its expansion toward Southeast Asia and the Far East was carried out through a combination of formal and informal enterprises. The process of 'informal colonization', spurred by adventurers, renegades, merchants, missionaries, and pirates, who created "pockets of Portuguese across Asia from the Levant to China",[14] created settlements that either were eventually formally integrated into the empire, as with Macau (founded in 1557),[15] or led to communities of Portuguese that lived under foreign rule, as with Nagasaki (founded in 1570).[16] The trade routes themselves came under imperial jurisdiction with the establishment of the *nau do trato*, an annual voyage that connected Goa with Japan via Macau, under the auspices of the Portuguese Crown and led by a *Capitão-Mor*. The *Capitão-Mor* not only enjoyed jurisdiction over the ships of the voyage but, until 1623, also acted as the interim Governor of Macau during

11 Subrahmanyam, *The Portuguese Empire in Asia, 1500–1700*, 262 ff.

12 Hespanha, "Uncommon Laws: Law in the Extreme Peripheries of an Early Modern Empire", 193; Details in: Brockey, *Journey to the East: The Jesuit Mission to China, 1579–1724*; Didier, *Le Portugais au Tibet: Les Premières Relations Jésuits (1624–1635)*; Flannery, *The Mission of the Portuguese Augustinians to Persia and Beyond (1602–1747)*; Menegon, *Ancestors, Virgins, & Friars: Christianity as a Local Religion in Late Imperial China*.

13 This occurred through the circulation of *casos de conciencia* and opinions, as shown in the chapters by Luisa Coutinho, Rômulo Ehalt, and Marina Torres Trimállez in this volume (Chapters 6, 8, and 9), but also through the production of doctrinal treatises. On the latter, see Duve, Egío and Birr (eds.), *The School of Salamanca: A Case of Global Knowledge Production*.

14 Russell-Wood, "Patterns of Settlement in the Portuguese Empire", 178. For some detailed depictions of this process, see Disney, *A History of Portugal and the Portuguese Empire: From Beginnings to 1807*, vol. 2, chap. 21; Hespanha, *Filhos da terra*; Subrahmanyam, *The Portuguese empire in Asia, 1500–1700*, especially chap. 9.

15 Boxer, *Portuguese Society in the Tropics: The Municipal Councils of Goa, Macao, Bahia, and Luanda, 1510–1800*.

16 Subrahmanyam, *The Portuguese empire in Asia, 1500–1700*, 110.

his stay in port and had jurisdiction over the Portuguese community in Nagasaki.[17] Here, one sees to what extent the empire was represented not only by territorial control, but also "by floating networks of maritime routes, where the seat of power could be the mobile deck of a military or trade vessel".[18] The Spanish informal empire, for its part, was represented by more or less successful missions launched from Manila toward East Asia and Southeast Asia,[19] and to the Mariana Islands (1668) and the Caroline Islands (1710) in the Pacific.[20] The Iberian presence in Asia was thus not always marked by a guided process of 'empire-building' but also included tenuous and interstitial jurisdictions guided by disparate interests and governed by different centers of power.

The Iberian empires in Asia set in motion a profound process of normative production and change throughout the region, but the empires themselves were never monolithically in control of how this process unfolded. This volume thus proposes a look at the Iberian empires in Asia to think about *norms beyond empire* in a dual sense. First, it seeks to move the historiographical focus *beyond empire* to highlight the ways in which law-making and local normativities operated beyond colonial rule. Second, it suggests a focus on *norms* as a way of escaping the often too narrow concept of law and to highlight the manifold underlying assumptions, deep-seated convictions, and cultural paradigms that shaped the way people governed, worshiped, and organized collective life.

The remainder of this introductory chapter lays out the historiographical debates about empire and law that shape this discussion and suggests that legal-historical research has reached a point where it should move toward a decentered history of law. The contributions in this volume draw on cases from South India, China, Japan, and the Philippines to illustrate different ways of dealing with these historiographical challenges, shedding light on how the history of the Iberian empires in Asia can be revisited with a focus on the law-making power of local normativities.

2 From Imperial History to Law

There has been much discussion about whether the Iberian experience, in Asia and elsewhere, was an imperial experience at all. Anthony Pagden has

17 Boxer, *The Great Ship from Amacon*.

18 Hespanha, "Uncommon Laws", 189.

19 Martínez Shaw and Alfonso Mola, "The Philippine Islands: A Vital Crossroads during the First Globalization Period", 32 ff.

20 Coello de la Rosa, *Jesuits at the Margins: Missions and Missionaries in the Marianas (1668–1769)*.

noted that in Europe until the 17th century the word 'empire' was only used to denote the Holy Roman Empire or as an equivalent of the idea of sovereignty: "Neither the Spanish nor the Portuguese, nor even the French, ever spoke of 'empire' [as an extended and detached empire] and the British only began doing so consistently after the loss of America".[21] During the process of territorial consolidation that began through the conquest of the Muslim lands of the Iberian peninsula, the ideas of 'kingdom' (*reino*) and 'Crown' (*corona*) became commonly used in Portugal and Spain, respectively, to designate the idea of a superior territorial and jurisdictional power. Though the notion of empire constituted a powerful idea that guided the overseas expansion, neither Spain nor Portugal ever officially designated their possessions as composing an empire.[22] At the height of the 16th century, the image that Spain still cultivated for its European and overseas possessions was that of a composite monarchy—a kingdom that ruled over various kingdoms.[23] António Manuel Hespanha has called attention to the titles of the Kings of Portugal and Spain to reveal the composite nature of their rule, encompassing claims to territorial dominion, immaterial jurisdiction, and vague geographical references—including an indefinite "etc." for "unlisted and virtual political jurisdictional claims".[24]

While in Portugal the use of the idea of 'empire' became tied to nationalist and imperialist political discourses of the 19th and 20th centuries, the historiographical use of 'Spanish empire', according to a recent survey, was only introduced by British historian J. H. Parry in the 1960s.[25] Since then, it has become increasingly common to speak of a Portuguese or a Spanish 'empire',[26]

21 Pagden, "Afterword: from Empire to Federation", 259.

22 Cardim and Hespanha, "A Estrutura Territorial das duas Monarquia Ibéricas (Séculos XVI-XVIII)", 76.

23 Elliott, "A Europe of Composite Monarchies"; Koenigsberger, "Monarchies and Parliaments in Early Modern Europe Dominium Regale or Dominium Politicum et Regale".

24 The official title of the Portuguese Kings, as provided by Hespanha, was as follows: "Pela Graça de Deus, Rei de Portugal e dos Algarves, d'Aquém e d'Além-Mar em África, Senhor da Guiné e da Conquista, Navegação e Comércio da Etiópia, Arábia, Pérsia e Índia, etc.". The title of the Spanish Kings: "Pela Graça de Deus, Rei de Castela, de Leão, de Aragão, das Duas Sicílias, de Jerusalém, [de Portugal,] de Navarra, de Granada, de Toledo, de Valência, da Galiza, de Maiorca, de Sevilha, da Sardenha, de Córdova, da Córsega, de Múrcia, de Jáen, dos Algarves, de Algeciras, de Gibraltar, das Ilhas de Canária, das Índias Orientais e Ocidentais, Ilhas e Terra Firme do Mar-Oceano, Conde de Barcelona, Senhor da Biscaia e de Molina, Duque de Atenas e de Neopátria, Conde de Rossilhão e da Cerdanha, Marquês de Oristano e de Gociano, Arquiduque de Áustria, Duque da Borgonha, do Brabante e de Milão, Conde de Habsburgo, da Flandres e do Tirol, etc.". See Hespanha, "Uncommon Laws", 188.

25 Hausser and Pietschmann, "Empire: The Concept and its Problems in the Historiography on the Iberian Empires in the Early Modern Age", 11.

26 Disney, *A History of Portugal and the Portuguese Empire*; Flores, "The Iberian Empires, 1400 to 1800"; Subrahmanyam, *The Portuguese Empire in Asia, 1500–1700*.

though the ideas of 'expansion',[27] 'monarchy',[28] and 'world'[29] are still used as alternatives. The more recent proliferation of the idea of empire has followed other historiographical trends of the past 30 years, particularly those related to the critique of methodological nationalism. To a certain extent, following the rise of Atlantic and global history, the concept of empire became a way to both broaden historical research beyond the borders of the nation state and construct new units of comparison. This has led to a multiplication of studies that explore the development of single empires, inter-imperial competition in a regional perspective,[30] diachronic and synchronic comparisons between empires,[31] and empires in their connections.[32]

Agreement on a concept of empire has, however, remained elusive. Being more of an analytical category than a historical one, linked to a more recent 'imperial turn', it is perhaps important to recall what the idea of empire is meant to convey. Of course, this is not a straightforward issue, since the concept is intended to make both diachronic and synchronic comparisons possible, thus integrating a temporally and geographically wide range of political formations. The question also poses issues of commensurability across cultures—a question posed by Jack Fairey and Brian P. Farrell: "are *tianxia* in Chinese, *pādhsāhī* in Persian, and *samrājya* in Sanskrit, for example, all interchangeable words for 'empire', or did they describe fundamentally different kinds of entities?".[33] The issues of commensurability are not restricted to differences between, but also apply to differences within world regions; the Dutch, French, British, and other European empires were not exactly congruent political formations.[34] Even despite their cultural affinities, Portugal and Castile constructed two quite distinct forms of empire, and the American often contrasted starkly with the Asian experience.[35]

27 Bethencourt and Curto (eds.), *Portuguese Oceanic Expansion, 1400–1800*; Boxer, *Igreja Militante e a Expansão Ibérica 1440–1770*; Hespanha, *Filhos da terra.*

28 Xavier, Palomo and Stumpf (eds.), *Monarquias Ibéricas em Perspectiva Comparada (Séculos XVI-XVIII): Dinâmicas Imperiais e Circulação de Modelos Político-Administrativos.*

29 Bouza, Cardim and Feros (eds.), *The Iberian World: 1450–1820.*

30 Brunero, Fairey and Farrell (eds.), *Empire in Asia: A New Global History.*

31 Alcock et al. (eds.), *Empires: Perspectives from Archaeology and History*; Burbank and Cooper, *Empires in World History: Power and the Politics of Difference.*

32 Subrahmanyam, *Empires between Islam and Christianity, 1500–1800.*

33 Fairey and Farrell, "Reordering an Imperial Modern Asia", 4.

34 Pagden, "Afterword: From Empire to Federation".

35 Biedermann, *The Portuguese in Sri Lanka and South India: Studies in the History of Diplomacy, Empire and Trade, 1500–1650*, 34; Subrahmanyam, *Empires between Islam and Christianity, 1500–1800*, 6–7.

Despite these difficulties, it may be possible to combine the diverse definitions of empire into two groups: a metropolitan and a cosmopolitan image of empire. The metropolitan image of empire hinges on the idea of a center that is capable of subordinating the territories under its rule. This idea is based on the experience of what Pagden has called the 'second European empires', typical of the colonial projects of the mid-19th and 20th centuries and ideologically shaped more by nationalism than by Roman universalism.[36] Empire, in this image, is primarily defined through distinctions between center and periphery or metropole and colony, and is characterized by the center's capacity to unilaterally impose political, economic, and cultural control over its periphery.[37] This is, for example, the implicit view observed in much of the literature reviewed by Christian Hausser and Horst Pietschmann: "the latest works continue to be based above all on the most recent conjuncture of 'empire' and as such follow the same lines as the usual fuzzy concepts – a political structure of immense scale, often transcontinental, oriented politically, economically and also in part culturally toward a centre that itself radiates towards the periphery".[38] The center in this notion of empire tends to be equated with Europe and has not only been used to describe the imperial experiences of the 19th and 20th centuries, but has also been transposed to the early modern period, particularly in international law scholarship.[39]

In the cosmopolitan image, by contrast, empire is understood as a form of political rule defined by expansive and expansionist territorial dominion, often achieved through conquest, by composite and layered distribution of political power, and by higher or lower tolerance of ethnic, cultural, and religious diversity.[40] This image of empire has been used to include a wide range of imperial experiences from all over the world and from antiquity until the early 19th century. Underlying this view is often—though not always—a con-

36 Pagden, *Lords of All the World: Ideologies of Empire in Spain, Britain and France c. 1500–c.1800*, 9.

37 Subrahmanyam, *Empires between Islam and Christianity, 1500–1800*, 6.

38 Hausser and Pietschmann, "Empire", 7.

39 See, for example, Halperin and Palan, "Introduction: Legacies of Empire", 10; Also: Maier, *Among Empires: American Ascendancy and Its Predecessors*; Roper and Van Ruymbeke (eds.), *Constructing Early Modern Empires: Proprietary Ventures in the Atlantic World, 1500–1750*.

40 Cooper, *Colonialism in Question: Theory, Knowledge, History*, chap. 6; Fairey and Farrell, "Reordering an Imperial Modern Asia", 5; Howe, *Empire: A Very Short Introduction*, 30; Kumar, *Visions of Empire: How Five Imperial Regimes Shaped the World*; Subrahmanyam, "Written on Water: Designs and Dynamics in the Portuguese Estado da Índia", 2001, reprint 2005, 43; Wendehorst (ed.), *Die Anatomie frühneuzeitlicher Imperien: Herrschaftsmanagement jenseits von Staat und Nation Institutionen, Personal und Techniken*.

trast with the homogenizing tendencies of the nation-state, emphasizing the plural and differentiated distribution of power that characterized the political forms before the 19th century. Jane Burbank and Frederick Cooper have synthesized this point as follows: "The concept of empire presumes that different peoples within the polity will be governed differently".[41] Unlike the metropolitan perspective, which focuses on the influences of the center on its periphery, this approach highlights the internal diversity and fluidity of the imperial system and thus allows for a plural—but not for this reason less violent—articulation between the different regions, networks, and interests that composed the imperial space. The cosmopolitan and the metropolitan images, thus, share the idea of asymmetrical integration and the use of violence and force as means for political control.

This distinction between the metropolitan and the cosmopolitan images are meant to convey how historians tend to think, either explicitly or implicitly, about the problem of empire. While the former understands empire in terms of centralization and standardization, the latter focuses on its internal complexity, the fluidity of its territories and composite parts, and the general flexibility it had as a form of political rule. In a way, one could argue that the cosmopolitan image was meant to provide an alternative to the metropolitan view as a growing variety of political models, world regions, and historical periods have been included in the historiography of empire. As Sanjay Subrahmanyam has noted, the issue at the heart of this has been, "namely, that various sorts of imperial polities have existed in the past, which do not all conform to a single profile, with a contiguous landmass, centralized fiscal and cadastral organizations, and powerful and continuous military presence in peripheries that are rigorously controlled from a well-defined center".[42] Zoltán Biedermann has, perhaps, framed it most eloquently by arguing that, in political models characterized by complexity and uncertainty, "it is crucial that we allow the words 'empire' and 'imperial' sufficient space to breathe".[43]

Even though these differing concepts of empire present quite divergent images of how rule was organized, within this literature law has often been restricted to a metropolitan image. The relative consistency of legal systems throughout the contemporary world is often seen as the outcome of a process though which European law was imposed on the non-European world through imperialism. This view was synthesized in Wolfgang J. Mommsen's introduction to the volume *European Expansion and Law*, published in 1992:

---

41 Burbank and Cooper, *Empires in World History*, 8.

42 Subrahmanyam, "Written on Water", 44.

43 Biedermann, *The Portuguese in Sri Lanka and South India*, 34.

> There is no doubt that during the period of European expansion the introduction of Western principles of law, although through the back door of special colonial law designed originally to maintain colonial control, had a lasting impact upon the societies in the non-Western world, and still continues to do so, which in hindsight may be judged at least in part as beneficial.[44]

In the same volume, Jörg Fisch argued that this outcome was not in all cases an intended effect of empire. European law moved across the world, sometimes, as a concomitant effect of migration and, other times, as an explicit instrument of rule. Ultimately, according to this view, "law was certainly not only a stabilizing factor for European rule but also an important agent for extending it, whether in the political or in the economic field".[45] Europe was thus placed at the center of empire, and law was seen as radiating, in diverse manners, toward a non-European world that was conceived as a periphery.

This volume was seminal in its focus on the relationship between law and empire and anticipated the formation of a field that, since the 2000s, has rapidly grown in significance.[46] This emerging field has expanded research to include postcolonial perspectives while attempting to move the focus of law from the center of empire toward its peripheries.[47] Unlike the characterization presented above, the more recent historiography of law and empire tends to take a more critical view of European law.[48] Antony Anghie, for example, has pointed to the colonial origins of international law and shown how the violence and discrimination inherent to its 'civilizing mission' continues to pervade international law until today.[49] Lauren Benton's work has taken the 'colonial origins' perspective in a different direction, detaching international law from its supposedly European origin and making it the result of an "ordered and contested multiculturalism"[50] that played out in the practice of solving conflicts across different local scenarios.[51] Other recent ways of understanding the

44 Mommsen, "Introduction", 13.

45 Fisch, "Law as a Means and as an End: Some Remarks on the Function of European and Non-European Law in the Process of European Expansion", 33.

46 Benton, "AHR Forum: Law and Empire in Global Perspective: Introduction", 1092.

47 Especially: Anghie, *Imperialism, Sovereignty, and the Making of International Law*; Benton, *Law and Colonial Cultures: Legal Regimes in World History, 1400–1900*; Benton, *A Search for Sovereignty: Law and Geography in European Empires, 1400–1900*.

48 Among others: Koskenniemi, Rech and Jiménez Fonseca (eds.), *International Law and Empire: Historical Explorations*; Pitts, *Boundaries of the International: Law and Empire*.

49 Anghie, *Imperialism, Sovereignty, and the Making of International Law*.

50 Benton, *Law and Colonial Cultures*, 7.

51 A good overview can be found in: Benton, "Made in Empire: Finding the History of International Law in Imperial Locations".

relation between law and empire can also be found in the connections established between imperial history and legal pluralism: "pluralistic legal structures were the norm [...] inside empires, both in spaces considered homeland [...] as well as in more distant regions into which empires expanded".[52]

The idea of law in this more recent literature is, however, still tied to a metropolitan image of empire. First, despite its more critical view, the literature of international law views international law, but also increasingly private law, as an instrument of empire.[53] Second, in a related manner, it shares with Mommsen and Fisch the idea that law is a European cultural achievement that was diffused to the non-Western world through violence and coercion in the process of colonization. The focus on certain treatises and authors (Grotius, Vitoria, Vattel, to name a few) tends to place the creation and development of law in Europe—even if it was shaped through the colonial experience.[54] Third, though legal pluralism is recognized as a basic feature of law in empire, the assumption is that this is the case because it was *allowed* by power holders. Legal pluralism is thus simply seen as another way in which the metropolis governed. Finally, though Benton's displacement of law-making from the metropolis to the periphery is certainly an important methodological step in the right direction, the interest still remains more prevalent in empire than in law. On the one hand, this is due to a narrow concept of law, reduced to the way in which law is mobilized in 'political' conflict and struggle. Thomas Duve has labeled this approach "a history of colonial laws of empires".[55] On the other hand, the focus on 'legal practice' explicitly requires historians to ignore norms and the "'normative structures' operating in deep background to legal behavior and utterances"[56] while, at the same time, restricting legal behavior to courts and other formal instances of legal decision-making.[57]

52 Burbank and Cooper, "Rules of Law, Politics of Empire", 281; Also, more generally: Benton and Ross (eds.), *Legal Pluralism and Empires, 1500–1850*; Duindam et al. (eds.), *Law and Empire: Ideas, Practices, Actors*; For a good overview of this in the context of Central Europe, see: Härter, "Das heilige römische Reich deutscher Nation als mehrschichtiges Rechtsystem, 1495–1806".

53 Koskenniemi, "Introduction: International Law and Empire: Aspects and Approaches".

54 For an interesting example of a different approach, including the literature therein cited, see: Weststeijn, "Provincializing Grotius: International Law and Empire in a Seventeenth-Century Malay Mirror".

55 Duve, "What is Global Legal History?", 30.

56 Benton, "In Defense of Ignorance: Frameworks for Legal Politics in the Atlantic World", 280. Two critical comments of this approach can be found in: Duve, "What is Global Legal History?"; Herzog, "What Natives Said and How Europeans Responded in Late-Seventeenth- and Eighteenth-Century Portuguese America", in Owensby; Ross, *Justice in a New World*.

57 Especially, Benton, "The Legal Regime of the South Atlantic World, 1400–1750: Jurisdictional Complexity as Institutional Order".

3 From Legal History to Empire

The idea of law that dominated the Iberian worldview was nevertheless broader than an 'imperial' image may suggest. Law was a pervasive presence. Thought to derive from God, it had a quasi-ontological quality and was understood as an ordering force that could be found both in nature and in all kinds of human institutions and practices.[58] Animals, for example, were thought to have legal capacities—in substance equal or analogous to those of humans—and stood in legal relationships with each other and with other things. Thus, lands, animals, and things could be 'punished' or enjoy rights and privileges.[59] Colors equally conveyed legal meanings and were to be worn on certain parts of the body or were reserved to specific dignitaries.[60] And within the human realm, etiquette, manners, rituals, ceremonies, and all kinds of behaviors were considered to convey legal meaning and, if improperly performed, could lead to injury and liability. Social relationships were linked to emotions and affections and were, accordingly, performed and reinforced through external manifestations: "To bow or to stand, to kiss the hands or the face, to take off the hat or to put it on were corporal dispositions from which one could infer corresponding internal dispositions".[61] Honor, duty, obedience, freedom, and faith were not only meant to be important ideals, but also had to be publicly performed and seen.[62] This "pan-juridification of the world", as Hespanha has called it, meant that law acted more as a cultural paradigm, "so deeply rooted that it extend[ed] over a wide set of normative discourses, like moral theology, ethics, economy [...] and politics".[63]

This juridical worldview has been reconstructed in the past three decades by Spanish, Portuguese, and Italian legal historians, who have tried to move away from legalist and statist conceptions of contemporary law to rediscover the alterity of the *ancien régime* by drawing on its peculiar anthropology.[64] In this

58 Grossi, *El Orden Jurídico Medieval*.

59 Girgen, "The Historical and Contemporary Prosecution and Punishment of Animals"; Humphrey, "Bugs and Beasts before the Law".

60 Hespanha, "As Cores e a Institução da Ordem no Mundo de Antigo Regime".

61 Hespanha, "Early Modern Law and the Anthropological Imagination of Old European Culture", 196.

62 To understand how this is embodied and practiced by the magistrate, see: Vallejo, "Acerca del Fruto del Árbol de los Jueces: Escenarios de la Justicia en la Cultura del Ius Commune".

63 Hespanha, "Early Modern Law and the Anthropological Imagination of Old European Culture", 201.

64 Clavero, *Tantas Personas como Estados: Por una Antropología Política de la Historia Europea*; Clavero, *Antídora: Antropología Católica de la Economía Moderna*; Grossi, *El Orden Jurídico Medieval*; Hespanha, *Como os Juristas viam o Mundo. 1550–1750: Direitos, Estados,*

worldview, law was guided by two underlying principles that fundamentally differ from what we understand as its central underpinnings today. First, in this normative order, law was understood to derive not from the state or political power, but from divine creation and, as such, preceded and transcended human intervention. This helps explain the pervasive view of law: God created order from chaos and gave its place to everything that was in the world, and thus humans, animals, and things, and the relations between and among them, were governed in substance by the same rules. This was a holistic conception in which law was not considered to be substantively different from natural and social reality itself.

Second, human existence was not understood as oriented toward the unfolding of the individual but was rather tied to the ontological and juridical primacy of the community and the corporative organization of society. Society was composed of corporate bodies (*corpora*) of diverse natures, organized around profession, trade, or territorial adscription, each of which had a different legal status and possessed great autonomy and capacity for self-regulation.[65] Guilds, parishes, villages, cities, universities, dioceses, religious orders, and the kingdom are some examples of these corporations.[66] These ideas can be considered the 'deep background to legal behavior and utterances', which was so obvious to early modern Iberian imagination that legal historians have had to parse through the "surface of the text" to reveal the worldview "encrypted behind the discourse, composed of convictions that were so fundamental that they did not need to be explicitly uttered for whomever was immersed in that 'other' society".[67]

The capacity to transform the divine, natural order into human law was at the root of the *ancien régime*'s conception of political power and was encompassed under the concept of *iurisdictio*, as the power to 'declare the law' and

Pessoas, Coisas, Contratos, Ações e Crimes; Hespanha, *La Gracia del Derecho*: *Economía de la Cultura en la Edad Moderna*; Hespanha, *Vísperas del Leviatán*: *Instituciones y Poder Político*; Petit, *Pasiones del Jurista*: *Amor, Memoria, Melancolía, Imaginación.*

65 Bastias Saavedra, "Jurisdictional Autonomy and the Autonomy of Law: End of Empire and the Functional Differentiation of Law in 19th-Century Latin America".

66 Agüero, "Las Categorías Básicas de la Cultura Jurisdiccional", 27; Hespanha, *História das Instituições*: Épocas Medieval E Moderna, chap. 6.

67 Agüero, "Las Categorías Básicas de la Cultura Jurisdiccional", 23. Of course, beyond these ontological foundations, almost every aspect of law was riddled with implicit background assumptions such as, for example, the virtues and qualities—nobility, wisdom, experience, prudence, patience, humility, eloquence, to name a few—a judge had to possess to pass just judgements. These virtues and qualities in turn were also grounded in underlying norms. On this, see: Vallejo, "Acerca del Fruto del Árbol de los Jueces".

'establish fairness' (*aequitas*).[68] As such, human law-making was always a process of declaring or revealing—but not creating—the law already handed down by the divine order.[69] This conception tied the legitimate exercise of power to the theological notion of justice, thus subordinating political power to the original normative order and making every act of authority an expression of that order. In this judicial model of government, the power to rule was inseparable from the power to judge.[70]

This manner of conceiving political power was also coherent with the corporative structure of society in which diverse holders of jurisdiction operated simultaneously and exercised varying magnitudes of power over partially or totally coinciding territories or groups of persons.[71] The holder of jurisdiction, as the head of the social body, was understood to exercise the aptitude of self-government that was inherent to every human community.[72] And insofar as the legitimacy of the exercise of jurisdictional power within each corporation arose from within itself, each sphere of jurisdiction was considered to have an autonomous—not delegated—origin.[73] It may be important to note that this corporate structure meant that jurisdiction was not only limited to the state and the Church; jurisdiction was widely distributed across all corporate bodies outside of the family which, though being the most basic and perfect corporation, was not a space governed by justice.[74]

The law-making capacities of political power were thus subordinated to a transcendent order, on the one hand, and to the corporate structure of traditional society, on the other, both acting as ontological premises that served as structural limitations to the 'centralization' of power.[75] The Monarch could not dispose of the law at will but could only act so as to sustain the natural order through justice or perfect it by grace.[76] But the power of the Crown was also limited by the jurisdictional structure of government which, although

68 Hespanha, *Como os Juristas viam o Mundo. 1550–1750*, 35. For a more detailed analysis, see: Costa, *Iurisdictio: Semantica del Potere Politico nella Pubblicistica Medievale (1100–1433)*; Vallejo, *Ruda Equidad, Ley Consumada: Concepción de la Potestad Normativa, (1250–1350)*.

69 For an insightful essay on the transformative power of law-making, see: Vallejo, "El Cáliz de Plata: Articulación de Órdenes Jurídicos en la Jurisprudencia del Ius Commune".

70 Agüero, "Las Categorías Básicas de la Cultura Jurisdiccional", 31; Garriga, "Orden Jurídico y Poder Político en el Antiguo Régimen", 18.

71 Vallejo, "Power Hierarchies in Medieval Juridical Thought: An Essay in Reinterpretation", 3.

72 Grossi, *El Orden Jurídico Medieval*, 67.

73 Vallejo, "El Cáliz de Plata", 11.

74 Zamora, *Casa Poblada y Buen Gobierno: "Oeconomía" Católica y Servicio Personal en San Miguel de Tucumán, Siglo XVIII*.

75 Garriga, "Orden jurídico y Poder Político en el Antiguo Régimen", 8.

76 Hespanha, *Como os Juristas viam o Mundo. 1550–1750*, 66.

organized through relations of super- and subordination, precluded a unitary and hierarchical integration of political power.[77] This premise has been used to show how the increasing importance of monarchical power after the 15th century, rather than expanding the executive functions of the Prince, produced a progressive specialization in the exercise of jurisdiction.[78] The consolidation of the early modern monarchies thus occurred through the development of a dual jurisdictional order: that of the king and his judge-administrators and that of the traditional corporative social structure.[79] As such, "the corporative society grows and develops alongside the modern monarchy, in a tight bond that will only be dissolved with the advent of the liberal State".[80] These features of the relation between law and political power in the Iberian monarchies were shared with other early modern monarchies and empires.[81]

Law-making was not only limited to the holders of jurisdiction, but was also a capacity of jurists and theologians, whose prestige, authority (*auctoritas*), and knowledge of the textual tradition made them important sources of normativity. Though they were not vested with *iurisdictio*, and thus could not declare the law in the same sense as a holder of jurisdiction, the jurist (in canon or civil law) and, beginning in the 16th century, the moral theologian shared the hermeneutical capacity to transform the divine order into law through *interpretatio*. Law-making was, by definition, interpretative, and there was therefore no substantive difference in the *interpretatio* of the Prince, of the community through its customs, of the judge in the administration of justice, or as the conceptual construction of the jurist and the theologian.[82] The difference, however, was that the *interpretatio* of the scholars was not general nor necessary, only probable—the binding force of their opinions was authoritative and persuasive, showing ways to find the right solutions without providing the solutions as such.[83] But this scholarly law was not merely theoretical or confined to books and universities; it also found different forms of practical use, either through the condensation of this knowledge into pragmatic literature

---

77 Vallejo, "El Cáliz de Plata", 8.

78 Mannori, "Justicia y Administración entre Antiguo y Nuevo Régimen", 132.

79 Hespanha, "Centro e Periferia nas Estruturas Administrativas do Antigo Regime", 55.

80 Agüero, *Castigar y Perdonar Cuando Conviene a la República: La Justicia Penal de Córdoba del Tucuman, Siglos XVII y XVIII*, 36–37.

81 Härter, "Das heilige Römische Reich deutscher Nation als mehrschichtiges Rechtsystem, 1495–1806", 345–346.

82 Grossi, *El Orden Jurídico Medieval*, 168 ff.

83 On how textual and practical knowledge was involved in producing these norms, see: Duve, "Pragmatic Normative Literature and the Production of Normative Knowledge in the Early Modern Iberian Empires (16th–17th Centuries)", 12.

for practitioners or through the opinions produced by jurists and theologians to solve specific issues that arose in different contexts.[84] The jurist/theologian thus mediated between the realms of concepts and facts, meaning that *interpretatio* had a creative function in the sense that it could modify the formal reservoir of normative knowledge—the legal doctrine of the *ius commune* and canon law, Scripture, and the 'ancient wisdom' taken from the authors of classical antiquity—to create new norms that reflected existing and new states of affairs.[85]

Two important preliminary conclusions for understanding the relation between law and empire can be drawn from this new legal historiography. First, it stresses the impossibility of conceiving of a centralized political power. Political power, insofar as it was based on *iurisdictio*, was widely fragmented and, though organized in higher- and lower-orders of power, excluded the possibility of a unitary political structure. The idea of governing by difference, stressed by the more recent imperial history, was a feature of such a political system, not only because it was efficient, but also because it is the way in which the exercise of political power was fundamentally conceived. Second, following this logic, law-making was not a monopoly of the ruler but was a capacity that was also widely fragmented and distributed. However, in a strict sense, it is a mistake to conceive this law in terms of legal pluralism because it was, in fact, a unitary order based on hierarchies, inequalities, and difference—which, as we have seen, encompassed the natural and supernatural world created by God—and it thus tended toward plurality rather than uniformity. Accordingly, law could manifest itself in many forms—in principle, in as many concurrent forms as there were *corpora*.[86] It is therefore perhaps better to speak of multinormativity with the understanding that human behavior was (and is) ordered by different techniques of both formal and informal regulation[87]—ranging from the implicit and deep-seated convictions about the world and the

84 On the former, see the articles in: Duve and Danwerth (eds.), *Knowledge of the Pragmatici: Legal and Moral Theological Literature and the Formation of Early Modern Ibero-America*. On the latter, see chapters 6, 8, and 9 in this volume.

85 Grossi, *El Orden Jurídico Medieval*, 174.

86 Donlan and Heirbaut (eds.), *The Law's Many Bodies: Studies in Legal Hybridity and Jurisdictional Complexity, C. 1600–1900*.

87 Duve, "Was ist Multinormativität? Einführende Bemerkungen". The idea of multinormativity may even include what Christopher Tomlins has called 'legality', understood as "a condition with social and cultural existence" produced not only in formal settings but "generated in the course of virtually any repetitive practice of wide acceptance within a specific locale, call the result rule, custom, folkway or pastime, popular belief or protest". Tomlins, "The Many Legalities of Colonization: A Manifesto of Destiny for Early American Legal History", 2–3.

cultural conventions outlined at the beginning of this section to aesthetic and linguistic standards, customs, royal edicts, and legal doctrine, including even the regulation of time and the life cycle, as discussed by Fupeng Li (Chapter 10) in this volume.

This basic model of law and government accompanied the Portuguese and Castilian crowns as they extended their rule to other parts of the Iberian Peninsula, as well as to Africa, Asia, and the Americas.[88] The Castilian system of *Audiencias* and Chancillerías, developed in the 14th and 15th centuries to represent the person of the king and guarantee the juridical order of the kingdom, was consolidated and perfected in America and the Philippines from the 16th century. Insofar as they stood in for the king—speaking with his voice and occupying his place in the definition of justice—the *Audiencias* were fundamental in defining the configuration of the political space of the Crown. They were also the way in which the military power of the conquistadors was tempered through the civil power of the king's magistrates. However, neither the *Audiencias* nor the other offices established for the government of the Indies should be understood as executive or administrative arms of the metropolis, but rather as jurisdictional bodies: i.e., performing, at once and without clear distinctions between them, the functions of government and justice. These magistrates and officers of the Crown, insofar as they enjoyed jurisdiction, were authorized by, and even protected against, royal orders,[89] and thus acted at the same time as "*instruments* of and *obstacles* to royal policy".[90] The royal institutions of the Portuguese monarchy functioned essentially under the same logic.[91]

The jurisdictional logic, however, was not only deployed by royal institutions, but was also replicated through the corporate structure of society, tied to the corporations that accompanied the expansion of the Iberian empires—the Church, the Inquisition, brotherhoods, religious orders, *cabilidos* and *cámaras*, guilds, cities, provinces, etc.—and to the corporations that organized local rule—*pueblos, gaunkaris*, and *barangays*, to name a few.[92] These corporations sometimes acquired explicit privileges granted by the monarch, such

88 Cardim and Hespanha, "A Estrutura Territorial das duas Monarquia Ibéricas (Séculos XVI-XVIII)".

89 Hespanha, "Antigo Regime nos Trópicos? Um Debate sobre o Modelo Político do Império Colonial Português", 46.

90 This section follows: Garriga, "Las Audiencias: Justicia a Gobierno de las Indias", 724. Emphasis in the original.

91 Hespanha, *Vísperas del Leviatán: Instituciones y Poder Político*, chap. 5.

92 On the *gaunkaris* and the *barangays*, respectively, see Xavier and Perez (Chapters 2 and 3) in this volume.

as the *forais*, but also developed their own local, unwritten norms based on longstanding practices and conventions.[93] The principle underlying this was that every community was endowed with an inherent capacity for self-government. Importantly, neither the laws of the king nor those of other instances of general law-making—e.g., the Church—could supersede or contravene the law and the law-making capacities of these corporations. In this conception, the "centrality of law was translated, in fact, to the centrality of local normative powers, both formal or informal, of the uses of the land, of 'rooted' situations (*iura radicata*), in the attention to the particularities of the case".[94] Outside of the king's jurisdiction, relations with foreigners and foreign rulers, with allied potentates through *amistad* (friendship), and with enemies were also regulated by the *ius gentium*, creating different sets of norms that, though beyond the power of the monarch, were not foreign to the unitary framework of the juridical order of the *ancien régime*.

The law of empire, therefore, rather than creating the conditions for voluntary, central rule, supported and reinforced the dispersion of and limitations to law and political power:

> Empire's law was a chaotic compound of legal regimes, combining the diversity of the very Metropolitan law with a wide array of particular legal orders, local usages and judicial styles. […] Rather than representing a hierarchical legal order dominated by a common set of imperial prescriptions, imperial law was a lacing machinery knotting legal threads of different colors and resistance, assisted by a disperse and incoherent body of officers, applied with the most diverse intensity to diversely dependent subjects.[95]

The localism and contextualization of law thus endowed the countless local situations of the empire with a political and juridical autonomy that precluded a pervasive rule and determination from the metropolitan center.

Therefore, in the case of the Iberian empires, if one can speak of the transference of a metropolitan model to the colonies at all it was in the way the *ancien régime* logic of law and government of the Peninsula was replicated under new conditions. The outcome of this process was not the transposition of European law to the non-European world but a 'normative overload', as the needs of imperial government required the creation of new norms through the

93 Hespanha, "Antigo Regime nos Trópicos?", 55.
94 Hespanha, "Depois do Leviathan", 57.
95 Hespanha, "Uncommon Laws", 186.

adjustment to local forms of social and political reproduction. This normative overload was a consequence of the logic of norm-production in the early modern world, in which new norms did not derogate older ones, thus leading to an ever-growing accumulation of normative information. And this information grew exponentially as the Iberian empires extended their rule. In *each* new place, kings enacted decrees and bestowed privileges; officials handed down rules; jurists, clerics, and theologians—not only in Salamanca and Rome, but also in Goa, Mexico City, Lima and Manila—drew on bodies of law, authorities, and classics to produce normative solutions for new situations; magistrates had to reach judgements; and cities, villages, and other territorial communities created or sustained their own norms and customs. Both before and after the 15th century, the existence of contradictory norms was the rule. The solution to navigating this normative complexity was simple: learning the facts inductively, respecting the particularities of the case, and aiming to sustain the interests of each party as they were understood to be—justice could only ever be local and particular, regardless of its place within the political structure of the empire.

4 Norms beyond Empire: Decentering the History of Law

The insights of this recent 'imperial turn' in legal historical research provide both an invitation and a challenge. On the one hand, they form an invitation to explore the complexities of local norm-production, giving it the central position that it had in the early modern period. On the other hand, they form a challenge insofar as this historiography leaves us with incomplete tools and concepts to take the next step: namely, how to analyze and interpret the ways in which vernacular normative orders and non-European and non-Christian local practices helped shape and order life in the Iberian empires. Despite the nuance and complexity it offers, the doctrinal corpus of the *ius commune*, which has helped legal historians understand the alterity of the European *ancien régime*, is still a blunt instrument for understanding what happened once the Iberian world moved beyond the Atlantic and the Mediterranean. Legal history is no longer simply confronted with the otherness of the early modern mentality, but is now also challenged with understanding and finding ways to integrate the different traditions, pasts, and histories of the peoples that, in one way or another, encountered and suffered under the Iberian empires.

These are the challenges faced by a legal history that is no longer European but global, and addressing them requires constructing appropriate conceptual and methodological frameworks.[96] Conceptually, the focus of legal history moves toward the idea of normativity. This serves to move legal history away from the often Eurocentric and narrow concept of *law* toward the less culturally charged idea of *normativity*, which highlights different orders of norms, their interactions, and their internal dynamics.[97] Further, since norms are never straightforward, but rather respond to different kinds of expectations, interact in variegated manners, and are layered upon each other, normativity should always be understood as *multinormativity*. This draws particular attention to the manifold underlying rules, assumptions, and conditions of possibility for the production of norms.[98] Tamar Herzog probably had a similar idea in mind when analyzing the interactions between the Portuguese and natives of the Brazilian interior: "I argue that beyond what was said and done, silently operating in the background were rules that linked speech and action to certain consequences. These rules anchored in culture and experience, were legal in the sense that they were normative. They prescribed which actions could be taken, which words could be pronounced, and what their results might be".[99]

Methodologically, the frame of reference is also not Europe, nor the connections between Europe and other world regions, but global.[100] However, this does not mean taking a macro perspective, but in fact demands the prioritization of the local. This is not only because a local perspective is consequent with the logic of law-making of the *ius commune* culture, as outlined above, but also because it is the only way to access the variation, selection, and transformation of normative options: "only by observing the smallest units can the processes of law-making be reconstructed, only from this vantage point can regional or global connections be accessed".[101] The focus on the local also means giving preference to local practices.[102] Because norms were not only produced by

96 Duve, "Von der Europäischen Rechtsgeschichte zu einer Rechtsgeschichte Europas in globalhistorischer Perspektive".

97 Other legal historians have proposed solving this problem, rather, by avoiding having an a piori concept of law. See: Garriga, "¿De qué Hablamos los Historiadores del Derecho cuando Hablamos de Derecho?"; Hespanha, "Is there a Place for a Separated Legal History? A Broad Review of Recent Developments on Legal Historiography".

98 Duve, "Was ist Multinormativität?", 92 ff.

99 Herzog, "What Natives Said and How Europeans Responded in Late-Seventeenth- and Eighteenth-Century Portuguese America", 62.

100 Duve, "What is Global Legal History?"; Duve, "Global Legal History a Methodological Approach".

101 Duve, "Von der Europäischen Rechtsgeschichte zu einer Rechtsgeschichte Europas in globalhistorischer Perspektive", 49.

102 Duve, "Von der Europäischen Rechtsgeschichte zu einer Rechtsgeschichte Europas in globalhistorischer Perspektive", 51.

rulers, scholars, and courts, and because they were not only experienced by people as litigants, but were also lived, embodied, expressed as convictions, and practiced, the production and reproduction of normativity can only be read through sources that shed light on these cultural and social practices.

All of this points to decentering the history of law in both an epistemological and methodological sense. This perspective means that *each* case study becomes its own center from which meanings and connections are drawn and reconstructed. Each place, as its own center, reveals the ways in which it interacts with the wider world—and these interactions are unique. Instead of leading to a fragmentation of local case studies, it opens the possibility of understanding how law was simultaneously and globally co-constructed through the loose interaction of the "fragile threads"[103] that connected different normative systems over the last five centuries. This draws inspiration from Subrahmanyam's appeal to delink certain global shifts from a supposedly European trajectory and agency, stressing that they actually have "many different sources and roots, and – inevitably – many different forms and meanings depending on which society we look at it from".[104] The "structural similarities"[105] and the "quasi-commensurability"[106] between the Iberian juridical worldview and that of the people submitted to their rule in Africa, Asia, Europe, and the Americas allowed for the interweaving of normative traditions that ultimately resulted in new configurations that were both no longer European and no longer native.

The chapters in this volume illustrate this approach by showing how local normativities were central to law-making in early modern Iberian Asia. First, this means integrating into the analysis different normative textual traditions, beyond imperial laws and the *ius commune*, and interrogating the ways in which these traditions interacted. Ângela Barreto Xavier (Chapter 2) reflects on the ways in which *Dharmaśāstra*, *Smṛti*, and other Brahmanical treatises may have influenced the customs of Goan villages before the arrival of the Portuguese and how they were integrated into the nascent Portuguese imperial order, especially in rules concerning inheritance and land sales. Luisa Stella de Oliveira Coutinho Silva (Chapter 6) similarly discusses how marriage practices in 16th-century Japan can be seen from the vantage point of the missionaries' conceptions of canonical marriage, as well as from the perspective of

103 Subrahmanyam, "Connected Histories: Notes towards a Reconfiguration of Early Modern Eurasia", 762.
104 Subrahmanyam, "Connected Histories", 737.
105 Benton, "The Legal Regime of the South Atlantic World, 1400–1750", 48.
106 Biedermann, *The Portuguese in Sri Lanka and South India*, 35.

a long tradition of Japanese norms that regulated families and households, from those codified in the *Ritsuryō* in the 7th century to the House Laws of the Sengoku period. The construction of Christian marriage practices in Japan in the 16th century necessarily drew from these different textual traditions. Li (Chapter 10) seeks to redefine the imperial calendars in the late Ming and early Qing dynasties as "manuals of rituals" that combined and incorporated both Chinese and European knowledge. The calendars combined the astronomical knowledge of the Jesuits, traditional Chinese numerology, and Confucian and Taoist philosophy to construct a ritual order that synthesized multiple orders: the natural order, the order of the empire, and the organization of everyday life.

Second, local practices and institutions should be highlighted to better understand how colonial rule and Christianity were anchored in the long-term persistence of local normativities. Marya Svetlana T. Camacho (Chapter 5) provides an excellent example of this, showing how the Bisayan *bugay* and the Tagalog *bigay-kaya* remained central institutions in marriage between natives in the Philippines even after conversion. The chapter argues that even though Spanish sources tended to speak of *dote* (dowry) and religious authorities tried to adjust local marriage practices to Church precepts, natives actually 'localized' Christian marriage in the Philippines by sustaining the practice of *bugay*/*bigay-kaya* throughout the centuries. Xavier (Chapter 2) also draws attention to the "several layers of experience" that constituted the multinormative Portuguese imperial order in Goa, based on administrative institutions of the Bijapur Sultanate, the local government of the *gaunkaris*, norms drawn from Brahmanical scholarship, and the efforts to consolidate the primacy of Portuguese law and Christian precepts. Abisai Perez Zamarripa (Chapter 3) also draws attention to the "indigenous jurisdiction hidden beneath Spanish rule", showing how colonial governance in the Philippines was built upon a layer of local normativities through the integration of repurposed pre-Hispanic institutions (*barangays* and *datus*) and customs. These examples point to the existence of 'subaltern normativities' that lived alongside and fed into the rule-making and institution-building processes of Iberian colonialism.

Third, the chapters in this volume help decenter the idea of empire by showing the internal complexity of imperial polities. As we have seen, the Iberian empires were less monolithic and more internally fragmented than the metropolitan image of empire may suggest. Xavier (Chapter 2) illustrates how the policy of conversion reshaped the Portuguese imperial order in Goa, Salcete, and Bardez, moving from a more pluralistic approach to local societies to one less so. Xavier thus demonstrates that the Portuguese imperial order had to balance the—sometimes aligned and sometimes divergent—interests of the Crown with those of the Church. Further, Patricia Souza de Faria (Chapter 4), by looking at the guardianship of orphans of Gentile parents, reveals that these tensions between the fiscal interests of the Crown and the spiritual interests of the Church tempered the policies of conversion. She argues that non-Christian merchants, craftsmen, and shopkeepers used their positions to take advantage of the tensions between the secular and religious interests of the *Estado da Índia* and were able to uphold their customs and gain certain exemptions from Christian obligations. Perez (Chapter 3) similarly illustrates how indigenous jurisdiction in the Philippines resulted from the way in which conflicts between the *encomenderos*, natives, the Crown, and the Bishopric of Manila were ultimately negotiated. The competing interests within the Spanish colonial structure gave indigenous *principales* a way to build alliances and reshape their relations with the Crown and the colonial government of the archipelago.

Fourth, this volume also discusses the ways in which, more than providing laws and rules for application, 'European law' provided a 'grammar' that allowed the production of new norms according to new conditions. Miguel Rodrigues Lourenço (Chapter 7) discusses the construction of a specific vocabulary for religious transgression and dissent by the Goa Inquisition, which was built on a long tradition of categories to address and punish religious offences—heresy, idolatry, sect, superstition, etc. The tendency of Goan converts, the *cristãos da terra*, to revert to their former rituals and practices—dressing in the "manner of a 'Moor'", removing their shoes when entering temples "in the manner of the Gentiles", or washing their bodies "in the fashion of the infidels", to name some examples—led the Holy Office to create *gentilidade* as a category of offence that could allow the inspection of a variety of behaviors, rituals, and ceremonies that reflected the specific circumstances of Christians in the territory. Rômulo da Silva Ehalt (Chapter 8) studies the role of missionary casuistry in defining the rules for professing the faith in Japan during the persecution of Christians under Tokugawa rule: could Japanese Christians lie about their faith if it meant saving their own lives and that of their co-religionists? The answer to this question—central to avoiding sins of commission—was important for guiding the practice of Christians in Japan and thus missionaries had to find ways to reconcile the needs generated by local conditions with the sources of normative authority. Lastly, Marina Torres Trimállez (Chapter 9) highlights the different sources of authority, and the varying degrees of importance assigned to them, used by missionaries in China to argue for and against the use of headwear during mass and confession. Despite the existence of a papal authorization that, against Tridentine precepts, allowed the use of headwear during mass in China, this rule was subject to debate and revision by the missionaries themselves. Torres Trimállez shows how missionaries drew on available normative knowledge to design rules for the discussion and modification of

Tridentine and papal rules and how, in turn, these discussions were built upon different sources of normative authority, ranging from experience and local custom to moral theology and divine and natural law.

Finally, the chapters of this volume also propose different methodological approaches to addressing local normativities. Xavier (Chapter 2) addresses the lack of written, archeological, and epigraphic sources for Goa by taking a 'regional approach' which makes use of anthropological studies of the broader West Konkan region of which it was a part. Also, as a way of overcoming the lack of pre-colonial sources, Camacho (Chapter 5) looks at anthropological research concerning the practice of bridewealth to understand the institutions of *bugay* and *bigay-kaya* in the Philippines. Coutinho Silva (Chapter 6) draws on the field of women's history to understand the transformation in marriage practices in Japan by looking at the way women's roles in the family and in society changed over time. Further, Perez (Chapter 3) and Lourenço (Chapter 7) use comparisons with the Iberian colonies in America to both fill gaps in knowledge and reveal regional variations in the treatment of similar problems. While Perez explores the literature on indigenous judicial systems in Spanish America to draw parallels to their development in the Philippines, Lourenço explores the treatment of cases of heresy and idolatry in Brazil to underscore the uniqueness of *gentilidade* as a category of religious offence by the Goa Inquisition.

Taken together, the chapters in this volume reveal that, even if the presence of the Iberian empires in Asia produced the disruption that set in motion a vast process of normative change, the outcome was not something that could be shaped in their image. Ultimately, the making of law in Iberian Asia was a decentralized process of normative production that tied different communities together, connected different layers of norms, and eventually shaped a wide variety of local orders.

Bibliography

Agüero, Alejandro, "Las Categorías Básicas de la Cultura Jurisdiccional", in Marta Lorente (ed.), *De Justicia de Jueces a Justicia de Leyes: Hacia la España de 1870*, Madrid 2007, 21–58.

Agüero, Alejandro, *Castigar y Perdonar cuando Conviene a la República: La Justicia Penal de Córdoba del Tucuman, Siglos XVII Y XVIII*, Madrid 2008.

Alcock, Susan, Terence D'Altroy, Kathleen Morrisson and Karla Sinopoli (eds.), *Empires: Perspectives from Archaeology and History*, Cambridge 2001 (repr. Cambridge 2005).

Angeles, F. Delor, "The Philippine Inquisition: A Survey", in *Philippine Studies* 28, no. 3 (1980): 253–283.

Anghie, Antony, *Imperialism, Sovereignty, and the Making of International Law*, Cambridge 2005.

Bastias Saavedra, Manuel, "Jurisdictional Autonomy and the Autonomy of Law: End of Empire and the Functional Differentiation of Law in 19th-Century Latin America", in *Rechtsgeschichte – Legal History* 26 (2018): 325–337.

Benton, Lauren, "The Legal Regime of the South Atlantic World, 1400–1750: Jurisdictional Complexity as Institutional Order", in *Journal of World History* 11, no. 1 (2000): 27–56.

Benton, Lauren. *Law and Colonial Cultures: Legal Regimes in World History, 1400–1900*, Cambridge 2004.

Benton, Lauren, *A Search for Sovereignty: Law and Geography in European Empires 1400–1900*, New York 2010.

Benton, Lauren, "AHR Forum: Law and Empire in Global Perspective: Introduction", in *The American Historical Review* 117, no. 4 (2012): 1092–1100.

Benton, Lauren, "In Defense of Ignorance: Frameworks for Legal Politics in the Atlantic World", in Owensby; Ross, *Justice in a New World*, 273–290.

Benton, Lauren, "Made in Empire: Finding the History of International Law in Imperial Locations", in *Leiden Journal of International Law* 31, no. 3 (2018): 473–478.

Benton, Lauren and Richard Ross (eds.), *Legal Pluralism and Empires, 1500–1850*, New York 2013.

Bethencourt, Francisco and Diogo Ramada Curto (eds.), *Portuguese Oceanic Expansion, 1400–1800*, New York 2007.

Biedermann, Zoltán, *The Portuguese in Sri Lanka and South India: Studies in the History of Diplomacy, Empire and Trade, 1500–1650*, Wiesbaden 2014.

Bouza, Fernando, Pedro Cardim and Antonio Feros (eds.), *The Iberian World: 1450–1820*, New York 2019.

Boxer, Charles R., *Portuguese Society in the Tropics: The Municipal Councils of Goa, Macao, Bahia, and Luanda, 1510–1800*, Madison 1965.

Boxer, Charles R., *The Great Ship from Amacon*. Macau 1988.

Boxer, Charles R., *Igreja Militante e a Expansão Ibérica 1440–1770*, São Paulo 2007.

Brockey, Liam Matthew, *Journey to the East: The Jesuit Mission to China, 1579–1724*, Cambridge 2007.

Brunero, Donna, Jack Fairey and Brian P. Farrell (eds.), *Empire in Asia: A New Global History*, London 2018.

Burbank, Jane and Frederick Cooper, *Empires in World History: Power and the Politics of Difference*, Princeton 2010.

Burbank, Jane and Frederick Cooper, "Rules of Law, Politics of Empire", in Lauren Benton and Richard Ross (eds.), *Legal Pluralism and Empires, 1500–1850*, New York 2013, 279–293.

Cardim, Pedro and António Manuel Hespanha, "A Estrutura Territorial das duas Monarquia Ibéricas (Séculos XVI–XVIII)", in Barreto Xavier, Ângela, Federico Palomo and Roberta Stumpf, *Monarquias Ibéricas em Perspectiva Comparada (Séculos XVI–XVIII)*, Lisboa 2018, 51–95.

Clavero, Bartolomé, *Tantas Personas como Estados: Por una Antropología Política de la Historia Europea*, Madrid 1986.

Clavero, Bartolomé, *Antídora: Antropología Católica de la Economía Moderna*, Milano 1991.

Coello de la Rosa, Alexandre, *Jesuits at the Margins: Missions and Missionaries in the Marianas (1668–1769)*, Taylor and Francis 2015.

Cooper, Frederick, *Colonialism in Question: Theory, Knowledge, History*, Berkeley 2005.

Costa, Pietro, *Iurisdictio: Semantica del Potere Politico nella Pubblicistica Medievale (1100–1433)*, Milano 2002.

Didier, Hugues, *Le Portugais au Tibet: Les Premières Relations Jésuits (1624–1635)*, Paris 2002.

Disney, A. R., *A History of Portugal and the Portuguese Empire: From Beginnings to 1807*, vol. 2. Cambridge 2009.

Disney, A. R., *The Portuguese in India and other Studies, 1500–1700*, Farnham 2009.

Donlan, Seán Patrick and Dirk Heirbaut (eds.), *The Law's Many Bodies: Studies in Legal Hybridity and Jurisdictional Complexity, C. 1600–1900*, Berlin 2015.

Duindam, Jeroen, Jill Harries, Caroline Humfress and Nimrod Hurvitz (eds.), *Law and Empire: Ideas, Practices, Actors*, Leiden 2013.

Duve, Thomas, "Rechtsgeschichte als Geschichte von Normativitätswissen?", in Augsberg, Gunnar Folke and Ino Schuppert (eds.), *Wissen und Recht*, Baden-Baden, forthcoming.

Duve, Thomas, "Von der Europäischen Rechtsgeschichte zu einer Rechtsgeschichte Europas in globalhistorischer Perspektive", in *Rechtsgeschichte – Legal History Rg* 20 (2012), 18–71.

Duve, Thomas, "Global Legal History a Methodological Approach", in *Max Planck Institute for European Legal History Research Paper Series*, no. 4 (2016).

Duve, Thomas, "Was ist Multinormativität? Einführende Bemerkungen", in *Rechtsgeschichte – Legal History* 25 (2017): 88–101.

Duve, Thomas, "Pragmatic Normative Literature and the Production of Normative Knowledge in the Early Modern Iberian Empires (16th–17th Centuries)", in Duve, Thomas and Otto Danwerth (eds.), *Knowledge of the Pragmatici: Legal and Moral Theological Literature and the Formation of Early Modern Ibero-America*, Leiden 2020, 1–39.

Duve, Thomas, "What is Global Legal History?", in *Comparative Legal History* (2020): 1–43.

Duve, Thomas and Otto Danwerth (eds.), *Knowledge of the Pragmatici: Legal and Moral Theological Literature and the Formation of Early Modern Ibero-America*, Leiden 2020.

Duve, Thomas, José Luis Egío and Christiane Birr (eds.), *The School of Salamanca: A Case of Global Knowledge Production*, Leiden 2021.

Elliott, J. H., "A Europe of Composite Monarchies", in *Past and Present* 137, no. 1 (1992): 48–71.

Fairey, Jack, and Brian P. Farrell, "Reordering an Imperial Modern Asia", in Brunero, Donna, Jack Fairey and Brian P. Farrell (eds.), *Empire in Asia: A New Global History*, London 2018, 1–8.

Fisch, Jörg, "Law as a Means and as an End: Some Remarks on the Function of European and Non-European Law in the Process of European Expansion", in Mommsen, Wolfgang and Jaap de Moor (eds.), *European Expansion and Law*, Oxford 1992, 15–38.

Flannery, John M., *The Mission of the Portuguese Augustinians to Persia and Beyond (1602–1747)*, Leiden 2013.

Flores, Jorge, "The Iberian Empires, 1400 to 1800", in Bentley, Jerry H., Sanjay Subrahmanyam and Merry Wiesner-Hanks (eds.), *The Construction of a Global World, 1400–1800 CE*, The Cambridge World History 6, Cambridge 2015, 271–296.

Garriga, Carlos, "Las Audiencias: Justicia y Gobierno de las Indias", in Barrios, Feliciano (ed.), *El Gobierno de un Mundo: Virreinatos y Audiencias en la América Hispana*, Cuenca 2004, 711–794.

Garriga, Carlos, "Orden Jurídico y Poder Político en el Antiguo Régimen", in *Istor. Revista de Historia Internacional* 16 (2004): 3–44.

Garriga, Carlos, "¿De qué hablamos los Historiadores del Derecho cuando hablamos de Derecho?", in *Revista Direito Mackenzie* 14, no. 1 (2020).

Girgen, Jen, "The Historical and Contemporary Prosecution and Punishment of Animals", in *Animal Law Review at Lewis & Clark Law School* 9, no. 1 (2003): 97–133.

Grossi, Paolo, *El Orden Jurídico Medieval*, Madrid 1995.

Gruzinski, Serge, *Las Cuatro Partes del Mundo: Historia de una Mundialización*, México D.F. 2010.

Halperin, Sandra and Ronen Palan, "Introduction: Legacies of Empire", in Halperin, Sandra and Ronen Palan, *Legacies of Empire: Imperial Roots of the Contemporary Global Order*, Cambridge 2015, 1–24.

Härter, Karl, "Das Heilige Römische Reich deutscher Nation als mehrschichtiges Rechtsystem 1495–1806", in Wendehorst, Stephan, *Die Anatomie frühneuzeitlicher Imperien: Herrschaftsmanagement jenseits von Staat und Nation, Institutionen, Personal und Techniken*, Berlin 2015, 327–347.

Hausser, Christian and Horst Pietschmann, "Empire: The Concept and its Problems in the Historiography on the Iberian Empires in the Early Modern Age", in *Culture & History Digital Journal* 3, no. 1 (2014): 7–16.

Herzog, Tamar, "What Natives Said and How Europeans Responded in Late-Seventeenth- and Eighteenth-Century Portuguese America", in Owensby, Brian P. and Richard J. Ross (eds.), *Justice in a New World: Negotiating Legal Intelligibility in British, Iberian, and Indigenous America*, New York 2018, 61–88.

Hespanha, António Manuel, *História das Instituições: Épocas Medieval e Moderna*, Coimbra 1982.

Hespanha, António Manuel, "Centro e Periferia nas Estruturas Administrativas do Antigo Regime", in *Ler História* 8 (1986).

Hespanha, António Manuel, *Vísperas del Leviatán: Instituciones y Poder Político (Portugal, Siglo XVII)*, Madrid 1989.

Hespanha, António Manuel, *La Gracia del Derecho: Economía de la Cultura en la Edad Moderna*, Madrid 1993.

Hespanha, António Manuel, "Early Modern Law and the Anthropological Imagination of Old European Culture", in Marino, John A., *Early Modern History and the Social Sciences: Testing the Limits of Braudel's Mediterranean*, Kirksville 2002, 191–204.

Hespanha, António Manuel, "Depois do Leviathan", *Almanack Braziliense* 5 (2007): 55–66.

Hespanha, António Manuel, "Antigo Regime nos Trópicos? Um Debate sobre o Modelo político do Império Colonial Português", in Fragoso, João L. R. and Maria d. F. Gouvêa, *Na Trama das Redes: Política e Negócios no Império Português, Séculos XVI–XVIII*, 43–93, Rio de Janeiro 2010.

Hespanha, António Manuel, "Uncommon Laws: Law in the Extreme Peripheries of an Early Modern Empire", in *Zeitschrift der Savigny-Stiftung für Rechtsgeschichte: Germanistische Abteilung* 130, no. 1 (2013): 180–204.

Hespanha, António Manuel, *Como os Juristas viam o Mundo. 1550–1750: Direitos, Estados, Pessoas, Coisas, Contratos, Ações e Crimes*, Lexington 2015.

Hespanha, António Manuel, "As Cores e a Instituição da Ordem no Mundo de Antigo Regime", in Hespanha, António M. (ed.), *A Ordem do Mundo e o Saber dos Juristas: Imaginários do Antigo Direito Europeu*, Lisboa 2017, 341–370.

Hespanha, António Manuel, *Filhos da Terra: Identidades Mestiças nos Confins da Expansão Portuguesa*, Lisboa 2019.

Hespanha, António Manuel, "Is there a Place for a Separated Legal History? A Broad Review of Recent Developments on Legal Historiography", in *Quaderni Fiorentini per la Storia del Pensiero Giuridico Moderno* 48 (2019): 7–28.

Howe, Stephen, *Empire: A Very Short Introduction*, Oxford 2002.

Humphrey, Nicholas, "Bugs and Beasts Before the Law", in Humphrey, Nicholas (ed.), *The Mind Made Flesh: Essays from the Frontiers of Psychology and Evolution*, Oxford 2002, 235–254.

Koenigsberger, H. G., "Monarchies and Parliaments in Early Modern Europe Dominium Regale or Dominium Politicum et Regale", in *Theory and Society* 5, no. 2 (1978): 191–217.

Koskenniemi, Martti, "Introduction: International Law and Empire: Aspects and Approaches", in Koskenniemi, Martti, Walter Rech and Manuel Jiménez Fonseca (eds.), *International Law and Empire: Historical Explorations*, Oxford 2017, 1–18.

Koskenniemi, Martti, Walter Rech, and Manuel Jiménez Fonseca (eds.), *International Law and Empire: Historical Explorations*, Oxford 2017.

Kumar, Krishan, *Visions of Empire: How Five Imperial Regimes Shaped the World*, Princeton 2019.

Maier, Charles S., *Among Empires: American Ascendancy and its Predecessors*, Cambridge 2006.

Mannori, Luca, "Justicia y Administración entre Antiguo y Nuevo Régimen", in *Revista Jurídica Universidad Autónoma de Madrid* 15 (2007): 125–146.

Martínez Shaw, Carlos and Marina Alfonso Mola, "The Philippine Islands: A Vital Crossroads during the First Globalization Period", in *Culture & History Digital Journal* 3, no. 1 (2014): 27–42.

Menegon, Eugenio, *Ancestors, Virgins, & Friars: Christianity as a Local Religion in Late Imperial China*, Cambridge 2009.

Mommsen, Wolfgang J, "Introduction", in Mommsen, Wolfgang J. and Jaap de Moor (eds.), *European Expansion and Law*, Oxford 1992, 1–14.

Mommsen, Wolfgang J. and Jaap de Moor (eds.), *European Expansion and Law: The Encounter of European and Indigenous Law in 19th- and 20th-Century Africa and Asia*, Oxford 1992.

Owensby, Brian Philip and Richard Jeffrey Ross (eds.), *Justice in a New World: Negotiating Legal Intelligibility in British, Iberian, and Indigenous America*, New York 2018.

Pagden, Anthony, *Lords of all the World: Ideologies of Empire in Spain, Britain and France c. 1500–c.1800*, New Haven 1995.

Pagden, Anthony, "Afterword: From Empire to Federation", in Balachandra Rajan and Elizabeth Sauer, *Imperialisms Historical and Literary Investigations*, New York 2004, 255–271.

Paiva, José Pedro, "The Inquisition Tribunal in Goa: Why and for What Purpose?" *Journal of Early Modern History* 21 (2017): 565–593.

Petit, Carlos, *Pasiones del Jurista: Amor, Memoria, Melancolía, Imaginación*, Madrid 1997.

Pitts, Jennifer, *Boundaries of the International: Law and Empire*, Cambridge 2018.

Roper, Louis H. and Bertrand van Ruymbeke (eds.), *Constructing Early Modern Empires: Proprietary Ventures in the Atlantic World, 1500–1750*, Leiden 2007.

Russell-Wood, A. J., R., "Patterns of Settlement in the Portuguese Empire", in Bethencourt, Francisco and Diogo R. Curto, *Portuguese Oceanic Expansion, 1400–1800*, 161–96, New York 2007.

Spate, O. H. K., *The Spanish Lake*, Minneapolis 1979.

Subrahmanyam, Sanjay, "Connected Histories: Notes towards a Reconfiguration of Early Modern Eurasia", in *Modern Asia Studies* 31, no. 3 (1997): 735–762.

Subrahmanyam, Sanjay, "Written on Water: Designs and Dynamics in the Portuguese Estado da Índia", in Alcock, Susan et al. (eds.), *Empires: Perspectives from Archaeology and History,* Cambridge 2001 (repr. Cambridge 2005), 42–69.

Subrahmanyam, Sanjay, *The Portuguese Empire in Asia, 1500–1700: A Political and Economic History*, Sussex UK 2012.

Subrahmanyam, Sanjay, *Empires Between Islam and Christianity, 1500–1800*, Albany 2019.

Thomaz, Luís Filipe, *De Ceuta a Timor*, Lisboa 1998.

Tomlins, Christopher, "The Many Legalities of Colonization: A Manifesto of Destiny for Early American Legal History", in *The Many Legalities of Early America*, Tomlins, Christopher and Bruce H. Mann, Chapel Hill 2001, 1–20.

Vallejo, Jesús, "Power Hierarchies in Medieval Juridical Thought: An Essay in Reinterpretation", in *Ius Commune* Sonderdruck (1992): 1–29.

Vallejo, Jesús, *Ruda Equidad, Ley Consumada: Concepción de la Potestad Normativa, (1250–1350)*, Madrid 1992.

Vallejo, Jesús, "Acerca del Fruto del Árbol de los Jueces: Escenarios de la Justicia en la Cultura del Ius Commune", in *Anuario de la Facultad de Derecho de la Universidad Autónoma de Madrid* 2 (1998): 19–46.

Vallejo, Jesús, "El Cáliz de Plata: Articulación de Órdenes Jurídicos en la Jurisprudencia del Ius Commune", *Revista de Historia del Derecho* 38 (2009): 1–13.

Wendehorst, Stephan (ed.), *Die Anatomie frühneuzeitlicher Imperien: Herrschaftsmanagement jenseits von Staat und Nation Institutionen, Personal und Techniken*, Berlin 2015.

Weststeijn, Arthur, "Provincializing Grotius: International Law and Empire in a Seventeenth-Century Malay Mirror", in Koskenniemi, Martti, Walter Rech and Manuel Jiménez Fonseca (eds.), *International Law and Empire: Historical Explorations*, Oxford 2017, 21–38.

Xavier, Ângela Barreto and Fernanda Olival, "O Padroado da Coroa de Portugal: Fundamentos e Práticas", in Xavier; Palomo; Stumpf, *Monarquias Ibéricas em Perspectiva Comparada (Séculos XVI–XVIII)*, 123–160.

Xavier, Ângela Barreto, Federico Palomo and Roberta Stumpf (eds.), *Monarquias Ibéricas em Perspectiva Comparada (Séculos XVI–XVIII): Dinâmicas Imperiais e Circulação de Modelos Político-Administrativos*, Lisboa 2018.

Zamora, Romina, *Casa Poblada y Buen Gobierno: "Oeconomía" Católica y Servicio Personal en San Miguel de Tucumán, Siglo XVIII*, Buenos Aires 2017.

CHAPTER 2

Village Normativities and the Portuguese Imperial Order: The Case of Early Modern Goa

Ângela Barreto Xavier

1 Introduction

Upon visiting the villages of the 'Old Conquests' of Goa today—the territories that included Tiswadi, Salcete, and Bardez—it would be clear that they are very different from those of Portugal. Dominated by the Portuguese for 450 years, one could conceivably expect more similarities. Their 'Indianness', particularly in what concerns their religious normativity, was reconstructed during the 19th and 20th centuries. However, before the 19th century, the 'Lusitanization' of these villages—that is to say, the incorporation of Portuguese-style practices into village life—was more explicit in very specific dimensions, namely the administrative, legal, and religious ones. This chapter addresses some of the dimensions of this process from the perspective of the life and afterlife of a Portuguese imperial document of 1526, the *Foral dos usos e costumes dos Gancares e Lavradores da Ilha de Goa e outras annexas a ella*, better known as *Foral de Mexia*, henceforth referred to as *Foral*.[1]

Since the 16th century, Portuguese imperial administrators and, later, scholars have collected a large body of knowledge about Goan normative orders and their cultural differences in relation to the Portuguese normative orders they were familiar with (which included their African dominions). Following this, European travelers, missionaries, and merchants have also registered information about the rules that operated in different parts of Western India, particularly those relating to religion, marriage, hereditary offices, and land. The relationship between these normativities and the Portuguese imperial order, however, still needs further study.

Normativities, as defined by Thomas Duve, are the sets of juridical, religious, social, and economic norms which guide individuals, groups, and peoples in

1 There are several published versions of this. In this text, I use the version provided by Cunha Rivara in the Fasc. 5, vol. 1 of *Archivo Portuguez Oriental* (henceforth APO), referred to in the footnotes as *Foral dos usos e costumes*.

their relationships with others and the world.[2] This chapter focuses on normativities related to the political, administrative, and judicial order of the Goan villages, while acknowledging that their delimitation—nowadays explicit—is difficult to define given the overlaps between those normativities and other spheres of power, like the religious one, for example.

Scholars have argued that many of the political, administrative, and judicial institutions found by the Portuguese in the territories they conquered not only survived imperial conquest, but were also crucial to constructing the imperial order. For these authors the case of Goa was paramount.[3] Seized in 1510 from the Sultanate of Bijapur, the preservation of many of the institutions belonging to the previous Muslim dominion was evident. Similarly, the primary forms of administration in the Goan villages—namely the *gaunkaris* (an agrarian association dominated by specific lineages and their members) and the *gaunkars*, that controlled the lands and ritual life in the villages—had also been kept.[4]

The first document to systematically address the organization of the Goan villages was the *Foral* of 1526. This compiled a selection of the "uses and customs" of these villages relating to the rules that governed them, particularly concerning the judicial system as well as uses of land and inheritance. Although the most crucial aim of the *Foral* was to guarantee the tax revenue due to the Portuguese Crown, it also provided a platform of communication between the local villages and the imperial rule by integrating local forms of organization into the imperial order.

Recent scholarship considers the *Foral* an example of the legal and administrative pluralism that characterized the early modern Portuguese imperial order. The *Foral*, in this view, translated the "well-knit economic and legal system based on Hindu jurisprudence"[5] into the Portuguese rule of Goa. This argument can be found explicitly in the work of António Manuel Hespanha, for example, and was later used by Lauren Benton.[6] This narrative dates back to the 19th century when, in the context of the municipal reforms that took place in Portugal from 1834, Goan elites reacted against the possibility of transposing those reforms to the Goan villages. Filipe Nery Xavier, one of the major figures

---

2 Duve, "European Legal History – Concepts, Methods, Challenges", 57–58; Rocher, *Studies in Hindu Law and Dharmaśāstras*, 83–102.

3 Madeira-Santos, "As Instituições Indígenas no Império Português", 278–289; Hespanha, *Panorama da História Institucional*..., 39–40; Thomaz, "A estrutura político-administrativa do Estado da Índia", 228, 237.

4 On the characteristics of this type of agrarian association in the Western Deccan see Guha, "The Political Economy of Village Life", 83–116.

5 Souza, *Legal Systems in Goa*, vol. 2, 59–60.

6 Hespanha, *Panorama da História Institucional*, 40; Benton, *Law and Colonial Cultures*, 51.

of this movement, presented the *Foral* as the written source of a thousand-year-old form of organization that had not and could not be changed.[7] Xavier and others—like the Portuguese administrator Cunha Rivara[8]—converged with two British colonial officials, Charles Metcalfe and Thomas Munro. Metcalfe and Munro also defended the immutability of the system operating in the Indian villages, a perception that found echoes in many other texts of the period.[9] These two lines of reasoning came together in the publication of an English version of the *Foral* by B. H. Baden-Powell, seen since then by Goans involved in politics and agrarian debates [10] as a 'written constitution' of the Goan villages.[11]

In contrast with this narrative, the *Foral* has also been considered only "a small inroad" to assessing the system that operated in the Goan villages.[12] Other authors stress the biased nature of the *Foral*, as it reflected the interests of imperial rulers as well as those of the local elites that constituted the *gaunkaris*. Moreover, they refer to this document as a 'construction' rather than a 'description'. This argument can be found not only in the work of Carlos Renato Gonçalves Pereira, Paul Axelroad and Michelle Fuerch, Teotónio de Souza, and Sanjay Subrahmanyam,[13] but also in two unpublished PhD dissertations and two recent articles which have been fundamental in rethinking this issue. In his thesis, for example, Remy Dias argues that the Portuguese imperial presence stimulated an internal reorganization of the Goan villages, particularly concerning the uses of land, thus impacting the economic power inside the village. For Dias, this process started in the 16th century, with the *Foral*, and intensified during the 18th century. Later, Manuel de Magalhães called attention to other narratives about the origins of the Goan elites that questioned those presented in the *Foral*, defending the predominantly imperial character

7 Xavier, *Collecção de Bandos, e Outras Differentes Providencias*, 3 vols., *passim*; Xavier, *Bosquejo Histórico das Communidades das Aldeias*, 3 vols. 1903–1907, *passim*; Xavier, Jr., *Collecção das Leis Peculiares das Communidades Agricolas das Aldeas*, *passim*. On that, see also Pinto, "The Foral in the History of Communidades", 191–192.

8 Rivara (ed.), "Foral dos usos e costumes dos Gancares e Lavradores da Ilha de Goa e outras annexas a ella". On this, see Dias, *A Socio-Economic History of Goa*, 12–18.

9 Inden, *Imagining India*, chapter 4.

10 See Kosambi, "The village communities in the Old Conquests", 63–78.

11 Baden-Powell, "The Villages of Goa in the Early Sixteenth Century", 261–291.

12 Souza, *Legal Systems in Goa*, vol. 2, 59–60.

13 Pereira, *História da Administração da Justiça*, vol. 1, 59–60. Axelroad and Fuerch, "Portuguese Orientalism", 439–476; Axelroad, "Living on the edge", 553–580; Souza, *Medieval Goa*, chapter 2; Subrahmanyam, "O romântico, o oriental e o exótico", 29–43. See also Viegas, *As Políticas Portuguesas na Índia*.

of the document.[14] More recently, Rochelle Pinto argued that the *Foral* accommodated the "needs of the sovereign" to "the socio-ecological conditions in the region where they were distributed", making it a hybrid document. Catarina Madeira-Santos has likewise stressed the changes in the local order entailed by the writing of the *Foral*. This author considered it as not merely a register of the local rights, but an expression of an imperial customary law, since the local rights had changed when integrated into an imperial framework.[15] The *Foral*, as the first mapping of Goan village order, is, nevertheless, an unavoidable source for those who intend to gain a deeper understanding of the Goan village normativities. While this scholarship confirms that the *Foral* is, in fact, "a small inroad" to assessing this order, it has not yet said much about its nature.[16]

To better understand the relationship between the villages' normativities and the Portuguese imperial order, sections two and three of this chapter focus on the context of the *Foral*'s production, the contributions from local elites, and the *Foral* as the first mapping of the Goan villages' order. The following questions thus arise: To what extent does the *Foral* allow us to assess the local order? How does it describe the local uses and customs? What were the interferences and distortions introduced to local normativities by imperial power through the *Foral*? And did it contribute to the construction of the normativities that operated in Goan villages from 1526 onward? To contribute toward answering these questions, section four provides a short inquiry into the multinormativity of the Goan order at the time of the Portuguese arrival as well as its past roots.

Following this, the subsequent sections focus on the uses of the *Foral* and its persistence in changing historical contexts.[17] Assuming that the *Foral* was a description of the local political, administrative, and judicial order, how much was it used during the early modern period? Section five focuses on what happened in the territories annexed 15 years after the completion of this document, and whether it fully applied to them. The final section deals with the role

14 Dias, *A Socio-Economic History of Goa*, 24–25; Magalhães, *Pequenos Reis e Grandes Honras*, 44–46, 238.

15 Pinto, "The Foral in the History of the Communidades", 185–212; Madeira-Santos, 282.

16 In his PhD dissertation, Manuel de Magalhães (*Pequenos Reis e Grandes Honras*) argues that the village order replicated, on a micro level, the logics of kingship. Therefore, the head of the village, the main *gaunkar*, had the authority of and behaved like a "little king"—a thesis that is hard to accept. In the villages under analysis in this essay, seldom are there references to a "main *gaunkar*". Instead, the reference to *gaunkars* (in plural) is often found pointing toward a collective rule of the village.

17 On the afterlife of the *Foral*, see Fernandes, "Invoking the Ghost of Mexia", 9–25.

of the *Foral* in a Christianized Goa, when the equivalence between *generatio* (birth) and *regeneratio* (baptism) transformed the locals into a-kind-of-Portuguese who therefore submitted to Portuguese law. This leads again to the term 'Lusitanization', which was a *top-down* model and ideal that remained, however, permanently incomplete. Its counterpart, always present, was the indigenization of the Portuguese imperial rule, already expressed in the *Foral*, many other documents, and many practices, as this chapter also demonstrates.

Before proceeding, some theoretical and methodological issues require attention. The first refers to the almost complete lack of a local written archive for studying the Goan normative order at the time of the arrival of the Portuguese. Besides the European sources, Goan written sources are scarce and archaeological and epigraphic sources are limited when compared with other parts of India, allowing little more than an impression of Goa's past before the Portuguese presence. A 'regional' approach to the history of Goa (i.e., observing these territories as part of a vaster region, the West Konkan, that shared some institutions and historical processes) can be useful to overcome such difficulties. This 'regional' approach thus takes into consideration the findings of the vast anthropological literature on this part of India as well as the processes of construction of colonial knowledge, of which the work of Bernard S. Cohn, among others, is fundamental. Second, connected to this, a 'subaltern perspective' is also needed; that is to say, these processes are analyzed by taking into consideration not only the 'voices from below', but also the local dynamics that existed and persisted within and beyond the Western imperial framework. Finally, these two approaches relate to recent scholarship on the legal history of India, some of which is referred to in this chapter.[18] In addition, this chapter is also inspired by comparative and connected methodological perspectives, favoring the relationship between the Portuguese empire and Indian polities as well as their relationship with the Spanish and the British empires. A final methodological issue refers to the use of the words: 'Goa', 'Goan(s)', 'Hindu(s)', 'India', 'Indian(s)', 'Europe', 'European(s)', 'Muslim(s)', and even 'Portuguese'.[19] Although it is problematic to use these terms when speaking of the 16th and 17th centuries since they refer to identities that did not exist then as they are recognized today, they are nevertheless used throughout this chapter to facilitate understanding.

---

18 Besides Cohn's *Colonialism and its forms of knowledge*, the scholarship on these issues is so vast that it cannot be referenced here. An example of the combination of all these approaches applied to the Portuguese empire in early modern India can be found in Xavier and Županov's *Catholic Orientalism*.

19 In his recent book *Os Filhos da Terra*, António Manuel Hespanha discusses thoroughly what "being Portuguese" could mean in this period, questioning the uniformity of the concept. His findings are extremely relevant to the discussion of the concept of 'Lusitanization'.

2 The Apprenticeship of Empire:[20] Uses and Customs during Early Portuguese Rule in Goa

Afonso de Albuquerque, governor of the *Estado da Índia* between 1509 and 1515, conquered Goa in 1510 and established somewhat of a feudal pact with his Indian ally, Timmaya.[21] He assigned him with the offices of *aguazil-mor* (chief judicial and administrative officer) and captain-general of Goa, in exchange for the defense of Goa, the representation of the Hindu population's interests and 60,000 *pardaos* of gold per year. Later, Malhar Rao,[22] brother of the King of Honavar (and later himself the king), acquired the same offices in exchange for 40,000 *pardaos* of gold.[23] Sources from 1510 say very little about the political and administrative organization of Goa. It is likely that locals retained their ways of living, as was common in suzerainty, a term Luís Filipe Thomaz used to characterize this initial period.[24] Through these pacts with Timmaya and Malhar Rao, the Portuguese recognized the property rights of the 'collaborationist' locals and did not ask for more taxes than the ones they had previously paid to the Bijapur Sultanate. Local populations were probably accustomed to this kind of situation since, as in other parts of South India, it was common to produce contracts between the ruler and his interlocutors. This allowed the conservation of local chieftains as well as the sharing of political, administrative, judicial, and fiscal power.[25]

Later, this pact was terminated and, by 1515, King D. Manuel I (1495–1521) decided to adopt the procedures of the "kings and lords of the land from the time of the Moors" to govern the territories of Goa, but it is unclear if these procedures were Muslim at all.[26] The territories of Tiswadi, Diwar, Chorão, and Jua (which included the town of Goa) had only been under Muslim rule for 40 years. They knew 20 years of Bijapur dominion (1490–1510), another 20 of Bahmanid rule (1470–1490), and a dispersed dominion, during the 14th century, of the Delhi Sultanate. Bijapur classified the territories of Goa as *Muāmala*, i.e., lands belonging to the Sultan. A *havaldar*—the governor—ruled them, helped by a *thānedār* (the chief fiscal and police officer, who became *tanadar* in the Portuguese documents) and a *Deshpande* (the general scribe). All of them

20 This expression is inspired by Luis Filipe Alencastro's essay, "The Apprenticeship of Colonization". On that, see also Guerra, "L'État et les Communautés: Comment Inventer un Empire".

21 Timoja in the Portuguese sources.

22 Mel Rao in the Portuguese sources.

23 Shastri, "Gersoppa's hand in the capture of Goa", 39–42.

24 Thomaz, "A estrutura político-administrativa do Estado da Índia", 228.

25 Magalhães, *Pequenos Reis e Grandes Honras*, 26.

26 Madeira-Santos, "As Instituições Indígenas no Império Português", 273.

mediated the relationship with the villages of the region of Goa, a function that was later assumed by the Portuguese *tanadar*. Judicially, the Sultan was the final authority of the *Qazi* court, while regionally there were courts presided by *vizirs* and *amirs*.

The impact of Muslim rule was undoubtedly more substantial in the town of Goa than in rural areas. Still the Portuguese documentation identifies village institutions and officers that were also present in other territories of the Sultanate of Bijapur, like the *muqqadam*, the *kulkarni*, and the *nayak*.[27] It is also telling that the names of these offices were of Persian, Konkani, or Marathi origin, demonstrating that Bijapur rule already adopted offices and institutions that existed before their domination of Goa.[28] Thus, adoption of the procedures of the "kings and lords of the land from the time of the Moors" meant to adopt previous political and administrative experiences that were already plural, of which only the most recent was visible to the Portuguese in the first years after their arrival. This means that King D. Manuel I's statement was the result of the Portuguese's ignorance of the long and complex history of domination of these territories.

This (apparent) respect for local differences represented the initial pluralist political and legal culture of the conquerors. António Manuel Hespanha demonstrated long ago that, in what concerns the early modern Portuguese kingdom, the law of the Crown coexisted with and was sometimes complementary to other types of law, such as local law and the jurisprudence of the courts. Similarly, sovereignty was shared, in contrast to the monopoly of the Crown, which would characterize later periods. In this initial period, these principles somehow translated into the imperial territories in respect of the local institutions. In the legal arena—like in other parts of Europe and the Hispanic world[29]—the local/corporative norms had precedence over the law of the king if they conformed to the *ratio juris* or the morals of the Christian religion.[30] Again, this was a political and legal culture that somehow converged with the situation in early modern India: in cases of dispute between the prescriptions included in the *Dharmaśāstras* and local customs, the latter often prevailed in the moment of making judgements.

27 Fukazawa, "A Study of the Local Administration of Adilshahi Sultanate (A.D. 1489–1686)", 37–66; Fukazawa, "Rural servants in 18th century Maharastra. Demiurgic or Jajmani System?" 14–40; but also in Kulkarni, "The Indian village with special reference to Medieval Deccan (Maratha county)", 1–42.

28 Gune, *The Judicial System of the Marathas*, xxii–xxviii.

29 Agüero, "Local law and Localization of law. Hispanic Legal Tradition and Colonial Culture", 101–130.

30 Hespanha, *Panorama da História Institucional e Jurídica* 3, 20–22.

The practice of compiling uses and customs was renewed in early modern Europe through the long-distance voyages that sought to find better routes to the Indies. During the 16th century, identifying the uses and customs was familiar not only to jurists, but also to travelers, merchants, missionaries, and humanists interested in mapping such uses and customs of the 'newly discovered' parts of the world. In 1520, for example, Johannes Boemus published an *Omnium Gentium Mores, Leges et Ritus*, arguing for its usefulness. Boemus' book did not yet include the information assembled by the Portuguese and the Spanish as a result of their overseas expansion.[31] Similarly, travelers, merchants, and officers of the Portuguese Crown compiled the uses and customs of the Indian societies since the beginning of the 16th century. Letters, reports, or treatises like the one of Duarte Barbosa of 1516, "Descrição das Terras da India Oriental, e dos seos Uzoz, Costumes, Ritos e Leys", the *Summa Oriental* of Tomé Pires of 1515, and the *Chronica de los reys de Bisnaga*, of Domingos Paes about Vijayanagar were included.[32] In contrast with the jurists, who were more interested in the uses and customs that overlapped or complemented the field of the *ius commune*, these actors mainly inquired about other normativities: social, religious, and ritual.[33]

To record and keep these uses and customs—which were, from a jurist's perspective, the "practices followed by most members of the community for a sufficient length of time to become binding"[34] and recognized as *ius proprium*—the Portuguese Crown had first to know them. It was in this context that several royal letters, laws, and decrees, issued between 1510 and 1526, tried to map the new territories and their people. In the same decades, when the jurists of the School of Salamanca theorized about the nature of the relationship between the Spanish monarchy and its non-Christian subjects, Portuguese practitioners in early modern Goa were building this relationship based on their Iberian cultural encyclopedias and experiences. The main issue at stake then was to identify which were the political, administrative, and judicial bodies that operated locally. This was crucial for grasping which taxes were paid by the inhabitants of Goa, as well as identifying which local structures could be integrated into the imperial order.[35]

The rules of João Machado, the captain and the *thānedār* of Goa in 1515, are exemplary of the initial efforts of the Portuguese Crown. Acquainted with the

---

31 Boemus, *Omnium Gentium Mores, Leges et Ritus*, S. Grimm & M. Wirsung, *passim*.

32 Paes, *Chronica dos Reys de Bisnaga*, *passim*.

33 On this literature, see, *maxime*, Lach, *Asia in the making of Europe*, vol 1.

34 Herzog, *A Short History of European Law*, 124–130.

35 Miranda, "The center and the periphery in the administration of the Royal Exchequer", 1–14.

Sultanate of Bijapur, Machado had to figure out the best way of exacting taxes from the farmers of Goa. These would be registered in a book and should be the same they paid to the previous 'lord of the land' (the Sultan of Bijapur). Four years later, the new *thānedār*, Duarte Pereira, received a more detailed set of instructions. First, Pereira had to count the *gaunkars* (the elites of the villages) that lived in Tiswadi, Chorão, Dívar, and Jua. Then, he had to identify their lands and the taxes the villages paid, which lands belonged to the Muslims, as well as which were small or damaged. Finally, he should know which *gaunkars* sold their properties or moved from one village to another, "as they were used to doing", so he could prevent them from doing so. Pereira also had judicial powers: he was supposed to settle the disputes between these *gaunkars* on issues related to their lands, trees, and plantations. Furthermore, he had to travel twice a week to the island of Tiswadi, accompanied by guards, to watch over it so that no one would steal fruits from either the king's or the *gaunkars*' trees.[36]

While Pereira was doing this, the "Rules for the government of the town" of Goa, of 1519, stated that the city councilors should know the ordinations of the towns and villages, preserving them when useful and amending them if bad.[37] This understanding conformed to paragraph 29 of volume one of *Ordenações Manuelinas,* which established the preservation of local customs unless the king decided to alter them. Article 66 clarified, however, that while each municipality explained its 'old rules', the Crown only kept those that were 'good', excluding those that were inconvenient.[38] Unfortunately, there are no traces of these early compilations that witness the effort of knowing the land and synthesizing the uses and customs of Goa already in the second decade of the 16th century. The same principles that guided Machado and Pereira's activities were present in the rules of the next *thānedār*, the powerful Goan Brahman Krishna,[39] who was now supposed to keep the information collected in a book divided into different sections, each one concerning a different village.[40]

These were indeed times of the 'apprenticeship of the empire', in which the Portuguese agents were slowly delving into the Goan local order, attempting

36 APO, Fasc. 5, vol. 1, 35–36.

37 APO, Fasc. 2, 20–27.

38 Hespanha, *Como os Juristas viam o mundo,* 2.4.1.2. Posturas, costumes locais e lei.

39 Crisná in Portuguese. The choice of Krishna demonstrated the dependency of the Portuguese Crown on local collaboration. Moreover, it allowed, at least theoretically, depending on the genuine political loyalty of Krishna to the Portuguese, easier access to the local people and their dealings.

40 APO, Fasc. 5, vol. 1, 65–68; On that, see Rochelle Pinto, "The Foral in the History of the Communidades", 203–204.

to grasp it intellectually, in a process that increased in the following decade. When Viceroy Vasco da Gama was sent to India in 1524, accompanied by a new team of officers, with the mission of correctly organizing the administration of the *Estado da Índia*, he inherited the results of these processes of learning and recordings of local uses and customs from the previous decade.[41] Among the officers that arrived in India in 1524 was Afonso de Mexia, who had extensive experience as an officer of the king (he had been one of the royal scribes, as well as a scribe of the Royal Exchequer). Mexia would substitute Pedro Nunes in the office of *Vedor da Fazenda*, the institution that oversaw all the economic and fiscal matters of *Estado da Índia* and supervised the *thānedār* as well.

3 Local Uses and Customs and Imperial Order in the *Foral*

It was on the 16th of September of 1526 that the *Foral* was concluded, signed by Mexia, and made public.[42] Another document written by Mexia reiterates that the *Foral* had, above all, fiscal goals. He explained that he had seen the papers of *thānedār* João Machado and inquired about the rents to be paid by the villages.[43] As Susana Münch Miranda has pointed out, tax revenue—and the establishment of institutions that allowed it in the politically subjugated territories—was "a means of establishing sources of revenue" that enabled the king "to ensure the self-sustainability of the crown's intervention in Asia".[44]

The first part of the *Foral* (today lost) materialized this endeavor, critical in a moment when the inhabitants of these villages were not Christian. The Portuguese Crown did not have the right to extract from them the tithes that Christians of other parts had to pay. Without tithes, other tribute payments and rents, namely the *foros* (one-fifth of the agrarian rents) the villages had to pay to the Portuguese Crown, became more important for the financial sustainability of the Portuguese presence in Asia. The first part of the *Foral* was in harmony with the process known as *Reforma dos Forais*, during which almost 500 *forais* of the Portuguese kingdom were rewritten between 1495 and 1520. These *forais* also aimed to control the tax revenue to be paid by the Portuguese municipalities and villages to the Crown.[45]

41 *Apud* Loureiro, "Reconstituição da documentação produzida por Afonso de Mexia", 22.

42 APO, Fasc. 5, vol. 1, 114–117, 139–141; Magalhães, *Pequenos Reis e Grandes Honras*, 58.

43 APO, Fasc. 5, vol. 1, 133–134.

44 Miranda, "The center and the periphery in the administration of the Royal Exchequer", 3.

45 Coelho, "O Poder Concelhio em tempos medievais", 19–34; Neto, "O foral manuelino de Porto de Mós", 77–78; Oliveira, "O Foral de Faro e a Reforma dos Forais", 14–15.

In contrast with the new *forais* of the kingdom, the *Foral* had a second part that compiled the uses and customs of Goan villages. However, its encounter with alterity was more challenging than the ones faced by medieval and early modern European royal agents and jurists. In India, the Portuguese faced different forms of social organization, languages, religions, and uses and customs, of which Goa was only a small part. The process of knowing and assembling local uses and customs for the *Foral* was simultaneously similar and different from previous experiences in the kingdom and in Europe since it adapted the *Foral*, as Pinto remembered, to the "socio-ecological conditions" of the region of Goa.[46] Moreover, relying on information previously collected, Mexia also included documentation produced in the context of (and prior to) the Bijapur Sultanate, and information found in old books, registering the *nemos* (decisions of the *gaunkars*) on economic and fiscal matters.[47] The *Foral* also included fresh information provided by the *gaunkars* and the scribes of the villages, many of them of Brahman origin. Mexia and his officers thus had many cultural, legal, and administrative resources to draw on when compiling the uses and customs of the Goan villages.

As a "socially embedded community", South India's Brahmans' presence was usually constituted in temples, lineages, referential books, and ritual practices.[48] The same can be said for the territories of Goa, where the presence of Brahmans was significant.[49] A copper plate of 1391 reported that Madhav Mantri, Goa's governor under the rule of Vijayanagar, had founded a *brahmapuri* (a learning place inhabited by Brahmans) on the island of Diwar.[50] In 1510, the *brahmapuri* of Diwar was still very active, described by the Portuguese as the equivalent of the "Holy Land" for the local populations or Rome for the Christians.[51] Brahmans of Kushashtali in Salcete worked as scribes during the rule of Vijayanagar too, as well as in the Bijapur Sultanate in the late 15th and early 16th century. Their involvement with these royal courts allowed them to reinforce their local and regional positions, expressed, for instance, in the donations they made to their temples.[52] Kushashtali, as well as Keloshi in its neighborhood, had

46 Pinto, "The Foral in the History of the Communidades", 187, 195.

47 Viegas, *As Políticas Portuguesas*, 47.

48 Fischer, *Hindu Pluralism*, 13–14. See also Rao, *Cultures of Memory in South Asia*, 307.

49 On that, see Xavier, *A Invenção de Goa*, 279.

50 A summary of this copper plate, translated into Portuguese, can be found in Barros, *Décadas da Ásia*, vol. 2, 188.

51 *Documentação para a História do Padroado Português do Oriente* (henceforth DHMPPO), vol. 7, 85. See Xavier, *A Invenção de Goa*, 267, 289–296.

52 Pereira, *Gaunkaris*, 95; O'Hanlon and Minkowski, "What makes people who they are?", 381–416; Rao, Shulman and Subrahmanyam (eds.), *Textures of Time, passim*; Alam and Subrahmanyam, "The making of a munshī", 185–209.

Brahmanical centers of learning. Their pundits wrote versions of well-known epic poems *Mahabharata* and *Ramayana,* adapting the stories of Pandavas, Kauravas, Rama, and their brothers to the territories of Goa. Rescued and transcribed by the Jesuits, these few texts that survived the destruction campaigns of the mid-16th century witnessed the presence of *dharma*—the moral world of the heroes of *Mahabharata* and the *Ramayana*—in the Goan territories.[53] They also testify to the creative appropriations of 'classical texts', as well as the capacity of local Brahmans to disseminate their worldviews and, to a certain extent, what some scholars called their "regulatory project".[54]

As shown below, the *gaunkars* and scribes involved in the production of the *Foral* did not provide all the information they had about their uses and customs, namely those concerning the laws of inheritance. When later questioned, they argued that this was due to the rush with which Mexia had pursued the inquiry.[55] Another explanation, however, is that the concealment of specific dimensions was intentional and sought to preserve their normative autonomy. It is also plausible that this was the result of (un)expected misunderstandings;[56] interpreters were involved in the translation of the local language and political and administrative categories into the Portuguese ones, and they could have mistaken the intentions of both parts.[57] There was neither a wholly *bottom-up* control of information nor a *top-down* one in the production of the *Foral.*

Each of the participants in the process somehow interfered in the final arrangements of the document, which made it into somewhat of a bridge between the village order and the imperial one. Parts of the *Foral* clearly express the command of the Portuguese Crown, while others show the local elites' ability to defend their interests. Above all, the *Foral* was not only a hybrid document, but also a monument to a particular historical context, which, for several reasons, was later generalized.

---

53 Sama, *Koṃkaṇī Rāmāyaṇa, passim.* Also a *Shri Krishnachavitrakatha* was written in this period, today in the Archives of Braga. See Gomes, *Old Konkani language and literature,* 50–54. On the appropriations of the *Mahabharata,* see Pollock, *The Language of the Gods in the World of Men,* 223–237.

54 O'Hanlon, Minkowski, and Venkatkrishnan, *Scholar Intellectuals in Early Modern India,* Introduction. On these appropriations in early modern India, see, in general, Davis, jr., and Brick, "Social and Literary History of *Dharmaśāstra* – Commentaries and Legal Digests", in Olivelle and Davis (eds.), *Hindu Law: A New History* of *Dharmaśāstra,* 33; Mitchell, "The Practice of Hindu Law", 58–77. Lubin, "The theory and practice of property", 13.

55 APO, Fasc. 5, vol. 1, 157.

56 Galindo, "Legal transplants between time and space", 134 onwards.

57 Couto, "The Role of Interpreters, or Linguas, in the Portuguese Empire During the 16th Century", 1–10; Flores, "Le «língua» cosmopolite", 225–250; Deshpande, "Scripting the Cultural History of Language", 62–86.

How did the imperial agents interfere in the contents of the document? And how did these interferences contribute to constructing a new local order? The preamble of the second part of the *Foral* openly assumed the interference of the Crown by indicating that it assembled the "rights, uses, and customs" of the villages, which "we [the Crown] should keep". Further, those "rights, uses, and customs" were to be used in the manner the agents of the Portuguese Crown found appropriate. The appropriated institutions were, in this case, the existing political and administrative bodies, the *gaunkari*, and the members that composed them, the *gaunkars*. The latter, defined in the *Foral* as governors, ministers, and benefactors, belonged, the *Foral* said, to the lineages of the founders of the villages. They constituted the collective organism that headed the village, the *gaunkari*, which governed, as already mentioned, the land and rituals associated with it. The *gaunkari* also defined access to the privileges annexed to the *gaunkar*'s and other officers' lineages (the *vaṇgaḍ*), each one usually living in specific quarters of the village. In addition, the *gaunkari* had judicial powers, settling, in general, the disputes among villagers. It was up to the *gaunkari* to make the decisions that bounded all villagers collectively.

However, contrasting with the *Foral*'s explanation, possibly provided by the *gaunkars* themselves, most of the 16th-century *gaunkars* did not descend from the founders of the villages. An 11th-century document, for example, shows that a man called Chadamma received, as a grant, the village of Morumbi, perhaps at that time already depopulated. In 1526, the *gaunkars* of that village belonged to several lineages, but Chadamma's was not part of them. Chadamma's case, like others, is consistent with the narrative about the foundation of Goan villages presented in the *Décadas da Asia* by João de Barros, who argued that none but three of the lineages that controlled the *gaunkaris* of Goa were descendants of the founders.[58] The *Foral*'s narrative also did not consider the *gaunkars* that had abandoned their villages after the Portuguese conquest of Goa, settling down in the lands of the Sultanate of Bijapur. The Crown expropriated their lands, which were received either by relatives or, in their absence, by other people, who occupied their positions in the *gaunkari*.[59]

By assuming that the actual *gaunkars* descended from the founders of the villages, by recognizing new *gaunkars*, and by making their powers and honors permanent, the Crown crystallized for the future a situation that was not necessarily descriptive of the villages' past. As Pinto has pointed out, this perpetual

58 Moraes, *Kadamba Kula*, 400; Barros, *Décadas da Ásia*, vol. 2, 190–191.

59 Paragraphs 17, 18, 40 of the *Foral*; APO, vol. 5, 25. If they returned to their original villages, they could be given other lands that were vacant at that moment (APO, vol. 5, 25).

association reinforced the internal power of those that were the *gaunkars* at the time the *Foral* was written.[60]

It is likely that the Portuguese agents were merely pragmatic in applying to the villages of Goa the principle of indivisibility that operated in the kingdom since the *Lei Mental* in the previous century. This principle stated that honors and jurisdiction should not be separated (*dignitates et jurisdictiones non dividuntur*). In the early kingdom, this principle had helped to tie powerful families to the Crown, settling an interdependency between both.[61] In Goa, where the weakness of the power of the king and the lack of human resources was evident, the adoption of this principle was a way of attracting the loyalty of the village elites to the imperial power.

Besides expressing the shared and the specific political culture of each Portuguese agent, this arrangement also converged with the mutual dependency of the ruler and the local chiefs that characterized many South India polities. In these polities, *dāna* (gifts) in the form of *māṇya* (rents, plus honor and ritual supremacy, namely the right of heading the ritual sacrifices) and *rakṣaṇa* (protection) were exchanged for taxes.[62] The protection of the elites in exchange for their loyalty was essential to the conservation of the imperial power, particularly in what concerned the fulfilment of fiscal duties. It was the *gaunkars*' duty, the *Foral* said, to pay to the "Lord of the land", the taxes each village already paid to the previous ruler. Many paragraphs are concerned with this aspect, while others, directly or indirectly, also refer to tax revenue and the rights of the Crown concerning the immovable and movable properties of the villages and their inhabitants.[63]

In other matters, the power of the *gaunkars* was reshaped and/or reduced. Several clauses concerning other aspects of the relationship between the *gaunkars*, the *gaunkari*, and the imperial power make it evident: their almost complete submission toward the *thānedar*; their obligation of hosting the officers of the king when they wanted to stay in the village; their commitment to providing services to the city of Goa when asked to do so; and their obligation of registering their decisions by following writing protocols in use in Portugal.[64]

The *Foral* also prohibited the *gaunkars* from exercising *dāna*, an essential part of the social recognition and ritualization of their power, in their

60 Pinto, "The Foral in the History of the Communidades", 188, 211–212.

61 Hespanha, *Como os juristas viam o mundo*, 2.4.3.7. Transmissão dos direitos senhoriais.

62 Magalhães, *Pequenos Reis e Grandes Honras Culto*, 23–25, 34.

63 *Foral dos usos e costumes*, paragraphs 3–6, 9–10.

64 *Foral dos usos e costumes*, paragraphs 11, 14, 18, 21, 36, 37, 39.

relationship with the king's officers. This prohibition referred directly to paragraph 56 of volume 4 of the *Ordenações* of King D. Manuel I, which tried to control practices which we today identify as corruption. However, locally it meant stripping an essential part of the expression of their power. The interference in the symbolic authority of the *gaunkars* was present in other moments too. On the one hand, the governor had to authorize the use of torches and palanquins by new *gaunkars*, as well as pedestrian officers to accompany them, increasing their dependency on the imperial power. On the other, harvest rituals had to include a Christian vicar and a presentation of rice in the cathedral, reducing the religious autonomy of the village.[65]

All these cases demonstrate that the *Foral* definitively reshaped the local political and administrative order. The *gaunkars* continued to be the heads of the villages, as well as responsible for the decision-making. At the same time, some of their honors were abolished, increasing their dependency on the Portuguese Crown. Furthermore, their administrative processes included some procedures that followed the Portuguese style. In addition, the *Foral* also insisted on the need to maintain the local uses and customs; the expressions "following their uses and customs" or "general customs" are frequently invoked. Moreover, the *Foral* stated that the customs of villages that had different customs should be respected as well. Thus, which local uses and customs were kept and how were they kept?

Again, the *gaunkars* were the main interlocutors, and they certainly tried to keep the customs that were most favorable to them, expressing, in practice, what Sumit Guha has argued: that "custom would favour the powerful whose predecessors had made it".[66] The *Foral* kept their customary privileges of leasing paddy fields as well as of granting wastelands if they were to be used to cultivate betel trees. The same happened with the grants they gave to the village officers—priest, dancers of the temple, clerk, porter, washman, shoemaker, carpenter, blacksmith, renter, 'faraz', cleaner—as payment for their services to the village. The taxes to be paid by each type of land—paddy fields, areca tree orchards, wastelands—were also preserved in conjunction with the principle that the *gaunkars* should not pay more to the Portuguese king than they did to the previous ruler.[67] However, according to John Duncan Derrett, those concerning inheritance were influenced by the *Yājñavalkya Smṛti* (the second

65 *Foral dos usos e costumes*, paragraphs 19, 27–29, 45 and 49; see also Pinto, "The Foral in the History of the Communidades", 209–210. It was the Portuguese law that was applied in the cases of usury and thefts (clauses 25, 26) referring to Ord Man, L V, tt. XXXVII – Dos furtos…; Leis Extravagantes, tt. III – Dos furtos & Roubos; OrdMan, L IV, tt. XIV – Das usuras.

66 Guha, "An Indian Penal Regime", 106.

67 *Foral dos usos e costumes*, paragraphs 5, 6, 9, 10, 12, 20.

most crucial 'legal' *smṛti* after the *Manusmṛti*), through the commentaries of Vijñaneśvara and Aparāditya I, as well as of *Parāśara Smṛti* by Madhāva. Derrett found this influence in a dispute taking place between Hindus in the first decades of 18th-century Goa, where "Goan customary law" was recalled.[68] If this 'classical' inspiration was still present at the beginning of the 18th century, two centuries after the Portuguese influence, it was probably more visible in the previous centuries and thus expressed in the *Foral*.

The judicial system inscribed in the *Foral* also followed the local customs. Many of the legal situations referred to were to be solved by the *gaunkari*. Modes of proof—documents, witnesses, oaths—were similar to those operating, in general, in the Indian world. However, if classical Indian legal texts treated legal procedures very carefully (like the inclusion of other modes of proof, such as 'possession' and 'ordeals'), the information included in the *Foral* was sketchy in what concerned legal procedures. In litigations between inhabitants of the village related to immovable properties and inheritance, the *Foral* required the annexation of the deeds (*rājaśāsana* or other documents) and the books of the village concerning the object of litigation. Also, the procedures related to mortgages, their amounts, and types of proof needed to solve litigations between creditors and debtors retained the local ways of solving conflicts.

The same did not happen, however, in the cases involving significant misbehavior by the *gaunkars*. In those situations, it was the *thānedār*, or even the captain-general or the governor or viceroy (the ultimate judicial officer of appeal), who decided what kind of punishment ill-doers would receive. However, this could also reproduce a local practice, since at least under the Bijapur domination, the Sultanate regional courts or the Sultan himself solved harsh criminal cases.

The pages above illustrate how difficult it is to reconstruct the village normativities through an analysis of the earliest available document that systematically maps some of them, especially concerning the political, administrative, and judicial spheres. Besides being a selection of norms, the *Foral* also witnesses the hybridity of the norms it contained. Admittedly, parts of them already operated in the villages, as a result of prior experiences, but others were the outcome of negotiations between the rulers and the ruled. Writing down the results of these negotiations was novel and made of the *Foral*, in a sense, a 'written constitution' of the village normativities, though not in the sense scholarship has traditionally attached to this word. Instead, the *Foral* did *constitute* a kind of new village order, which was the result of older norms and practices and imperial selections and impositions.

68 Derrett, "Hindu law in Goa", 206, fn. 6.

4 Dharmaśāstras and the Smṛti in the Local Order of Goan Villages: The Multinormativity of the Foral

Stepping back in history can be enlightening in what concerns the potential sources of some of the normativities that were considered old uses and customs. The medieval territories of Goa were under the dominion of polities that had the *Dharmaśāstras* and their commentaries as part of their world of normative reference. The Western Chalukyas (1076–1156), the Goan Kadambas (1006–1356), and the Vijayanagar empire (1370–1469) were all under Brahmanical influence and promoted the commentators of the ancient texts.

It was during the Chalukya government of Vikramadatya VI (1076–1126) that the Brahman jurist Vijñaneśvara wrote the *Mitāṣksāra,* the most famous and most widely disseminated commentary on the *Yagnavālkya Smṛti.* By that time, the Goan territories were under the rule of the feudatory Jayakesi II, who was the Kadamba rāja of Goa between 1125 and 1147 and husband of one the daughters of Vikramadatya VI.[69] More or less in the same period, the *Apārarka*—another treatise on the *Yagnavālkya Smṛti*—was written by the ruler of the Silaharas, Aparaditya I (1170–1197), a polity of the north Konkan in the vicinity of Goa.[70]

It is still not possible to trace a direct link between these treatises and the customs included in the *Foral* that seem to refer to them. Still, the Brahmanical influence in the Goan territories since the 11th century allows us to suspect that they might have had an impact in these territories. In that century, for example, donations to Śivaite Brahmans reinforced the impression of a Brahman influence among the elites of medieval Goa. Those Śivaite Brahmans established centers of learning (*agrāharas*), where the *Vēdas* and the schools that interpreted them (the *Mīmāṃsā, Nyāya, Sāmkhya, Yoga,* and *Vedānta,* which was the last and the one that prevailed in 16th–century South India), were studied.[71] Similarly, other 'classical' texts—the *Dharmaśāstras,* the *Itihāsas,* and the *Purānas*—were taught, through methods of exegesis and analysis comparable to the Scholastic tradition in Europe.[72]

---

69 *Mitāṣksāra* became one of the most important medieval digests, translated into Tamil, Telegu, and Persian, at least. Another well-known digest was the *Dāyabhāga,* a treatise written by Jīmūtvahāna of Bengal of the 10th to 11th centuries, which proposed different interpretations concerning inheritance, property rights, women's rights, and other matters.

70 Kane, *History of the Dharmaśāstras,* vol. 1, 374–375.

71 Fischer, *Hindu Pluralism,* 5–6.

72 Moraes, *The Kadamba Kula,* 287–300. On that, see inscriptions from the time of the Kadambas in *Epigraphia Indica,* vol. 7; Herzog, *A Short History of European Law,* 78–79.

As Derrett has pointed out, some of the inheritance customs assembled in the *Foral* might have been local appropriations of the *Mitāṣksāra.* The principle that inheritance was due to the kinship between the owner of the wealth and the heir of it (father, son, grandson, and vice-versa)—what Vijñaneśvara called "unobstructed heritage"—ruled the majority of the succession norms present in the *Foral.*[73] Similar situations can be found in the clauses about the sale of land. Selling land was complicated since the agreement of all its heirs and other *gaunkars* was needed; in addition, cancelling the sale was also possible.[74] The same could be said concerning the *Mitāṣksāra* for the rules toward women, who were entirely unable to inherit from their fathers, grandfathers, and husbands.[75] Finally, the norm that stated that if any goods were "discovered" or "found", they belonged to the king, could also refer to *Mitāṣksāra* (or other treatises) paragraphs on forms of acquiring property.[76]

It is still unknown whether such uses and customs were transmitted orally or in writing. Documents produced under Portuguese domination in the early 16th century do refer to the existence of ancient scriptures and books of law in the villages of Goa. Were these books simply compilations of uses and customs without reference to the classical treatises, as some scholarship argues? Or were they mere apocryphal documents used to impress the new rulers? Many scholars contend that, instead of a normative textual tradition based on the *Dharmaśāstras* and the *Smṛtis,* customs were "the main source of court decisions", "which decided case by case without taking into consideration any normative text".[77] Practice and jurisprudence, not books, defined multiple and casuistic judicial architectures, where the very concept of enforceable law

73 *Foral dos usos e costumes*, paragraphs 22 and 30. However, the interference of Portuguese law was also visible in these sections. The paragraphs concerning the heritage of those dead without heirs provide an excellent case to observe: the inheritances belonged to the king, but he allowed the *gaunkars* to use or distribute them to other people.

74 *Foral dos usos e costumes*, paragraphs 15 and 16.

75 *Foral dos usos e costumes*, paragraphs 27, 30, 33.

76 *Foral dos usos e costumes*, paragraph 32. See *Dāya-Bhāga and Mitākṣarā*, 242; Bhattacharyya-Panda, *Appropriation and Invention of Tradition*, 21–22, and Rocher, *Jimutavahana's Dayabhaga*, 16.

77 Halpérin, "Transplants of European Normativity in India and in Japan", 150–157. These authors bring up examples from 14th–16th century Kerala, where *Dharmaśāstras* were never quoted. There were places where the *sāstric* prescriptions were not even invoked. In fact, practical law relied on *ācāra*, *samaya*, and *maryādā*, all words referring to customs and practices, without reference to the *śāstras*.
Davis, "Dharma, Maryāda and Law in Early British Malabar", 83, 119, 129 and 204; the *Manu Smrti* was known in the 18th-century courts of the Marathas kingdom. Gune, *The Judicial System of the Marathas*, 69. A similar understanding of these processes can be found in Guha, "An Indian Penal Régime", 101–126.

did not exist. In addition, other scholars have argued that these customs were "epitomes of past balances of social power".[78]

What was the status of the uses and customs compiled in the *Foral*? Were they only 'local customs' or, instead, did they witness the appropriation in Goa of the *Dharmaśāstras* and the *Smṛtis*? Moreover, if the latter is true, can it be said that *Tikās* and *Nibandhas* (treatises that were legal commentaries on the *Dharmaśāstras*) proliferated in 16th century Goa, like in the Islamicized territories of the Deccan or other Indian polities, by the time of the British arrival?[79] More detailed studies are needed to reconstruct the legal traditions that informed the administrative order of the Goan villages and to understand, with more rigor, the characteristics of this administrative order. Still, the examples presented above allow us to suppose that the village order that materialized in the *Foral* was constituted by several layers of experience, combining *genuinely local* uses and customs with local appropriations of classical Brahmanical treatises, transforming their rules into local customs. This diversity was undoubtedly related to the many dominations that had ruled the villages before the Portuguese. The Portuguese were merely another superimposed layer in an order characterized by multinormativity, which even hosted contradictory norms.[80]

5 The Uses of the *Foral* in the 16th and 17th Centuries

The coverage of the *Foral* reinforced its *constitutive* dimension: the "*gaunkars*, laborers, tributaries, inhabitants" and other people of the villages and town of Goa were supposed to be attached to its norms. Moreover, even if the document clearly defined its initial normative space—the 31 communities of Tiswadi, Chorão, Dívar, and Jua[81]—from 1543 it was extended to the inhabitants of the

78 Guha, "Wrongs and rights in the Maratha country", 26; Rocher, *Studies in Hindu Law and Dharmaśāstras, passim*; Mawani and Hussin, "The Travels of Law: Indian Ocean Itineraries", 735; see also Davis, *The boundaries of Hindu Law, passim.*

79 Bhattacharya-Panda, *Appropriation and Invention of Tradition*, chapter 1, 17; Lapidus, *A History of Islamic Societies*, 361–364; Hallaq, *An Introduction to Islamic Law, passim*; Coulson, *A History of Islamic Law, passim*; Davis, "Dharma, Maryāda and Law in Early British Malabar", 51–70; Rocher, "Hindu Conceptions of Law", 1283–1284.

80 On the superimposition and substitution of different layers and the overlapping of sources of justice in early modern India, see Guha, "The qazi, the dharmadhikari and the judge Political authority and legal diversity in pre-modern India: Premodern Europe and India in Comparison (13th–18th Centuries)", 97–115.

81 Pinto, "The Foral in the History of the Communidades", 200–201.

villages of Salcete and Bardez, which meant that 99 more villages came under its influence. Concerning these territories, a document of 1595 declared that Salcete followed most of the uses and customs of Tiswadi, but it is not clear whether the same applied to Bardez.[82] In fact, concerning land, for example, a 1619 report explained that all property of Salcete belonged to the ruler, who rented it for short periods to the villages, while in Bardez, the document said it was the inhabitants of the villages who owned the land.[83] How did these statements unite with the norms of the *Foral* concerning the land and its ownership? The *Foral* was imposed on territories and people with different historical experiences, thus freezing the diversity of these experiences in favor of a process of essentialization of village life, which was mainly useful for the relationship between the imperial power and those villages. Was the *Foral* efficient in this endeavor?

A petition of 1534 sent to the Governor of Goa is particularly enlightening: on the one hand, this petition demonstrates that the judicial system of the village was considered insufficient to solve all conflicts, especially when the solution provided by the village courts did not satisfy one of the litigants. Perhaps this explains why one of the parties involved in the litigation decided to petition to the imperial court. On the other hand, this petition also demonstrates that, by 1534, some local inhabitants started to refer to the norms included in the *Foral* to settle conflicts between them, even if this discredited the validity of the document in relation to specific situations.[84]

The *Sentença sobre as partilhas dos naturaes da terra,* signed by the Governor of the *Estado da Índia,* Nuno da Cunha (1529–1538), on August 14, 1534, refers to a conflict between three brothers: Santu Sinay and Sau Sinay against their half-brother, Ramu Sinay. The conflict concerned the inheritance of their father. Sau and Santu complained about the division of their father's heritage into only two parts, based on the number of wives he had, rather than three, based on the number of sons. Their petition argued that the *Foral* was insufficient in the clauses concerning inheritance after the death of a father, regarding the rights of the sons, nephews, and relatives, or sons of different wives. They argued that the "books of their antique laws" contradicted the clauses included in the *Foral.*[85] To solve this contradiction, the two brothers suggested the governor send the principal officer of justice—the *Ouvidor* Pedro Álvares

82 Paes, *Tombo das Ilhas de Goa e das Terras de Salcete e Bardês*, 100.

83 ANTT, Armário Jesuítico, Mss. 89, no. 19, 42; AHU, India, Cx 6. no. 29, 1.

84 Pereira, *História da Administração da Justiça*, vol. 1, 61–65.

85 Jaffe, "The languages of petitioning in early colonial India", 581–597.

de Almeida—to listen to local "lettered men" (probably *prādviveka*)[86] about the various chapters concerning inheritance included in the "books" and "antique scriptures" of the land.[87]

The judicial sentence issued by the Governor did include information provided by "lettered men". They declared that the inheritance, both immovable and movable property, of a deceased father should be equally parted between his sons, though with an advantage for the eldest brother. They also said that the heirs should give some movable property to their mother, for her maintenance. The same principle applied in the case of multiple wives, but only when these were of the same caste as the deceased father. Some of these legal principles were present in the *Manusmṛti* and were repeated in other texts, like the *Dharmasutras* of Gautama and Baudhāvana and the *Smṛtis* of Yājñavalkya and Nārada.[88] As mentioned above, these were principles that circulated, directly or indirectly, among Brahmanical communities, and were probably appropriated by the "lettered men" of Goa and its surroundings.

These explanations, however, opposed clause 33 of the *Foral*, which explicitly stated that in cases with two wives the inheritance should be divided into two equal parts, even if one wife had one only child, and the other, two or more. Consequently, the *Ouvidor* decided to convene an assembly of the *gaunkars*, who eight years earlier had informed the Portuguese agents about the inheritance rules that operated in the villages of Goa. The Portuguese ruling explained that "the truth of their customs" motivated this decision. The *gaunkars* validated the two different customs; however, they said that in disputes like that of the brothers, the law was to be followed, thus contradicting the rule that customs had precedence over law. In addition, the *gaunkars* explained, as before, that they had not given this information to Mexia because he appeared to be in a hurry when questioning them about the rules of inheritance that operated in the villages.[89]

The *Ouvidor* conducted the process and wrote the conclusions, but the final ruling was Governor Cunha's. He accepted both customs as valid, arguing that both customs were "ancient in this land", and "both were used". He decided for the norm that stated that the inheritance should be equally divided among all sons, independently of the number of wives. He also agreed with the

86 Local expert on the *Dharmaśāstras* and their legal commentaries (*Tikās, Nibhandas*), as well as on local customs.

87 APO, Fasc. 5, vol. 1, 156.

88 Rocher, "Hindu conceptions of law", 39–58; Rocher, "Inheritance dāyabhāga", 172; Kane, *The History of the Dharmashastras*, vol. 2–1, 472,

89 APO, Fasc. 5, vol. 1, 157.

application of the same solution to comparable situations, possibly because this norm was most similar to Portuguese law, where all the sons had equal rights to their fathers' inheritance.[90] Cunha's decision converged with the tendency to expand Portuguese law—probably considered to embody the *ius commune* better than any other—to all subjects, in tension with the legal pluralism that was still present at the time of production of the *Foral*.

This petition and the corresponding decision are unusual for several reasons. On the one hand, the decision of the Governor illustrates a change that was taking place in the political culture of Portuguese elites. Parallel to the traditional pluralist culture, a trend favoring the homogenization of the societies under the rule of the same prince was emerging. Somehow, Cunha already embodied this, which, as will be discussed, had other and more dramatic expressions in the territories of Goa. On the other hand, this case demonstrates that the local elites (at least, Brahman elites) were well aware of the lacunae of the *Foral* and took advantage of this when possible.

Ultimately, not only were the local normativities more complicated than what was assembled in the *Foral*, but so was the vocabulary used by the locals to refer to them. The reference to the body of rules that was perceived and translated by the Portuguese as "law" is enlightening. To which "law" was it referring? Why did the Portuguese think that such "law"[91] could translate into the Portuguese word *lei*? The data available are insufficient to answer these questions. We can only hypothesize that the "lettered men" belonged to an *agrahara*[92] or *brahmapuri*, where there was possibly an archive with scriptures in which different customs and laws were compiled.

Like clause 33, other requirements of the *Foral* were open to interpretation. For example, paragraphs 17 and 18 expressed different customs about the inheritance of *gaunkars* who had abandoned their land, rights, and obligations. Clause 18 established that the relatives of a fleeing *gaunkar* inherited his properties, but, if they did not want to accept it or were absent, the inheritance would revert to the *gaunkaris*. However, clause 17 stated that the *gaunkars* could give those rights "to whom they want", paving the way for the entrance of other lineages into the *gaunkaris*,[93] as was later witnessed in three villages of Bardez (Calangute, Aldona, and Siolim) and one of Salcete (Raia). In these

90 APO, Fasc. 5, vol. 1, 153–159. On that case, see also Pinto, "The Foral in the History of the Communidades", 81–82; and D'Souza, *Legal Systems*, vol. 2, 73–74.

91 We only have access to the Portuguese translation, and not to the original word used by the *gaunkars* and the "lettered men".

92 Land given by a king or a noble person to Brahmans to maintain their temples and a pilgrimage site and to sustain their families.

93 *Foral dos usos e costumes*, paragraphs 17, 18, and 33.

villages, people that did not belong to the lineages of the actual *gaunkars*, but had rents or rights in the village or were powerful creditors, were promoted to the status of *gaunkars*, constituting new *vaṇgaḍs.*[94]

In contrast, other clauses were invoked by other *gaunkars* to counteract either the pressure of these powerful groups that tried to participate actively in the government of the village or, as would happen later, the policies of the Crown.[95] In 1572, the king received a collective petition against the public services that the government asked the *gaunkars* to provide. The *gaunkars* argued that these demands were against the *Foral:* Clause 21 established that they should only help in the construction and cleaning of the walls of the town of Goa and similar services.[96]

Seeing that the second part of the *Foral*, the one specifically related to the uses and customs, was challenged, the same happened with the first (missing) part. In 1533, Governor Cunha asked for the presence of the *gaunkars* of Goa and asked them to include in the *Foral* the *goddevrad,* a tax they paid to the former rulers of Goa. The *gaunkars* admitted that this tax was absent, declaring that they would pay it henceforth. Six years later, *Vedor da Fazenda* Fernão Rodrigues de Castelo Branco asked the scribes of the villages to include the *culcarna papoxi,* another tax they had formerly paid to Bijapur. In 1541, the same officer received information from the Sultanate of Bijapur about the *kushvarat,* a voluntary tax paid by the villages, calling the *gaunkars* again to settle this. As a result, an addendum was placed in the *Foral,* thus raising the taxes paid by the villages. Following this, the *kushvarat* was suspended by Governor Martim Affonso de Sousa in 1543 and reintroduced by Viceroy D. Luís de Athaíde in 1579, who said that this was to respect the *Foral* and the agreements made with the *gaunkars* in 1541. However, since this tax was only paid since 1579 by the people of Bardez, its *Câmara Geral* (the assembly of the most important villages of Bardez) petitioned against it, which led Viceroy Francisco de Mascarenhas to suspend it once more until its second reintroduction in 1595.[97] All these decisions were attached to the original document, making both parts of the *Foral* a palimpsest of the historical processes taking place in Goa, as well as demonstrating their plasticity.[98] One of these processes was the Christianization of Goa and its inhabitants.

94 APO, Fasc. 5, vol. 2, 844–846. *Vaṇgaḍs* were hierarchical divisions within the *gaunkar* and caste groups expressed in the spatial organization of the village.

95 Magalhães, *Pequenos Reis e Grandes Honras*, 63, 201.

96 APO, Fasc. 5, vol. 2, 844–846.

97 Miranda, *A Administração da Fazenda Real no Estado da Índia*, 59, fn. 16.

98 Paes, *Tombo das Ilhas de Goa e das Terras de Salcete e Bardês*, 9–17.

6 Christianity and Conversion: Religious Homogenization and the 'Lusitanization' of Village Normativities

The Portuguese elites' political culture had changed significantly by the time of the annexation of the territories of Salcete and Bardez in 1543. The religious conflicts taking place in Europe, at least since the formal excommunication of Luther by Pope Leon X in 1521, increased the political relevance of religious affiliation. The decision-makers feared that the political loyalty of people who did not share the same religion as their king was feeble. Consequently, while in the kingdom there were visible efforts of re-Christianization and to control orthodoxy (the Inquisition was one of the institutional expressions of this)[99]; in the imperial territories, Christianization became an essential tool to guarantee political preservation, particularly in those territories under the direct rule of the Portuguese king.

This change starts to materialize in Goa in the 1530s, already under the government of King D. João III (1521–1557).[100] The conversion to Christianity and the homogenization of Goa's inhabitants became systematic in the subsequent decades, with dramatic consequences for the life of the villages. The juridical principle that assimilated *regeneratio* (baptism) to *generatio* (birth) was associated with the conversion to Christianity and became an instrument of naturalization, that is to say, of 'Lusitanization' of the local people. After baptism, local Christians would enjoy, at least theoretically, the same legal rights and obligations of the Portuguese and they would submit to canon law and its precepts.[101]

It is therefore essential to visit the decade of 1540 to be able to assess the changing world of Goan villages and the transformation of the normativities that governed them. The systematic destruction of the temples, deities, and books of the villages and the expulsion of their priests started in 1540, severing the 31 villages of Tiswadi, Chorão, Dívar, and Jua, from one of their essential dimensions: the religious one. Knowing how the patronage of deities and temples and the performance of the rituals involved in this were relevant to the *gaunkars*' power, it is easy to deduce how this process of destruction

99 For an analysis of the strategies used by the Inquisition to stimulate and control orthodoxy in Asia, see Lourenço (Chapter 7) in this volume.

100 Xavier, *A Invenção de Goa*, chapter 1.

101 *Documentos Remetidos da Índia*, vol. 2, 66–67. The establishment of a High Court in 1544 also helped to enforce the efficacy of the new legislation as well as the reception of the decrees of the Council of Trent, which had been adopted as law of the kingdom since 1564.

had immediate consequences in the local economy of power.[102] Twenty years later, the territories of Salcete and Bardez were the object of the same policies, even if this violated the 1555 treaty established between the Portuguese government and the Sultanate of Bijapur that annexed them; this treaty had established that the inhabitants of those two regions should only convert to Christianity with freedom of choice, allowing them to keep their temples, rites, and devotions.[103]

It was in this context of Christianization that Fernão Rodrigues de Castelo Branco wrote a new *Foral*. This document was mainly concerned with taxes and was probably intended to substitute the first part of the *Foral de Mexia*. It established that the *gaunkars* would voluntarily (with "contentment" and without any obligation) pay to the Crown, "every year and forever", 2,000 *tangas brancas* taken from the rents of the lands and other properties that belonged to the temples, priests, and other temple servants who had been expelled from Goa. This money was intended to be used for promoting Christianity, the building of churches, convents, and monasteries, and the payment of priests.

The *Foral* of 1541 recognized that the *gaunkars* were the owners of those lands and that neither the governor nor the *Vedor da Fazenda*, or any other officer of the Portuguese Crown, could ever violate those rights.[104] Curiously, this agreement kept the financial control over the (now Christian) religious world in the hands of the *gaunkars*, which was essential for the symbolic recognition of their supremacy. This was the case even if only one of the signatories of this agreement (which included the *Vedor da Fazenda*, Krishna, the *thānedār*, Loqu Sinai, and Gopu, three of the principal Brahmans of Goa, as well as the *gaunkars* of 15 villages) was already a Christian.

Although it testified to the increasing interference of the imperial power in the life of Goan villages, this new *Foral* was also a testimony to a time in which the *gaunkars* of the villages were still in charge and able to control their most valuable lands. Fifteen years later, an inventory of the properties given to the temples and their servants was made with the help of the *gaunkars*, who, in general, continued to be Hindu.[105] However, this situation would not persist

102 APO, Fasc. 5, vol. 2, 508, 612–614; DI, I, 63–89; Priolkar, *The Goa Inquisition*, 71. At the same time, it was suggested to the viceroy that some powerful Brahman families, like those of Khrisna, Loqu, and Anu Sinai, should be put away in order to facilitate the conversion to Christianity.

103 APO, Fasc. 5, vol. 1, 267–278, 272.

104 APO, Fasc. 5, vol. 1, 161–170; Paes, *Tombo das Ilhas de Goa e das Terras de Salcete e Bardês*, 67–75.

105 APO, Fasc. 5, vol. 1, 286–290; the lands and rents of the temples continued to be disputed by different agents. For example, in 1603, António Rodrigues, a converted Indian, asked

for long, as demonstrated by other documents from the second half of the 16th century concerning these lands.[106]

The legal consequences of Christianization for life in the villages were critical. The royal decree of 1542 (confirmed in the following decades and expanded to the territories of Salcete and Bardez) defined the legal and political effects of the conversion of Indians. It openly expanded the privileges of the Portuguese living in Goa to people of "any other nation or generation" that married in Goa and set up house there, provided they were Christian.[107] This statement—"provided they were Christian"—became a juridical principle that would frame many of the subsequent imperial laws, provisions, and decrees.

Aspects such as marriage, family, orphanhood, women, inheritance, land, residence, labor, ownership, and political rights were now dependent on conversion. For example, conversion by one member of the family meant that inheritance would be regulated by Portuguese law, leading to conflicts among the members of the family regarding inheritance rights. As said before, the sections of the *Foral* on inheritance excluded women (widows) and daughters from family heritage.[108] However, Portuguese law stated that Christian women could access their own parents' legacy and take precedence over their non-converted male brothers. Christian widows could marry a second time and receive part of their husband's legacy. In the absence of sons, a man's heritage was divided among wives and daughters that were Christian and among other relatives that had converted to Christianity. Additional legislation against the *sati* prohibited women from burning themselves "on account of the death of her husband". The Portuguese ordinances would also regulate infidelity, prostitution, and other issues concerning morality.[109]

Additionally, a significant number of laws were explicitly discriminatory of the non-Christians, reducing their local power, social status, and economic standing. For example, in the leases of the paddy fields of the villages, Christians had an advantage over non-Christians. These decrees and laws were among many aimed at persuading the locals to convert to Christianity. Ecclesiastical norms, such as decree 27 of the First Provincial Council of Goa (1567), stated that "a non-believer shall not receive office, dignity, honor, pre-eminence, or

---

for the rents of the temples of the village of Margao, the most important village of Salcete, and received them (APO, Fasc. 5, vol. 3, 1095, vol. 1099)

106 APO, Fasc. 5, vol. 1, 182–183, 218–219, 230–234, 249–254, 330, 336–337; APO, Fasc. 5, vol. 2, 687–689, 835–837; APO, Fasc. 5, vol. 3, 993.

107 APO, Fasc. 2, 115–116; Fasc. 5, vol. 1, 386–387.

108 *Foral dos usos e costumes,* clauses 28–30 and 32.

109 APO, Fasc. 5, vol. 1, 171–173, 175, 178, 381–383, 410; APO, Fasc. 5, vol. 2, 543–545, 612, 903–903, 994–996.

domain over a believer".[110] In conjunction with this, non-Christians could not own Christian slaves and many Brahmans lost their power positions. These decisions were legitimated by the *Relação of Goa*, established in 1544 as a court of appeals, which was also charged with reviewing the *alvarás* and provisions issued by the governors and viceroys. Among these were those related to the advancement of Christianity.[111]

The Christianization of the economy of power inside Goan villages was gradual, even if many administrative practices were kept. However, a relevant change occurred in the decision-making process: *gaunkars* who did not convert to Christianity became unable to vote in the *gaunkaris* or participate in the elaboration of the *nemos* (the written decisions). This excluded them, in practice, from the government of the communities. The introduction of the *Livro das Communidades* by the end of the century, with paper coming from Portugal and kept in an arch located in the parish buildings, witnesses the ongoing process of 'Lusitanization' of the village life. From that moment onward, the *nemos* were registered in these books. The autonomy of the *gaunkari* also changed significantly. In 1633, the Viceroy Miguel de Noronha issued a provision that explicitly declared the loss of the status of *gaunkar* and the honors associated with it for all those that did not convert to Christianity. This decision responded to a joint petition by the *Câmara Geral*, the "Christian people" of Goa, and the "Christian ministers".[112]

There were also ambivalences concerning some decisions. For example, in 1561 D. Francisco Coutinho allowed the "gentiles" that had departed for Bijapur to return to their villages and receive their lands back. Though contradicting clause 17 of the *Foral,* this decision was prompted by the fact that many communities were deserted and the paddy fields became uncultivated, which meant significant decreases in tax revenue.[113] However, Viceroy D. Duarte de Meneses declared in 1585 that Christians could inherit these lands or, in their absence, "whomever the *gaunkars* wanted" (clause 17), thus reaching a kind of compromise between the *Foral* and the policy of conversion. Furthermore, in

110 APO, Fasc. 5, vol. 2, 319–320, 543–545.

111 Pereira, *História da Administração da Justiça*, vol. 1, 160.

112 APO, Fasc. 5, vol. 3, 1399–1402.

113 APO, Fasc. 5, vol. 2, 521–523, 543–545. The same viceroy attributed in 1563 all the lands belonging to deceased Muslims, Jews, or "gentiles" without heirs, of all Goa, to the construction of the cathedral of Santa Catarina (because this was one of his priorities) and, in another decree, decided to expel many Brahmans and "gentiles" of Goa that opposed the conversion processes (APO, Fasc. 5, vol. 2, 580–581).

other cases, the Crown protected the rights of the Christian *gaunkars*, invoking, when needed, the *Foral*.[114]

The policy of conversion also changed the judicial system that operated in the village. On the one hand, as mentioned above, Portuguese law applied to the converted. On the other, Christian agents gained influence in the judicial sphere of the village.[115] During the government of Francisco Barreto (1555–1558), António Martins, the *Pai dos Cristãos* (Father of the Christians), could solve civil conflicts between Christians and between Christians and non-Christians involving a fine of up to five *xerafins*. His decisions had no right of appeal as was also the case with his jurisdiction for criminal cases where there had been no blood shed. In 1560, Pius IV's bull, *Pro salubri regnorum*, renewed for King D. Sebastião (1554–1578) the rights of the monarchy to enlist ecclesiastics in civil affairs, such as judging cases of crime. In an *alvará* of 1563, Viceroy Coutinho extended this jurisdiction to "the rectors of the parishes and confraternities of the churches".[116] They could "listen to the Christians of the land and the gentiles, in their conflicts". The fines imposed were up to a certain amount of money and their decisions were not open to appeal or grievance. From 1566 onward, a Judge of Orphans exclusively dealt with the inheritance of the orphans of non-Christians and converted Indians.[117] Again, a competence previously divided between the *gaunkari* and the Crown in the *Foral* was now assumed entirely by institutions of the Crown. In the following decade, a clause required that if the rectors knew "the people in those lands and islands worshipped idols, or engaged in other forms of gentile acts prohibited by the Council", they were obliged to inform the competent judge. This provision ensured that these rectors were charged not only with religious power to resolve matters of minor importance but were also expected to denounce the ill-doers.[118]

However, after an initial period of judicial interdependence between the Crown and the regular clergy, there was a gradual push to revoke the priests' judicial powers. In 1581, the judicial power of the missionaries in the villages was limited through the creation of the office of *Conservador e Juiz dos Cristãos da Terra* (Judge of the Christians of the Land). This official had to investigate

114 APO, Fasc. 5, vol. 1, 489; APO, Fasc. 5, vol. 2, 602–603, 903–903; APO, Fasc. 5, vol. 3, 1397–1398, 1403–1404.

115 *Quadro Elementar*, XIII, 124.

116 APO, Fasc. 5, vol. 2, 512–513. Pereira, *História da Administração da Justiça*, vol. 1, 120.

117 See Faria (Chapter 4) in this volume.

118 APO, Fasc. 5, vol. 3, 1429–1431; APO, Fasc. 5, vol. 2, 903–904. Pereira, *História da Administração da Justiça*, vol. 1, 125.

and resolve all cases among the newly converted. When this official was not present, these functions were handed over to the captains of the forts, as was the case in the territories of Salcete and Bardez.[119]

7 Final Remarks

Almost 500 *forais* were rewritten in the Portuguese kingdom between the last decades of the 15th century and the first decades of the 16th. The aim of this administrative reform was to map the tax revenue that the Portuguese municipalities had to pay to the king. While this process was still taking place in the kingdom, a similar one started in Goa, ending with the compilation of the *Foral* in 1526. As mentioned above, this document was simultaneously similar and different from the Portuguese ones: it had a first part (today missing) about the taxes to be paid to the king and a second part compiling a selection of local uses and customs, which recovered a practice that had already taken place in the kingdom in the medieval period. Since there are no other documents comparable to the *Foral* in other parts of the Portuguese empire, it can reasonably be said that the *Foral* was a singular document and a testimony to the particular relationship established by the Portuguese Crown with the Goan territories and people in the first decades of the 16th century, during the period of the 'apprenticeship of empire'. At this time, what was the role of Goan village normativities in the making of the Portuguese imperial order? How can we assess these normativities through the *Foral*, the earliest imperial document to map some of them? How did it constitute and construct the normativities taken by the Portuguese imperial agents (and, later, scholars) as the village normativities? Furthermore, given that it was a document produced for a non-Christian Goa, what was its relevance in a Christianized Goa?

Let us return to the idea that the *Foral* is only a "small inroad" to assessing the village's normativities. The pages above have demonstrated that what we today call the *Foral* was only the second part of a document that included, in the first part, the taxes that the villages of Goa had to pay to the Portuguese Crown in 1526. Even if later documents compiled these taxes, the first part of the *Foral* would undoubtedly be useful for connecting the fiscal duties of the villages with the uses and customs selected to be included in the second part.

---

119 APO, Fasc. 5, vol. 3, 974–975. See also the documentation published by Abranches Garcia (Garcia, *Arquivo da Relação de Goa*) and Pereira, *História da Administração da Justiça*, vol. 2, 311–312.

Nevertheless, this link is missing and with it so are some of the meanings of the *Foral*.

This aspect related to the production of the *Foral* converges, in a very evident way, with the notion of its selective nature, stressing the idea that the *Foral* has to be used very cautiously when studying the normativities operating in the Goan villages. The selective nature of the second part of the *Foral* was the result of several variables. On the one hand, the *Foral* was the outcome of a continuous process by the Portuguese imperial agents of becoming acquainted with the land of Goa. As mentioned above, the *thānedārs* of Goa collected much of the information included in the *Foral* since 1515. This means that the contents of the *Foral* are also the result of their processes of getting to know the land, which involved Portuguese agents and local informants. Little is known, however, about these previous processes. In addition to the filters and layers of information already identified in the process of production of the *Foral*, its contents were submitted to other various other filters and layers about which we know almost nothing. Moreover, as the *Sentença* of 1534 states, the work of Mexia was probably done "in a rush". Not knowing how much time Mexia did dedicate to the material production of the *Foral*, it is clear that this was mainly a pragmatic document that selected as much as it excluded.

Unlike Mexia, other officers were more cautious and "professional" when gathering information, thus, the diversity of attitudes is evident, particularly considering the imperial agents' local interlocutors. Though we know almost nothing about who the interlocutors of the *thānedārs* were, the same applies to the *gaunkars* of the villages of Goa that were convoked by Mexia. Who were these *gaunkars*? Who did the *gaunkars* involved in the production of the *Foral* truly represent? Knowing that, in 1541, only the *gaunkars* of 15 villages contributed to the creation of a new *Foral*, one can hypothesize that the same happened during the creation of the original *Foral*. We know nothing, either, about the castes of the *gaunkars* involved in the process, even if we do know that the scribes of the villages were Brahman. Nevertheless, we do know that the villages of Tiswadi had *gaunkars* belonging to different castes: Brahmans dominated some of them, Charodos (who considered themselves of Kshatriya descent) and Sudras dominated others. Some villages had mixed *gaunkaris*, too. Did the *gaunkars* involved in the production of the *Foral* belong to different castes? If so, did their different ways of living shape the contents of the *Foral*? These and many other questions remain open.

The little knowledge we do have about the production of this document is telling about its status as a historical source, particularly considering all the missing information about its contexts of production. It is also telling, however, about the relevance it acquired after its production. The diversity of voices involved in the *Foral* were somehow frozen and homogenized since the moment of its writing. Yet, this very process meant that some village normativities did play a role in contributing to the Portuguese imperial order. It is true that the mere act of writing down the norms agreed between some local informants and some Portuguese agents meant an interference in the local order. However, it also contributed to establishing specific rules, certain procedures, and, overall, the power of the local elites that had been recognized by the Portuguese as their privileged informants. Is it possible that these local informants had invited royal interference in order to reinforce their local power? If so, this would have meant that the gap between the contents of the *Foral* and the people it applied to is even more meaningful than what scholarship has assumed until now. In that sense, the *Foral* became, ironically (but also understandably), the 'written constitution' of the Goan villages that simultaneously satisfied Portuguese power and the local elites.

However, this equilibrium changed dramatically with the Christianization of the Goan villages, making it clear that the Portuguese Crown had two different approaches in their relationship with the local populations during the 16th century. The first, which roughly corresponds to the government of King D. Manuel I and the first decade of the government of King D. João III, was more secular, less concerned with religious issues, and more 'pluralistic'. For example, the *Foral* accepted the existence of bigamy and polygamy among the Goan people, even if these practices contradicted Portuguese rule and Christian values. Moreover, the *Foral* is almost absent in what concerns religious matters in general, accepting the Hindu organization of the local order. In that sense, the *Foral* was still an expression of the legal pluralism that characterized the Portuguese political order as well as the idea that the laws that organized each political community should be respected.

The second approach, more religious and less open to cultural differences, started to become visible in the decade of 1530, shortly after the production of the *Foral*. It meant the destruction of the religious and ritual life in the villages and the Christianization of the local populations. Due to the equivalence between *generatio* and *regeneratio*, converted Goans would be fully covered by Portuguese law from the moment of conversion onwards. This meant that the clauses of the *Foral*, which contradicted Portuguese law and Christian values, were applied less and less. In addition, from that moment onwards, there was an expansion of the law of the kingdom and the contraction of the local customs, namely those included in the *Foral*. Predictably, since then, Christian judicial officers started to solve minor conflicts and crimes either between the converted or between the converted and non-converted.

If these policies already limited the applicability of the *Foral* in the 16th century, by 1720 the *Foral* faced an entirely new local reality when the Portuguese law applied to 92.2 per cent of the Goan population.[120] This situation was in deep contrast with the moment of its production. At that time, most of the population of Goa was composed by non-Christians and was supposed to be governed by the *Foral*. This change in the demography of Goa meant that the norms included in the *Foral* that only covered the non-Christians applied to increasingly fewer people. Carmo D'Souza was probably right when he wrote that "Portuguese jurisprudence seemed to have prevailed over the indigenous system in the Old Conquests by the seventeenth century".[121] This 'Lusitanization' of the relationship between the Portuguese administrative and legal order and the village normativities was sealed in a set of rules known as the *Regimento* of 1735 when the Portuguese Crown made new norms for the government of the villages, which would substitute the ones included in the *Foral*. This does not imply, however, that this process fully succeeded and that local orders did not continue to operate in parallel with the imperial order. Nevertheless, it witnesses the intentionality of the Portuguese Crown in imposing onto the local normativities what was considered, by then, the 'Portuguese way' of doing things.

Does this mean that the *Foral* is unreliable in recovering specific dimensions of the normativities that organized the Goan villages? This chapter argues that, despite its shortcomings, the *Foral* and all it entails is still necessary for assessing some aspects of the local order. The very fact that it voiced the interests and expectations of some (possibly Brahmanical) local elites provides an insight into the local order and its dynamics. A step back in history and a movement in geography are also useful for understanding whether there were links between some of the norms included in the *Foral* and more general South Indian juridical traditions. Derrett's intuition was probably right: in a complex and contradictory way, the *Foral* evoked, namely in the clauses concerning inheritance, the Indian classical traditions. However—as this chapter demonstrates—the information about the appropriation of these traditions is almost completely lacking, and further research is needed to verify the existence of linkages between these traditions and the *Foral*.

In any case, the status eventually attributed to the *Foral* by 19th-century scholars and local elites was, therefore, a convenient fantasy, projecting on the past a narrative that was different from that of the agents genuinely involved

120 Matos, "O numeramento de Goa de 1720", 321–324.

121 D'Souza, *Legal Systems of Goa*, vol. 2, 114.

in the production of the *Foral*. As mentioned at the beginning of this chapter, these 19th-century readings did contribute to shaping subsequent scholarship by overstating the descriptive power of the *Foral* and overlooking its constructive nature. By doing this, this scholarship contributed to a particular "vision of community",[122] as well as 'invent[ing] a tradition' that has persisted until today in the commonsense of the Goan people.[123] Furthermore, it gave legitimacy to the idea that legal and administrative pluralism characterized all of the Portuguese imperial experience in Goa, and that the Portuguese imperial order largely preserved the village normativities. As the previous pages have demonstrated, this was predominantly untrue. Even if legal pluralism was characteristic of the first two decades of the Portuguese imperial presence in Goa, and plural normativities coexisted in Goa in different times and modalities. This plurality was of a different nature to what is usually included under the label of legal pluralism.

Acknowledgements

Previous versions of this essay were presented at the "Norms and Empires Lecture Series" coordinated by Manuel Bastias Saavedra at the Max-Planck Institut für Rechtsgeschichte und Rechtstheorie, Frankfurt; at the "History and Historiography of Brazil Seminar", coordinated by Laura de Mello e Souza in the Université de Sorbonne I, Paris; in the "Reading Seminar" of the Research Group "Empires, Colonialism, and Post-Colonial Societies" of the Instituto de Ciências Sociais da Universidade de Lisboa; and in the II Encontro Hispano-Luso de História do Direito, Lisboa. I would like to thank the audience of these seminars for their comments and suggestions. I am also truly indebted to the insightful and critical reading and comments by Manuel Bastias Saavedra and Sumit Guha, as well as the anonymous reviewers of this text. Finally, I would like to thank Genevieve Beech for the English revision, which much improved the text. This is part of the project Legal Pluralism in the Portuguese Empire (18th–20th centuries), PTDC/DIR–OUT/30873/2017 coordinated by Cristina Nogueira da Silva in CEDIS–UNL and funded by the Fundação para a Ciência e Tecnologia. All translations from documents and scholarship in Portuguese or languages other than English are mine.

---

122 Kroppenberg and Linder, "Coding the Nation. Codification History from a (Post)Global Perspective", 67–99.

123 On that, see the article of Fernandes, "Invoking the Ghost of Mexia", 9–25.

Abbreviations

APO	*Archivo Portuguez-Oriental*
HAG	Historical Archives of Goa
IAN/TT	Instituto Nacional de Arquivos/Torre do Tombo
AHU	Arquivo Histórico Ultramarino
Fasc.	Fascículo
OrdMan	*Ordenações Manuelinas*

Bibliography

Manuscripts

Arquivo Histórico Ultramarino (AHU), Lisbon, India: Cx 6, no. 29.

Historical Archives of Goa (HAG), Assentos da Relação de Goa, no. 8779, no. 79

Instituto Nacional de Arquivos / Torre do Tombo (IAN/TT), Lisbon, Armário Jesuítico, Mss. 89, no. 19.

Printed Sources

Archivo Portuguez Oriental, ed. by Joaquim Heliodoro da Cunha Rivara, 6 vols., repr. in Delhi 1992.

Barros, João de, *Décadas da Ásia*, 3 vols., Lisboa 1988–1994.

Boemus, Johannes, *Omnium Gentium Mores, Leges et Ritus* ex multis clarissimis rerum scriptoribus, sn., sl., 1520.

Dāya-Bhāga and Mitākṣarā. *Two Treatises on the Hindu Law of Inheritance*, trans. H. T. Colebrooke, repr. in Delhi 1984.

Documentação Remetida da Índia ou Livros das Monções, ed. by Raymundo António de Bulhão Pato, 10 vols., Lisboa 1880–1982.

Documentação para a História do Padroado Português do Oriente: Índia, ed. by António da Silva Rego, 12 vols., Lisboa 1947–1958.

Epigraphica Indica, vol. 7, Delhi 1980.

Foral dos usos e costumes dos Gancares e Lavradores da Ilha de Goa e outras annexas a ella, in Rivara, Joaquim Heliodoro da Cunha, in *Archivo Portuguez Oriental*, Fasc. 5, vol. 1, Delhi 1992.

Ordenações Manuelinas, 5 vols., Lisboa 1984.

Paes, Domingos, *Chronica dos Reys de Bisnaga: manuscrito inedito do século XVI*, ed. David Lopes, Lisboa 1887.

Paes, Francisco, *Tombo das Ilhas de Goa e das Terras de Salcete e Bardês*, ed. P.P. Pissurlencar, Goa 1952.

Pires, Tomé, *Summa Oriental*, in *The Suma Oriental of Tomé Pires (...) and the Book of Francisco Rodrigues (...)*, trans. Armando Cortesão, London 1944.

Sama, Krsnadasa, *Komkaṇī Rāmāyaṇa: kristī dharmaprasārakāmcyā hātāmtalyāna dhvanyātmaka romīkaraṇa*, ed. Olivinho Gomes, Goa 1996.

The Book of Duarte Barbosa, 2 vols., ed. by Mansel Longworth Dames, London 1918.

Wicki, Joseph, S.J., *Documenta Indica* (DI), 12 vols., Rome 1948–1972.

Literature

Agüero, Alejandro, "Local law and Localisation of law. Hispanic Legal Tradition and Colonial Culture (16th–18th Centuries)", in Meccarelli, Massimo and Maria Julia Solla Sastre (eds.), *Spatial and Temporal Dimensions for Legal History. Research Experiences and Itineraries, Global Perspectives on Legal History*, Frankfurt am Main 2016, 101–130.

Alam, Muzzafar and Sanjay Subrahmanyam, "The making of a munshī", in Sheldon Pollock (ed.), *Forms of Knowledge in early modern Asia. Explorations in the Intellectual History of India and Tibet 1500–1800*, Durham and London 2011, 185–209.

Axelroad, Paul e Michelle Fuerch, "Portuguese Orientalism and the making of the Village Communities in Goa", in *Ethnohistory* 45:3 (Summer 1998): 439–476.

Alencastro, Luiz Filipe, "The Apprenticeship of Colonization", in Patrick Manning, *Slave Trades, 1500–1800, Globalisation of Forced Labour*, Aldershot/Burlington USA/Singapore/Sydney, 1996, 83–106.

Axelroad, Paul, "Living on the edge: The village and the state on the Goa-Maratha frontier", in *The Indian Economic and Social History Review* (Dec. 2008): 553–580.

Baden-Powell, B. H., "The Villages of Goa in the Early Sixteenth Century", in *Journal of The Royal Asiatic Society* 32: 2 (1900): 261–291.

Benton, Lauren, *Law and Colonial Cultures: Legal Regimes in World History, 1400–1900*, Cambridge 2002.

Bhattacharyya-Panda, Nandini, *Appropriation and Invention of Tradition: The East India Company and Hindu Law in Early Colonial Bengal*, Delhi 2008.

Cohn, Bernard S., *Colonialism and its forms of knowledge: The making of British India*, Princeton, 1996.

Coelho, Maria Helena da Cruz, "O Poder Concelhio em tempos medievais – o 'deve' e 'haver' historiográfico", in *Revista da Faculdade de Letras — HISTÓRIA*, III Série, vol. 7 (2006): 19–34.

Coulson, Noel J., *A History of Islamic Law*, 2nd ed., New Brunswick and London 2011.

Couto, Dejanirah, "The Role of *Interpreters*, or Linguas, in the Portuguese Empire During the 16th Century", *E-Journal of Portuguese History* 1:2 (Winter 2003): 1–10.

D'Souza, Carmo, *Legal Systems in Goa (1510–1986)*, Panaji 2012.

Dasgupta, Sashi Bushan, *Obscure Religious Cults as Background of Bengali Literature*, Calcutta 1946.

Davis, Donald R., "Dharma, Maryāda and Law in Early British Malabar. Remarks on words for 'Law' in the Tellicherry records", in *Studien zur Indologie und Iranistik* 23 (2002): 51–70.

Davis, Donald R., Jr., and David Brick, "Social and Literary History of *Dharmaśãstra* — Commentaries and Legal Digests", in Patrick Olivelle and Donald Richard Davis, Jr. (eds.), *Hindu Law: A New History* of *Dharmaśãstra*, Oxford 2018, 30–45.

Davis, Donald Richard, "Introduction", in Patrick Olivelle and Donald Richard Davis, Jr. (eds.), *Hindu Law: A New History* of *Dharmaśãstra*, Oxford 2018, 1–11.

Davis, Donald Richard, Jr., *The boundaries of Hindu Law: tradition, politics and custom in Medieval Kerala*, Torino 2004.

Derrett, John Duncan Martin, *Essays in Classical and Modern Hindu Law. Dharmaśãstra and Related Ideas*, Leiden 1976.

Derrett, John Duncan Martin, "Law and social order before the Muhammadan conquests," in *Journal of the Economic and Social History of the Orient* 7:3 (1964): 73–120.

Derrett, John Duncan Martin, "Hindu law in Goa: A contact between Natural, Roman and Hindu Laws", in Derrett, John Duncan Martin, *Essays in Classical and Modern Hindu Law: Consequences of the Intellectual Exchange with the Foreign Powers*, Leiden 1977, 131–165.

Derrett, John Duncan Martin, *Essays in Classical and Modern Hindu Law: Consequences of the Intellectual Exchange with the Foreign Powers*, Brill 1977.

Deshpande, Prachi, "Scripting the Cultural History of Language: Modi in the Colonial Archive", in Chatterjee, Partha, Tapati Guha-Takurti and Bodhisattva Karr (eds.), *New Cultural Histories of India: Materiality and Practices*, Delhi 2014, 62–86.

Dias, Remy, *A Socio-Economic History of Goa with Special reference to the Communidade System, 1750–1910* (PhD Thesis), Goa 2004.

Duve, Thomas (ed.), *Entanglements in Legal History: Conceptual Approaches, Global Perspectives on Legal History*, Frankfurt am Main 2014.

Duve, Thomas, "European Legal History — Concepts, Methods, Challenges", in Duve, Thomas (ed.), *Entanglements in Legal History: Conceptual Approaches, Global Perspectives on Legal History*, Frankfurt am Main 2014, 29–66.

Fernandes, Jason Keith, "Invoking the Ghost of Mexia: State and Community in Post-Colonial Goa", in *Ler História* 58 (2010): 9–25.

Fischer, Elaine M., *Hindu Pluralism. Religion and the Public Sphere in the Early Modern South India*, Oakland 2017.

Flores, Jorge, "Le «língua» cosmopolite. Le monde social des interprètes hindous de Goa au XVIIe siècle," in Lefèvre, Corinne, Ines G. Županov and Jorge Flores (eds.), *Cosmopolitismes en Asie du Sud sources, itinéraires, langues, XVIe–XVIIIe siècle, in Purushártha* 33 (2015) : 225–250.

Fukazawa, Hiroshi, "A Study of the Local Administration of Adilshahi Sultanate (A.D. 1489–1686)", in *Hitotsubashi Journal of Economics* 3:2 (1963): 37–66.

Fukazawa, Hiroshi, "Rural servants in 18th century Maharastra. Demiurgic or Jajmani System?", in *Hitotsubashi Journal of Economics* 12:2 (1972): 14–40.

Galindo, George Rodrigo Bandeira, "Legal transplants between time and space", in Duve, Thomas (ed.), *Entanglements in Legal History: Conceptual Approaches, Global Perspectives on Legal History,* Frankfurt am Main 2014, 129–148.

Gomes, Olivinho, *Old Konkani language and literature: the Portuguese role: Chandor,* Goa 1999.

Gordon, Stuart N., *Marathas, marauders, and state formation in eighteenth century India*, London 1994.

Guerra, François-Xavier, "L'État et les Communautés: Comment Inventer un Empire. Introduction", in Serge Gruzinski and Nathan Wachtel (dirs.), *Le Nouveau Monde. Mondes Nouveaux. L'Expérience Américaine*, Paris 1992, 351–364.

Guha, Sumit, "The Political Economy of Village Life", in Guha, Sumit, *Beyond Caste, Identity and Power in South Asia. Past and Present*, Leiden-Boston 2013, 83–116.

Gune, Vithal Trimbak, *The Judicial System of the Marathas*, Poona 1953.

Hallaq, Wael B., *An Introduction to Islamic Law*, Cambridge 2009.

Halpérin, Jean-Louis, "Transplants of European Normativity in India and in Japan: a Historical Comparison", in *Rechtsgeschichte – Legal History* 22 (2014): 150–157.

Herzog, Tamar, "Colonial law: Early Modern Normativity in Spanish America", in Tellekamp, Jörg Alejandro (ed.), *A Companion to Early Modern Spanish Imperial and Political Thought,* Leiden-Boston 2020, 105–127.

Hespanha, António Manuel, *Como os Juristas viam o mundo, 1550–1750, Direitos, estados, pessoas, coisas, contratos, ações e crimes*, Lisboa 2015.

Hespanha, António Manuel, *Panorama da História Jurídica de Macau*, Macau 2005.

Hespanha, António Manuel, *Os Filhos da Terra. Identidades Mestiças nos confins da expansão portuguesa*, Lisboa 2019.

Inden, Ronald, *Imagining India,* Oxford 1990.

Jaffe, James A., "The languages of petitioning in early colonial India", in *Social Science History* 43 (2019): 581–597.

Jois, Mandagadde Rama, *Legal and Constitutional History of India: Ancient, Judicial and Constitutional System*, Delhi 2004.

Kane, Pandurang Vaman, *History of the Dharmaśāstras*, vol. 1, Poona 1940.

Kosambi, Damodar Dharmanand, "The Village Community in the 'Old Conquests' of Goa", *Journal of the University of Bombay* 15, no. 4 (1947): 63–78.

Kroppenberg, Inge and Nikolaus Linder, "Coding the Nation. Codification History from a (Post-)Global Perspective", in Duve, Thomas (ed.), *Entanglements in Legal History: Conceptual Approaches, Global Perspectives on Legal History,* Frankfurt am Main 2014, 67–99.

Kulkarni, A. R., "The Indian village with special reference to Medieval Deccan (Maratha county): General presidential address", in *Proceedings of the Indian History Congress* 52 (1991): 1–42.

Kumar, Raj, *Essays on Legal Systems in India*, Delhi 2003.
Lach, Donald F., *Asia in the making of Europe*, 3 vols., Chicago 1965–1977.
Lapidus, Ira M., *A History of Islamic Societies*, Cambridge 2002.
Lariviere, Richard W., "*Dharmaśāstra*, Custom, 'Real Law', and 'Apocryphal' *Smrtis*", in *Journal of Indian Philosophy* 32:5–6 (2004): 611–627.
Lingat, Robert, *Les sources du droit dans le système traditionnel de l'Inde*. Paris 1967.
Loureiro, Sara, "Reconstituição da documentação produzida por Afonso de Mexia, escrivão da Câmara e da Fazenda Real de D. Manuel I e D. João III", *Cadernos do Arquivo Municipal de Lisboa*, 1ª série, no. 9 (2007): 1–49.
Madeira-Santos, Catarina, "As Instituições Indígenas no Império Português", in Xavier, Ângela Barreto, Federico Palomo and Roberta Stumpf (coord.), *Monarquias Ibéricas em Perspectiva Comparada. Dinâmicas Imperiais e Modelos Administrativos (Séculos XVI–XVIII)*, Lisbon 2018, 271–302.
Magalhães, Manuel, *Pequenos Reis e Grandes Honras Culto, Poder e Estatuto na Índia Ocidental* (PhD Thesis), Lisbon 2013.
Matos, Paulo Lopes, "O numeramento de Goa de 1720", in Anais de História de Além-Mar, 8 (2007), 241–324.
Mawani, Renisa and Iza Hussin, "The Travels of Law: Indian Ocean Itineraries", in *Law and History Review* 32:4 (2014): 733–747.
Meccarelli, Massimo and Maria Julia Solla Sastre (eds.), *Spatial and Temporal Dimensions for Legal History. Research Experiences and Itineraries, Global Perspectives on Legal History*, Frankfurt am Main 2016.
Menski, Werner F., *Hindu Law: Beyond Tradition and Modernity*, Delhi 2003.
Miranda, Susana Münch, *A Administração da Fazenda Real no Estado da Índia (1517–1640)* (PhD Thesis), Lisbon 2007.
Miranda, Susana Münch, "The center and the periphery in the administration of the Royal Exchequer of the Estado da Índia (1517–1640), in *E-Journal of Portuguese History* 7:2 (2009): 1–14.
Mitchell, Axel, "The Practice of Hindu Law," in Davis, Donald Ronald Jr. and Javanth K. Krishnan, *Hinduism and Law: An Introduction*, Cambridge 2010, 58–77.
Mitragotri, V. R., *Socio-Cultural History of Goa, From Bhojas to Vijayanagar*, Goa 1999.
Moraes, George, *The Kadamba Kula: A History of Ancient and Mediaeval Karnataka*, Bombay 1931 (repr. Delhi 1990).
O'Hanlon, Rosalind and Christopher Minkowski, "What makes people who they are? Pandit networks and the problems of livelihood in early modern Western India", in *India Economic and Social History Review* 45:3 (2008): 381–416.
O'Hanlon, Rosalind, Christopher Minkowski and Anand Venkatkrishnan (eds.), *Scholar Intellectuals in Early Modern India: Discipline, Sect, Lineage and Community*, London 2017.
Oliveira, Luís Filipe, "O Foral de Faro e a Reforma dos Forais", in *O Foral de Faro de 1504: Apresentação e Edição*, Faro 2017, 9–20.

Olivelle, Patrick and Donald Richard Davis, (eds.), *Hindu Law: A New History* of *Dharmaśāstra*, Oxford 2018.

Olivelle, Patrick, "Social and Literary History of *Dharmaśāstra* — The Foundational Texts", in Olivelle, Patrick and Donald Richard Davis (eds.), *Hindu Law: A New History* of *Dharmaśāstra*, Oxford 2018, 17–29.

Pereira, Carlos Renato Gonçalves, *História da Administração da Justiça no Estado da Índia*, Lisbon 1964.

Pereira, Rui, *Gaunkaris* (*The old villages associations*), Goa 1978.

Pinto, Rochelle, "The Foral in the History of the Communidades de Goa," in *Journal of World History* 29:2 (2018): 185–212.

Pollock, Sheldon (ed.), *Forms of Knowledge in early modern Asia. Explorations in the Intellectual History of India and Tibet 1500–1800*, Durham and London 2011.

Pollock, Sheldon, *The Language of the Gods in the World of Men. Sanskrit, Culture, and Power in Premodern India*, Berkeley/Los Angeles/London 2006.

Priolkar, Anant Kakba, *The Goa Inquisition*, Bombay 1961.

Rao, Velcheru Narayana, David Shulman and Sanjay Subrahmanyam (eds.), *Textures of Time. Writing History in South India 1600–1800*, Delhi 2003.

Rao, Velcheru Narayana, David Shulman and Sanjay Subrahmanyam, "A new imperial idiom in the Sixteenth Century. Krishnadevaraya and His Political Theory of Vijayanagara", in Sheldon Pollock (ed.), *Forms of Knowledge in early modern Asia. Explorations in the Intellectual History of India and Tibet 1500–1800*, London and Durham 2011, 69–111.

Rao, Venkat, *Cultures of Memory in South Asia. Orality, Literacy and the Problem of Inheritance*, New Delhi/Heidelberg/New York/Dordrecht/London 2014.

Rocher, Ludo, *Jimutavahana's Dayabhaga: The Hindu Law of Inheritance in Bengal*, New York 2002.

Rocher, Ludo, "Hindu Conceptions of Law", *The Hastings Law Journal* 29 (1978), 1283–1305.

Rocher, Ludo, "The theory of proof in ancient Hindu Law", in Davis, Donald R. (ed.), *Studies in Hindu Law and Darmaśāstra*, New York 2012, 39–58.

Rocher, Ludo, *Studies in Hindu Law and Dharmaśāstras*, Davis, Donald R. (ed.), New York 2012.

Rocher, Ludo, "Inheritance dāyabhāga", in Olivelle, Patrick and Donald Richard Davis, (eds.), *Hindu Law: A New History* of *Dharmaśāstra*, Oxford 2018, 164–178.

Shastri, B. S., "Gersoppa's hand in the capture of Goa", in B. S. Shastri, *Goa-Kanara Portuguese relations, 1498–1763*, Porvorim 2000, 24–36.

Sobral Neto, Margarida, "O foral manuelino de Porto de Mós: processo de elaboração, conteúdo e aplicação", in *Revista de História da Sociedade e da Cultura* 6 (2006): 155–176.

Souza, Teotónio de, *Medieval Goa: A Socio-Economic History*, Goa 1979.

Stein, Burton, *Vijayanagar*, vol. 1.2 of *The New Cambridge History of India*, Cambridge/New York/Port Chester/Melbourne/Sydney 1989.

Subrahmanyam, Sanjay, "O romântico, o oriental e o exótico: notas sobre os portugueses em Goa", in Rosa Maria Perez (ed.), *Histórias de Goa*, Lisboa 1997, 29–43.

Thomaz, Luis Filipe, "Estrutura política e administrativa do Estado da Índia no século XVI", in Thomaz, Luis Filipe, *De Ceuta a Timor*, Carnaxide 1994.

Viegas, Valentino, *As Políticas Portuguesas na Índia e o Foral de Goa*, Lisboa 2005.

Xavier, Ângela Barreto, *A Invenção de Goa, Poder Imperial e Conversões Culturais nos séculos XVI e XVII*, Lisboa 2008.

Xavier, Ângela Barreto and Županov, Ines G., *Catholic Orientalism. Portuguese Empire, Indian Knowledge (16th–18th centuries)*, Delhi 2015.

Xavier, Ângela Barreto, Federico Palomo and Roberta Stumpf (coord.), *Monarquias Ibéricas em Perspectiva Comparada. Dinâmicas Imperiais e Modelos Administrativos (Séculos XVI-XVIII)*, Lisboa 2018.

Xavier, Filipe Nery, *Bosquejo Histórico das Communidades das Aldeias dos Concelhos das Ilhas, Salsete e Bardez*, 3 vols., Bastorá 1903–1907.

Xavier, Filipe Nery, *Collecção de Bandos, e Outras Differentes Providencias Que Servem de Leis Regulamentares para o Governo Economico e Judicial das Provincias Denominadas das Novas Conquistas, Precedida da Nocao da sua Conquista*, 3 vols., Pangim 1840.

Xavier, Filipe Nery, *Collecção das Leis Peculiares das Communidades Agricolas das Aldeas dos Concelhos das Ilhas, Salsete e Bardez*, Nova Goa 1855–1877.

CHAPTER 3

The *Principales* of Philip II: Vassalage, Justice, and the Making of Indigenous Jurisdiction in the Early Colonial Philippines

Abisai Perez Zamarripa

1 Introduction

In early May, 1590, native chief Don Felipe Tuliao of Guagua (Pampanga, the Philippines) testified, at the request of Spanish Governor Gómez Pérez Dasmariñas, about the current state of local justice. A year before, Dasmariñas had mandated to summarily conduct, i.e. resolve orally without keeping written records, all the local lawsuits, and he requested that the Crown make his order irrevocable. To achieve his goal, the governor resorted to the testimonies of *principales*, as the Spaniards called the indigenous rulers of the Philippines. According to *principal* Tuliao, since "the lawsuits are determined verbally without writing", natives no longer filed "unjust lawsuits proven with false witnesses" or spent their goods on "the many fees that the judges and their officials" required. In Tuliao's opinion, a royal confirmation of summary justice "would be a particular *merced* (favor) to these islands" because it dealt with two obstacles in the dispensing of justice explored in this paper: the shortage of colonial magistrates and the abuses that they performed against the natives.[1] Tuliao's testimony provides insight into the dispensing of justice by the Spanish Crown to its Philippine subjects—a key strategy for keeping the newly conquered islands under its control. Thus, the question arises, which principles governed the administration of justice in the early colonial Philippines and how did the Crown manage this?

1 "este testigo ha conocido ha visto oír de todos los pleitos así civiles como criminales [...] con que los indios unos a otros se ponían demandas injustas probando con testigos falsos [...] gastando en ello sus haciendas por los muchos derechos que los jueces y sus oficiales pedían [...] y ha visto que los demás pleitos se determinan verbalmente sin escribir y lo que se escribe es con mucha brevedad que todo le ha parecido a este testigo muy bien [...] sería particular merced para todas estas islas que su majestad confirmase la dicha orden". AGI, Filipinas, 34, n. 91, fols. 1014r–1028v. The translation of all quotations used in this chapter are mine.

DOI:10.1163/9789004472839_004

As legal historians, such as António Manuel Hespanha, Carlos Garriga, Tamar Herzog, Víctor Tau Anzoátegui, and Lara Semboloni, have extensively demonstrated, the early modern Iberian empires rested upon a judicial model of government.[2] In the Spanish Monarchy, to govern essentially meant to mete out justice, being that the king's main function was to sustain and reestablish an original normative order provided by God.[3] Similarly, in Iberian political culture, government involved judgment following the principle of justice: God endowed the world with a perfect order that guaranteed each person what he or she was entitled to.[4] Humanity had organized itself into communities receiving from God's *iurisdictio* (jurisdiction), operating under the mandate of exercising justice over community members in order to preserve the harmony dictated by divine will.[5] Drawing from this idea of justice, Spanish political culture acknowledged the monarch as the sovereign and supreme guarantor of justice of his realm because the communities handed him their jurisdiction.[6] Since the king stood out as the highest judge in the kingdom, his main duty was to dispense justice by reestablishing equity among all his subjects.

This paper traces the role of these political principles in the development and management of justice in the early colonial Philippines, by tracking how the Spanish Crown incorporated Philippine natives as vassals, administered justice over them, and acknowledged the jurisdiction of the indigenous nobility. The first section introduces the origins of the contractual relationship between the Spanish king and Philippine natives. In explaining the legal grounds that guided the conquest of the archipelago, this section shows that the Spanish Crown branded Philippine natives as vassals, drawing from the theological and juridical concept of friendship. The second section analyzes how the colonial authorities organized the jurisdictions in the Philippines in line with the governor's authority and Spanish settlement patterns. It also explains the problems in the administration of justice because colonial magistrates owned *encomiendas*—indigenous labor drafts granted by the Crown to Spanish conquistadors. The third section explores the recognition of the jurisdiction of native elites resulting from the lobbying for and formation of local customs by ecclesiastical actors. It also suggests that, although indigenous magistrates were the cornerstones of daily local justice, substantial records do

2 Hespanha, *As vésperas*; Garriga, "Sobre El Gobierno"; Herzog, *Los ministros*; Tau Anzoátegui, *El Jurista*; Semboloni, *La construcción*.

3 Vallejo, "El Cáliz de Plata"; Bastias Saavedra, "Jurisdictional Autonomy".

4 Agüero, "Las Categorías Básicas"; Garriga, "Sobre el Gobierno".

5 Agüero, "Las Categorías Básicas".

6 Fioravanti, "Estado y Constitución".

not exist due to the preeminence of the oral culture among Philippine peoples and the historical contingency that precipitated the absence of archival evidence.

Since there is a lack of testimonies by indigenous actors from the early colonial period, this research adopts two strategies. First, it draws upon imperial legislation and official correspondence between Spanish agents and the Crown to read between the lines following the indigenous experience in the face of Spanish colonization. The decrees issued to protect indigenous vassals and the reports on their mistreatment by the colonizers reveal the recurrent concerns and challenges that shaped the administration of justice during the early colonial Philippines. Second, this paper juxtaposes the developments in the archipelago with the Spanish American experience. Since the beginning of the conquest and colonization, the Spanish Crown attempted to reproduce in the Philippines the legal structure that it previously implemented in its American dominions. Accordingly, this paper attempts to understand and reconstruct the elusive role of Philippine native elites in the colonial justice system through the analysis of the strategies and reactions that unfolded in Spanish America.

So far, research on the role of Philippine natives under Spanish rule mainly focuses on social and economic issues. John L. Phelan, Patricio Hidalgo, and Luis Alonso Álvarez argue that the Crown decided to preserve the nobility status of the *datus* (native chiefs, also called *principales* in Spanish) and to maintain the *barangay* institution—a kinship-oriented community formed by 40–50 households and led by a *datu*—merely for economic reasons.[7] Indeed, both the *barangay* and the *datus* became key instruments not only in the organization and collection of indigenous tribute payments, but also in the formation of the colonial militias that sustained Spanish rule.[8] Consequently, scholarship has overlooked the indigeneity of the process: native elites and native customs were critical components in the administration of justice. They permitted the management of daily justice at a local level without the presence of Spanish agents. This paper proposes that, in line with the ideological background of Spanish legal culture, the Philippine *principales* wielded indigenous jurisdiction, which involved the ability to mete out justice among native subjects concerning minor crimes within their *barangays*.[9] Despite the lack of

7 Phelan, *The Hispanization of the Philippines*; Hidalgo Nuchera, *Encomienda, tributo y trabajo*; Hidalgo Nuchera, *La recta administración*; Alonso Álvarez, *El costo del imperio*, 93–142.

8 See the recent works of Borao Mateo, "Contextualizing the Pampangos"; Mawson, "Philippine Indios"; Crossley, "Dionisio Capulong".

9 Another definition of indigenous jurisdiction that dovetails with the specific features of colonial Mexico is offered in Premo and Yannakakis, "A Court of Sticks".

Spanish agents throughout the colonial period, the Crown was able to govern an archipelago of 7,000 culturally and geographically diverse islands thanks to the indigenous jurisdiction hidden beneath Spanish rule.[10]

2 Conquest through *Pacificación*: Friendship, Vassalage, and Conversion

Spanish imperial ambitions in Asia prompted the colonization of the Philippines; when Hernán Cortés defeated the Mexica in 1521, the Crown supported his explorations toward the Pacific Ocean aimed at establishing contact with the mythical *Catay* and *Cipango* (China and Japan).[11] The Portuguese conquests of Malacca (1511) and Ternate (1512) drove the Spaniards to redouble their efforts in establishing a secure trade route with Asia. The first Spanish endeavors to connect Asia and America unfolded with the circumnavigation voyage of Fernando Magallanes and Sebastián Elcano (1519–1522) and two failed campaigns (in 1527 and 1542) in the Maluku Islands (eastern Indonesia).[12] Since these journeys paved the way for the conquest of the Philippines, scholarly literature tends to overemphasize the objective of establishing a commercial route between the two continents. It therefore overlooks the Crown's key concern regarding how to integrate the indigenous peoples into its realm.[13] A careful analysis of the instructions that Captain Miguel López de Legazpi followed when conducting the colonial enterprise reveals the Spanish Crown's early strategy to bestow upon Philippine natives the status of vassals.

By the time of Legazpi's journey (1564), the Crown's approach to securing new domains differed from the one proclaimed during the early 16th century. Initially, Spanish monarchs justified the possession of their overseas domains by considering them donations from the Pope since he commended to them the religious conversion of indigenous peoples who were regarded as heathens. Complying with this papal mandate, since 1514 Spanish conquistadors had to perform the Crown's protocol of *requerimiento*, which justified the conquest

10 Ethnohistorical research has demonstrated the prevalence of customs in local daily life as well as how natives partially adopted the culture of the colonizers. See Scott, *Barangay*; Concepcion, "Negotiating Land".

11 León-Portilla, "Lo que supo y no supo Hernán Cortés"; Gruzinski, *El águila y el dragón*, 52–59.

12 Bernabeú, "Magallanes: retrato de un hombre"; Knauth, "Los dos Fernandos"; Andaya, "Los primeros contactos de los españoles".

13 Cervera, "¿Las Molucas o China?"; Ollé, "A inserção das Filipinas"; Gruzinski, *El águila y el dragón*, 94–139.

of natives by just war. It demanded that indigenous peoples provide unconditional and immediate recognition of the Spanish kings as their "superior lords [...] by virtue of the said donation". If they refused to comply, the conquistadors became authorized to wage war against them and take them as slaves without any moral constraint reasoning that all "the deaths and damage that occurred" were the natives' fault.[14]

In the mid-16th century, pro-Indianist theologians Francisco de Vitoria and Bartolomé de Las Casas contested the *requerimiento*'s principles. Both Dominican thinkers argued that natives were conscious human beings who possessed the right to self-determination; regardless of their ignorance of Christian religion, indigenous peoples were the rightful owners of the land they inhabited and could thus neither be enslaved nor stripped of their properties by force.[15] Such arguments undermined the legitimacy of the papal donation and the *requerimiento* and urged the Crown to halt the violent conquests unfolding in the New World. Las Casas questioned whether God would approve of the reading of *requerimientos* to "the peaceful and quiet *indios*" and the destruction that Spaniards carried out when natives refused to obey a "king who they never heard or saw", particularly when royal envoys were "so cruel, so ruthless, and horrible tyrants".[16]

In response to pro-Indianist criticism, in 1556 the Crown decreed a new approach to colonial expansion. In that year, Emperor Charles V forwarded the Viceroy of Perú, Marqués de Cañete, the *Instrucciones para las nuevas poblaciones y descubrimiento* to conduct new colonial enterprises following the strategy of *pacificación* (pacification), i.e., conquest through pacts of friendship. The orders established that Spaniards should found new settlements "close to the lands of the natives who until now are not subjugated", without "taking anything from the *indios* without their consent". Once the Spaniards settled, they must seek "peace and friendship with the *indios* who dwell on that land" by treating them well, protecting them, "reducing them to *buena policía* (order)", and converting them to Catholicism. While the *requerimiento* demanded that the natives surrender, the *pacificación* sought to persuade them through good actions. If, after three attempts of inducement, the indigenous peoples still refused to welcome the Spaniards, the invaders could then wage war against them, "defending themselves from the said *naturales* (natives) without doing any more harm than was necessary".[17] Supposedly, Spaniards would no longer

---

14 Encinas, *Cedulario Indiano*, vol. IV, 226–227.

15 Phelan, "Some Ideological Aspects"; de la Hera, "El dominio español"; Wagner, "Francisco de Vitoria".

16 Las Casas, *Tratados*, vol. I, 51.

17 AGI, Lima, 567, L.8, fols. 148r–151v.

pursue aggressive conquests, but defensive wars instead. Yet, the same goal prevailed: the religious conversion of indigenous peoples.

The shift from conquest to pacification could therefore appear inconsequential, since ultimately the new approach similarly legitimized Spanish subjugation over the natives in God's name, either by persuasion or force. But contrary to the *requerimiento*, the *pacificación* introduced a legal-theological concept that changed how Spaniards now perceived and should treat indigenous peoples: friendship. As historiography widely explains, pro-Indianist thought of the 16th-century Iberian world was inspired by Thomas Aquinas' idea of natural law.[18] Aquinas considered that the human being, as a rational and free being by God's design, must follow his own natural inclinations dictated by reason.

Sociability and friendship were seen as rational inclinations since people attain the common good—the improvement of the spirit and the salvation of the soul—only by living in community and establishing relationships of respect and mutual help.[19] By stating that the Spanish king's main purpose was to "form friendships with them [the natives] and teach them to live politically and know God",[20] the *pacificación* recognized that indigenous peoples were able to act as rational human beings. If they accepted Spanish friendship, natives would demonstrate their rational capacity to live within the king's realm, the community that guaranteed them protection, and, more importantly, Christian salvation. If natives refused such a friendly invitation, then they showed a lack of rationality. It was inconceivable to reject Christ's religion of love, which Aquinas regarded as a feeling that all rational beings pursue. Thus, while the *requerimiento* regarded natives as barbarians who should be subjugated by force, the *pacificación* considered them free and rational peoples able to embrace Spanish friendship, but only if they accepted Christianity.

The instructions that Legazpi received from the *Real Audiencia* (royal court) of Mexico to conduct the Philippine expedition reveal that the Crown planned to integrate Philippine natives following the pacification strategy. Drafted by Viceroy Luis de Velasco, and later approved by the Spanish king, Legazpi's instructions stated that his main objective was to "bring the natives of those parts to the knowledge of our holy Catholic faith and to discover the return route to this New Spain". Like the *Instrucciones* forwarded to the Viceroy of Perú in 1556, Legazpi's instructions emphasized the mission of establishing "with the natives all good friendship and peace".[21] As Pedro Cardim explains,

18 Duve, "La Escuela de Salamanca".
19 Cortés Pacheco, "La amistad política".
20 AGI, Lima, 567, L.8, fol. 148v.
21 AGI, Patronato, 23, r. 12, fol. 34r–34v.

friendship, as a legal and theological category, dictated guidelines of behavior whereby the monarch must express his love and respect to his subjects and other rulers.[22] Since Legazpi's instructions reflected this Thomistic notion of friendship, they also set rules of behavior for the Spaniards when encountering the indigenous peoples of the archipelago.

Generosity and respect were two key elements that set the grounds for friendship. According to the instructions, during the first encounter, Legazpi must give "to the *señores principales* (native chiefs) [...] the gifts you think convenient and give them all good treatment" to demonstrate the king's generosity. In doing so, Spaniards were showing that their monarch regarded the indigenous chiefs as *señores principales* (sovereign lords), emphasizing the expedition's purpose to establish peaceful relationships between equal sovereigns. The instructions specified that "the natives of those lands [...] are *gente política y rica* (rich and organized people) where there are great princes" with whom the "powerful King of Castile" desired to "have all good friendship and brotherhood so that among the subjects and vassals there could exist communication and trade".[23] Yet, a commercial agreement was not the main purpose of the expedition but was in fact the first step toward the Spaniards befriending the natives and gaining their confidence. Thus, Legazpi and his crew had to primarily act as royal envoys, not as conquistadors.

Once captain Legazpi had befriended the natives, then he could proceed to settle there. If the expedition found "such rich and high quality [land] that you must populate it", Legazpi must do it "in the part and place that best suits and where best friendship" has been established with the indigenous peoples. If, for some reason, Legazpi was unable to remain in the new settlement, "some religious people and some Spaniards" must stay in order to secure "the conversion of the natives as to preserve the friendship and peace that you will leave settled with them".[24] Occupying the land not only strengthened the friendship between the Spanish king and the natives, but it also guaranteed the possession of the land through the subjugation of its inhabitants. Accepting Spanish friendship implicitly conveyed Christian conversion, obedience to a new sovereign, and, consequently, incorporation into a new polity: the Spanish Monarchy.

The instructions of pacification projected that the conquest of the Philippines required the acquiescence of local populations and Legazpi fitted the profile of leader for such an enterprise. Unlike the Spanish conquistadors who fought in the New World, Legazpi was not a soldier; however, he was well-versed

22 Cardim, "Amor e amizade".

23 AGI, Patronato, 23, r. 12, fol. 13v.

24 AGI, Patronato, 23, r. 12, fol. 33r.

in Spanish legal culture and had served as the main notary of the *cabildo* and *Casa de Moneda* (mint) of Mexico City.[25] Despite his lack of maritime experience, Legazpi became the leader of the expedition because his private wealth greatly contributed to the journey. In addition, he was a close friend of Friar Andrés de Urdaneta, the veteran campaigner of the Spanish expansion toward Southeast Asia.[26] Legazpi had also worked as one of the personal notaries of New Spain's Archbishop and Inquisitor Juan de Zumárraga, who had carried out an aggressive persecution against the indigenous nobility to erase their ancient beliefs.[27] Before he turned into the leader of the Philippine expedition, Legazpi had therefore been a close eyewitness of the religious persecution against natives and the gradual enforcement of laws to protect them. Given his experience, the Crown expected that he would treat indigenous peoples with "a lot of respect as if they were people of our *policía* (order)" because they are "men of good reason [...] and white like us".[28] As a skilled notary, Legazpi would be expected to comply with the royal instructions.

The expedition reached the Philippines in early April, 1565 and by the end of that month it arrived at the city-port of Cebu, whose subjugation Legazpi depicted as a sublime act of friendship. Initially, Tupas, lord of Cebu, fiercely repelled the invaders, but he and his people had to flee to the mountains. After a skirmish, the Spaniards captured "two women and two girls of the nobility [that were] kept with great care". The women were relatives of chief Simaquio, Tupas' close ally. Simaquio tried to free his wife and daughters, offering in exchange his life and that of his followers so the Spanish captain could "do his will and hold them as slaves or sell them or send them to Castile". Legazpi responded that the only thing he wanted was "peace, friendship, and favor, and help and protection which he had offered to them in the name of His Majesty", stressing his selfless intention of serving only the Spanish king. Since friendship conveyed protection and mutual respect, Legazpi highlighted that the captive women's honor had been defended and that he had lodged them "as if he had them in his own house". Such good treatment only revealed, according to Legazpi, all the "good deeds and favors in His Majesty's name" that Philippine natives could receive once they accepted becoming "vassals of the King of Castile".[29]

---

25 Sanz y Díaz, *Legazpi*; Muro, *La expedición Legazpi–Urdaneta*, "Título escribano público de México: Miguel López de Legazpi", AGI, Patronato, 180, r. 56.

26 Barandica, "Andrés de Urdaneta".

27 Greenleaf, *Zumárraga*; AGNM, Inquisición, vol. 72, exp. 32.

28 AGI, Patronato, 23, r. 12.

29 AGI, Patronato, 23, r. 22.

In order to persuade chief Simaquio, Legazpi allowed him to see and speak with his captive family. After his wife told him about "the good actions and *merced* (courtesy) she had received from the governor", Simaquio then accepted "to be friend and vassal of the King of Castile and to settle peace and friendship perpetually".[30] Furthermore, he promised to convince Tupas and the other *principales* of Cebu to do the same, which was eventually achieved.

Ultimately, to become the friend of the Spanish king meant becoming his vassal. Vassalage was a contractual relationship that stemmed from a pact between a lord and a free man, who voluntarily accepted to obey and serve the lord in exchange for protection. Spanish friendship, as stated in the *pacificación* instructions, set the grounds for a relationship of vassalage based on obedience and a promise of safeguard. First, since friendship was a rational inclination of free peoples, when natives accepted to befriend the king, it was assumed that they were acting voluntarily and freely. Thus, the first condition of a contract of vassalage was that the person becoming a vassal was free to enter into it. In addition, the *pacificación* instructions stated that the friendship offered by the king also involved his protection, meaning that the free man's consent was the second condition for vassalage, i.e., a free man requested and accepted protection from a lord.[31]

The contractual nature of indigenous vassalage involved mutual responsibilities. The king must guarantee the wellbeing of his indigenous vassals by protecting them, hearing their petitions through his representatives—i.e. the Viceroy, the *Real Audiencia*, the *protector de indios*—forbidding their enslavement, and recognizing some of their prehispanic practices as legitimate sources of law.[32] Thus, royal tutelage was meant to be under the king's jurisdiction: the king, and not a private person, was the supreme judge who could decide what was in the best interest of his native vassals. In exchange for the king's protection, the natives had to render him obedience, allegiance, and loyalty. All these obligations were comprised in the payment of tributes which sustained the king's realm.[33] While the king provided protection, native vassals primarily helped him with their labor: either producing for the king's treasury or working in his estates or public works.

Spanish legal culture acknowledged the reciprocal relationship between the king and his vassals, highlighting the royal authority and the virtue of loyalty. The *Siete Partidas* stated that the lord "has commandment and power over

30 AGI, Patronato, 23, r. 22.

31 Ganshof, *El feudalismo*, 111–160; Reynolds, *Fiefs and Vassals*, 17–19.

32 Ruiz Medrano, *Mexico's Indigenous Communities*, 11–68.

33 Menegus, "Alcabala o Tributo".

all those who live in his land", while vassals "receive honor and benefit from [their] lords" as long as they fulfill their duty "to love and honor and keep" their lord.[34] Sebastián de Covarrubias' dictionary states that a vassal "is the one who lives in the land of a lord whom he recognizes and respects as such [...] insofar as he promises to be faithful", while the lord wields authority "to honor and benefit who is virtuous and to punish and reduce the one who is cruel."[35] As Xavier Gil notes, Spanish political culture stressed the value of loyalty because it guaranteed the keeping and safeguarding of the polity.[36] As vassals, natives also became members of a community that they had to keep and safeguard, particularly because the Spanish Monarchy carried out the providential mission to expand and defend the true faith.

Because religion justified the subjugation of indigenous peoples and conditioned their membership to the polity, the religious identity of Philippine natives was an essential issue within the pacification strategy. After the conquest of Cebu, Legazpi informed King Philip II that numerous *moros*—as the Spaniards called the Muslims—inhabited the archipelago. Still, he considered that most of them had "little knowledge of the law which they profess, beyond practicing circumcision and refraining from pork". For this reason, he claimed, natives could be "easily converted to our holy Catholic faith".[37] Such observations were relevant at a time when the Crown had enforced harsh policies against Muslims and Jews in its dominions while it struggled in the Mediterranean against the Ottoman Empire.[38] Aspiring to become the defender of Christianity, the Spanish Monarchy endorsed the slavery and dispossession of Muslims.[39] Therefore, downplaying the Muslim faith of Philippine natives was instrumental in achieving their peaceful integration into the Spanish Crown.

The Spanish king insisted on the *pacificación* as a way to subjugate Philippine natives, whom he regarded as heathens waiting for evangelization. Soon after receiving the first news from the archipelago, King Philip II reminded Legazpi of his "sensible policy in not waging war [...] unless you should be provoked and in your own defense". He ordered that the expedition should attempt "by all good means to attract the natives to the service of God our Lord and mine". If the *moros* "come for the purpose of spreading their cursed Mahometan worship" then Legazpi should proceed with a defensive war,

34 *Siete Partidas*, title 25, laws 1 and 6.

35 Covarrubias, *Tesoro de la lengua*, "vasallo".

36 Gil Pujol, "The Good Law".

37 López de Legazpi, "Relation of the Filipinas Islands and of the Character and Conditions of their Inhabitants", vol. 34, 54–61.

38 Hess, "The Moriscos'; Constable, *To Live like a Moor*, 1–14.

39 González Arévalo, "Cautiverio y esclavitud".

which gave him the right to seize their property and enslave the captives. But the king strictly forbade the slavery of "those who were *indios* who may have adopted the worship of Mahomet" through a reminder that the main objective was "to persuade them to accept our holy Catholic faith".[40]

King Philip II's resolve in favor of the *pacificación* strategy derived from his idea that among Philippine natives there existed *moros* "by birth and nation" and "*indios*" who had converted to Islam.[41] While the first were enemies of the empire and responsible for Muslim proselytism, Philippine natives—labeled as *indios*—were acknowledged as heathens; Muslims had known and rejected the true faith, whereas natives were considered to have overlooked the Christian faith and were therefore waiting for redemption through evangelization. Thus, for King Philip II, although some Philippine *indios* had been corrupted by Islam, they were mostly considered pagans who he could bring "to a civilized life and [...] separate them from their vices, sins, and evil customs".[42]

King Philip II's stance made the pacification of Manila possible, even though its rulers professed Islam. As some scholars have suggested, Manila's rulers not only professed Islam, but they were also relatives of Brunei's royal family.[43] Foreseeing the strategic position of Manila, which connected the archipelago with South China, the Indian Ocean, and the Maluku islands, Legazpi sent a small expedition under the command of Martín de Goiti to "pacify" the city in mid-1570. After Goiti failed to subjugate the city, Legazpi personally commanded a new expedition in May of 1571, accompanied this time by hundreds of Cebuano warriors. Although Manila's dwellers fled inland burning their houses behind them, Legazpi settled in the city. A few days later, he received the indigenous rulers of Manila and Tondo, Raja Ache and his heir Raja Soliman, and Raja Sibanao Lakandula.

The encounter between the Spanish captain and the native chiefs epitomized the subjugation of Manila as a pact of vassalage. The Spanish account, called "protocol of pacification", described the meeting in line with the principles that sustained the incorporation of Manila's inhabitants as vassals of the Spanish Crown. The first principle was the voluntary election of a new sovereign. Manila's *principales* assembled with other native lords of neighboring towns to discuss "whether it would be good for them to make peace and friendship with the Spaniards and be His Majesty's vassals". They then agreed

40 King Philip II, "Reply to Miguel López de Legazpi", vol. 34, 230–235.

41 King Philip II, "Reply to Miguel López de Legazpi".

42 King Philip II, "Instructions given to Miguel de López de Legazpi", ed. Emma H. Blair and James A. Robertson, vol. 34, 242.

43 Santiago, "The Houses of Lakandula, Matandá and Solimán"; Majul, *Muslims in the Philippines*; Saunders, *A History of Brunei*, 49–53.

that "with common consent, they wanted to be vassals of the King of Castile".[44] Through this action, the protocol highlighted the natives' free will to become vassals on the basis of a voluntary election of a new lord: King Philip II. On account of the nature of the sources, however, one can only speculate about the Spanish expectations and it cannot be affirmed that natives voluntarily became subjects of the Crown. What the document however does reveal is that the normative foundation of Spanish justifications for conquest had shifted from the *requerimiento* to pacts of vassalage.

The second principle of the protocol emphasized the providential mission that justified the Philippine expedition. Legazpi explained that he "came to these villages by command of His Majesty the King of Castile Don Felipe (King Philip II)", who wanted to "make [the Philippine rulers] know the true almighty God". After hearing that the king's central aim was to propagate "the holy Catholic faith so that they might be saved and not condemned", the *principales* responded "happily to be His Majesty's vassals", implicitly accepting religious conversion.[45]

The third principle meant that the protocol guaranteed *principales* the king's protection as a result of the vassalage compact. The Spanish captain explained that "if any Spaniard or any other person in his company does any harm to them or takes anything from them by force and against their will", he would act on behalf of the king as judge to "maintain peace and justice [among the natives] as vassals of His Majesty".[46] Thus, the protocol of pacification sealed the pact of vassalage promising the eventual establishment of laws, institutions, and magistrates able to guarantee their wellbeing. On paper, the benefits for indigenous vassals appeared attractive. In practice, however, adherence to the contract proved difficult for the Crown. Lack of human resources and the rapid growth of the *encomenderos*' hegemony in the archipelago, explained in the following section, hindered the Crown's pledge to dispense justice to its native vassals.

3 Justice in the Early Colonial Philippines

The idea of justice fashioned the development of the judicial model of government in the Philippines. The Spanish king held supreme jurisdiction, which was represented in the Philippines by different officeholders. Since the

44 AGI, Patronato, 24, r. 24, fol. 1r.
45 AGI, Patronato, 24, r. 24, fol. 1r.
46 AGI, Patronato, 24, r. 24, fol. 1v.

beginning of the colonial era, the governor stood at the apex of the institutions. Legazpi's pacification instructions had entitled him, as the supreme representative of royal authority, "governor general appointed by His Majesty".[47] After the conquest of Cebu, the Crown invested him and his successors with supreme judicial authority in royal ordinary justice, i.e. "civil and criminal justice",[48] over all the inhabitants of the islands. Since then, the governor's main function was to "execute [the king's] royal justice there [the Philippines]".[49] Having full ordinary jurisdiction, the governor could "open and determine all lawsuits and civil and criminal cases"[50] concerning both the Spaniards and the natives. In addition, he and his delegates could remand "the foresaid [natives]" to make "any inquiries about the cases of rights, premises, and all other things [that] you consider are for the service of the royal justice".[51]

This delegation determined that the exercise of justice in the islands orbited and stemmed from the governor. His influence increased when the Crown granted him the right to allocate *encomiendas*—assignments of indigenous labor drafts to Spanish conquistadors in exchange for their military services and support in providing Christian education to their indigenous wards. In 1568, the Crown gave Legazpi and his successors the right to "*encomendar* (grant *encomiendas*) and distribute the towns you deem necessary, in accordance with the laws of succession of the *indios*".[52] Governors leveraged this decree to benefit their close relatives and friends—a situation that favored the rapid growth of the *encomiendas* in the archipelago.[53]

As a result, during the first decade after the conquest of Manila, the *encomiendas* populated the Philippine landscape. In 1582, Spanish conquistador Miguel de Loarca reported to the Council of the Indies that Spanish soldiers together with their indigenous allies had conquered most of the archipelago. Analysis of the report reveals that indigenous male tributaries amounted to 141,840. Of this number, 100,520 were allocated as *encomiendas* to about 120 Spanish conquistadors, while the remaining 41,320 were direct tributaries of the Crown. In the entire Philippines, only 800 indigenous inhabitants in Cebu were exempt from tributes "for having always been in favor of the Spaniards and helping to gain part of the other islands".[54] Thus, Loarca concluded that almost "all the

47 AGI, Patronato, 23, r. 12. fol. 8r.

48 AGI, Filipinas, 339, L.1, fol. 24r.

49 AGI, Filipinas, 339, L.1, fol. 24r.

50 AGI, Filipinas, 339, L.1, fol. 24v.

51 AGI, Filipinas, 339, L.1, fols. 24v–25r.

52 AGI, Filipinas, 339, L.1, Fols. 1r–2v.

53 Hidalgo Nuchera, *Encomienda, tributo y trabajo*, 58–58.

54 AGI, Patronato, 23, r. 9. Philippine *principales* and their descendants were exempt from tribute payment because of their nobility status. Thus, the exemption granted to Cebu's indigenous commoners is a unique case in the entire Philippines.

islands and populations that are at the service of His Majesty"[55] were allocated as *encomiendas*.

In advancing the pacification of the archipelago, Spanish governors founded five settlements, where the few Spanish colonists settled to manage their *encomiendas*. The towns were Manila (Central Luzon), Cebu (Cebu island), Villa de Arévalo (Panay island), Villa de Cáceres (Bicol, southern Luzon), and Villa Fernandina (Ilocos, northern Luzon). Each of these organized the administration of justice and the management of indigenous tribute payments in the early colonial Philippines. As a result, there were seven major provinces in the archipelago: Manila (39,880 tributaries, subject to Manila), Cebu (24,100 tributaries, subject to Cebu), Panay (25,060 tributaries, subject to Villa de Arévalo), Bicol (28,7000 tributaries, subject to Villa de Cáceres), Pangasinan (14,300 tributaries), Mindoro (no data), and Ilocos (12,200 tributaries)—the last three subject to Villa Fernandina.

Each of these Spanish towns and the settlements enjoyed limited self-government: they had a *cabildo* formed by *regidores*, who were deputies in charge of the urban management, and *alcaldes ordinarios*, who were local judges administering justice within the town. The towns were also the seat of provincial authorities—the *alcalde mayor* and the *corregidor*—who carried out the fundamental mission of tribute payment collection and held jurisdiction over the natives living in the countryside.

Each Spanish province governed extensive territorial areas and thus the indigenous tributaries greatly outnumbered the available magistrates. The provinces of Cebu, Panay, Bicol, Pangasinan, Mindoro, and Ilocos only had one *alcalde mayor* each. As a result, only six magistrates were available to dispense justice over more than one hundred thousand indigenous subjects.

In Manila and its surroundings, the situation was slightly different. Given that Central Luzon was the most populated and richest region of the islands, since 1576 the Crown had been taking most of the indigenous tributaries from the *encomenderos* to put under its dominion.[56] To improve tribute payment collection, the Crown organized the region into ten jurisdictions managed by eight *alcaldes mayores* (Calompit, Candaba, Lubao, Bulacan, Tondo, Bahi, Cavite, and Laguna Bay) and two *corregidores* or provincial judges (Batan and Balayan). In the entire archipelago, the total of the tributary population (141,840) divided by the total of colonial magistrates (15) results in an average of one Spanish judge to 10,313 tributaries—not counting women, young people, and the elderly. Loarca's report reasoned that all the Spanish authorities were *encomenderos*, "because if they were not *encomenderos* they could not sustain

---

55 AGI, Patronato, 23, r. 9.

56 Hidalgo Nuchera, *Encomienda, tributo y trabajo*, 79–81.

themselves". *Alcaldes mayores* visited the indigenous communities under their jurisdiction once a year to collect taxes and attend the "Indian lawsuits (*pleitos de indios*) [...] and other commissions committed to justice".[57] Although the Crown mandated that Spanish colonists with *encomiendas*, including the authorities, must reside in their estates, all of them preferred to settle in one of the Spanish towns.

Such an imbalance between magistrates and population and the fact that the former held *encomiendas* posed two major challenges that prevented the natives from receiving proper justice. First, magistrates failed to meet the demands of the indigenous population given the large number of cases that they had to attend each year. In the words of Don Pedro Lumano, a Pampanga *principal*, it was common that the indigenous communities "were worn out and destroyed among themselves in disputes and differences of the past".[58] When the *alcaldes mayores* arrived at the indigenous towns to administer justice, they and their notaries merely registered the lawsuits in writing without issuing a decision. The lack of resolutions reached the point that, according to *principal* Don Juan Lisin, the judge died or was replaced by a new one and then he "heard [the cases] again and every day the lawsuits and the *pleitantes* (litigants) grew". Lisin also declared that this led the natives to invest a lot of resources and time in demanding justice, since "the *indios* of this land are *noveleros* (novices) [and] they put forward unreasonable lawsuits among themselves [...] spending their goods on this".[59] The colonial magistrates benefited from this situation by registering the disputes without resolving them, while the *indios* became impoverished because they tended to leave "their houses and plots [...] all of them giving [the judges] large sums in fees because the *naturales* did not know about tariffs".[60]

Second, there were exploitations committed by the colonial administration against natives, which both secular and ecclesiastical agents extensively reported to the Crown. As *encomenderos*, the magistrates naturally put their personal interests first at the expense of the proper administration of justice. After Legazpi's sudden death in 1572, the *encomenderos* took advantage of the freedom to exploit and deprive the natives. Conquistador Guido de Lavezaris, who succeeded Legazpi as governor, granted both *encomiendas* and justice posts to his fellow conquistadors. Missionary Martín de Rada explains that the natives arrived at Manila "to ask for justice but are badly heard and attended

57 Filipinas, 339, L. 2, fols. 134r–134v.
58 AGI, Filipinas, 34, n. 91, fols. 1014r–1028v.
59 AGI, Filipinas, 34, n. 91, fol. 1015v.
60 AGI, Filipinas, 34, n. 91, fol. 1016r.

to because the governor and his officials are *encomenderos*".[61] In Rada's opinion, the *encomenderos*' greed eroded the contractual relationship of vassalage: rather than vassals, Philippine natives had been turned into slaves.[62]

A decade later, since the mistreatments persisted, Manila's *procurador* (solicitor), Gabriel Rivera, made three propositions before the Council of the Indies to solve the mismanagement of justice in the islands. First, he proposed that the governor should be the only judge in charge of hearing and deciding on the indigenous lawsuits. As "most of the *alcaldes ordinarios* have *encomienda*" and it is common that the natives "receive many grievances and justice is not given to them",[63] the governor should be more active in dispensing justice in his capacity as the highest judge in the islands. Second, the Crown should appoint a *protector de indios* to provide the natives with legal aid in their demands for justice. The *indios*, as "newly converted and pacified people [...] have no understanding or ability to defend themselves", and are thus in need of a "*protector general defensor* (general solicitor defender) with enough power" to take the natives' causes before the royal courts.[64] Third, Rivera requested the creation of a *Real Audiencia* in Manila "for the *Audiencia* of Mexico to which [the inhabitants of the Philippines] go on appeal is so far away and this thus lacks justice".[65] As Garriga explains, since the Crown proclaimed the New Laws in 1542 to protect its indigenous vassals, the *Reales Audiencias* became the highest provincial court embodying the supreme jurisdiction of the king. A *Real Audiencia* mainly served as a regional court of appeal for both civil and criminal cases and its main objective was to "correct" the judgments that colonial magistrates may have reached in bad faith.[66]

At this time, there was no *Real Audiencia* in the Philippines as "the appeals concerning the cases and litigation dealt with by the governor of the said islands take place in the *Real Audiencia* of Mexico". When Manila became capital of the archipelago in 1574, the Crown mandated that it was "fair that the government there was united and dependent on the government of New Spain" so that "the laws concerning government and justice keep the same order they

61 "toman por la fuerza de las armas lo que encuentra en los pueblos [...] es demasiado e insoportable el tributo [in gold] que se les lleva según la miseria de los naturales [...] y aunque vienen a pedir justicia [the natives] son muy mal oídos y despachados, al fin como así el gobernador y sus oficiales son todos encomenderos". AGI, Filipinas, 84, n. 4, fols. 1r–1v.

62 AGI, Filipinas, 84, n. 4, fol. 1v.

63 AGI, Patronato 25, r. 2, fol. 3v.

64 AGI, Patronato 25, r. 2, fol. 4r.

65 AGI, Patronato 25, r. 2, fol. 1r.

66 Garriga, "Sobre El Gobierno".

have" in New Spain.[67] The incorporation of the Philippines into the jurisdiction of the Mexican *Audiencia* made judicial appeals extremely costly and complicated because of the huge distance between Manila and Mexico City. Only wealthy individuals could appeal to the king's court, while the indigenous subjects, who were neophytes in Spanish legal culture and had been exploited by the *encomenderos*, could not afford long-distance litigation.

Aiming to bring the king's justice to the distant Philippines, in 1584 the Crown established the *Real Audiencia* of Manila. Aside from attending appeals filed by Spaniards, the *Audiencia* also had to "take great care to be informed of the crimes and abuses which shall be committed, or have been committed, against the *indios* who shall be under our royal Crown". In consequence, the *fiscal* of the *Audiencia* was the main person in charge of assisting the "poor *indios* in the suits being carried out, and seeing to it on their behalf that they are not oppressed, maltreated, or wronged".[68]

The *Audiencia* also acted as advisory council to the governor, which caused bitter confrontations between them. The struggle for power led to the suppression of the tribunal in 1590 and the creation of a new one six years later. The first *Audiencia* not only engendered disputes with the highest official in the islands—the governor—but was also unable to provide legal aid to indigenous subjects. From 1598–1600, the second *Audiencia* and the governor produced the first laws to reform the behavior of the colonial government and to improve the conditions of Philippine natives.[69] Yet, the huge gap between the number of inhabitants and the magistrates available remained. Such a situation—not exceptional, but rather common in the empire—did not impede the Spanish Crown from governing over thousands of diverse indigenous communities scattered across the archipelago. Beneath the jurisdiction held by Spanish magistrates there was a different level of government that assured the regular collection of tribute payments and the daily administration of justice: indigenous jurisdiction.

4 The Making of Indigenous Jurisdiction: *Principales* and *Barangays*

The acknowledgement of indigenous jurisdiction in the Philippines dates to the conquest of Cebu in 1565. In the vassalage compact between Legazpi and

67 AGI, Filipinas, 339, L.2, fol. 49r.

68 Blair, Emma H. and James A. Robertson, "Foundation of the Audiencia of Manila", vol. 5, 261–304.

69 See Hidalgo Nuchera, *Los autos acordados*, 19–37.

Cebu's natives, the Spanish captain set up a clause specifying that "if any *indio natural* of this island commits any crime or evil against any Spaniard [...] the *principales* are compelled to catch them and bring them as prisoners before the governor so he can punish them and put them on trial".[70] Thus, Legazpi confirmed the *principales*' authority as petty justice agents in charge of apprehending indigenous delinquents. Yet, the *principales* were not recognized as judges, although Spaniards acknowledged that, before they arrived at the archipelago, only the *principales* "are defenders and executors" of the public order, who "punish the crimes and also give laws" to their communities.[71] The jurisdiction or the ability to dispense justice was reserved for the governor and, in consequence, his lieutenants, who were the *alcaldes mayores*.

This paralleled the Spanish American experience, where the Crown had seized the administration of justice from the indigenous nobility by creating a Spanish provincial government. From 1550, the Crown invested the *corregidores* and *alcaldes mayores* with judicial authority to "know of the grievances that were done to *indios*, punish those who do them, and dispense justice".[72] The same judicial model functioned in the Philippines during the first three decades (1565–1595) of colonial dominion.

In royally appointing provincial magistrates, the Crown pursued two objectives. First, it aimed to enforce and expand the royal jurisdiction to the detriment of the *encomenderos* by appointing a judiciary that would resolve and punish "crimes committed between some *españoles* and others, and between *indios* and *españoles*".[73] Second, the new provincial magistrates would end the "tyrannies" that the indigenous nobility supposedly committed against its subjects, who frequently claimed that not only the *encomenderos*, but also their *caciques* maltreated them.

At the same time that the provincial Spanish magistrates came on the scene, the Viceroys of New Spain and Peru introduced the *cabildo* in the indigenous towns. Native deputies and judges, annually elected to manage each town and the corresponding daily dispensation of justice involving minor crimes, formed the indigenous *cabildo*.[74] The creation of *cabildos* meant that native agents outside the traditional nobility class upheld civil jurisdiction within their towns for the time they served in the town council. The strategy allowed the Crown to assert control over the labor and tribute of its indigenous vassals,

70 "Relación sobre los sucesos de Cebú", AGI, Patronato 23, r. 22, fol. 4r.
71 AGI, Patronato, 23, r. 9.
72 Encinas, *Cedulario Indiano*, vol. III, 19.
73 Encinas, *Cedulario Indiano*, vol. III, 19.
74 Haskett, *Indigenous Rulers*, 77–82.

while the representatives of the indigenous communities acquired limited civil jurisdiction to dispense justice over the indigenous members of the town.[75]

A similar process of empowerment of indigenous agents as judges unfolded in the Philippines from the 1580s, however in this case the indigenous nobility did not lose its jurisdiction but recovered it. Dominican friar and theologian Domingo de Salazar, the first Bishop of the Philippines, stood out as the main defender of the indigenous subjects and the Philippine *principales*. As Guillaume Gaudin explains, the creation of the Bishopric of Manila (1579) and the appointment of Salazar in the episcopal see of the archipelago sought to moderate the power of the governor, to reaffirm the royal authority over the monastic orders, and to grant justice to natives.[76] As missionary and solicitor of the Dominican order in New Spain, Salazar demonstrated a combative spirit in favor of the peaceful conversion and submission of the natives.[77] When he arrived in Manila, he rapidly became the most formidable opponent to the *encomenderos* and the colonial government by denouncing their actions directly to the king.

In 1582, Salazar celebrated a synod that gathered all the secular and religious authorities of the Philippines. The synod's purpose was to solve the major problem facing the indigenous vassals: that *alcaldes mayores* were also *encomenderos*. Salazar's main concern was that this combination prevented the natives from receiving proper administration of justice and religious education.[78] Through the synod of Manila, Salazar expected to effect change by setting norms of behavior for the Spanish colonizers and asking for the judicial empowerment of the Philippine *principales*.

In the council, Salazar drew two radical conclusions. First, Spanish conquistadors had conducted military campaigns without respecting the pacts of friendship and vassalage established in the pacification instructions. Therefore, all the goods they had taken from the natives should be restituted by investing in the construction of churches for the missionary enterprise, since Spanish dominion's primary purpose was that of Christian conversion. If the governor and the officials did not comply with such restitution, Salazar would denounce that the conquest of the Philippines had been attained illegally.[79]

Second, Salazar suggested that Spaniards "caused the *indios* great harm by thinking they are not capable of governing themselves, because [Spaniards]

75 Menegus, *Del señorío a la república de indios*, 77–93; Mumford, *Vertical Empire*, 75–80.
76 Gaudin, "Estableciendo la autoridad del rey".
77 Porras Camúñez, *Sínodo de Manila*, 36–49.
78 Porras Camúñez, *Sínodo de Manila*, 9–11.
79 Salazar, *Suma de una junta*, lib. 1, cap. 7, 16.

neither understand them nor know their language and their customs". Salazar went even further, stating that, if Spaniards understood indigenous peoples, "we would see that they could govern themselves as well as we do, and that perhaps we are more barbaric to them than they are to us".[80] Although the bishop and his religious companions asserted that Philippine peoples lacked "good government", they considered that a better comprehension of indigenous customs would improve the justice and conversion of Philippine natives.[81]

In denouncing the barbaric ways in which Spaniards treated the natives, Salazar demanded the restitution of the *principales*' jurisdiction within their communities by empowering them as local magistrates. He urged the governor "to appoint Indian judges, elected by the *indios* themselves, in the more populated villages", so that native subjects "could ask for common justice and *policía* (order) and ordinary cases" before their own authorities. Such a proposal, Salazar highlighted, was according to "the natural law, since nature itself shows that even brute animals [...] have governors and heads of their same *república* (republic)" and not from a different one. The bishop thought it necessary "that the governor [of the natives] must be of the same kind when the conditions allowed it", and that the granting of justice must "be trusted to an *indio*, by giving him jurisdiction over the rest" of the indigenous population. A good judge and governor needed to possess a "knowledge of his *república* and its laws, customs, and abuses". For all these reasons, Salazar concluded, "the governor should, under pain of mortal sin, appoint these Indian judges" as a means to restitute all the injustices that Spaniards had brought upon indigenous peoples.[82]

As expected, Salazar's project faced strong challenges in finding its place in the colonial institutions. Both the *encomenderos* and the *Real Audiencia* of Manila rejected the synod's proposal. Yet, the major challenge of the bishop's plan to create autonomous indigenous jurisdictions was that, as he stated in the synod, Spaniards ignored indigenous customs. The restitution of the *principales*' jurisdiction required knowledge of indigenous customs since they

---

80 Anon., *Junta y congregación*, lib. 1, cap. 1, § 11–13.

81 Salazar, *Suma de una junta*, lib. 1, cap. 1, 6.

82 "Supuesto es justa la jurisdicción del Rey y su Gobernador en esta tierra, decimos que el gobernador, fuera de los alcaldes mayores, debe poner en los pueblos mayores y más asentados jueces indios elegidos por los mismos indios [...] porque es derecho natural, que la misma naturaleza enseña aún a los brutos animales, y así vemos que las grullas, hormigas y abejas tienen gobernador y cabeza de su misma república y no de otras; y entre los mismo del cuerpo que gobierna es uno de ello [...]. Y por esta razón pareció debía el Gobernador, bajo pecado mortal y restitución de los daños que se siguieren, poner estos jueces indios donde hubiese disposición". Salazar, *Suma de una junta*, lib. 1, cap. 17, 24–25.

delineated both the territorial limits and the legal matters that indigenous nobility would oversee.

In the Spanish colonization of America, the endorsement of an indigenous judiciary accompanied the incorporation of indigenous customs into the normative corpus of the Spanish empire. In 1555, a royal decree mandated to preserve the "good customs and laws that the *indios* used to have for their governance and *policía*" as long as they were not contrary to the Christian faith.[83] As Hespanha explains, Iberian jurists conceived indigenous customs as "rustic law" (*direito rústico*). According to him, indigenous customs, were considered an inferior legal reality since they derived from the ignorance of barbarian peoples. Still, indigenous customs were a legitimate source of law because they aimed to preserve the wellbeing of their communities. Therefore, royal magistrates should incorporate, through a process of compilation and selection, those elements of "rustic law" considered useful for the welfare of indigenous peoples that did not contradict Catholic morality.[84]

Salazar's proposal to recognize indigenous jurisdiction became reality when Franciscan Friar Juan de Plasencia met the task of compiling the Philippine indigenous custom. In 1589, Plasencia handed the *Real Audiencia* of Manila two works—*Costumbres antiguas de los naturales de estas islas* and *Costumbres de los naturales de la provincial de Pampanga*—in which he described the most important aspects of "government, justice, bequests, slaves, and dowries" according to the traditions and customs of the Tagalog and Pampangos, who inhabited Luzon island.[85] Plasencia's works served as a guide for the *Audiencia*'s magistrates concerning the ancient ways of justice among Philippine natives so they could "keep the customs that the foresaid *naturales* used to have and currently have in the foresaid lawsuits so they may be preserved as His Majesty commands".[86]

83 Encinas, *Cedulario Indiano*, 355.

84 Hespanha, "As fronteiras do poder".

85 "he juntado indios de diferentes partes hombres viejos y los de más capacidad que yo conocía y sacada la verdad en limpio dejadas muchas impertinencias acerca de su gobierno y justicia, herencias y esclavos y dotes es lo que hay aquí". Since Plasencia reported before the Royal Audiencia de Manila, his works are inserted in a collection of decrees—*reales cédulas* and *autos de buen gobierno*—mandated by royal tribunal. "Cédulas sobre Filipinas, 1581 a 1594", BLAC, G56, fols. 51r–56v.

86 "conviene que los abogados y procuradores de esta Real Audiencia aleguen las costumbres de los dichos naturales que antes tenían y tienen en los dichos pleitos para que les sean guardadas como su majestad manda". "Cédulas sobre Filipinas, 1581 a 1594", BLAC, G56, fol. 45v. Historiography has considered these works as key ethnographic sources, but Plasencia's original purpose was to compile the indigenous customs of Central Luzon. A

Plasencia's research emphasizes the role of the *barangay* as the basic unit of social organization and, hence, of indigenous jurisdiction. He explains that the Tagalog "always had *principales*, whom they call *datus*, who ruled them", and who also wielded justice over a certain number of families; this set of households "is called *barangay*".[87] A similar situation existed among the peoples of Pampanga. Plasencia explains that "they never had a head whom in general all the peoples obeyed but, in each *barangay*, they only obeyed one chief". Native commoners presented "their lawsuits to their *principal*", who sought to reconcile the opposing parties through oral trials with the participation of witnesses.[88] Plasencia's inquiries show that the Tagalog and Pampanga peoples possessed customs in which the *datus* or *principales* played a central role in the exercise of justice, which supported Salazar's plan to restitute indigenous jurisdiction.

Plasencia's reports also demonstrate that the *principales*' jurisdiction encompassed the *barangay*. Regarding the Tagalog peoples, he explains that the *datu* was responsible for "judging and inquiring" about the crimes committed "within his *barangay*". A *principal* was the only judge within his community unless the native chiefs invited another *principal* from a neighboring *barangay* to act as an impartial judge. When "one of the parties felt aggrieved, they all agreed to appoint an arbiter judge from another *barangay* or town" so the neighboring *principal* could judge "the truth according to their customs". When the *principales* of the same *barangay* confronted themselves, or when two distinct *barangays* had disputes, the native chiefs also tended to "appoint arbiter judges".[89] Plasencia perceived that Philippine customs, in a similar way to the Spanish legal tradition, resorted to consultative meetings to dispense justice on the grounds of a common agreement among the magistrates. The *barangay* constituted the social unit that defined the limits of the *principales*' jurisdiction, but the *principales* could also assemble to form advisory councils to solve community conflicts.

---

short review of Plasencia's work to explain the concept of *barangay* and other notions of Tagalog and Pampanga peoples is in Scott, *Barangay*, 1–6.

87 Plasencia, *Costumbres antiguas*, fol. 51r.

88 Plasencia, *Costumbres de los naturales*, fol. 54v.

89 The complete title expresses: "El juzgar y averiguar sus competencias el dato lo hacía entre los de su barangay. Y si alguna de las partes se sentía agraviada, de conformidad todos nombraban un juez árbitro de otro barangay o pueblo, fuese dato o no, que para esto había ya algunos conocidos por hombres desapasionados y que decían y juzgaban la verdad según sus costumbres; y si era el pleito entre dos principales, cuando querían excusar guerras nombraban también jueces árbitros; y si era entre dos de diversos barangays, así mismo". Plasencia, *Costumbres antiguas*, title 9.

Plasencia's works not only served as a guide for Spanish magistrates dealing with "Indian lawsuits", but also enhanced Salazar's project of recognizing indigenous jurisdiction, which the Crown finally endorsed in 1594. That year, a royal decree from King Philip II declared that, "having been informed that the *indios principales* were deprived of the *señorío* [dominion] they had in their gentility [...] I command you to treat them well and entrust them, in my name, with the government of the *indios* of which they were lords".[90] Finally, the Crown recognized *principales* as legitimate governors of their *barangays* and, hence, guarantors of local justice since they were "lords" of their communities and held jurisdiction over them. Later, by the 1640s, the colonial government developed the post of *gobernadorcillo* in line with the conciliar system that Plasencia described. In addition, the *barangays* now had to have a *cabeza de barangay* who represented his community (formed by 45–50 households), and each year the *cabezas* of a set of *barangays* assembled to elect a *gobernadorcillo*, who collected tribute payments and solved minor disputes in the communities that elected him.[91] In creating the elective post of the *gobernadorcillo*, the Crown endorsed the "impartial arbiter" that Philippine communities used to recognize in their daily administration of justice.

Neither the royal decree that restituted the *principales*' jurisdiction nor any other later colonial decree specified in which legal matters and how the native chiefs could intervene. When the Crown reinstalled the *Real Audiencia* of Manila in 1596, it specified that, when possible, the "Indian lawsuits" at all jurisdictional levels must "be summarily determined, keeping their habits and customs as long as they were not clearly unjust".[92] The insertion of Plasencia's works in the *autos de buen gobierno*—provisions of government collegially decided among all the members of the *Audiencia*—suggests that the colonial magistrates in the Philippines took them as reference to determine at their discretion which customs were "not clearly unjust". Ultimately, Spanish magistrates indistinctly drew from the opinions of jurists, from royal decrees and ordinances, and from custom—including the indigenous customs—to dispense justice in each case: giving each person what they were entitled to without custom or written law having precedence over the other.

---

90 "Cédulas sobre Filipinas, 1581 a 1594", BLAC, G56, fol. 175v.

91 Sánchez-Gómez, "Elecciones Locales Indígenas"; Sánchez-Gómez, "Estructura de Los Pueblos"; Alonso Álvarez, *El costo del imperio*, 124–134.

92 "Mando que los dichos mi presidente y oidores tengan mucho cuidado de no dar lugar que en los pleitos que entre indios o con ellos se hagan procesos ordinarios no haya largas sino que sumariamente sean determinados guardando sus usos y costumbres no siendo claramente injustos y los dichos mis oidores tengan cuidado que estos mismos se guarden por los jueces inferiores". AGI, Filipinas, 339, L.2, fols. 183v–185r.

Unfortunately, there is little archival evidence available to decipher the practice and scope of indigenous jurisdiction in the Philippines; two aspects explain this gap. First, a substantial portion of documents concerning the colonial era perished because of the bombing and looting that unfolded during the Second World War. As Bruce Cruikshank notes, it is highly probable that the Philippine National Archives contained the records of the *Real Audiencia* of Manila, including thousands of "Indian lawsuits", that were destroyed amid the chaos of war.[93]

Second, in 1590, before the second *Audiencia*'s orders, the Crown had already mandated the Spanish magistrates to "avoid any lawsuits and to solve them by good means without them reaching trial". When lawsuits had to be solved by trial, they had to be "brief and to the point without the ordinary deadlines and terms [...] to save expenses to the *indios*". Seeking to enhance the administration of local justice, the Crown stipulated that the provincial judges must proceed "summarily in civil matters and that minor cases should not be recorded in writing". Equally, if the Spanish judiciary was not required to keep written records on minor trials, it is also likely that, given the well-rooted oral culture of Philippine peoples, indigenous magistrates also did not think it necessary to record the daily dispensation of justice.[94] Pending further archival discoveries, Spanish records are the only evidence available to assist with understanding indigenous jurisdiction and customs in the Philippines. Hidden and often ignored because of the lack of sources, justice imparted by Philippine *principales* was probably one of the cornerstones for the Spanish Crown in its governance and maintenance of its Asian possession for more than three centuries.

5 Conclusion

In 1596, two years after the restitution of the *principales*' jurisdiction, the Crown mandated the renewal of the pacts of friendship between the king and the Philippine peoples. From 1599–1600, through the mediation of missionaries, the *principales* performed the oath of vassalage pledging allegiance to the Spanish monarch while symbolically electing him, again, as their true and

93 Cruikshank, *Filipiniana in Madrid*, 1–7.

94 "su majestad en su real instrucción [has] mandado y ordenado que en estas islas se procure evitar cualesquiera pleitos y concordaos a buenas sin que lleguen a tela de juicio y que los pleitos que hubiere y no se pudieren excusar sean breves sumarios sin los plazos y términos ordinarios y que para evitar costas a los indios y otras molestias y gastos en ellos se proceda sumariamente mayormente en los civiles y que algunos de poca importancia no se escriban [...]." AGI, Filipinas, 34, n. 91, fols. 1014r–1028v.

perpetual sovereign.[95] The "Philippine referendum"—as defined by Phelan and Fidel Villarroel—vindicated the promise made by the protocols of pacification and the pacts of friendship from the conquest period: that the vassalage relationship between the king and the indigenous rulers was based on mutual obligations.

This paper traces the foundations of the pact and its impact on the development of the administration of justice and the colonial institutions in the early colonial Philippines. Before Legazpi arrived on the shores of the Philippines, the Crown had already projected to bestow upon Philippine natives the legal status of vassals. Drawing from the Thomistic concept of friendship, the Crown mandated to recognize Philippine native rulers as equal sovereigns to the Spanish king, a relationship that conveyed mutual responsibilities: protection and conversion in exchange for tribute payments. The friendship pacts between the natives and the king that unfolded during the conquest set the stage for the later development of a government that would ideally anticipate the protection and Christian conversion of the indigenous vassals. Yet, Spanish conquistadors soon took over the archipelago, by not only seizing indigenous labor through *encomienda* assignments, but also occupying the offices that supposedly guaranteed natives the king's protection. The abuses and mistreatments by the colonial government prompted Salazar, the first bishop of the Philippines, to effect change. In the Synod of Manila (1582), Salazar proposed to restitute the *principales*' jurisdiction, which meant to recognize them as local judges in charge of daily justice within their communities. Only when Franciscan Friar Plasencia compiled the customs of Tagalogs and Pampangos, which supported Salazar's proposal, did indigenous jurisdiction become another jurisdictional level in the Philippines that allowed the Spanish Crown to manage its Asian possession. The *principales* and their *barangays* became a key component of the institutions that assured Spanish rule in an archipelago of more than 7,000 scattered islands with extensive geographical and cultural diversity.

Acknowledgements

Research for this article has been possible thanks to the generous support of the Tom and Martha Ward Endowed Fund, the Department of History at the University of Texas at Austin, and the ConTex Doctoral Fellowship. I want to

95 Villarroel, "Philip II"; Phelan, "Some Ideological Aspects".

express my gratitude to Ann Twinam, Nicholas Sy, Grace Concepcion, and my wife, Stephannie Coeto Coix, for their kind support. Their insightful comments and expertise have improved this study in innumerable ways. I also want to thank Manuel Bastias Saavedra and the two anonymous reviewers for their suggestions. All errors are mine.

Bibliography

Manuscripts

Archivo General de Indias, Sevilla (AGI), Filipinas, 34, n. 91.
Archivo General de Indias, Sevilla (AGI), Lima, 567, L.8, fols. 148r–151v.
Archivo General de Indias, Sevilla (AGI), Patronato, 23, r. 12.
Archivo General de Indias, Sevilla (AGI), Patronato, 180, r. 56.
Archivo General de la Nación, México (AGNM), Inquisición, vol. 72, exp. 32.
Archivo General de Indias, Sevilla (AGI), Patronato, 24, r. 24.
Archivo General de Indias, Sevilla (AGI), Patronato, 23, r. 22.
Archivo General de Indias, Sevilla (AGI), Filipinas, 339, L. 1.
Archivo General de Indias, Sevilla (AGI), Filipinas, 339, L. 2.
Archivo General de Indias, Sevilla (AGI), Filipinas, 84, n. 4.
Benson Latin American Collection, Austin (BLAC), Genaro García Collection, G56.

Printed Sources

Anon., *Junta y congregación*, ed. Porras Camúñez, José Luis, Madrid 1988.
Alfonso X, *Las siete Partidas* […], ed. Real Academia de la Historia, Madrid 1807.
Blair, Emma H., Robertson, James A., *The Philippine Islands* […], Cleveland 1909.
Covarrubias, Sebastián de, *Tesoro de la lengua* […], ed. Luis Sánchez, Madrid 1611.
Encinas, Diego de, *Cedulario Indiano*, ed. García Gallo, Alfonso, Madrid 1990.

Literature

Agüero, Alejandro, "Las categorías básicas de la cultura jurisdiccional", in Lorente, Marta (ed.), *De Justicia de jueces a justicia de leyes: hacia la España de 1870*, Madrid 2006, 19–58.
Alonso Álvarez, Luis, *El costo del imperio asiático. La formación colonial de las islas Filipinas bajo dominio español, 1565–1800*, México 2009.
Andaya, Leonard Y., "Los primeros contactos de los españoles con el mundo de las Molucas en las Islas de las Especias", in *Revista Española del Pacífico* 2:2 (1992): 62–85.
Bastias Saavedra, Manuel, "Jurisdictional Autonomy of Law: End of Empire and the Functional Differentiation of Law in 19th-Century Latin America", in *Rechtsgeschichte-Legal History* 26 (2018): 325–337.

Barandica, Luis Abraham, "Andrés de Urdaneta en la Nueva España", in Barrón, Ma. Cristina (ed.), *Urdaneta Novohispano: la Inserción del mundo hispano en Asia*, México 2012, 35–66.

Bernabeú, Salvador, "Magallanes: retrato de un hombre", in Yuste López, Carmen and Pinzón Ríos, Guadalupe (eds.), *A 500 años del hallazgo del Pacífico: la presencia novohispana en el Mar del Sur*, México 2016, 21–52.

Borao Mateo, José E., "Contextualizing the Pampangos (and Gagayano) Soldiers in the Spanish Fortress in Taiwan (1626–1642)", in *Anuario de Estudios Americanos* 70:2 (2013): 581–605.

Cardim, Pedro, "Amor e Amizade Na Cultura Política Dos Séculos XVI e XVII", in *Lusitania Sacra* 11 (2000): 21–57.

Cervera, José Antonio, "¿Las Molucas o China? Filipinas y los planes para la expansión hispana a Asia Oriental desde la Nueva España en el siglo XVI", in Yuste López, Carmen and Pinzón Ríos, Guadalupe (eds.), *A 500 años del hallazgo del Pacífico: la presencia novohispana en el Mar del Sur*, México 2016, 101–124.

Conception, Grace L., "Negotiating Land in the Spanish Philippines: Cases of Land Donations and Boundary Disputes in Laguna, Seventeenth and Eighteenth Centuries", in *Philippine Studies: Historical and Ethnographic Viewpoints* 67:3 (2019): 285–313.

Constable, Olivia Remie, *To Live like a Moor: Christian Perceptions of Muslim Identity in Medieval and Early Modern Spain*, Philadelphia 2018.

Cortés Pacheco, Carmen, "La amistad política en Santo Tomás de Aquino: entre la Justicia y la misericordia", in *Espíritu: Cuadernos Del Instituto Filosófico de Balmesiana*, no. 151 (2016): 101–127.

Crossley, John N., "Dionisio Capulong and the Elite in Early Spanish Manila (c. 1570–1620)", in *The journal of the Royal Asiatic Society* 28:4 (2018): 697–715.

Cruikshank, Bruce, *Filipiniana in Madrid: Field Notes on Five Major Manuscript Collections*, Honolulu 1984.

Duve, Thomas, "La Escuela de Salamanca: ¿un caso de producción global de conocimiento?: Consideraciones Introductorias Desde Una Perspectiva Históricojurídica y de la historia del conocimiento", in Duve, Thomas (ed.), *The School of Salamanca. A Digital Collection of Sources and a Dictionary of Its Juridical-Political Language*, Working Paper Series No. 2018–02.

Fioravanti, Maurizio, "Estado y Constitución", in Fioravanti, Maurizio (ed.), *El Estado moderno en Europa: instituciones y derecho*, trans. Manuel Martínez, Madrid 2004, 13–44.

Ganshof, François L., *El feudalismo*, trans. Feliu Formosa, Madrid 1979.

Garriga, Carlos, "Sobre el gobierno de la justicia en Indias (siglos XVI–XVII)", in *Revista de Historia Del Derecho* 34 (2006): 67–160.

Garriga, Carlos, "Las Audiencias: justicia y gobierno de las indias" in Barrios Pintado, Feliciano (ed.), *El gobierno de un mundo: virreinatos y audiencias en la América hispánica*, Cuenca 2004, 711–794.

Gaudin, Guillaume, "Estableciendo la autoridad del rey católico en Asia oriental: la erección del obispado de Manila (años 1570–1590)", in *Caravelle*, no. 113 (2019): 125–138.

Gil Pujol, Xavier, "The Good Law of a Vassal: Fidelity, Obedience and Obligation in Habsburg Spain", in Elliott, John H. and Arrieta, Jon (eds.), *Revista internacional de estudios vascos,* serie cuadernos 5 (2009): 83–106.

González Arévalo, Raúl, "Cautiverio y esclavitud en el reino de Granada (siglos XIII–XVI)", in *Vínculos de Historia*, no. 3 (2014): 232–257.

Greenleaf, Richard E., *Zumárraga y la Inquisición mexicana, 1536–1543*, México 1988.

Gruzinski, Serge, *El águila y el dragón: desmesura europea y mundialización en el siglo XVI*, trans. Mario Zamudio, México 2018.

Haskett, Robert S., *Indigenous Rulers: An Ethnohistory of Town Government in Colonial Cuernavaca*, Albuquerque 1991.

Hera, Alberto de la, "El dominio español en indias", in Sánchez Bella, Ismael, Alberto de la Hera and Carlos Díaz Rementería (eds.), *Historia del derecho Indiano*, Madrid 1992, 109–164.

Herzog, Tamar, *Los ministros de la Audiencia de Quito (1650–1750)*, Quito 1995.

Hespanha, António Manuel, "As fronteiras do poder. Os mundos dos rústicos", in *Seqüência*, no. 51 (2005): 47–105.

Hespanha, António Manuel, *As vésperas do leviathan. Instituições e poder político: Portugal- séc. XVII*, Coimbra 1994.

Hess, Andrew C., "The Moriscos: An Ottoman Fifth Column in Sixteenth–Century Spain", in *The American Historical Review* 74:1 (1968): 1–25.

Hidalgo Nuchera, Patricio, *Encomienda, tributo y trabajo en Filipinas, 1570–1608*, Madrid 1995.

Hidalgo Nuchera, Patricio, *La recta administración. Primeros tiempos de la colonización hispana en Filipinas: la Situación de la población nativa*, Madrid 2001.

Hidalgo Nuchera, Patricio, *Los Autos acordados de la Real Audiencia de las Islas Filipinas de 1598 y 1599*, Madrid 2012.

Knauth, Lothar, "Los dos Fernandos: prerrogativas comerciales y afán territorial en los proyectos transpacíficos", in Barrón, Ma. Cristina (ed.), *Urdaneta Novohispano: la Inserción del mundo hispano en Asia*, México 2012, 19–34.

León-Portilla, Miguel, "Lo que supo y no supo Hernán Cortés acerca del océano Pacífico", in Yuste López, Carmen and Guadalupe Pinzón Ríos (eds.), *A 500 años del hallazgo del Pacífico: la presencia novohispana en el Mar del Sur*, México 2016, 53–82.

Majul, Cesar A., *Muslims in the Philippines*, Quezon City 1999.

Mawson, Stephanie, "Philippine Indios in the Service of Empire: Indigenous Soldiers and Contingent Loyalty, 1600–1700", in *Etnohistory* 63:2 (2016): 381–413.
Menegus Bornemann, Margarita, "Alcabala o tributo. Los indios y el fisco (siglos XVI al XIX). Una encrucijada fiscal", in Jáuregui, Luis and Antonio Serrano (eds.) *Las Finanzas Públicas En Los Siglos XVIII–XIX*, México 1988, 110–130.
Menegus Bornemann, Margarita, *Del señorío a la república de indios: el caso de Toluca, 1500–1600*, Madrid 1991.
Mumford, Jeremy R., *Vertical Empire: The General Resettlement of Indians in the Colonial Andes*, Durham 2012.
Muro, Luis, *La expedición Legazpi–Urdaneta a las Filipinas (1557–1564)*, Mexico 1975.
Ollé, Manel, "A inserção das Filipinas na Ásia Oriental (1565–1593)", in *Review of Culture* 7 (2033): 7–22.
Phelan, John L., "Some Ideological Aspects of the Conquest of the Philippines", in *The Americas* 13:3 (1957): 221–239.
Phelan, John L., *The Hispanization of the Philippines: Spanish Aims and Filipino Responses, 1565–1700*, Madison 1959.
Porras Camúñez, José Luis (ed.), *Sínodo de Manila de 1582*, Madrid 1988.
Premo, Bianca and Yanna Yannakakis, "A Court of Sticks and Branches: Indian Jurisdiction in Colonial Mexico and Beyond", in *American Historical Review* 124:1 (2019): 28–55.
Reynolds, Susan, *Fiefs and Vassals: The Medieval Evidence Reinterpreted*, Oxford 1994.
Ruiz Medrano, Ethelia, *Mexico's Indigenous Communities: Their Lands and Histories, 1500–2010*, trans. Russ Davidson, Boulder 2010.
Sánchez-Gómez, Luis A., "Elecciones locales indígenas en Filipinas durante la etapa hispánica", in Rodao, Florentino (ed.), *Estudios sobre Filipinas y las Islas del Pacífico*, Madrid 1989, 53–61.
Sánchez-Gómez, Luis A., "Estructura de los pueblos de indios en Filipinas durante la etapa española", in Rodao, Florentino (ed.), *España y el Pacífico*, Madrid 1989, 81–116.
Santiago, Luciano P. R., "The Houses of Lakandula, Matandá and Solimán (1571–1898): Genealogy and Group Identity", in *Philippine Quarterly of Culture and Society* 18:1 (1990): 39–73.
Sanz y Díaz, José, *Legazpi: conquistador de Filipinas*, 2nd ed., Madrid 1959.
Saunders, Graham E., *A History of Brunei*, New York 1994
Scott, William H., *Barangay: Sixteenth-Century Philippine Culture and Society*, Manila 1994.
Semboloni, Lara, *La construcción de la autoridad virreinal en Nueva España, 1535–1595*, México 2014.
Tau Anzoátegui, Víctor, *El jurista en el Nuevo Mundo: pensamiento. Doctrina. Mentalidad*, Frankfurt am Main 2016.

Vallejo, Jesús, "El cáliz de plata. Articulación de órdenes jurídicos en la jurisprudencia del Ius Commune", in *Revista de historia del derecho*, no. 38 (2009): 1–13.
Villarroel, Fidel, "Philip II and the 'Philippine Referendum' of 1599", in Lario, Dámaso de (ed.), *Re-Shaping the World: Philip II of Spain and His Time*, Manila 2008, 93–133.
Wagner, Andreas, "Francisco de Vitoria", in Domingo, Rafael and Javier Martínez-Torrón (eds.), *Great Christian Jurists in Spanish History*, Cambridge 2018, 84–96.

CHAPTER 4

Catholics and Non-Christians in the Archbishopric of Goa

Provincial Councils, Conversion, and Local Dynamics in the Production of Norms (16th–18th Centuries)

Patricia Souza de Faria

1 Introduction

In 1567, the First Provincial Council of Goa was held in the city that became the seat of the homonymous Archbishopric and capital of the Portuguese conquests located in Asia. Within the scope of the Portuguese overseas empire, the Provincial Councils of Goa stand out for the relative regularity with which they were held, totaling five councils celebrated between 1567 and 1606, and for their role in the production of ecclesiastical legislation to be applied in territories and societies as diverse as those under the jurisdiction of the Archbishopric of Goa.

This chapter analyzes how the relationship between Catholics and non-Christians was intended to be governed by the Church and the Portuguese Crown in the Archbishopric of Goa. By analyzing the decrees of the Provincial Councils of Goa as well as some specific regulations utilized in the *Estado da Índia*, the actions aimed at promoting the conversion of local populations and eradicating non-Christian beliefs can be examined. Simultaneously, it is necessary to consider the multiple concrete circumstances in which Catholics and non-Christians coexisted and interacted in the territories of the *Estado da Índia.*

The first section discusses the nature of the Portuguese presence in the Indian Ocean and its establishments, demonstrating that the ecclesiastical organization of the *Estado da Índia* was built amid a diversity of establishments and communities under the influence—directly or indirectly—of the Portuguese Crown. The second section summarizes the historical contexts and main products of the five Provincial Councils of Goa. Additionally, the essence of the decrees contained in the Second Action of the minutes from these councils are analyzed, with attention to the regulations aimed at dealing with non-Christian social groups and the idealized means for promoting conversions to Catholicism in the Archbishopric of Goa. The determinations contained in the minutes of the councils concerned with favoring the conversion of those the Portuguese Crown called "Gentile vassals" who lived in the Portuguese Asian empire are also considered.

The last section analyzes the complex and dynamic process of the production of norms in the Archbishopric of Goa by emphasizing how the decrees of the Provincial Councils of Goa, and other laws of the *Estado da Índia*, dealt with the issue of guardianship of orphans of Gentile parents, one of the means adopted to stimulate the conversion of native populations. The conversion policy of orphans is examined considering aspects from the context in which the first norms on the matter were formulated, in the 16th century, to the debates that took place in the context of the transformations of the *Estado da Índia*, between the decades of 1670 and 1720.

Accordingly, this chapter presents an overview of the establishment of the Archbishopric of Goa and the Provincial Councils before focusing on the analysis of the minutes from these councils—and other laws of the *Estado da Índia*—looking at how they dealt with a very controversial topic within the scope of the religious policy adopted in the Archbishopric of Goa: the withdrawal of orphaned children of Gentile parents from the kin group to be given to Christian tutors. It was believed that this practice would have a significant potential to multiply conversions, not only because orphaned boys and girls would be instructed in the Christian faith, but also because family members would be encouraged—coerced—to convert to Catholicism so that the children were not taken from them. This chapter also situates the roles of two local agents whose functions were inextricably linked to the converted native populations and the orphans of non-Christian parents: the *Pai dos Cristãos* (Father of Christians) and the *Conservador e Juiz dos Cristãos da Terra* (Judge of the Christians of the Land).

Within the broad possibilities related to the conversion policy, this study focuses on the issue of orphaned children of Gentile parents, not only because it allows a glimpse of a very conflicting facet of the relationship between Christians and non-Christians; the controversies surrounding the laws aimed at the conversion of these children and their relatives also allow for the analysis of rulemaking in the *Estado da Índia*, considering the role of different local agents (judges, the *Pai dos Cristãos*, viceroys, Gentile families) in the construction of norms. As mentioned, the minutes of the Provincial Councils of Goa, as well as royal letters, orders from viceroys of the *Estado da Índia*, opinions from theologians, and petitions of the native population that were transmitted to the authorities of the *Estado da Índia* or to the King of Portugal are consulted and cross-checked as documentary sources.

2 Norms for a Multifaceted Empire

Before a closer analysis of conversion policies and the decrees of the Provincial Councils of Goa, it is necessary to consider the nature of the Portuguese presence in the Indian Ocean and its establishments. Essentially, the *Estado da Índia* was a network (a communication system across various spaces), marked by the heterogeneity of institutions and the imprecision of its territorial and legal limits, that supported agreements, conquests, and Portuguese sovereignty in the East Africa and Asia.[1] The formal empire was characterized by areas directly controlled by the Portuguese Crown, such as the region of Goa, or forts and cities under the jurisdiction of the viceroy of the *Estado da Índia*. With regard to the informal empire, there were communities of Portuguese people with autonomous status who adopted Portuguese civil institutions; Portuguese people who acquired land, villages, and jurisdiction over populations in regions outside the formal borders of the empire; and Portuguese mercenaries who acted according to individual interests or those of the African or Asian armies they served.[2]

Pontifical documents gave shape to the rights of patronage in the Portuguese overseas territories so that the King of Portugal, as administrator of the Order of Christ, became the main agent responsible for evangelization in his conquests, for the creation and maintenance of the local churches,[3] and for exercising the prerogative to propose the creation of dioceses and the appointment of bishops, subject to the Pope's confirmation.[4] In 1534, the Bishopric of Goa was created, which came to have spiritual jurisdiction over territories from the East African coast to the Far East. According to the author Catarina Madeira-Santos, the introduction of diocesan jurisdiction corresponded to the duplication of Goa's centrality with it becoming both a political and ecclesiastical center of the *Estado da Índia*.[5] In 1557, the Bishopric of Goa was elevated to the status of Archbishopric, while the ancient geographical domains under its administration were dismembered to form the suffragan dioceses of Cochin and Malacca. In 1575, the diocese of Macau was created, covering the

---

1 Thomaz, *De Ceuta a Timor*, 207–210.

2 Newitt, "Formal and Informal Empire in the History of Portuguese Expansion".

3 The *Padroado* corresponded to privileges associated with certain obligations that the Church granted to the founders of churches, chapels, or benefits, such as, the presentation of candidates for an ecclesiastical office and the administration of tithes. Gonçalves, "Padroado"; Xavier and Olival, "O Padroado da Coroa de Portugal: Fundamentos e Práticas".

4 Sá, "Estruturas Eclesiásticas e Acção Religiosa", 267.

5 Madeira-Santos, *Goa é a Chave de Toda a Índia. Perfil Político da Capital do Estado da Índia (1505–1570)*, 201.

Christianity of China and Japan, and this was dismembered in 1588 with the creation of the diocese of Funai (Japan). In short, the Archbishopric of Goa had jurisdiction over the Bishoprics of Cochin, Meliapor, Malacca, Macau, and Funai, as well as the Territorial Prelature of Mozambique (created in 1612) and the Bishoprics of Nanjing and Beijing (created in 1690).[6]

The territorial circumscription of the dioceses varied over time. The Archbishop of Goa had ordinary jurisdiction over the Portuguese possessions of Goa, Daman, and Diu, regions where the Portuguese *Padroado* established parishes; missions founded in Konkan and Karnataka, south and east of Goa; and churches built under the *Padroado*, north of Goa, and in Vasai and Bombay. The diocese of Cochin administered ecclesiastical affairs in southern India and Ceylon until it was dismembered in 1606, giving rise to the diocese of Saint Thomas of Mylapore. The diocese of Angamale was created in 1600 but transferred to Cranganor five years later, in addition to incorporating almost all the Saint Thomas Christians (Syrian-Malabar rite) who were forced to adopt the Roman Catholic rite.[7]

When analyzing the rules adopted in this multifaceted Portuguese Asian empire, one finds "a chaotic compound of legal regimes, combining the diversity of a very metropolitan law with a wide array of particular legal orders, local usages and judicial styles".[8] Following the considerations of António Manuel Hespanha, Madeira-Santos states that the legal and jurisdictional pluralism of Portuguese origin became expandable to the empire's spaces, with its potential for adaptation.[9] This flexibility became advantageous in the management of the empire, which combined a multiplicity of kingdoms, protectorates, neighboring kings (allies or enemies), and populations less integrated in the empire's borders, which could be managed pragmatically based on the human and economic resources available.[10] It should be added that evangelization in

---

6 Coutinho, *Le Régime Paroissial des Diocèses de Rite Latin de l'Inde des Origines (XVIe Siècle) à nos Jours*; Sá, "Estruturas Eclesiásticas e Acção Religiosa".

7 The Diocese of Angamale-Cranganor resulted from the incorporation of communities of native Christians from the Malabar Coast. From the papal brief *In supremo militantis ecclesiae* (1600), the diocese came to belong to the Portuguese *Padroado* (from 1600), but the imposition of the Latin rite encountered difficulties since the majority of the Christians of that community lived outside the Portuguese domains. Bethencourt, "A Igreja", 376.

8 Hespanha, "Uncommon Laws. Law in the Extreme Peripheries of an Early Modern Empire", 86.

9 Madeira-Santos, "O Império Português Face às Instituições Indígenas (Estado da Índia, Brasil e Angola, Séculos XVII–XVIII)", 276.

10 Hespanha, "Uncommon Laws. Law in the Extreme Peripheries of an Early Modern Empire", 201.

the context of missions meant that Christian populations located beyond the borders of Goa and the *Estado da Índia*, because they were subjected to the canonical jurisdiction of Portuguese bishops, indirectly became subjects of the King of Portugal to some extent.[11]

The decrees of the Provincial Councils of Goa have provisions considering the different statutes of the territories, the different degrees of vassalage, and the different confessional ties. In the first place, a good part of the decrees clearly focuses on the conquests and peoples that were subjected to the political-military control of the Portuguese Crown. However, it is necessary to consider that within these settlements there were distinct human groups under which specific norms, restrictions, or privileges fell: Catholics of European origin; Saint Thomas Christians or other Christians who did not follow the Latin rite; natives converted to Catholicism; and non-Christians (Jews, Muslims, Gentiles).

Finally, it is worth noting that a local institution was created in the 1530s to deal with conversion issues. The *Pai dos Cristãos* was a lay position, however, it came to be occupied by members of religious orders in the main conquests and fortresses administered by the Portuguese Crown in the *Estado da Índia*. The main duties of the position involved preventing the practice of "idolatry", granting favors and privileges to those who converted, teaching Christian doctrine, guaranteeing the baptism of catechumens, and supporting converts. The *Pai dos Cristãos* had to visit the villages to learn about the orphans and catechumens—orphans who were children of "infidels" would be collected at the *Colégio de São Paulo*.[12]

According to Joseph Wicki, the institution of the *Pai dos Cristãos* existed exclusively in the Portuguese missions in the East. In a way, it can be considered a singular office associated with the Portuguese presence in Asia. However, there are some similarities in relation to other offices established in the spaces of Iberian colonization as local ways of dealing with indigenous populations, such as the case of the *Procurador de Índios* in Brazil[13] or the *protector de indios* in Hispanic America.[14] The *Procurador de Índios* in Brazil acted as an assistant and lawyer for the indigenous people, however, he had no jurisdic-

11 Xavier and Olival, "O Padroado da Coroa de Portugal: Fundamentos e Práticas", 146–147.

12 Wicki, *O Livro do Pai dos Cristãos*, 14–17.

13 Ferreira, "Nas Malhas da Liberdade: O Tribunal da Junta das Missões e o Governo dos Índios na Capitania do Maranhão (1720–1757)", 90; Mello, "Sobre as Apelações de Liberdade dos Índios na Amazônia Portuguesa no Século XVIII".

14 Cardim, "Os Povos Indígenas, a Dominação Colonial e as Instâncias da Justiça na América Portuguesa e Espanhola".

tional function, forwarding cases to the governor and Crown judge.[15] In India, the Governor Francisco Barreto issued a provision that attributed to the *Pai dos Cristãos* of Goa the role of judging the quarrels between Christians, as long as they were minor.[16] In this sense, according to Hespanha, the *Pai dos Cristãos* acquired the role of "private judge of the Christianized indigenous people".[17]

Ângela Barreto Xavier considers that, in a second conjuncture in 1581, an attempt was made to reduce the religious action established in the villages of Goa so that the position of *Conservador e Juiz dos Cristãos da Terra*, responsible for judging cases involving native Christians, was created.[18] The provision determined that the viceroy should appoint a literate judge to hold this position.[19] Although it is possible to locate provisions that continued to grant such assignments to the *Pai dos Cristãos*, in the 1680s, permits reiterated the role of viceroys in appointing judges to serve as *Conservador e Juiz dos Cristãos da Terra*,[20] whose Rules of Procedure are analyzed at the end of this chapter, in the midst of the controversies surrounding the conversion of orphaned children of Gentile parents.

3 Ordering the Province: The Provincial Councils of Goa

This section situates the context in which the norms related to the conversion policy in the Archbishopric of Goa were formulated. Some scholars affirm that, in the initial decades that followed the conquest of Goa (in 1510), a religious policy prevailed which was characterized by the tolerated coexistence of Catholics and non-Christians.[21] Around the 1540s, there was a turning point in religious politics[22] that coincided with the political-religious reform that had developed during the reign of D. João III.[23] Thus, a second phase, roughly between the decades of 1540 and 1570, was characterized by the broad incen-

15 Mello, "Sobre as Apelações de Liberdade dos Índios na Amazônia Portuguesa no Século XVIII".
16 Xavier, *A Invenção de Goa: Poder Imperial e Conversões Culturais nos Séculos XVI e XVII*, 183.
17 Hespanha, *Cultura Jurídica Europeia – Síntese de Um Milênio.*
18 Xavier, *A Invenção de Goa: Poder Imperial e Conversões Culturais nos Séculos XVI e XVII*, 101 and 184.
19 Wicki, *O Livro do Pai dos Cristãos*, 71–74.
20 Wicki, *O Livro do Pai dos Cristãos*, 292–294 and 300.
21 Mendonça, *Conversions and Citizenry: Goa under Portugal. 1510–1610*, 250–255.
22 Tavares, *Jesuítas e Inquisidores em Goa.*
23 Xavier, *A Invenção de Goa: Poder Imperial e Conversões Culturais nos Séculos XVI e XVII.*

tive to proselytize, in which context the Jesuits arrived in India (in 1542) and the Court of the Holy Office of Goa was created (in 1560).

During the reign of D. João III, the regency of D. Catarina, and the reign of D. Sebastião, anti-Hindu laws and decrees were produced, leading to the establishment of decrees in favor of Christianity, including laws that prevented non-Christians from occupying offices in the *Estado da Índia*, in addition to granting other privileges exclusively to converts. Laws passed during the government of D. Pedro Mascarenhas (1554–1555) maintained the focus of stimulating conversions and preventing Hindu or Muslim religious ceremonies, as well as determining that orphans of Hindu parents should be removed from the relationship with their relatives and receive a Christian education.[24] Thus, except for Francisco Barreto, between 1550 and 1560, the governors were closely aligned with bishops—and later with archbishops—and with Jesuits concerning the religious policy favorable to conversions.[25]

The laws instituted in the 1540s and 1560s contained some central guidelines that were recorded in the minutes of the First Provincial Council of Goa in 1567 and were taken up again in later Provincial Councils. When the First Council was called, D. Gaspar de Leão was leading the Archbishopric of Goa, but he received the Pontiff's consent in relation to his resignation request, whereby D. Jorge Themudo became his successor in conducting the activities and concluding the minutes of the council. The First Council was celebrated when D. Antão de Noronha (1564–1568) was governor of the *Estado da Índia*, during which he received several royal letters determining that he would prioritize conversions in India. One of the actions in favor of the conversions adopted in his government was the approval of the law that determined the surrender of orphans of Gentile parents to the Jesuits.[26] The minutes of the First Council were sent to the governor so that they were examined and gave rise to the letter passed in legal form by him[27] approving almost all of the decrees, demonstrating the complex overlap between political and ecclesiastical powers in the construction of norms in the *Estado da Índia*.

After the First Provincial Council of Goa in 1567, four other councils were held. One of the determinations of the Council of Trent was the periodic

24 Araújo, "O 'Pay Dos Christãos'. Contribuição para o Estudo da Evangelização da Índia", 306; Mendonça, *Conversions and Citizenry: Goa under Portugal. 1510–1610*, 258–259.

25 Vila-Santa, "O Vice-Reinado de D. Antão de Noronha no Contexto da Crise do Estado da Índia de 1565–1575".

26 Vila-Santa, "O Vice-Reinado de D. Antão de Noronha no Contexto da Crise do Estado da Índia de 1565–1575", 91.

27 Rego, *Documentação para a história das Missões do Padroado Português do Oriente*, vol. 10, 334–335 (hereafter: "DHMPPO"). Vila-santa, "O Vice-Reinado de D. Antão de Noronha no contexto da crise do Estado da Índia de 1565–1575".

holding of synods and provincial councils. Indeed, Session XXIV of the Council of Trent reestablished the holding of provincial councils in the places where they had been abolished, with triennial regularity.[28] Prelates were to meet and draft constitutions associated with the sacraments, religious rituals, tasks and responsibilities of the clergy, and administration of patrimony and justice, as well as sins and moral deviations.[29] In Europe, the Kingdoms of Portugal and Spain were among the first to recognize the Tridentine decrees. Meetings were held in 1566 in Portugal, Lisbon, and Braga and the following year in Évora. From the Iberian kingdoms, the decrees of the Council of Trent were disseminated to the respective colonial spaces.[30]

Thus, the Second Provincial Council was celebrated in Goa in 1575 during the government of Antônio Moniz Barreto (1573–1577).[31] As a result of the death of D. Jorge Themudo, Pope Gregory XIII ordered that D. Gaspar would resume the role of Archbishop of Goa, conducting the Second Provincial Council. In the midst of political disputes, D. Gaspar was the one who executed the royal order of deposition of the Viceroy D. António de Noronha in 1573, who was succeeded by Barreto. Barreto supported the role of the archbishop in the Second Provincial Council, but it was D. Gaspar's last attempt to try to apply the conversion policy more austerely, through the close connection between political and religious power.[32] The Third Provincial Council of Goa took place in 1585 under the leadership of Archbishop D. Vicente da Fonseca during the government of Viceroy D. Duarte de Meneses (1584–1588). The Fourth Council was held in 1592, conducted by D. Mateus de Medina and the Fifth was celebrated in 1606, under the leadership of Archbishop D. Aleixo de Meneses.[33]

These three Provincial Councils took place in the context of the Iberian Union (1580–1640), during the third phase of the religious policy adopted in the Archbishopric of Goa, when the reorientation of the *Estado da Índia* was taking place, with emphasis on the growing concern about the territorial expansion that, according to Sanjay Subrahmanyam, predates the Habsburg government itself.[34] This search for the territorial expansion of the *Estado da Índia* encountered obstacles because of the new political order formed in Asia, exemplified by the expansion of the Mughal Empire. Moreover, the Dutch

28 *Sacrosanto, e Ecumênico Concílio de Trento*, sess. 24, cap. 2, 267.

29 Boschi, "Estruturas Eclesiásticas e Inquisição".

30 Silva, "Recepção Do Concílio de Trento em Portugal"; Paiva, "A recepção e aplicação do Concílio de Trento em Portugal".

31 Rivara, *Archivo Portuguez-Oriental*, fasc. 4, 86 (hereafter: "APO").

32 These statements are based on Vila-Santa, "Revisitando o Estado da Índia nos Anos de 1571 a 1577".

33 Wicki, "Die Konzilien der Kirchenprovinz Goa: 1567–1895".

34 Subrahmanyam, *O Império Asiático Português. 1500–1700*.

and English presence in Asia rivaled Portuguese commercial interests in the Indian Ocean. In this context of external and internal challenges, D. Duarte de Meneses complained about the lack of financial resources as a result of the emigration of Hindus from the lands controlled by the Crown partly due to anti-Hindu laws.[35] Thus, laws that encouraged conversion continued to be enacted in the period, but governors and viceroys needed to consider their impact on the *Estado da Índia*'s finances in the context of such military and economic challenges.

The expectation surrounding the regularity of such meetings is evident in the minutes of the Fifth Provincial Council of Goa, which determined that the Sixth would be celebrated in January 1616.[36] If one compares the Church's legislative activity in Portuguese Asia and Portuguese America, the difference is striking; there are no known compilations of ecclesiastical legislation in Brazil in the 16th and 17th centuries.[37] In this manner, the Church's legislative activity in the Archbishopric of Goa is more similar to that adopted in the Spanish overseas domains, due to the recurrence of comparable meetings, such as the Provincial Councils of Lima (1551–1552, 1567–1568, 1582–1583) and Mexico (1555, 1565, 1585), the joint gathering celebrated in Manila (in 1582), and the First Episcopal Synod held in the Philippines, in Cebú, in 1600.[38]

One of the main objectives of the Provincial Councils was to legislate, according to canon law and the reform implemented by the Council of Trent. Broadly speaking, the minutes of the Provincial Councils of Goa can be divided into four parts: The first contains the presentation of the council, its objectives, and the Tridentine Profession of Faith; the second focuses on the conversion of non-Christians and the treatment of converts; the third addresses ecclesiastical matters, the administration of the sacraments, divine worship, and the behavior of the clergy; while the fourth deals with the reform of customs. In this sense, the Provincial Councils dealt with everything considered convenient to the ecclesiastical provincial, such as provision for the vacancies of churches, absolution of irregularities, promotion of preaching of the Gospel, overseeing the moral behavior of laypeople, fostering of episcopal seminars, and protocols for marriages, masses, and other sacraments.[39]

---

35 Mendonça, *Conversions and Citizenry: Goa under Portugal. 1510–1610*, 183 and 267.

36 APO, fasc. 4, 278. The Sixth Provincial Council of Goa only took place in 1894.

37 Boschi, "Os escritos de D. Frei Manuel da Cruz e as Constituições Primeiras do Arcebispado da Bahia", 399–400.

38 Martínez López-Cano, *Concilios Provinciales Mexicanos*. Época Colonial; Porras Camúñez, *Sínodo de Manila de 1582*; Grignani, "La Legislación Eclesiástica de Toribio Alfonso de Mogrovejo, Segundo Arzobispo de Lima: La Regla Consueta y Los Sínodos Diocesanos".

39 Moutin, "Producing Pragmatic Literature in the Third Mexican Provincial Council (1585)", 285–286.

In addition to decrees, the Provincial Councils were responsible for producing other documents "that acquired normative value".[40] During the First Provincial Council of Goa, the Constitutions of the Archbishop of Goa were also examined and were printed in 1568. D. Gaspar, in the Prologue to the Constitutions, asserted that each vicar had acted as he saw fit, which was why efforts to standardize ecclesiastical activities were necessary.[41]

The search for standardization in the way of providing instruction in the Catholic faith, celebrating divine offices, and administering the sacraments[42] among other matters, was one of the objectives of the Provincial Councils, materialized in the form of decrees, Constitutions, and even what Thomas Duve has called "pragmatic literature"—as a legal tool for evangelization, with an emphasis on "their juridical origin" as "canonical documents arranged for a practical use".[43] By way of comparison, the Third Provincial Council of Mexico approved three catechisms, a directory for confessors and penitents, and a ritual for administering the sacraments. The bishops of the Third Mexican Council asked theologians to develop a catechism for Indians, Africans, and Spaniards, not for the lack of catechisms but in order to search for instruction in the matters of the Christian faith in a standardized way.[44]

Similarly, the First Provincial Council of Goa established that bishops would be in charge of compiling a compendium of Christian doctrine.[45] Almost twenty years later, the Third Provincial Council of Goa ordered a compendium of Christian doctrine to be created in Portuguese, translated into the native languages, in addition to a brief Tridentine catechism adjusted to the peoples of Asia and approved by the Council.[46] The Third Council also ordered the production of a summary of the Constitutions and decrees approved in the Provincial Councils of Goa to be handed over to the Bishop of Angamale, in addition to the translation of the Missal and Roman Breviaries, a catechism,

40 Moutin, "Producing Pragmatic Literature in the Third Mexican Provincial Council (1585)".

41 Rego, DHMPPO, Constituições do Arcebispado de Goa, 1568, vol. 10, 484; Xavier, "Gaspar de Leão e a Recepção do Concílio de Trento no Estado da Índia", 145.

42 Rego, DHMPPO, vol. 10, Constituições do Arcebispado de Goa (1568).

43 Duve, "Pragmatic Normative Literature and the Production of Normative Knowledge in the Early Modern Iberian Empires in the 16th–17th Centuries", 20–22; Moutin, "Producing Pragmatic Literature in the Third Mexican Provincial Council (1585)," 292.

44 Moutin, "Producing Pragmatic Literature in the Third Mexican Provincial Council (1585)", 288.

45 Rego, DHMPPO, vol. 10, 366 (1st Council, action 2, dec. 46).

46 APO, fasc. 4, 139 and 188. BNP, cod. 176, fl. 75r. In the list of books composed by the Jesuits in Asia, it appears as: "Cathecismo, ou práticas, da doutrina Christã [...] feitas pera christãos novamente convertidos destas partes da Índia [...] collegidas do Cathecismo Romano, e universal, e de outros, por ordem do 3.º Conçilio Provincial de Goa por hum Padre da Companhia de Jesus em Português".

a sum of cases (for the use of confessors), and a preaching book to guide priests—documents that aimed to fit the Saint Thomas Christians into the rites and doctrines of the Catholic Church.[47]

The Provincial Councils of Goa ordered and approved the documents cited, but one of their main products was the decrees. Of particular interest are those contained in the Second Action, which sought to establish the norms that would regulate the relations between Catholics and non-Christians, as well as define which principle(s) would demarcate the boundary between means considered lawful and unlawful when seeking conversions.

In summary, the decrees contained in the Second Action have four points worth highlighting. The first is the granting of privileges and favors to converts, such as access to positions in the *Estado da Índia*, inheritance, and land, while non-Christians would be subject to restrictions, loss of status, and even expulsion from territories administered by the Portuguese Crown.[48]

The second aspect is that although the focus of the decrees was on the prohibition of the use of force, provisions that had the purpose of carrying out coercions in search of conversions predominate. In this sense, one of the orders was that bishops oblige all "infidels" who lived in their diocese and who were over 15 years old to attend preaching in church on Sundays. If the infidels did not do so they could be deprived of trade with the Christians.[49] Regarding these conciliar decrees, the Viceroy D. Antão de Noronha ordered the production of lists of Gentiles residing in Goa, Vasai, Cochin and Malacca. The purpose of these lists was to define in which parishes the Gentiles had to attend preaching. However, wealthy Hindu merchants who brought income to customs and physicians were excluded from the obligation to listen to the preaching and were not included in these lists.[50]

The third aspect refers to orders for the destruction of images and temples dedicated to local cults.[51] Christians were forbidden to participate in the rites, celebrations, and weddings of the Gentiles.[52] The First Provincial Council ordered the expulsion of all "infidels" who held offices equivalent to those of priests or masters of the local religious systems from the territories adminis-

47 APO, fasc. 4, 149.

48 Mendonça, *Conversions and Citizenry: Goa under Portugal. 1510–1610*; Xavier, *A Invenção de Goa: Poder Imperial e Conversões Culturais nos Séculos XVI e XVII*; Faria, "Os Concílios Provinciais de Goa: Reflexões sobre o Impacto da 'Reforma Tridentina' no centro do Império Asiático Português (1567–1606)".

49 Rego, DHMPPO, vol. 10, 344.

50 Rego, DHMPPO, vol. 10, 406.

51 Rego, DHMPPO, vol. 10, 346–347 (1st Council, action 2, dec. 9).

52 Rego, DHMPPO, vol. 10, 346–348 (1st Council, action 2, dec. 9 and 10).

tered by the Portuguese Crown.[53] Lastly, the fourth aspect was to try to avoid the cohabitation of Christians with non-Christians, with the hope of avoiding the "contamination" of Christian faith and habits.

According to Luís Filipe Thomaz, the anti-Hindu legislation adopted in Goa could never be put into practice in the places located in the territory of allied Gentile kings in which Portugal did not exercise sovereignty. Similarly, the Portuguese ecclesiastical and civil authorities were unable to implement this legislation in Diu, an important commercial center, where it was essential to maintain forms of coexistence with the merchants operating in the region by guaranteeing them freedom of worship.[54]

It is important to highlight that the general principle present in the minutes of the Provincial Councils of Goa was a prohibition on the use of force in search of conversion, so that the Gentiles could only be led to adhere to the Catholic faith voluntarily. This prohibition is found in the minutes of the First Council,[55] was repeated at subsequent ones, and is present in the Archbishop of Goa's constitutions.[56]

Ecclesiastics and other participants in the discussions held during the Provincial Councils of Goa faced this fundamental issue, essential in the organization of relations between Catholics and non-Christians, widely addressed by theologians and jurists since medieval times. In the 16th century, theologians discussed this in the legal-theological debates that took place in the Iberian Peninsula. Francisco de Vitoria, for example, postulated about circumstances where there were infidels subjected to Christian princes or those who lived in Christian countries. In such circumstances, should infidels be compelled to receive the Christian faith? In short, Vitoria followed the conclusions of Saint Thomas Aquinas on the prohibition of compelling infidels to accept the Christian faith and baptize children (under the age of reason) against the will of unfaithful parents because, according to natural law, children are governed by parents.[57]

Decrees of the Provincial Councils of Goa that defined the legal means to obtain the conversions would address the aforementioned traditional issues[58] but what stands out in the decrees is how practices adopted by missionaries

53 Rego, DHMPPO, vol. 10, 345–348 (1st Council, action 2, dec. 6 and 9).
54 Thomaz, "Amchi Bhas: O paradoxo linguístico de Goa".
55 Rego, DHMPPO, X, 341 (1st Council, action 2, dec. 1).
56 Rego, DHMPPO, X, 499.
57 Hernández, *Derechos Humanos en Francisco de Vitoria: Antología*, 179–185; Aquino, *Suma Teologica*, ed. Ferreira, IIª–IIª, q. 10, a. 8 and 12 and IIIª, q.68, a. 10.
58 Rego, DHMPPO, vol. 10, 343 (1st Council, action 2, dec. 3); APO, fasc. 4, 93 (2nd Council, action 2, dec. 5).

locally, as they caused scandals and raised great doubts about the nature of conversions, were then banned.[59] In this sense, the First Council ordered that none of the highest caste could eat or drink with those of the lowest and that, if they did, they would soon lose their caste "and remain in the rank and honor of the lowest with which they ate".[60] This decree determined that "no one should feed these Gentiles against their will, if they do not want to become Christians".[61] Missionary actions that led to the loss of caste were classified as illicit means of conversion. Regarding the removal of orphaned children of Gentile parents, debates tended to focus on whether it was lawful to baptize children (before the age of reason) without parental consent (a traditional question mentioned above), as well as the definition of an orphan, meaning that this type of conversion was not considered violent and illicit in itself.

4 The Conversion of Orphaned Children of Gentiles: Laws, Customs, and Local Agency

To analyze in more detail the complex process of production of norms in the *Estado da Índia*, the following section places an emphasis on how the decrees of the Provincial Councils of Goa and some laws dealt with the issue of guardianship of orphans of Gentile parents. In the first place, children were not considered to be legal entities as they were under the power of the *pater familias*, in that the power was an attribute of the father and, if he could not exercise it, he would preferably be replaced by another man. Portuguese law defined that the position of orphan judge should be instituted in all locations that had more than 400 residents and that this judge should appoint a guardian to look after the orphans' assets.[62] In Goa, boys (up to 14 years old) and girls (up to 12 years old) whose father had died would be handed over to tutors to be educated based on Christian principles. Furthermore, this tutelage also had the

59 Tavares, *Jesuítas e Inquisidores em Goa*. Missionaries were denounced for exploiting the food bans of Indian populations, forcing them to eat certain foods that made them "unclean". If they lost their caste, they would be rejected by their group of origin. To survive, they would need to convert to Catholicism seeking any favors that the local Church granted to converts. This type of measure to stimulate baptism could cause "scandals", that is, the idea that conversion to Catholicism would not result from the neophyte's will.

60 Rego, DHMPPO, X, 342 (1st Council, action 2, dec. 1).

61 Rego, DHMPPO, X, 342 (1st Council, action 2, dec. 1).

62 Gandelman, "Entre a Cura das Almas e o Remédio das Vidas: O Recolhimento de Órfãs da Santa Casa da Misericórdia do Rio de Janeiro (ca. 1739–1830)", 151; Coates, *Degreados e Órfãs: Colonização dirigida pela Coroa no Império Português. 1550–1755*, 196 and 256.

consequence of controlling the assets that orphans would inherit.[63] In effect, in 1556, Barreto, the Governor of the *Estado da Índia*, determined that children of Gentile parents would be removed from their families when their father died even when their Hindu mother and relatives were still alive. The orphans would then be handed over to a Christian tutor until they reached the age of reason or 14 years old.[64]

In 1559, the reactions of the non-Christian native population pressured Queen Regent D. Catarina to change the 1556 law, instituting a new decree which determined that only the children of Gentiles in the city and on the islands of Goa who remained without a father or mother and without a grandfather or grandmother, or any other ascendants, and who were under 14 years of age were to be taken by the orphan judge to the *Colégio de São Paulo*, where they would be indoctrinated in the Catholic faith and routed to the learning of a craft.[65] In 1564, the Viceroy D. Antão de Noronha, on behalf of King D. Sebastião, confirmed this decree.[66]

At the First Provincial Council, the authorities present alluded to the aforementioned laws on orphans but asked the King of Portugal to determine that every son of an infidel, after his father's death, at an age that was considered an orphan (according to royal ordinances) be handed over to a Christian tutor or guardian.[67] Thus, the First Council decree sought to reverse the laws of 1559 and 1564, which determined the removal of orphans only if, in addition to the father, they had no other living relatives.[68]

Much of the clergy believed that the coercion linked to the removal of orphans from the mother's care favored her subsequent conversion. The authorities gathered at the Fifth Council asked the viceroy to enforce the laws so that the children, as soon as their Gentile father died, be handed over to a Christian tutor, who could consent to the baptism of orphans who had not reached the age of reason, even against the wishes of the mother or grandparents.[69] In 1646, forty years after the Fifth Council, the Viceroy D. Filipe de Mascarenhas (1644–1651) reiterated decrees of the First and Fifth Provincial Councils, establishing that the consent of the Christian tutor was enough for

---

63 Robinson, *Conversion, Continuity and Change*, 48.

64 Mendonça, *Conversions and Citizenry: Goa under Portugal. 1510–1610*, 205–206.

65 APO, fasc. 5, part. I, 335; Wicki, *O Livro do Pai dos Cristãos*, 98–99.

66 APO, fasc. 5, part. II, 577; Mendonça, *Conversions and Citizenry: Goa under Portugal. 1510–1610*, 207.

67 Rego, DHMPPO, vol. 10, 350 (1st Council, action 2, dec. 13).

68 Rego, DHMPPO, vol. 10, 350 (1st Council, action 2, dec. 13); Mendonça, *Conversions and Citizenry: Goa under Portugal. 1510–1610*, 207.

69 APO, fasc. 4, 208 (5th Council, action 2, dec. 7); Mendonça, 207–208.

the orphan of Gentile parents to be baptized before reaching the age of reason, even if the mother and other ascendants were opposed to the conversion.[70]

After the aforementioned 1646 decree of D. Filipe de Mascarenhas, the norms that regulated the conversion policy of orphans who were children of Gentiles had another significant change in late 1670. In the meantime, between the promulgation of the decree of D. Filipe and the junta which met in 1677 to examine the question of orphans, the *Estado da Índia* and the administration of the Archbishopric of Goa experienced many challenges. In addition to the creation of the Congregation of the Propaganda Fide (in 1622) that brought challenges to the Portuguese *Padroado*, a long period of suspension of relations between the Holy See and the Portuguese Crown began after the Portuguese Restoration (1640). In addition, between 1652 and 1670, the Archbishopric of Goa became a vacant seat.

After the surrender of Bombay to the British (in 1665) and the revision of the peace agreements with the Dutch (in 1669), the conjuncture of the 1670s, during the regency of D. Pedro, marked the beginning of a neutral policy for the Portuguese Crown relative to other European powers in maritime Asia. There was a need for an economic reorientation to compensate for the losses of the *Estado da Índia* and one of the responses was to explore the growing demand for Brazilian tobacco in Goa, Macau, and other parts of Asia. Tobacco became the most relevant item in the Lisbon-Goa trade from the end of the 17th century until the end of the 18th century, so that Hindu merchants dominated this lucrative trade. At the same time, importation of different goods in Asia was being resumed, led mainly by Indo-Portuguese, Christian Goans, Saraswat Brahmins, and Banianes.[71]

The regency of D. Pedro and the action of the viceroys and governors of the period (D. Luís de Mendonça Furtado, D. Pedro de Almeida, Antônio Paes de Sande) took place among the seeking of both administrative changes and a balance capable of maintaining religious proselytism, but without economic damage to the *Estado da Índia*, so that the demands of Gentiles who occupied relevant economic positions could not be neglected. In a letter written in 1671, more than 30 Gentile merchants from Baçaim reported to the Viceroy D. Luís de Mendonça Furtado what they considered to be abuses regarding the compulsory withdrawal of orphans. In 1676, after a new petition from the Gentiles sent to D. Pedro, the regent ordered a board to be convened to examine the topic.[72]

---

70 APO, fasc. 6, 1265.

71 Disney, *A História de Portugal e do Império Português*, vol. 2, 457–467; Antony, *The Goa–Bahia Intra-Colonial Relations*.

72 Ames, "Serving God, Mammon, or Both?: Religious Vis-à-Vis Economic Priorities in the Portuguese Estado Da India, c. 1600–1700".

Regarding laws designed to encourage the conversion of orphans of Gentile parents, three controversial issues can be highlighted that were frequently discussed in the minutes of the Provincial Councils and in the legislation adopted by the *Estado da Índia*. The first was whether it was lawful to baptize orphaned children of Gentile parents before they reached the age of reason. The second was that, although the orphan judge was the official responsible for ensuring the removal of orphans (children of infidels) from their relatives' homes and handing them over to a Christian guardian, other agents ended up becoming involved in this task, such as the *Pai dos Cristãos* and the inquisitors of Goa, despite in principle it not being something under their jurisdiction. Maria Manso has demonstrated the involvement of the *Pai dos Cristãos* in situations of forced withdrawal of young people from such families, which encouraged complaints about this procedure.[73] In 1646, the Viceroy D. Filipe determined that the *Pai dos Cristãos* and other Jesuits, in places where there was an orphan judge, could only take the orphans if they had authorization from the viceroy or the orphan judge and were accompanied by a court official.[74] However, the analysis below demonstrates that the *Pai dos Cristãos* was often accused of failing to comply with such determinations thereby exceeding the limits of his performance established by the laws, which displeased both the authorities of the *Estado da Índia* and the native population.

Regarding the involvement of the inquisitors in the issue of Gentile orphans, it is worth mentioning that the Goa Inquisition classified the habit of hiding orphans from Gentile families as a practice that was under the jurisdiction of the Holy Office and, for this reason, it persecuted "infidels" who hid orphans as they were seen as an obstacle to granting baptism to the orphans.[75] In the 1640s, the archive of the Inquisition of Goa kept the records relating to the *Pai dos Cristãos* (Father Antônio Serqueira) and the orphans of the deceased Malagaro, who took up the right of customs collection on tobacco, as well as a certificate regarding the request of Recu Many, Gentile widow of Beru Chatim, against this measure—both examples of petitions presented by the disaffected Gentile population.[76]

The third issue to highlight in these controversies was the clash over the definition of who was to be considered an orphan. In general, as already discussed, the tendency was to consider anyone whose father had died as an

73 Manso, *A Companhia de Jesus na Índia*, 191.

74 APO, fasc. 6, 1265–1267.

75 Lopes, "Goa: A simbiose luso-Oriental", 109.

76 Wicki, *O Livro do Pai dos Cristãos*, 304–305. ANTT, Tribunal do Santo Ofício, Conselho Geral, mç. 36, no. 7; Faria, "A Inquisição de Goa e a Conversão Compulsória de Órfãos"; Chaturvedula, "Imperial Excess: Corruption and Decadence in Portuguese India", 271.

orphan, even if his mother and grandparents were alive, which provoked several demonstrations of discontent among the non-Christian population. The decrees maintained the same nature of coercion of widows and relatives of Gentile orphans until 1677, coincidentally the same year in which an extremely violent episode occurred that led to the murder of a *Pai dos Cristãos* (a Franciscan) who, under orders from the Goa Inquisition, tried to remove orphans from their non-Christian families.[77] The many complaints, petitions, and violent reactions prompted state officials in India to seek change in the practices and laws adopted.

Indeed, the Viceroy Antônio de Melo de Castro opposed the actions of the Goa inquisitors and interfered in the matter by asking them to release Mangoji Sinai, a tobacco contractor (*rendeiro da Chancelaria e do tabaco de Bardez*) condemned in the *auto-da-fé* celebrated in Goa on March 26, 1662, for having taken three orphans, his grandchildren, to the land of infidels and hiding them from the Portuguese authorities. The viceroy argued that the Inquisition disregarded royal provisions on orphans and interfered with the jurisdiction of the orphan judge. He explained that the kings of Portugal attributed the task, of taking the orphan boys and girls, to the orphan judge, while leaving it to the *Pai dos Cristãos* to learn about the Gentile parents who had died. The viceroy said that the Goa Inquisitor, Paulo Castelino, wanted this jurisdiction himself. However, an orphan was taken in Diu, a region where the Portuguese and ecclesiastical authority did not carry the same weight as they did in Goa, "as in that city there are greater privileges, and this introduction of the inquisitors was something new, it created such astonishment, that the next day three thousand or so residents moved to the land of the Moors".[78]

Glenn Ames has shown that complaints against the position adopted by the inquisitors were sent to the Kingdom of Portugal, due to the indirect financial losses suffered by the *Estado da Índia*, as the removal of orphans, would have been one of the stimuli for native merchants to leave for lands of neighboring kings (Muslims and Hindus) or for the English enclave of Bombay.[79] The pressures exerted by the Gentiles could be carried out in several ways. Sometimes, they were individual petitions to receive exemption so that they did not need to comply with the standard, as was the case with Ramogy Sinay Cottary,

77 Faria, "A Inquisição de Goa e a conversão compulsória de órfãos"; Mendonça, *Conversions and Citizenry: Goa under Portugal. 1510–1610*.

78 Baião, *A Inquisição de Goa: Tentativa de História de Sua Origem, Estabelecimento, Evolução e Extinção*.

79 Ames, "Religious Life in the Colonial Trenches: The Role of the Pai dos Christãos in Seventeenth Century Portuguese India, c. 1640–1683".

a Brahmin who served the Portuguese Crown as interpreter of the *Estado da Índia* and a resident of Bicholim, who stated that he wished to move to Goa. He was "wanting to bring his wife, children and more family to this city, and live in it".[80] Then, he requested permission to live in the lands of the Portuguese Crown and that after his death his descendants would not be taken as if they were orphans, nor would their property be confiscated. In addition, he requested that his children's mother be able to maintain their guardianship and that none of his relatives be harassed because of the orphans.

Jorge Flores explains that Cottary made the aforementioned claim after having watched the confiscation of the assets of the deceased Krishna Sinai, whose son-in-law, Vitoji Sinai, was Cottary's nephew. Additionally, Cottary would also have acted alongside the viceroy to prevent the Gentile Mangoji Sinai from having his sentence of exile to Mozambique executed.[81] These two examples refer to the existence of important local groups of Hindus, whose objective was to "increase the share of the income held by a particular community", protecting the interest of its members. Michael N. Pearson studied the networks formed by such "holders of *rendas*, and their relatives and caste associates", identifying, among such tenants, the role of Mangoji Sinai in the midst of these networks of Hindu relatives and guarantors.[82]

In addition to petitions like those of Cottary, other forms of protest were collective. On March 30, 1677, the Prince Regent reported having learned of a petition by the "Gentile people" against the compulsory withdrawal of orphans from the guardianship of their Gentile relatives.[83] In December of 1677, the Viceroy D. Pedro de Almeida—under the order of the Prince Regent—summoned a board that met in Goa to evaluate the petition of the Gentile people, who wanted the application of legislation on orphans based on the aforementioned law of 1559 which considered children orphans only if they had no father, mother, or other living ascendants. Apart from the Goa Inquisitor Francisco Delgado e Matos, the opinions of those present at the board favored the application of the 1559 law.

Chancellor Manuel Martins Madeira pointed out that according to "civil and national law" (*direito civil e pátrio*) those with no father were considered orphans, even if they had a living mother and grandparent. However, his opinion was favorable to the 1559 law as it was created by the king to be applied to

80 Pissurlencar, *Assentos do Conselho de Estado*, fasc. 4, 33–34.

81 Flores, "Religião, 'Nação', Estatuto: Os Desafios de uma 'Dinastia' de Intérpretes Hindus na Goa Seiscentista", 555

82 Pearson, "Coastal Western India: Studies from the Portuguese Records", 101.

83 ANTT, Tribunal do Santo Ofício, Conselho Geral, liv. 102, fol. 16v.

the Christianity formed by his vassals who lived in the East.[84] Thus, the chancellor defended the primacy of a particular law (that instituted by D. Sebastião for his vassals in the East) over the general (civil law, Ordinances of the Kingdom of Portugal).[85]

One argument used by the Chancellor and the Chief Revenue Superintendent, António Paes de Sande, was based on issues concerning "the political government, and the conservation of this state", so that both highlighted the negative impact of the withdrawal of orphans from Gentile families on the finances of the *Estado da Índia*.[86] However, some arguments presented by civil and ecclesiastical authorities were stated in accordance with the assumptions of "Catholic politics" or "prudent theology" (*Theologia prudente*), as a Jesuit active in Goa called it.[87] Prudent theology considered both "state reasons" (*razões de Estado*) and "supernatural reasons" (*razões sobrenaturais*) in order to achieve the supreme purpose, that is, to stimulate conversion. It was based on political foundations, as it aimed to avoid disturbances in the republic. Thus, political action conformed to justice, defined in a Christian way as the peace of the various interests unified in the common good.[88] In the following statement by Chancellor Madeira, the maintenance of the Gentiles and their business in Portuguese territories was the *sine qua non* condition to create a viable rise in conversions: if the lands managed by the Crown are sustained with rent and goods, the conversion of Gentiles can be hoped, which would be impossible if they left for the lands of Muslim or Hindu kings.

The archbishop of Goa accommodated the temporal and spiritual reasons in a balanced way. He considered that, although civil law and the Ordinances of the Kingdom of Portugal defined orphans as only those who did not have a living father, princes could "lay down particular laws in derogation from general ones", defending the prevalence of the particular over the general, as the Chancellor had done. In addition, he evoked the principles of legal pluralism and localism, which adjusted to imperial contexts, in which sovereigns could adopt different laws, according to the diversity of territories and the nature of their vassals.[89] Soon, the law of 1559 was adjusted to the diversity that existed in the *Estado da Índia*.

---

84 Pissurlencar, *Assentos do Conselho de Estado*, vol. 4, 280–287.

85 See: Hespanha, "Depois do Leviathan", 57; Hespanha, *Cultura Jurídica Europeia – Síntese de um Milênio*.

86 Pissurlencar, *Assentos Do Conselho de Estado*, vol. 4, 280–287.

87 APO, fasc. 6, supp., 25. Father Manuel de Sá, S.J. (1713). "[…] razão política canonizada por santa em toda a Theologia […]".

88 Hansen, "Razão de Estado", 147.

89 "que os príncipes possão estatuir leis particular em derrogação das gerais, não padece dúvida […] além de ser máxima dos Príncipes conquistadores, que dominam várias

A second board met on January 12, 1678, which maintained the precedent opinion that Gentiles who had a mother, grandparents, or other living Gentile ascendants were not to be considered orphans.[90] In the final years of the 17th century and in the first decades of the following one, the pressures of the native population encouraged the adoption of a more favorable definition of "orphan" for the Gentiles. In addition, the documentation demonstrates how the native population constantly denounced the way in which agents (judges, *Pai dos Cristãos*, inquisitors) acted, which was perceived locally as affronts to their customs or abuses by Crown officials who acted without the backing of royal laws. In the latter case, Gentiles were not refusing to obey the royal order, but rather what they considered to be the wrong forms of its application, associated with what they considered to be disrespect and affronts perpetrated by some officials. Concerning the abuses, at the beginning of the 18th century the Gentiles of Goa sent a complaint to the King of Portugal to denounce the *Pai dos Cristãos*, who was removing boys and girls from the bosom of Gentile families, even those who had a father and other living ascendants, that is, without observing the royal legislation itself.[91]

It is also interesting to note that Gentiles began to demand certain procedures from the officials of the *Estado da Índia* when they went to pick up the orphans—procedures that were not provided for in the minutes of the provincial councils or in the royal legislation: "When we took some orphans, the Gentiles used to require we ask them questions to know whether or not they want to be Christians". It was a procedure that the Gentiles wished to impose on the Portuguese authorities, even though the kings of Portugal never ordered them "to ask such orphans such questions".[92] The actions of the *Pai dos Cristãos* sought to put into practice the decrees of the Provincial Councils of Goa, which established the obligation for the Gentile vassals of the Portuguese Crown to hear preaching regularly. Another determination that the *Pai dos Cristãos* sought to implement was the creation of Gentile rosters in order to learn, above all, of the existence of their orphaned children. However, the context in which the *Pai dos Cristãos* was denounced by the Gentiles, the early years of the 18th century, was different from that in which the Provincial Councils of Goa were celebrated, when several determinations were approved to force the Gentile vassals to have contact with Christian doctrine, like the one regarding preaching.

Províncias e estados, [podem] regê–los e governá–los com diferentes leis, conformando–se com a diferença natural dos sogeitos, e vassalos que nelle vivem". Pissurlencar, *Assentos do Conselho de Estado*, vol. 4, 285.

90 Pissurlencar, vol. 4, 299–304.

91 APO, fasc. 6, supp., 4, Lisbon, March 21, 1709.

92 APO, fasc. 6, supp., 6.

To demonstrate their discontent, there were many complaints which the Gentiles sent to the King of Portugal. A controversy that occurred in 1715 centers on one of the practices denounced by the Gentiles; Gentile vassals of the Portuguese Crown reacted to what they considered to be disrespect, abandoning the Portuguese conquests and going to neighboring lands, after the *Pai dos Cristãos* (Father Afonso da Costa) asked the Cathedral Chapter of Goa for authorization for a vicar to enter their homes in order to draw up a list of the names of the orphans. According to the customs of the Gentiles, when lists were made, they had to be made by *mazanes* (or *cabeças*)[93] who were designated for "such lists, as they have often been used without repugnance", because the Gentiles felt affronted if "Christians or Ministers of the Church" entered "their homes, *which has never been practiced,* nor should it be practiced, because it is an affront".[94]

Indeed, the Jesuit Manuel de Sá was consulted on the matter and explained that the custom was that the *mazanes* were the agents responsible for the creation of the rolls with the names of the Gentiles: "When the viceroys ordered these people to be rostered, it was by calling the *mazanes*, or the heads, and they themselves went through the neighborhoods [...] putting all the Gentiles on the list*: this was always the style observed, and it was always done".* However, the procedure adopted by the *Pai dos Cristãos*, not following the traditional way of producing the rolls, caused great discontent: "now what was done [...] was entering [...] the most secret chambers of these men's homes" where "their wives and daughters are, which is a most serious injury". [95]

In addition, according to *"the national customs of these Gentiles"*, it was enough that "someone from another caste see the pot where they cook for them to not use it anymore".[96] The manner in which priests entered their houses to make the rolls caused many troubles for the Gentiles. Father Manuel de Sá considered that "it cannot be argued that this, and other customs that [the Gentiles] observe, are barbaric, because *whether it is barbaric or not, it is their custom*. And if they enter his interior houses, or force him to show his women, he has this for affront and injury, and is reviled among the most as a man without honor".[97] In short, Manuel de Sá stated that the Gentiles did not

---

93 Mazanes (*mahâ jan*, that is, great men) are the notables of the Hindu community. Thomaz, "Amchi Bhas: O paradoxo linguístico de Goa", 179.

94 APO, fasc. 6, supp., doc. 12, 20. January 10, 1716. Emphasis added to highlight the idea of novelty and the introduction of changes that affronted the Gentiles and did not respect their customs.

95 APO, fasc. 6, supp., 45–46. Emphasis added.

96 APO, fasc. 6, supp., 45. Emphasis added.

97 APO, fasc. 6, supp., 45. Emphasis added.

repudiate the law instituted by the King of Portugal, but to the way the *Pai dos Cristãos* tried to enforce it, neglecting the socially accepted customs and offending their honor.

The viceroy requested opinions from the State Council and religious officials on the subject. In addition, he stressed that the law itself that established the mandatory attending of preaching and the inclusion of the names of Gentiles on lists did not apply to all Gentiles.[98] One of the appraisers, Manuel de Sá, also recalled the privileges granted to some of the Gentile vassals of the Crown, such as tenants, high-skilled artisans, and shopkeepers, who were exempt from the aforementioned obligations.[99]

Regarding the incident of 1715, the King of Portugal, through the advisers of the Overseas Council, expressed his support for the decision made by the Viceroy to suspend the procedures that were being adopted by the *Pai dos Cristãos*, in relation to the obligation of the Gentiles to listen to preaching and the creation of the Gentile rosters without respecting local customs.[100] In general, the Viceroy had determined that the Gentiles could return to the Portuguese conquests in a safe manner, without having to attend preaching and that the rolls would be executed at the time he deemed convenient.[101]

The controversies surrounding the laws aimed at the conversion of orphaned children of Gentile parents and their relatives allow for the unravelling of the complex plot concerning the construction of rules and their application in the *Estado da Índia*. If in the normative scope the problem had institutions, agents, and their jurisdictions supposedly well defined, as the decree of the Fifth Provincial Council of Goa emphatically defended,[102] the interpretation of the norm concerning orphans and its application, in turn, have been the subject of intense disputes over the decades and centuries, involving judges of orphans, the *Pai dos Cristãos*, inquisitors, viceroys, vicars, and, of course, family members of the orphans. It can be said that the pressures exerted by the Gentile families (writing of petitions to the King of Portugal, abandonment of Portuguese lands, acts of murder against the agents who took the orphans) led local authorities of the *Estado da Índia* to seek ways to compromise on the rules through recognizing the legitimacy of part of the demands of the Gentiles, including respect for their customs, such as being included in rosters made only by the *mazanes*, which was agreed on at the beginning of the 18th century.

98 APO, fasc. 6, supp., 26. Manuel de Sá was a Jesuit and Patriarch of Ethiopia.

99 APO, fasc. 6, supp., 25–27. Goa, July 3, 1715.

100 APO, fasc. 6, supp., 71–73. Lisbon, January 14, 1717.

101 APO, fasc. 6, supp., 22. Goa, January 10, 1716.

102 APO, fasc. 4, 207 (5th Council, action 2, dec. 7).

5 Final Considerations

This chapter has analyzed the responses that ecclesiastics and other authorities present in the provincial councils sought to give to local challenges in search of the establishment of norms that would regulate the relations between Christians and non-Christians in the Archbishopric of Goa, in parallel with the efforts to promote the conversion of local populations that were quite diverse. The conciliar decrees, therefore, intended to build norms to try to control this multiplicity of presences, belongings, and statutes.

The minutes from these councils also express very clearly that without the support of different justices, agents, and powers it would be impossible to implement the idealized norms to order the relations between Christians and non-Christians in the Archbishopric of Goa. In this sense, the minutes of the Provincial Councils of Goa are replete with requests to the King of Portugal or to the viceroy (or governor) for specific regulations to be drawn up or for efforts to be made to comply with existing laws regarding matters in which the secular and spiritual domains were highly interwoven. The normative production over non-Christian populations was therefore the result of the interaction between different agents and institutions.

Although the political and economic contexts related to the Kingdom of Portugal and the *Estado da Índia* underwent changes between the celebration of the First (1567) and the Fifth Provincial Council of Goa (1606), the conciliar decrees maintained the same tone, sustaining the ambition to promote the systematic conversion of local populations, at least in the central and more controlled spaces of the *Estado da Índia*. At the discursive level, the supposed confluence of political and religious interests is combined in the minutes of the five provincial councils—although the positions of civil and ecclesiastical agents revealed different inclinations in other contexts of normative production, embracing a more austere or moderate policy of proselytism.[103]

In the context of the late 17th century and the early decades of the 18th century, when the *Estado da Índia* itself had already changed its configuration, civil and ecclesiastical authorities emphasized that it was imperative to review actions in search of conversions, being difficult to maintain the evangelical fervor typical of the period in which the first provincial councils took place. The issue of conversions was accompanied by considerations about the nature of political actions that guaranteed the conservation of the *Estado da Índia*. In a memorial written at the end of the 17th century, Manuel Gonçalves Guião—judge of the Court of Appeal of Goa who was appointed *Conservador e Juiz dos*

103 Mendonça, *Conversions and Citizenry: Goa under Portugal. 1510–1610*; Xavier, *A Invenção de Goa: Poder Imperial e Conversões Culturais nos Séculos XVI e XVII*.

Cristãos da Terra[104]—was in favor of prudence and diplomacy, recommending good correspondence with the Gentile and Moorish kings who authorized the presence of Christians in their lands, but who were scandalized when their vassals were oppressed. Despite having held a position at the local institution more radically associated with religious Christianization projects—the Inquisition of Goa—Guião argued that the ministers of the Holy Office needed to be endowed, above all, with "prudence, speech, and politics" (*prudência, discurso, e política*) to achieve the preservation of Christianity in the East, arguing that the loss of a rebellious soul is less important than the loss of all Christianity.[105]

Another conclusion is that the assignments of the *Pai dos Cristãos* were subject to dynamic normative construction throughout the period under investigation, that is, from the 1530s, when the position was created, to the 1720s, when the Rules of Procedure were drawn up for the *Conservador e Juiz dos Cristãos da Terra*. The offices of *Pai dos Cristãos* and *Conservador e Juiz* were instituted locally and dealt with very specific issues related to conversion, including judicial action in cases involving native Christians and the treatment of issues related to orphaned children of Gentile parents.

After the order of D. João V, the Rules of Procedure for the Newly Converted and Gentile Orphans was created (1724), on the basis of which the *Pai dos Cristãos* should only notify the *Conservador e Juiz* of the existence of orphaned children of Gentiles, without being able to remove them from their homes. According to the Rules, the *Conservador e Juiz* would have the same powers as the orphan judge (for example, preparing inventories) and would act as a private judge in civil cases or crimes involving converted natives or Gentile orphans, while the *Pai dos Cristãos* would have his functions reduced to spiritual matters.[106]

In practice, the aforementioned Rules of Procedure and other forms of regulation do not seem to have prevented some *Pais dos Cristãos* from continuing to act in spheres that, according to the regulations, never or no longer belonged to them, causing constant dissatisfaction from authorities and native populations. This was responsible for several denunciations of possible abuses, in the case of the practice of preparing rosters with the names of Gentiles, entering their homes, and cutting off the *sendy* (tail they wore on their heads) so that they would lose their caste and be baptized, that is, an action in search of conversions that had been prohibited since the First Provincial Council of Goa.[107]

---

104 On Manuel Guião, see: Lourenço, "Uma Inquisição Diferente. Para uma leitura institucional do Santo Ofício de Goa e do seu distrito (séculos XVI e XVII)".

105 ANTT, Conselho Geral do Santo Ofício, mç. 36, no. 29, fol. 1r. Guião was appointed *promotor* and, later, inquisitor of the Holy Office of Goa.

106 APO, fasc. 4, supp., 113–118; "Regimento dos novamente convertidos, e órfãos gentios".

107 APO, fasc. 6, 305.

The threats exerted by the Gentiles did not lead to the total repeal of the law that authorized the removal of orphans from the home of their Gentile relatives. This means that the withdrawal of such orphans did not come to be understood by agents of the Portuguese Crown and the Church as an undoubtedly violent action—used to stimulate baptisms—which needed to be prohibited to be in line with provincial councils that prevented the use of force to favor conversions. However, it is important to recognize the role of the native population itself in the construction of norms, more precisely, in the issues that involved the removal of orphans from their kin groups. In this chapter, some Gentiles emerge in petitions involving the controversial orphan conversion policy: Mangoji Sinai, who took up the right of customs collection on tobacco; Malagaro, tax-collector of the Bardez Customs; Many, widow of Beru Chatim;[108] and Cottary, an interpreter and diplomatic agent of the *Estado da Índia*. They were merchants, tax collectors, financiers, that is, people who had an important economic or diplomatic role for the *Estado da Índia*, whose actions demonstrate the capacity of such local groups to explore existing legal spaces and that their demands were considered in the interpretation and decision of cases.

When the minutes of the Provincial Councils of Goa are compared with other documentary sources, one sees how the social pressures exerted locally impacted the reformulation (or rejection) of some norms that tried to order the relationship between Christians and non-Christians. Thus, in the last quarter of the 17th century, the interpretation that brought more contentment to the local non-Christian population was that the Gentile orphan would be liable to be handed over to a Christian guardian if he or she had no living paternal or maternal ascendants, that is, this interpretation prevailed over some of the decrees of the Provincial Councils of Goa which advocated handing over the orphans to a guardian after the death of the Gentile father, even though the boys and girls had other living ascendants. From a diachronic perspective, it can be considered that local pressures played an important role in the way in which the norms concerning orphans were interpreted in Goa. In short, local interests and challenges faced by Portuguese institutions and agents established in Asia, as well as complaints and other forms of contestation of such rules by native populations, led to changes in the interpretation of such laws, resulting in the definition of norms that suggested forms of compromise or efforts toward accommodation of Gentile customs.

---

108 Chatim was a term used to designate merchants or more specifically a type of rich gemstone merchant.

Acknowledgements

I would like to thank Manuel Bastias Saavedra and the two anonymous reviewers for their suggestions. I also thank Genevieve Beech for her work on the English version of this text.

Bibliography

Manuscripts

Arquivo Nacional da Torre do Tombo, Lisbon (ANTT), Tribunal do Santo Ofício, Conselho Geral, mç. 36, nc. 7.

Arquivo Nacional da Torre do Tombo, Lisbon (ANTT), Tribunal do Santo Ofício, Conselho Geral, liv. 102.

Arquivo Nacional da Torre do Tombo, Lisbon (ANTT), Conselho Geral do Santo Ofício, mç. 36, no. 29.

Biblioteca Nacional de Portugal, Lisbon (BNP), Cod. 176.

Printed Sources

Aquino, Tomás de, *Suma Teológica*, ed. Pereira, Joaquim, São Paulo 2001.

Pissurlencar, Panduronga, *Assentos do Conselho de Estado*, Bastorá 1953.

Rego, António da Silva, *Documentação para a História das Missões do Padroado Português do Oriente*, vol. 10, Lisboa 1995.

Rivara, Joaquim Heliodoro Da Cunha, *Archivo Portuguez-Oriental*, Delhi 1992.

Sacrosanto, e Ecumênico Concílio de Trento, em Latim e Portuguez, Lisboa 1781: Na Officina Patriarc. de Francisco Luiz Ameno.

Wicki, Joseph, *O Livro do Pai dos Cristãos*, Lisboa 1969.

Literature

Ames, Glenn, "Serving God, Mammon, or Both?: Religious Vis-à-Vis Economic Priorities in the Portuguese Estado da India, c. 1600–1700", in *The Catholic Historical Review* 86, no. 2 (2001): 193–216.

Ames, Glenn, "Religious Life in the Colonial Trenches, The Role of the Pai dos Christãos in Seventeenth Century Portuguese India, c. 1640–1683", in *Portuguese Studies Review* 16, no. 2 (2008): 1–23.

Antony, Philomena, *The Goa-Bahia Intra-Colonial Relations*, Tellichery 2004.

Araújo, Maria Benedita, "O 'Pay dos Christãos'. Contribuição para o Estudo da Evangelização da Índia", in *Missionação Portuguesa e Encontro de Culturas. Actas do Congresso Internacional de História*, Braga 1993, 305–324.

Baião, António, *A Inquisição de Goa: Tentativa de História de Sua Origem, Estabelecimento, Evolução e Extinção*, Lisboa 1945.

Bethencourt, Francisco, "A Igreja", in Bethencourt, Francisco and Kirti Chaudhuri (eds.), *História da Expansão Portuguesa*, Navarra 1998, 369–386.

Boschi, Caio, "Estruturas Eclesiásticas e Inquisição", in Bethencourt, Francisco and Kirti Chaudhuri (eds.), *História da Expansão Portuguesa*, Navarra 1998, 426–459.

Boschi, Caio, "Os Escritos de D. Frqıei Manuel da Cruz e as Constituições Primeiras do Arcebispado da Bahia", in Feitler, Bruno and Evergton Sales Souza (eds.), *A Igreja no Brasil: Normas e Práticas durante a Vigência das Constituições Primeiras do Arcebispado da Bahia*, São Paulo 2011, 399–424.

Cardim, Pedro, "Os Povos Indígenas, a Dominação Colonial e as Instâncias da Justiça na América Portuguesa e Espanhola", in Domingues, Ângela, Maria Leônia Chaves de Resende and Pedro Cardim (eds.), *Os Indígenas e as Justiças no Mundo Ibero-Americano (Sécs. XVI–XIX)*, Lisboa 2019, 29–84.

Chaturvedula, Nandini, *Imperial Excess: Corruption and Decadence in Portuguese India* (PhD Thesis), Columbia 2010.

Coates, Timothy, *Degreados e Órfãs: Colonização dirigida pela Coroa no Império Português. 1550–1755*, Lisboa 1998.

Coutinho, Fortunato, *Le Régime Paroissial des Diocèses de Rite Latin de l'Inde des origines (XVIe Siècle) à nos jours*, Louvain 1958.

Disney, Anthony, *A História de Portugal e do Império Português*, Lisboa 2011.

Duve, Thomas, "Pragmatic Normative Literature and the Production of Normative Knowledge in the Early Modern Iberian Empires in the 16th–17th Centuries", in Duve, Thomas and Otto Danwerth (eds.), *Knowledge of the Pragmatici: Legal and Moral Theological Literature and the Formation of Early Modern Ibero-America*, Leiden 2020, 1–39.

Faria, Patricia Souza de, "Os Concílios Provinciais de Goa: Reflexões sobre o impacto da 'Reforma Tridentina' no centro do Império Asiático Português (1567–1606)", in *Topoi* 14, no. 27 (2013): 218–238.

Faria, Patricia Souza de, "A Inquisição de Goa e a Conversão Compulsória de Órfãos", in Silva, Marco Antônio Nunes da Silva and Suzana Maria de Sousa Santos Severs (eds.), *Estudos Inquisitoriais: História e Historiografia*, Cruz das Almas (Brazil) 2019.

Ferreira, André Luís Bezerra, *Nas Malhas da Liberdade: O Tribunal da Junta das Missões e o Governo dos Índios na Capitania do Maranhão – 1720–1757* (MA Thesis), Belém 2017.

Flores, Jorge, "Religião, 'Nação', Estatuto: Os desafios de uma 'Dinastia' de intérpretes hindus na Goa Seiscentista", in Monteiro, Rodrigo Bentes, Bruno Feitler, Daniela Calainho, and Jorge Flores (eds.), *Raízes do Privilégio: Mobilidade Social no Mundo Ibérico do Antigo Regime*, Rio de Janeiro 2011, 537–565.

Gandelman, Luciana Mendes, *Entre a Cura das Almas e o Remédio das Vidas: O Recolhimento de Órfãs da Santa Casa da Misericórdia do Rio de Janeiro – ca. 1739–1830* (MA Thesis), Campinas 2001.

Gonçalves, Nuno da Silva, "Padroado", in Azevedo, Carlos Moreira, *Dicionário de História Religiosa de Portugal*, Lisboa 2001, 364–368.

Hansen, João Adolfo, "Razão de Estado", in Novaes, Adauto (ed.), *A Crise da Razão*, São Paulo 1999, 135–156.

Hernández, Ramón, *Derechos Humanos en Francisco de Vitoria: Antología*, San Esteban 1984.

Hespanha, António Manuel, "Depois do Leviathan", in *Almanack Braziliense* 0, no. 5 (2007): 55.

Hespanha, António Manuel, *Cultura Jurídica Europeia – Síntese de um Milênio*, Coimbra 2012.

Hespanha, António Manuel, "Uncommon Laws. Law in the Extreme Peripheries of an Early Modern Empire", *Zeitschrift Der Savigny-Stiftung Fur Rechtsgeschichte, Germanistische Abteilung* 130, no. 1 (2013): 180–204.

Lopes, Maria de Jesus dos Mártires, "Goa: A Simbiose Luso-Oriental", in Serrão, Joel and António Henrique de Oliveira Marques (eds.), *Nova História Da Expansão Portuguesa: O Império Oriental: 1660–1820*, Lisboa 2006.

Lourenço, Miguel Rodrigues, "Uma Inquisição Diferente. Para uma Leitura Institucional do Santo Ofício de Goa e do Seu Distrito (Séculos XVI e XVII)", in Lusitania Sacra 31 (2015): 129–164.

Madeira-Santos, Catarina, *Goa é a Chave de Toda a Índia. Perfil Político da Capital do Estado da Índia (1505–1570)*, Lisboa 1999.

Madeira-Santos, Catarina, "O Império Português Face às Instituições Indígenas (Estado Da Índia, Brasil e Angola, Séculos XVII–XVIII)", in Xavier, Ângela Barreto, Federico Palomo and Roberta Stumpf, *Monarquias Ibéricas em Perspectiva Comparada (Sécs. XVI–XVIII)*, Lisboa 2018, 271–302.

Manso, Maria de Deus Beites, *A Companhia de Jesus na Índia (1542–1622). Actividades Religiosas, Poderes e Contactos Culturais*, Macau 2009.

Martínez López-Cano, María del Pilar (ed.), *Concilios Provinciales Mexicanos. Época Colonial*, Ciudad de México 2014.

Mello, Márcial Eliane Alves de Souza e, "Sobre as Apelações de Liberdade dos Índios na Amazônia Portuguesa No Século XVIII", in *II Jornada Nacional de História do Trabalho,* Florianópolis 2004.

Mendonça, Délio de, *Conversions and Citizenry: Goa under Portugal. 1510–1610*, Delhi 2002.

Moutin, Osvaldo R., "Producing Pragmatic Literature in the Third Mexican Provincial Council (1585)", in Duve, Thomas and Otto Danwerth (eds.), *Knowledge of the Pragmatici: Legal and Moral Theological Literature and the Formation of Early Modern Ibero-America*, Leiden 2020, 282–295

Newitt, Malyn, "Formal and Informal Empire in the History of Portuguese Expansion", in *Portugueses Studies* 17 (2001): 1–21.

Paiva, José Pedro, "A Recepção e Aplicação do Concílio de Trento em Portugal", in Paiva, José Pedro, Savid Sampaio Barbosa and António Camões Gouveia (eds.), *O Concílio de Trento Em Portugal e Nas Suas Conquistas: Olhares Novos*, Lisboa 2014, 13–40.

Pearson, Michael N., *Coastal Western India: Studies from the Portuguese Records*, Delhi 1981.

Pissurlencar, Panduronga, *Assentos do Conselho de Estado*, Bastorá 1953.

Porras Camúñez, José Luis, *Sínodo de Manila de 1582*, Madrid 1988.

Robinson, Rowena, *Conversion, Continuity and Change*, Delhi 1998.

Sá, Isabel dos Guimarães, "Estruturas Eclesiásticas e Acção Religiosa", In Bethencourt, Francisco and Diogo Ramada Curto (eds.), *A Expansão Marítima Portuguesa, 1400–1800*, Lisboa 2007, 265–292.

Silva, Amélia Maria Polónia da, "Recepção do Concílio de Trento em Portugal: As Normas Enviadas pelo Cardeal D. Henrique aos Bispos do Reino, em 1553", in *Revista da Faculdade de Letras – História* 7 (1990): 133–144.

Subrahmanyam, Sanjay, *O Império Asiático Português. 1500–1700*, Lisboa 1995.

Tavares, Célia Cristina da Silva, *Jesuítas e Inquisidores em Goa*, Lisboa 2004.

Thomaz, Luiz Filipe, *De Ceuta a Timor*, Lisboa 2004.

Thomaz, Luís Filipe, "Amchi Bhas: O Paradoxo Linguístico de Goa", in *Povos e Culturas* 20 (2017): 145–214.

Vila-Santa, Nuno, "O Vice-Reinado de D. Antão de Noronha no Contexto da Crise do Estado da Índia de 1565–1575", in *Anais de Historia de Além-Mar*, no. 10 (2010): 7–48.

Vila-Santa, Nuno. "Revisitando o Estado da Índia nos anos de 1571 a 1577", in *Revista de Cultura* 36 (2010): 88–112.

Vila-Santa, Nuno, "Resistência e Contemporização: Tensões Políticas na Implementação da Contra-Reforma no Estado da Índia (1557–1580)", in Avelar, Ana Paulo, Margarida Lalanda, and Paulo Lopes (eds.), *Martinho Lutero e Portugal: Diálogos, Tensões e Impactos*, Lisboa 2019, 153–172.

Wicki, Joseph, "Die Konzilien Der Kirchenprovinz Goa : 1567–1895", in *Annuarium Historiae Conciliorum* 12 (1983): 155–270.

Wicki, Joseph, *O Livro do Pai dos Cristãos*, Lisboa 1969.

Xavier, Ângela Barreto, "Gaspar de Leão e a Recepção do Concílio de Trento no Estado da Índia", in Paiva, José Pedro, David Sampaio Barbosa, and António Camões Gouveia (eds.), *O Concílio de Trento em Portugal e nas Suas Conquistas: Olhares Novos*, Lisboa 2014, 133–159.

Xavier, Ângela Barreto, *A Invenção de Goa: Poder Imperial e Conversões Culturais nos Séculos XVI e XVII*, Lisboa 2008.

Xavier, Ângela Barreto and Fernanda Olival, "O Padroado Da Coroa de Portugal: Fundamentos e Práticas", in Xavier, Ângela Barreto, Federico Palomo and Roberta Stumpf, *Monarquias Ibéricas em Perspectiva Comparada (Sécs. XVI–XVIII)*, Lisboa 2018, 123–160.

CHAPTER 5

"Que los indios no puedan vender sus hijas para contraer matrimonio": Understanding and Regulating Bridewealth and Brideservice in the Spanish Colonial Period of the Philippines

Marya Svetlana T. Camacho

1 Introduction

In his seminal work on the process of hispanization in the first century and a half of Spanish rule in the Philippines, John Leddy Phelan concluded that the Spaniards had succeeded in Christianizing matrimony; however, he acknowledged that socioeconomic aspects of prehispanic marriage persisted in the first century of Spanish colonization, particularly those of brideprice and bride-gift. According to Phelan, these practices "smacked of fathers selling their daughters, perhaps against the latter's will, to the highest bidder".[1] While Phelan differentiated between dowry and brideprice as Philippine indigenous practices, an examination of Spanish sources, ethnographic and otherwise, shows that what the Spaniards called 'dowry' (*dote*) corresponds to brideprice; that is, these two marriage prestations were actually the same. The application of European nomenclature obscured the meaning of the original indigenous referent (*bugay* in Bisaya and *bigay-kaya* in Tagalog, two Philippine languages), and so, like early modern Spanish authors in the field, Phelan appears to have confused these terms.

This chapter problematizes the conceptual translation of indigenous marriage prestations. It explores the perspectives of moral theologians and clergymen, and traces the normative means, both ecclesiastical and secular, and their juridical and moral underpinnings, to make native customs conform to Catholic matrimonial law and values. Likewise, it examines normative literature and judicial sources to discern the indigenous response to these efforts at transformation in the late 17th to 18th century. In sum, it traces the ways in which the institutions of *bugay/bigay-kaya* were practised, interpreted, contested, and integrated into the colonial matrimonial order.

1 Phelan, *The Hispanization of the Philippines*, 64–65.

Alain Testart's historical study on the shift from bridewealth to dowry among Indo-Europeans provides a theoretical lead. Having established the antiquity of bridewealth practiced alone or in combination with dowry, he attributes the wide-ranging change to ideologies, which includes religions and colonization. He states that Christianity "seems to have always considered bridewealth an anti-Christian institution".[2] The issues surrounding marriage endowments in the colonial Philippines appeared in the context of the introduction of Tridentine canonical marriage.

Ultimately, the question arises as to how closely the level of efficacy of the legal mandate to do away with bridewealth and brideservice was tied to the level of enforcement of the various laws and directives on the ground, taking into consideration the goals of the *cura animarum* (the care of souls) and experiential knowledge of indigenous culture and norms concerning marriage. At the end of the 18th century, Spanish colonial authorities continued to decry bridewealth and brideservice, indicating that these persisted, counter to the general tenor of secular and ecclesiastical prescriptions. This chapter deals with these questions. From a mainly anthropological perspective, the chapter begins with a short discussion of the meaning and functions of bridewealth and brideservice (alternate terms for brideprice and bride-gift) in different contemporary and historical societies in the world, and provides background to the ethnographic descriptions of Philippine indigenous marriage prestations in Spanish sources from the early modern period. This is followed by a summary of Castilian law regarding arrhae and dowry as the historical legal context for the interpretation of these institutions. The rest of the chapter consists of a historical outline of how bridewealth and brideservice were dealt with in legal texts and pragmatic normative literature in the Philippines, which naturally drew from the European and Catholic tradition. Although too few exist on which to base conclusive observations about judicial treatment of marriage prestations in the period covered, some 18th-century ecclesiastical court cases from Manila furnish specific details and afford an idea as to the extent in which they were regulated and subjected to either civil or ecclesiastical jurisdiction in various parts of the island of Luzon.

2 Meanings of Bridewealth and Brideprice

Before proceeding to the historiography of *bugay* and *bigay-kaya* in the earlier centuries of Spanish colonization, this section examines the nature of

2 Testart, "Reconstructing Social and Cultural Evolution", 41.

this marital institution drawing from contemporary scholarship that has used interdisciplinary methodology, thereby discerning meanings that transcend the understanding of European authors from the early modern period. The abundant literature on brideprice, bridewealth, brideservice, bride-gift, and dowry provides a comparative base that is geographically broad and longitudinal in some cases, albeit covering mainly Indo-European and African societies and generally excluding Austronesian cultures to which Philippine peoples belong.[3] Since these studies use a combination of anthropological, economic, and historical lenses, they are able to penetrate the intricate meanings as well as the multiplicity of factors affecting the prevalence of some forms of marriage prestations within a given society, as well as changes in them over time. Economic anthropology, in particular, has sought to explain the trends and prevalent forms of marriage transactions.[4] In addition, the literature allows conceptual comparisons that enrich the interpretation of comparable Philippine practices.

At the outset, the two related problems experienced chiefly in the colonial encounter, which Stanley J. Tambiah has identified, are taken into account. The first pertains to translation, i.e., assigning an English word to a local custom or institution that the writer or observer thinks he has sufficiently comprehended. The second is the unquestioned application of an anthropological category to the phenomenon, which turns out to be inadequate.[5] Thus, in this paper, the term 'brideprice' as well as 'dowry' are retained when used by the European colonial writers cited, to remain consistent with how they construed the referred marriage transaction.

In all other cases, 'bridewealth' will be used following the same reasoning as Edward E. Evans-Pritchard who maintained his preference for it over other terms denoting marital endowments in non-European societies and for which no English expressions correspond exactly.[6] This term is also in accordance with the practice prevalent in Philippine elite marriages as described below. Evans-Pritchard demonstrated that it better captured the range of socioeconomic functions and the significance of the institution without ignoring its economic value, while other terms focused only on one aspect. He therefore proposed it as an alternative to brideprice to de-emphasize the notion

3 Goody and Tambiah, *Bridewealth and Dowry*; Tambiah, "*Bridewealth and Dowry* Revisited"; Botticini, "Why Dowries?"; Testart, "Reconstructing Social and Cultural Evolution".

4 Bossen, "Toward a Theory of Marriage"; Botticini "Why Dowries?"; Anderson, "The Economics of Dowry and Brideprice".

5 Tambiah, "*Bridewealth and Dowry* Revisited", 414.

6 Evans-Pritchard, "An alternative term for 'bride-price'".

of purchase while maintaining continuity with that long-established term by emphasizing the role of the woman, instead of opting for a more general term like 'marriage-wealth'.[7]

Since Evans-Pritchard, anthropologists have made further conceptual distinctions. Beyond the civilizational and moral connotations of brideprice that earlier debates dealt with, bridewealth and brideprice have been differentiated in socioeconomic terms. Both are understood as a transaction between the groom's and bride's kin, in the direction of groom to bride.[8] The dynamic of kinship involvement and interest in the transmission of resources elucidates the Philippine practice of bridewealth historically considered below. In relation to bridewealth, Jack Goody created the notion of 'indirect dowry', by which gifts from the groom are received by the bride's father who eventually gives them to his daughter. Further research on pre-colonial Philippine bridewealth might find this a useful category as there is evidence that the bride possessed personal property inherited from parents.

Similarly grappling with the problem of translation of European terms, Bernard Vroklage tested whether brideprice and dower were synonymous concepts in Indonesia. He studied them through the indigenous meanings of the words associated with the corresponding practices and discovered that the indigenous terms equivalent to price and purchase in relation to marriage were not to be understood literally. While material value was indeed involved, and the relevant terms connoted the economic dimension, the woman was not a commodity of exchange per se. Instead, the brideprice was understood as a form of compensation for the cost (economic and otherwise) of the care of the bride—whose marriage represented the loss of a worker and a bearer of children—as well as for the sadness of parting. As compensation, it was not to be conflated with purchase, which implied subordination. Furthermore, the bride's family gifted their in-laws in turn, without seeking to match the value of the brideprice, as an expression of the social value of reciprocity. Vroklage concluded that various Indonesian ethnic groups had as complementary practices what would correspond to brideprice and dower which were very similar to Philippine marriage prestations under discussion here.[9]

---

7 Subsequent studies on indigenous societies made further inroads into comprehending the range of meanings and functions of these marriage transactions. For example, L. Bossen ("Toward a Theory of Marriage") points to the limitations of transaction terminology often applied to brideservice, bridewealth, and dowry, and the need to include women's economic interests in marriage transactions.

8 See J. Goody, *Bridewealth and Dowry*, 2.

9 Vroklage, "Bride Price or Dower", 135–137.

In her study on marriage in a highland community in Guatemala, Laurel Bossen outlined the economic implications of bridewealth. As in Indonesia, it was understood as compensation to the woman's family for raising her and for the loss of their daughter's economic contribution through her work. While bridewealth was a deterrent to separation for the man, it likewise guaranteed sustenance for the woman in case the marriage failed. Having afforded her family some economic advantage through the bridewealth received, she expected them to provide for her should she have to return to the family home. Lastly, bridewealth was the means by which parents arranged a wife for their son, who would contribute economically to the household through her work in partnership with her husband and in assistance to her mother-in-law in domestic tasks.[10]

In the context of maritime Southeast Asia, using archaeology and ethnohistory, Laura Lee Junker compared bridewealth as a normative practice among different ethnolinguistic groups and traced its continuance among non-Christianized indigenous groups in the Philippines today. Bridewealth payments were among the social prestige- and political power-building transactions that members of the elite performed and were an effective way of transferring luxury goods, obtained by local production, trading, or raiding.[11] In this connection, Fenella Cannell analyzed the initial stage of pre-colonial Visayan marriage arrangements thus: "the logic of courtship and brideprice suggested that the bride's side were in fact superior to the groom's side".[12] Bridewealth fulfilled the function of establishing equilibrium between the two kinship groups brought together by the marriage as it enabled the groom to match the bride's status. Furthermore, William Henry Scott translated the Visayan *bugay* as brideprice, citing three reasons for differentiating it from the Spanish dowry (*dote*): its size and kind was set by the bride's father, it was not a set value but subject to bargain "like goods in a marketplace," and, once given, it belonged to the woman and her family, not forming part of conjugal property.[13] The quality of the *bugay* was a major signifier of the prospective marriage's importance, particularly among people of high status for whom these unions created or strengthened alliances between their kinship groups. In the Tagalog regions the equivalent term was *bigay-kaya*.

10 Bossen, "Towards a Theory of Marriage", 137.

11 Junker, *Raiding, Trading, and Feasting*, 294–300.

12 Cannell, *Power and Intimacy*, 70.

13 Scott, *Barangay*, 140.

3 Bridewealth in the Philippines in the Early Colonial Period (1580–1660)

The Visayan islands in the central Philippines were the entry point of the Spaniards while the lowlands of the major island of Luzon in the north, where the colonial capital Manila was founded in the Tagalog region, would be the most intensively colonized areas from 1570s onwards.[14] The main sources about Visayan and Tagalog bridewealth are reports and historiographical works containing ethnographic sections, as well as dictionaries by Spanish authors. Accounts from the late 16th century identified the *dote*, using the Spanish equivalent of the indigenous institution, as the principal element in arranging marriages among the Visayans, "paid by the husband to the woman", according to the *conquistador* Miguel de Luarca.[15] Marriage proposals were normally initiated by the man's father through a representative who approached the prospective bride's father. Referring to the Visayans, but without using the Spanish term *dote*, the *Boxer Codex* also mentioned some sort of payment for the bride: "when a man wants to marry off his son to another man's daughter, the two fathers come to an agreement as to what the groom's father will pay for the marriage".[16] In addition, Juan de Plasencia's *relación* (report) on the customs of the Tagalogs and Kapampangans (the inhabitants of the region of Pampanga north of Manila) expressed the indigenous practice as *dote*, never using the vernacular term *bigay-kaya*. Accomplished upon the order of the *Audiencia* of Manila, his *relación* was intended to become the official reference for indigenous customs in litigation involving natives.[17] Furthermore, 17th-century lexicons, namely the Visayan-Spanish *Diccionario* by Alonso de Mentrida and the Tagalog-Spanish *Vocabulario tagalo* by Francisco de San Antonio, translated

14 Background on the conquest and colonization of the Philippines can be found in Perez (Chapter 3) in this volume.

15 Luarca, "Tratado de las Yslas Philipinas", cap. 10, 83. Luarca's account is dated 1582. "Despues qe ya esta conçertado el casamiento que despues de auerse conçertado en el qual paga el marido a la mugger". Note that Luarca did not mention the corresponding Visayan term *bugay*.

16 Donoso (ed.), *Boxer Codex*, 47.

17 Pérez, "Fr. Juan de Plasencia y sus relaciones", 55. Plasencia made the report upon the request of the Audiencia of Manila; he completed it in 1589. See the Audiencia of Manila's resolution of 7 January 1599 (Hidalgo Nuchera, *Los autos acordados de la Real Audiencia*, 82–83). Consistent with the differentiation he made between dowry and brideprice mentioned above, Phelan (*Hispanization of the Philippines* [64–65]), notes: "Plasencia's study did not mention bride-service and bride-price. Hence these customs did not come under the protection of the Spanish law courts".

"bugay" or "bugey" and "bigáy-caya" respectively as *dote*.[18] Thus, the usage of *dote* appears conceptually consistent across the sources for this period.

The ethnographic descriptions in Jesuit writings from the late 16th to mid-17th century, which enriched European knowledge of Philippine matrimonial practices, featured the term *dote* in the same sense. The chronicle of Pedro Chirino (1604) provided the earliest basic account of indigenous marriage, which Francisco Colin (1663) largely drew from while adopting a more juridical approach. Francisco Ignacio Alzina wrote a voluminous and exceptionally perceptive historical and ethnographical account of the Visayans whose chapters on marriage are unparalleled in detail.[19] A layman's publication from the period was Antonio de Morga's *Sucesos de las Islas Filipinas* with its final chapter—practically an appendix to what was chiefly a historical work—consisting of an ethnography of the Tagalogs, which he took mostly from earlier writers. Since his book was published in Mexico, it presumably circulated more widely in secular circles than the Jesuit publications did.[20]

Naturally, the Western juridical background of these authors structured their approach and description of marriage prestations. Their oftentimes comparative perspectives used canon law and the *ius commune* as point of reference, with a view to gauging the extent to which the indigenous institution approximated Christian marriage and therefore its aptness for conversion to the same. The Jesuit authors examined Philippine indigenous societies and cultures in the context of the history of civilizations as seen from a Christian and humanistic perspective, applying European standards of human dignity and social interaction as basis for what it meant to be 'civilized'.[21] On the matter of *dote*, Chirino cited classic authors such as Boethius who were familiar with similar customs in other nations: they "were accustomed to buy women to marry".[22] This notion of purchase and commodification would be reiterated in later religious historical works. A few decades later, in the succeeding Jesuit chronicle, Colin specified that such was the practice in Mesopotamia as well as other nations, "as if [they were] selling their daughters".[23] Similarly,

---

18 Mentrida, *Diccionario de la lengua bisaya*; San Antonio, *Vocabulario tagalo*. Note that most of the Spanish authors, except for Alzina and later on J. F. San Antonio, did not use the indigenous terms for which they used the terminological equivalent of *dote*.

19 Chirino, *Relación de las Islas Filipinas*; Colin, *Labor evangélica*; Alzina, *Una ethografía de los Indios Bisayas*.

20 Morga, *Sucesos de las Islas Filipinas*.

21 See Javellana, *The Jesuits*, 427; Rubiés, "The Spanish Contribution", 442 and 448.

22 Chirino, *Relación de las Islas Filipinas*, cap. 30, 70. The translation of all Spanish texts except the *Boxer Codex* in this chapter is mine.

23 Colin, *Labor evangélica*, lib. 1, cap. 16, 1663, 71. Echoing Colin almost a century later, the Franciscan San Antonio (*Chronicas*, parte 1, lib. 1, cap. 45, 169) was more biting: "por modo

Alzina did not mince words, stating that in the Philippine archipelago "more than marrying off their daughters, [they] sell them".[24] But then he went on to demonstrate that it was not an unusual tradition since it was the practice among the Jews as well as in Asian nations such as China, Japan, and Cambodia. With irony, he noted that in Europe dowries came from the woman's family to help support the cares of marital life (*ad sustendam honera matrimonii*), while in the Philippines they added to the burden (*ad augenda onera*).

Predictably, the ability to give bridewealth belonged to the high-status groups (*principales*), as a function of wealth and prestige. According to Luarca, ordinarily the brideprice amounted to a hundred taels' worth of gold in the form of slaves and household goods, equivalent to 500 or 600 pesos. Among the abovementioned authors, only he described marriage among the non-elite: the *timaguas* (*timawas*) or freemen celebrated in a much simpler manner for lack of means.[25] With regard to the value of the bridewealth, the *Boxer Codex* limited itself to stating "a certain quantity of gold or its [corresponding] value; as is best agreed between them according to the status of each one".[26] Describing the elaborate marriage negotiations among the Visayan elite, Alzina mentioned slaves, gold, and foreign prestige goods such as ceramic plates and metal bells as the usual components of bridewealth. In a society where labor—and not land—was highly prized and could be bought and sold, slaves represented potential for wealth generation, and accordingly carried the greatest value.[27] Alzina described the protracted process of courtship and the prestige that the negotiating parties accrued when they imparted the value of the bridewealth to the public.[28] Alzina[29] and San Antonio[30] noted that fathers usually asked for the same amount as the bridewealth they had given for their wives; but

de Comercio, vendiendo a la Hija [...] por precio justo". He described Tagalog marriage as it was in the period of contact with observations on how it had evolved since then.

24 Alzina, *Una ethografía de los Indios Bisayas*, lib. IV, cap. 12, 233.

25 Luarca, "Tratado de las Yslas Philipinas", cap. 10, 83–84.

26 *Boxer Codex*, 47.

27 On slaves in pre-Hispanic Philippines, see Scott, *Barangay*, 133–135; on land and property, 144–145.

28 Only Alzina (*Una ethografía de los Indios Bisayas*, lib. IV, cap. 12, 233–234) was able to distinguish that in the negotiation of the *bugay* some items were designated as symbolic and were not actually given (*holog*), while there were others to be given during the marriage if at all demanded (*lantai*), and another part which had to be delivered to the bride's house before the wedding (*idadatung* or the Hispanized term *ipacasal*). Alzina commented how important it was for judges as well as clergy to know these differences to be able to resolve quarrels over such matters.

29 Alzina, *Una ethografía de los Indios Bisayas*, lib. IV, cap. 12, 233.

30 San Antonio, *Chronicas*, parte I, lib. I, cap. 45, 169.

not all suitors could match this demand. The bride's side demanded a big sum to maintain its status, while the groom's ability to meet the demands elevated his side. From being initially asymmetrical, their respective statuses reached an equilibrium through bridewealth, and the transference of property could continue after the wedding.[31]

The Spanish chroniclers provide varying though not altogether discrepant details about the bridewealth and accessory gifts for the bride's immediate family, relatives, and other members of the household, even slaves. Their worth depended on the groom's socioeconomic status, and their kind ranged from small valuables to slaves.[32] The crucial role of kinship solidarity emerges: "the relatives help each other in this manner"[33]; those who received their share were in turn obliged to contribute to the *bugay* of their relatives' sons, either in the same amount or more.[34] Among the Tagalogs, however, the following gifts formed part of the *bigay-kaya*: *panhimuyat* or *panghimuyat* given to the mother as recompense for having raised the daughter and the *pasoso* (*pasuso*), denoting the act of suckling, for the wet nurse. These items were non-negotiable even in the absence of the *bigay-kaya*, so much so that non-fulfillment of these gifts could trigger litigation.[35] Among the Visayans, the equivalent of *panhimuyat* was *himirao* (literally, compensation for the sleepless nights spent in caring for the infant), usually in gold or silver, given to the mother, grandmother, or whoever had raised the woman. Separately from the *bugay,* the bride's family received gifts from the groom and his kin several more times during and after the wedding ceremony: as the bride left her house and afterwards, when she was to move to her new home, as if to persuade the bride to leave her parents' dwelling and to compensate for the place she was leaving behind.[36] This spatial representation highlighted that the woman's realm was the house; there she performed her main activities, such as weaving.

---

31 Cannell, *Power and Intimacy*, 70.

32 Chirino, *Relación de las Islas Filipinas*, cap. 30, 70; Colin, *Labor evangélica*, lib. I, cap. 16, 71; Alzina, *Una ethografía de los Indios Bisayas*, lib. IV, cap. 12, 233–235.

33 *Boxer Codex*, 46–47.

34 Alzina, *Una etnografía de los Indios Bisayas*, 242–243.

35 San Antonio, *Chronicas*, parte I, lib. I, cap. 45, 168–169.

36 Alzina, *Una ethografía de los Indios Bisayas*, lib. IV, cap. 12, 235; cap. 13, 237 and 240; Luarca, "Tratado de las Yslas Philipinas", cap. 6, 83. The Visayan term for the high-status bride was *binukot* which denoted her seclusion in a room, hence the reference to the empty space that her absence created. Cannell (*Power and Intimacy*, 70) theorized about the representation of space in the paternal home that the bride was leaving. Additionally, as mentioned above, much anthropological literature has explored the economic significance of the woman whose absence would be compensated by bridewealth or brideprice and

The Spanish authors readily understood that the *bugay/bigay-kaya* went to the bride's parents and family but they did not wholly grasp the significance of the familial involvement, which anthropologists have studied thoroughly. Generally, they gathered that eventually part of the property was given to the married couple at some vital stage. In the case of betrothals between children, they were given their share once they reached marriageable age or could start living together. Marriage being virilocal, other couples received their share when they began to have children or formed a separate household.[37] Among the Tagalogs, upon the death of the woman's parents the *bigay-kaya* was distributed equally among their children like the rest of their property unless they chose to give more to the daughter for whose marriage it was.[38] If the girl was an orphan, she received it when she married. And yet, as San Antonio derisively observed, her avaricious relatives, who acted as her guardians, and her wet nurse would often claim their share and leave her with nothing. His other objection was that parents spent excessively on the wedding celebration, so that little of the *bigay-kaya* remained.[39]

These accounts present how central the negotiation of the bridewealth was in arranging marriages, which culminated in a celebration when the parties arrived at an agreement. Among the Kapampangans, "this [bridewealth] was what made the marriage".[40] In the language of commodification typical of the Spanish authors, the *habilin* was given as an advance on the *bigay-kaya*, "as the token given in transactions of sale at the price agreed on, to prevent sale to another [party]".[41] Plasencia reported that half of the *bigay-kaya* was given even when the prospective spouses were still children, noting that this matter became complicated in cases when the reneging party had to pay the penalty set, which varied in value depending on the local custom and status of the parties involved. But if after the parents' death one of those betrothed as a child refused to honor the agreement upon reaching marriageable age, the bridewealth was merely returned to the groom's family without imposition of penalty. However, if the parents were still alive, the penalty remained in force since they arranged the marriage in the first place.[42] Among the Visayans, if

---

whose presence in the new household would contribute not only in economic terms but also in her childbearing capacity.

37 Luarca, "Tratado de las Yslas Philipinas", cap. 6, 83; *Boxer Codex*, 46–47.

38 Pérez, "Fr. Juan de Plasencia y sus relaciones", 69.

39 San Antonio, *Chronicas*, parte I, lib. I, cap. 45, 170. Although he wrote in the 18th century, San Antonio described marriage practices comparing his 'today' with the past, that is, closer to the previous century.

40 Pérez, "Fr. Juan de Plasencia y sus relaciones", 74.

41 San Antonio, *Chronicas*, parte I, lib. I, cap. 45, 169.

42 Pérez, "Fr. Juan de Plasencia y sus relaciones", 74.

the man reneged from the marriage already arranged, he lost whatever part of the bridewealth he had already given as a token, since "as they begin to arrange the marriage, they [also] begin to give the dowry".[43] *Hingisul* was the penalty that the party who had failed to keep the agreement was obliged to pay in gold, slaves, and other valuables. Alzina observed that in his day, that is, by the mid-17th century, it was enforced less rigorously than in the past. Aware that the penalty for reneging occasioned forced marriages, the clergy tried to limit its application to cases when the party who had broken the agreement had personally arranged it.[44] All this went in favor of freedom of consent that the Catholic Church required for valid marriage.

The Spanish authors went into detail concerning the *bugay* or *bigay-kaya* in case of divorce. Plasencia reported that among the Tagalogs, if the wife initiated the divorce before having children and she intended to remarry after the separation, she returned the *bigay-kaya* and an additional amount, as a form of penalty, to the husband; otherwise she returned only what she had received from the husband. If it was the husband who asked for the divorce, only half of the *bigay-kaya* was returned to him. If the couple had children, they inherited the entire *bigay-kaya* and penalty which the grandparents—or in their absence another trustworthy person—administered in the meantime. Among the Kapampangans, if the wife divorced her husband, she gave him back double the worth of the bridewealth even if the couple had children.[45]

Luarca shifted the attention from the party initiating the divorce to the legitimate causes of divorce and the consequences on the *bugay*, as recorded in the discourse of the elder presiding at a Visayan wedding:

> The man weds the woman but on the condition that if he became wayward and failed to support his wife, she can leave him and not return anything of the 'dowry' he has given her, and she will be free to marry another man; therefore, if she were a vile woman, [the husband] could get back the 'dowry' he gave her, leave her, and marry another woman. Be all of you my witnesses to this agreement.[46]

Morga followed Plasencia, adding that when the cause of separation was the husband's fault, he had no right to restitution of the *bigay-kaya*.[47]

---

43 Luarca, "Tratado de las Yslas Philipinas", 83.

44 Alzina, *Una ethografía de los Indios Bisayas*, lib. IV, cap. 11, 225–226.

45 Pérez, "Fr. Juan de Plasencia y sus relaciones", 69–70, 74.

46 Luarca, "Tratado de las Yslas Philipinas", cap. 10, 83.

47 Morga, *Sucesos de las Islas Filipinas*, cap. 8, 254: "Apartábanse y disolvían este casamiento por ligeras ocasiones, vista y juicio de los deudos de ambas partes y de los ancianos que intervenían a ello, y entonces volvía la dote recibida al varón, que llaman *vigadicaya*, si

Plasencia also recorded the Kapampangan normative practice as regards the destination of the bridewealth upon the death of the wife. If the couple had had no children at the time of the wife's death, it was entirely returned to the surviving husband. But if the couple already had children, whether the children were alive or dead at the time of the mother's demise, only half of the bridewealth was returned to the surviving husband. Plasencia noted that among the Tagalogs, if one of the spouses died less than a year after the wedding without leaving offspring, half of the bridewealth was returned, although more out of compassion than obligation, to the deceased husband's family, or if it was the wife who died, to the surviving husband.[48]

Since Plasencia's *relación* was intended to be the juridical reference on Tagalog and Kapampangan customs, the *dote*, as it was described (that is, as bridewealth) would have been recognized in the colonial legal system.[49] While bridewealth lay outside the jurisdiction of the ecclesiastical tribunal, tasked to implement the canonical form of marriage and promote Catholic matrimonial values, it inevitably surfaced in that forum in relation to promises of marriage. Alzina's occasional mention of his intervention in such affairs provides a glimpse of the special role of the parish priest and provincial vicar as a recognized arbiter in family and community conflicts. He highlighted how important it was for judges as well as members of the clergy to know the nuances of local conventions to be able to resolve quarrels over those matters. His writing reveals that he intervened as parish priest in these issues, discerning when to abide strictly by local normative practice and when to temper it to lessen the economic burden on the groom's kin, as when the bride's family demanded full payment of the bridewealth promised to follow after the wedding, or when the gifts to the bride's relatives came to cost as much as the bridewealth.[50] The experiences Alzina narrated provide an indication of how the clergy made use of their moral authority, particularly among Christianized groups, not only to introduce and implement Tridentine marriage, but also to shape notions of

---

no fuese que se apartaban por culpa del marido, que entonces no se la volvían y quedaban con ella los padres de la mujer". Note that Morga mentioned what would be an approximation of the vernacular term (*bigay-kaya*) which, as mentioned above, Plasencia never did.

48 Pérez, "Fr. Juan de Plasencia y sus relaciones", 69 and 74. San Antonio, *Chronicas*, parte I, lib. I, cap. 45, 169–170, echoed this point.

49 Here I differ with Phelan (*The Hispanization of the Philippines*, 64) who, consistent with his differentiation between dowry and brideprice (or bridewealth), states that Plasencia mentioned only dowry (*dote*) and therefore the colonial legal system did not recognize brideprice.

50 Alzina, *Una etnografía de los Indios Bisayas*, lib. IV, cap. 12, 234 and 236; cap. 13, 242.

justice in the direction of clemency and moderation of greed—in the particular case of bridewealth, in relation to the material advantages accruing from it.

4 Dowry and Arrha in Castilian Law

The Spanish authors, mostly missionaries, not only described Philippine marriage, but inevitably—some more than others—interpreted its constitutive elements at the same time. In this dual but overlapping process they used the categories known to them, articulated for the most part in Castilian as well as canon law. Plasencia's report highlighted that the issues and concerns arising from marriage and family, universal institutions in themselves, were familiar to Europeans and therefore lent themselves to being analyzed using European juridical language.

The principal query that emerges from a reading of the chronicles, reports, and other published works from the early colonial period involves the use of *dote* as a translation of bridewealth. Plasencia plainly stated, "The men give the dowry to the women, which belongs to the women's parents".[51] While this implies that the direction of the endowment was different from European practice, Alzina was more forthright about it: "contrary to our practice, which is that the bride's father gives the dowry (the general usage in Europe it seems), here he receives it".[52] Thus, it seems that these authors were using *dote* in the generic sense of a marriage prestation regardless of the direction of the transmission of property. However, the indigenous institution was not entirely the opposite of the European practice of dowry, which the woman in effect received from her parents, brought to the marriage, and entrusted to her husband while it remained her property; in the case of bridewealth, the bride's parents and kin received it without necessarily giving it to the bride, although indirectly it might contribute to her marriage when spent on preparations. Also, as mentioned above, the couple could be given part of it at a later stage in their married life. Furthermore, the woman's personal inheritance might include some items from the bridewealth.

Spanish authors logically tended to make sense of indigenous practices, concepts, and terms by homologizing them with those that existed in Castilian law. Later, in the 18th century, the Augustinian Casimiro Díaz recalled the debate among moral theologians on whether it was better for the man or woman to give the *dote*, with the woman's side mustering stronger arguments.

---

51 Pérez, "Fr. Juan de Plasencia y sus relaciones", 69.

52 Alzina, *Una etnografía de los Indios Bisayas*, lib. IV, cap. 12, 232–233.

But he cut himself short by stating that there was no such thing among the indigenous peoples as it was understood in Europe; rather, what existed was the money given by the groom to the bride's parents.[53] In the continuing discourse on this particular custom, the conceptual correspondence between *dote* and bridewealth seemed to derive from the appreciation of their common nature as marital endowments, consisting in the transmission of property or money, and was deemed critical to the negotiation of marriage agreements.

The laws governing marriage prestations during the early modern period in Spain evolved from various legal traditions (Germanic, Roman, and canonical) and corpora, successively incorporated into the juridical system. As a feature of the Germanic influence from the Visigothic legal code *Fuero Juzgo*, in its third book the arrha together with the father's authority over the daughter's marriage figured prominently. The bride's father or mother received the arrha from the groom; in their absence the bride's brothers or closest relatives received it on her behalf (title 1, law 7). The 13th-century *Fuero Real*, promulgated by Alfonso X el Sabio to implant royal law in the territories where it did not exist, took from the *Fuero Juzgo* much of its laws on marriage.[54] It specified that if the girl was not yet of marriageable age, her parents or brothers should keep the arrha intact until she came of age, and should demand it since it was to serve the couple in their marital life (book 3, title 2, law 3). Likewise, neither spouse could dispose of the arrha in their lifetime without permission from the other and upon their death their surviving children would inherit it. The value of the arrha was limited to the value of one-tenth of the groom's property. This law would be reiterated centuries later by a prohibition of its renunciation in the *Leyes de Toro* (law 50), compiled toward the end of the reign of the Catholic Kings. If the husband died, the woman was granted the capacity to dispose freely of the arrha if she did not have children (*Fuero Juzgo*, book 3, title 1, law 6); otherwise she kept only half of it, as her children had the right to inherit the other half. All this was on the condition of true marriage, indicated by the spousal kiss. This condition did not hold if it was the woman who died; then the arrha wholly went to the children (*Fuero Juzgo*, book 3, title 1, law 5). If she died without direct heirs, the arrha was to be returned to the husband or to his closest relatives if he was also deceased (*Fuero Juzgo*, book 3, title 1, law 6). Furthermore, the woman could lose the arrha if she committed adultery (*Fuero Real*, book 3, title 2, law 6). In the medieval legal corpora, the predominance of the arrha is evident, until the *Siete Partidas* introduced the Roman concept of dowry.[55]

---

53 Díaz, *Parrocho de Indios*, lib. I. cap. VI, § 8, no. 71, 54r.

54 *Fuero Real*, xxiv–xxv.

55 *Fuero Real*, xxv.

The *Siete Partidas* as royal law drew heavily from the *ius commune* and relegated local laws to a subsidiary level. In the fourth Partida, which deals with betrothals and marriage, the laws on marriage prestations are found in title 11. Five types of matrimonial endowments were explained: *dote, donation propter nuptias, arras, sponsalitia largitas,* and spousal gifts (law 1). The first two derived from Roman law; the *dote* (dowry) was defined thus: "It is something that the woman gives the husband on account of marriage [...] and is in the manner of an endowment with the understanding that it is intended for the support of and assistance to the marriage".[56] The dowry belonged to the woman although she entrusted it to the husband during the marriage—whose duty it was to preserve it—for her upkeep in case the couple separated or for her children to inherit once she died. The husband, as head of the household, administered the dowry which was meant to serve the marriage (law 7). The *donatio propter nuptias* is "what the man gives the woman on account of marriage [...] as an endowment that the man gives the woman because he marries her" (law 1).[57] Although this donation was called *arras* in Spain, the same law promptly clarified that ancient law had defined *arras* as an earnest for a marriage promise, so that whichever side failed to fulfill the promise forfeited it. The *sponsalitia largitas* was described as the gifts that the spouses might give each other before and after the wedding which should be made equally.[58] The *Siete Partidas* (law 2) maintained the Visigothic precept regarding the destination of the arrha upon the demise of one of the spouses.

The *Leyes de Toro* of 1505 compiled Castilian law hitherto in force, which included more aspects of private law in relation to women, particularly as regards legal transactions, inheritance, and property rights, marking a significant advancement as far as women's legal capacity was concerned.[59] Regarding the arrha (law 51), the woman's right to it, whether she had children or not, was unambiguously recognized, in continuity with *Fuero Juzgo*.[60] The Taurine laws echoed the *Fuero Juzgo, Fuero Real,* and the *Siete Partidas*, being explicit about betrothal (*matrimonio de futuro*) or marriage (*matrimonio de presente*) as the legitimizing factor for ownership of the arrha and other gifts given before the marriage. If the couple separated after the spousal kiss had been given but before marriage was consummated, the woman had the right to half of what the man had given her (*sponsalitia largitas*); absent the kiss, she did

56 López, *Siete Partidas*, 29r.

57 López, *Siete Partidas*, 29r.

58 López, *Siete Partidas*, 29v. "las dotes e las donaciones que faze el marido a la mujer, e la muger al marido [...] se pueden fazer ante que el matrimonio sea acabado, o después. E deven ser fechas egualmente".

59 Korthe and Flusche, 'Dowry and Inheritance", 396.

60 Reiterated in the Nueva Recopilación, lib. 5, tit. 2, ley 3.

not receive anything, all the gifts being restored to the man's heirs.[61] If the husband should die after the marriage was consummated and no arrha had been given, the wife retained everything she had received from the husband. If the arrha had been given before the husband died, the woman had 20 days after the husband's heirs asked her to decide which to keep, either the arrha or the other gifts; otherwise the choice was theirs (law 52).[62]

By the early modern period, the arrha had evolved from the Germanic bride-price to become the groom's tribute to the bride's virginity.[63] The arrha has also been interpreted as the husband's compensation for the marital rights over the wife that he acquired. This understanding of the arrha emphasized conjugal relations in which the importance of the wife was acknowledged even under the husband's dominion, by which marriage formed the core of family. Margarita María Birriel pointed out that despite the *Siete Partidas*' attempt to equate the arrha with the Justinian *donatio propter nuptias* defined above, Castilian juridical and notarial practice demonstrated otherwise, a difference which was reinforced in the *Leyes de Toro*. Nevertheless, the *Siete Partidas*, which had defined *arras* in two interrelated ways, became the basic reference for the definition of *arras* in 16th- and 17th-century Spanish dictionaries.[64]

A summary comparison of women's property rights with respect to the arrha and Philippine indigenous customs regarding bridewealth would yield commonalities particularly regarding the conditions for retaining or losing that marriage endowment as well as the children's right to inherit it. The Spanish authors in the colonial Philippines, however, preferred to use the term *dote* instead of *arras*, perhaps influenced by the value of bridewealth in Philippine society which paralleled the crucial importance of the *dote* in Europe in arranging marriages.

The *Nueva Recopilación de las leyes destos Reynos* of 1567, which posthumously fulfilled Queen Isabel's desire to compile and organize Castilian law, included only three laws related to arrhae taken from the *Leyes de Toro* (and therefore from the earlier codes of law) and a royal decree from 1534 regulating the value of dowries vis-à-vis income levels as well as the *sponsalitia largitas*, described above. The latter reveals that dowries needed to be regulated so as not to be an unreasonable hindrance to marriage; they had become inflated in their pivotal role in negotiating advantageous matches in the early modern

61 Mijancos (*La igualdad entre el varón y la mujer*, 138) interprets this measure as a way of protecting women against unfulfilled marriage promises since a spousal kiss received by an unmarried woman was an occasion of dishonor.

62 Reiterated in the Nueva Recopilación, lib. 5, tit. 2, ley 4.

63 Korthe and Flusche, 400.

64 Birriel, "Mujeres y matrimonio", 85–87.

period, not only in Spain but also in New Spain.[65] The provisions of the other earlier legal codes in regard to matrimonial property and inheritance continued to be in force. As in Spanish America, the laws of Castile and those promulgated for the Indies, as well as canon law, were applied to marriage in the Philippine colony where, with increasing experience and knowledge of indigenous socio-economic and cultural institutions, eventually local laws were enacted.

5 *Bugay* and *Bigay-Kaya* in the Framework of European Law: Juan de Paz's Translation

Some of the abovementioned authors directed their ethnographic writings to aiding judicial and spiritual administration by way of enlightening the Spaniards on indigenous practices and traditions. Although hitherto little is known of the jurisprudence from the period, which may shed further light on how European law grappled with indigenous normative practices, we do have the opinion of Juan de Paz (1622–1698), the renowned Dominican moral theologian in Manila, in a case involving *dote*.[66]

This case involved Mateo, who gave his betrothed Gerónima 20 pesos as *dote* and, in addition, promised ten pesos for her wedding dress. They agreed that if Mateo reneged from the marriage, he would forfeit the 20 pesos; if Gerónima did, she should return the same amount and 20 pesos more. In effect, they agreed on penalizing the party who failed to keep the agreement—a practice condemned by ecclesiastical and civil law. On the day of the wedding itself, Mateo brought her a secondhand wedding dress which the bride rejected. He then offered the ten pesos so she could purchase a wedding dress of her choice, but the bride and her parents still refused to proceed with the wedding. In the subsequent litigation, the judge sentenced Gerónima according to the terms of their betrothal, apparently in accordance with the counsel of Paz.

The main argument in the consultation (*consulta*) about this case was that canon law prohibited imposing a monetary penalty for breaking a betrothal

65 Owens ("El precio de la novia", 280–281) traces this trend in other parts of western Europe in the same period; on New Spain, see, for example, Gonzalbo Aizpuru, "Las cargas del matrimonio", 210.

66 Against the background of dearth of locally produced jurisprudential works in early Spanish colonial Philippines, Paz's *Consultas* was exceptional and responded to the need to have a stable corpus of cases for reference, particularly on questions and scenarios specific to the Philippines. Many unpublished consultations on the most varied issues are kept in the Archives of the University of Santo Tomas in Manila. Camacho, "'Mirando las cosas de cerca", 271–272, 275. For his earliest known biography, see Salazar, *Historia de la Provincia de el Santísimo Rosario*, 729–731.

because the financial burden could constrain the freedom of the reneging party. When asked to clarify the basis for his counsel, Paz cited other authors who held the opinion that imposing a penalty for breaking a marriage promise without reasonable cause was valid, but not in cases of justifiable cause. However, in the present case, Paz argued, what the woman forfeited was the *arras* and not the *dote*, and therefore the judge's decision lay within the bounds of law. The arrha was a sign of future marriage and therefore had to be returned if one of the parties went back on his or her word.[67]

Pursuing his argument, Paz explained that conflating the restitution of the *dote*, on the one hand, and the restitution of the arrha with an additional amount, on the other, made the sentence seem like a penalty and was therefore in violation of the freedom of marriage. However, the *consulta* maintained that the 20 pesos that Mateo had given Gerónima was *dote* and not *arras*; therefore, the additional 20 pesos the woman had to pay was a form of penalty and had nothing to do with the *arras*. Paz insisted that the man had given the woman a token of future marriage—the arrha—comparable to a purchase for which an earnest or an advanced amount was given. In the case at hand, the sum of 20 pesos was given as guarantee of future marriage and was thus tantamount to a contract. Regarding the additional 20 pesos paid by the woman, it was in keeping with the significance of the arrha; civil law penalized the woman who broke the betrothal by obliging her to return double the value of the arrha, which at any rate was usually less in value than the dowry.[68] Clearly, Paz chose to be guided by the *Siete Partidas*, whose definition of *arras* he used. The influence of the *ius commune* is evident in his argumentation on penalties for broken marriage promises while safeguarding the freedom of marriage, for which he relied heavily on the Justinian Code and canon law.

Paz's opinion would resonate with Pedro Murillo Velarde's in his *Cursus Juris Canonici, Hispani et Indici* published decades later (1743), in which arrha was unambiguously defined as a sign and token of marriage and could be given by both man and woman to each other. When applied to a marriage promise, however, it constituted a penalty imposed on the reneging party; as such it was merely promised and not given and usually amounted to more than the arrha so that it would be more obliging. Absence of a legitimate reason for not fulfilling the marriage promise justified the imposition of penalty without impairing the freedom of matrimonial consent.[69]

67 These connected cases are presented consecutively in the chapter Tercera clase (Simples promesas, mandatos, fideicomisos) as Consultas III, IV, and V (Paz, *Consultas y resoluciones*, 280–283).

68 Paz, *Consultas y resoluciones*, 282–283.

69 Murillo Velarde, *Curso de derecho canónico*, lib. 4, tit. 1, nos. 9 and 10.

The abovementioned case evinces the degree of confusion about indigenous marriage prestations and the terms applied to them, and, as Paz pointed out, the need to clarify concepts. The term *dote* was used to denote the sum given to the woman, which in accordance with indigenous norms was received by her parents; to jurists familiar with native Philippine culture, the referent of the translation would be distinct enough. Paz, then, homologized European and Philippine practices by translating the native *bugay/bigay-kaya* as the European arrha by virtue of the fact that the groom provided it. While in this way he respected the prevailing indigenous norm, he emphasized the meaning of the sum of money that Mateo had handed to Gerónima's parents: that it was a sign of commitment of both parties to marriage, serious enough to justify the imposition of a penalty without violating the freedom of marriage of the betrothed. He did not nullify the local customs which the litigating parties were following, and which penalized the breaking of marriage promises. However, by framing the case in Castilian law and translating indigenous notions into European categories, he focused on the meaning of *arrha*, which he qualified as more than merely a promise, and therefore justified the penalty.

Since this case was limited to the concept of arrha, it is unclear whether Paz complemented the translation of the *bugay/bigay-kaya* to *arras* with a corresponding concept for the Spanish *dote,* that is, for what the bride's family might give to the bride or to the couple. Except for Alzina, it seems that little or no attention was paid to a possible indigenous equivalent of the arrha understood as *donatio propter nuptias,* called *bantal,* which in olden times was expected to be double the *bugay*. Paz did not adequately capture the sociocultural meaning of the *bugay/bigay-kaya* in indigenous society—and it would be too much to ask of him to have known what modern anthropology has learned—when he limited his analysis to the meaning of arrha as an earnest. The impact of his legal translation on colonial jurisprudence and subsequent cases has yet to be verified. What is clear in the ecclesiastical and civil sources of the 17th and 18th centuries is that the term *dote* continued to be employed in the same sense as it had been used earlier by Plasencia and other authors during the early colonial period.

6 *Dote* and *Servicio Personal* in the Normative Discourse of the 18th Century

Although churchmen in the Philippines had long been cognizant of the effects of indigenous marital prestations considered detrimental to canonical marriage and had taken steps to mitigate them, the publication of the *Recopilación de de las leyes de Indias* in 1681 furnished colonial authorities with a firm secular basis for the reform of those customs. They found an apposite regulation in book 6, title 1, law 1, in which they recognized how the Maya categories and socioeconomic context of the original decree were analogous to those found in the Philippines.[70] From this point of departure, this section traces the history of ecclesiastical and civil legislation forbidding the *dote* and *servicio personal* in the 18th century and examines how it was applied through the lenses of litigation revolving around broken marriage promises in the ecclesiastical tribunal, specifically of the archdiocese of Manila. It ends with the colonial Church's endeavor to make marriage conform to Tridentine norms through conciliar and synodal decrees from the 1770s. In the last quarter of that century, the defense of freedom of marriage which lay behind its consistent denunciation of those two indigenous practices again surfaced in response to the royal decrees which strengthened parental authority or its equivalent over the choice of spouse in function of social order.

6.1 *Linking Maya and Philippine Marriage Practices: Religious and Secular Ordinances in the 18th Century*

Servicio personal or brideservice formed part of the *bugey/bigay-kaya*. Among the Visayans, brideservice (*pangagar*) of about a year was rendered by the son-in-law even if he had fulfilled the requirements of the bride's parents for the *bugay*. If he had not, then he served longer.[71] The groom, while still a minor or while waiting for the bride to come of age, worked for his future in-laws. In other parts, it was a post-wedding obligation with a duration which could range from a few years to a lifetime. It was a practice consonant with the traditional attachment of Visayan women to their family home, obliging the men to present them with gifts at every stage of the transfer to their new home. Although some parish priests found it difficult to curb this custom, considered oppressive, Alzina, with his deep knowledge of the Visayans, conceded that it was not altogether bad as long as it did not prevent the couple from enjoying marital relations.[72]

As to why the other chroniclers appear to have failed to observe the practice of brideservice and therefore made no mention of it is an unresolved question.

---

70 *Recopilación de las leyes de Indias*, 190: "Que los Indios no puedan vender sus hijas para contraer matrimonio".

71 Alzina (*Una ethografía de los Indios Bisayas*, lib. IV, cap. 13, 239–241) traced the etymology of this term to *humagar* or father-in-law, such that *pangagar* meant living in the in-law's house, in effect a temporary kind of uxorilocal residence, although in some cases it became permanent.

72 Luarca, "Tratado de las Yslas Philipinas", cap. 6, 83; Alzina, *Una ethografía de los Indios Bisayas*, lib. IV, cap. 13, 239–240.

It might be that they had not been sufficiently immersed in indigenous communities to discern that uxorilocal residence after marriage entailed brideservice. For example, if the bride was very young—as young as 12 years old—she was allowed to remain in her parents' home and much time could pass before the marriage was consummated. Alzina's ethnography was exceptional in its depth and breadth of knowledge of Visayan culture and norms, capturing details and nuances that no other missionary writing in the first century of colonization did. But, as will be seen below, the information it offers is not sufficient regarding brideservice.

While in the prehispanic period (continuing until the early colonial period) bridewealth was largely a status-building, alliance-forming practice among the elite, in colonial times it evolved into a generalized practice involving lower values and was more conspicuously accompanied by brideservice.[73] Although the early accounts were critical of bridewealth and drew attention to the notion of purchase and commodification it connoted, they did not dwell on the moral and canonical arguments that colonial authorities would invoke at the turn of the 17th century and throughout the 18th.[74] Alzina's description of brideservice as a post-marriage tradition diverged from the pre-marriage requirement that was severely disapproved of in the colonial normative order. Available sources do not allow us to establish whether such a change did take place in the 17th century, nor can we readily apply Alzina's observation to the other indigenous ethnolinguistic groups in the Philippines.

The reiteration of arguments from religious faith and morals, with corresponding disciplinary measures, points to an apparent inefficacy of the legal means enacted. The moral reasons for censure appeared repeatedly in secular and ecclesiastical law and in manuals for clergy and moral theological writings, in response to the common concern for public morals understood within the cultural matrix of Christianity.[75] Manuel del Río summarized the collaboration of authorities thus: "and so the Minister has to be vigilant in this matter, severely punishing those who are guilty of this, or notifying the *alcalde mayor* [provincial governor], who has been entrusted with this business by virtue of royal ordinances, or the *vicar forane* to whom this matter closely pertains".[76]

Aside from the licentious premarital relationships that brideservice propitiated, in *Parrocho de indios,* a manual for parish priests published in the mid-18th century, Díaz underlined its serious consequences affecting the freedom

---

73 Cannell, *Power and Intimacy*, 74.

74 Garcia, "Particular discipline on marriage", 20–24.

75 Díaz, *Parrocho de Indios*; Ortiz, *Práctica del ministerio*; AUST, lib. 62.

76 Río, *Instrucciones morales*, cap. 1, § 6, Del Sacramento del Matrimonio, 10r.

of marriage. The daughter was especially vulnerable when forced to marry the man whom her parents had chosen because he could afford to give more *dote*. Díaz clarified this *dubium* (doctrinal question) following the Tridentine teaching: although children ought to obey their parents' wishes regarding matrimony—to the extent these were reasonable—they enjoyed the freedom to marry whom they chose. He expressed openness to this indigenous custom even though he thought the bride's parents did not need to be compensated for carrying out their natural duties to their offspring, which was the purported rationale of the *bigay-kaya*. But precisely for the foregoing reasons affecting the validity and integrality of marriage, he included this topic in the chapter on "the abuses and bad habits of *Gentilidad*" in the celebration of matrimony.[77]

The decree of Governor Domingo de Zabálburu of 8 April 1704 was a collaborative effort with the Archbishop of Manila Diego de Camacho as an attempt to eliminate both bridewealth and brideservice in one sweep.[78] It cited book 6, title 1, law 1 of the *Recopilación de las leyes de Indias,* originally decreed by Philip IV for Guatemala (Madrid, 29 September 1628).[79] It prohibited parents from receiving anything from suitors, whether in money or in kind.[80] Given the similarity between Maya and Philippine marriage prestations, it is easy to see how colonial authorities appreciated the law's applicability halfway around the world. Like the Spanish accounts of indigenous Philippine cultures, the bishop of Yucatan Diego de Landa's description of Maya matrimonial customs in the mid-16th century used European categories: the parents of the prospective spouses—who were married at the young age of 12 or 13 at the time of Landa's writing—arranged the marriage by agreeing on the *dote* and *arras*, which were not much; the former was given by the boy's father to the girl's father, and in addition the boy's mother proceeded to prepare the dowry in the form of clothing for her son and daughter-in-law. After the wedding, the groom remained in the house of his in-laws where he worked for five to six years for his father-in-law. Negligence on his part was reason for his in-laws to make him leave the house and presumably dissolve the marriage.[81]

77 Díaz, *Parrocho de Indios*, lib. I. cap. 6, § 8, 54v–55r. On the notion of *Gentilidade* in Portuguese Asia, see Lourenço (Chapter 7) in this volume.

78 AUST, lib. 60, fols. 133v–134r.

79 The royal decree was preceded by the seventh ordinance of those issued by the *oidor* (royal judge) of the Audiencia of Guatemala Juan Maldonado de Paz on 19 December 1625. Tovilla, *Relaciones histórico-descriptivas*, chap. 22, De las ordenanzas por hoy se gobierna estos indios de la Verapaz, no. 7.

80 Modern-day Maya in highland Guatemala continue to practice bridewealth (Bossen, "Towards a Theory of Marriage", 137) the economic implications of which has been explored and may be applied, to some extent, historically.

81 Landa, *Relación de las cosas de Yucatan*, chap. 25.

The Philippine version of the law applied the same penalties as the original to the parents found guilty of admitting the forbidden practices: fifty lashes for the *timagua* (*timawa*) (*mecegal* [*macehual*] in the original), demotion of the *principal* to *timawa*, and ineligibility for public office.[82] The main motive for enacting the law was stated as follows:

> from which [custom] result many grave offenses to God our Lord, against chastity as well as against justice, because oftentimes when the agreement with the *indio* parents is dissolved, those [men] who were supposed to marry lose the payment due to their work, or of their own free will abandon the *indio* women who suffer the lamentable loss of their virginity, and the men [the loss of] their labor.[83]

This decree formed part of the ordinances issued by Zabálburu and subsequent governors general of the 18th century, such as Pedro Manuel de Arandía and José Raón.[84] The Augustinian Tomás Ortiz referred to the specific ordinance in a handbook for his confreres:

> The *indios* have the custom of serving the parents of the woman whom they wish to marry, from which many sins have ensued because that service is usually the proximate occasion [of sin] for the two who want to get married and, owing to that, several edicts have been issued to prohibit it. See the royal ordinance no. 42.[85]

This ordinance was among those selected by the *alcalde mayor* of the Tagalog province of Bulacan for local promulgation in 1733.[86] The concern for virtue

---

82 In the socioeconomic hierarchy at the period of contact, which Plasencia described as "estates", the *timawa* was below the *datu* (chieftain) or *maginoo* class; considered as freemen, they were followers of the *datu* and rendered him services including military. By the 18th century, with the gradual elimination of debt peonage, lowland indigenous society became two-tiered, consisting of the *principales* who were eligible for public office, and the *timawa* or commoner. See Scott, *Barangay*, 219–223.

83 AUST, lib. 60, fol. 133v.

84 Zabálburu, "Ordinances", *The Philippine Islands*, 216–217; AUST, Libros 60, fols. 133–134. In the 40th ordinance, Zabálburu explained that he had received a communication from the archbishop dated 26 January 1702 asking him to enforce the cited law from the *Recopilación de las leyes de Indias*. Note, however, the different number cited by Tomás Ortiz and Manuel del Río.

85 Ortiz, *Práctica del ministerio*, § 7, De la administracion del matrimonio, no. 77, 25. M. del Río, *Instrucciones morales*, cap. 1, § 6, Del sacramento del matrimonio, 101, also refers to the same ordinance.

86 AFIO 88/40, Ordenanzas circuladas por el Alcalde mayor de Bulacan, no. 7.

and to maintain freedom of marriage for both men and women also appeared in the ordinances issued for northern Luzon provinces Cagayan (1739) and Ilocos (1743) by the *oidor* of the *Audiencia* of Manila, Ignacio Arzadun y Rebolledo, resulting from the *visita a la tierra* that he conducted there. The 33rd ordinance condemned the *dote* as an abuse because it was set at prohibitively high values which were unattainable for most men, thereby discouraging them from getting married. The law underlined the coercive effect of those practices and applied, like Zabálburu's, the same penalties as the aforementioned law found in the *Recopilación de las leyes de Indias*, this time substituting the Ilocano term *caylian* for the Tagalog *timawa*.[87]

A quarter of a century later, however, Miguel García San Esteban (1768–1779), the bishop of the diocese of Nueva Segovia in northern Luzon, was still decrying this "abuse" which was particularly prevalent—as it had always been—among wellborn people. He was more explicit in describing the immoral consequences of brideservice of six months to one year or more, which among other things delayed marriage:

> oftentimes after a long service causing grave damage to his property, and greater [still] in his soul, he is dismissed on account of a small fault, and they withdraw from the wedding that was already arranged, and in this way parents convert their daughters into prostitutes, and sell them [...] [which] matters little to them, and they take no notice of the taint on their honor even if their daughter may have lost her maidenhood, becoming a most corrupt woman, not a woman for holy matrimony but [instead] a harlot exposed to reproach and ridicule. [88]

Bishop San Esteban was aware how difficult it was to extirpate these practices since the natives took care to hide them from the Spanish authorities. In his pastoral letter, quoted above, he prohibited prospective grooms from going to the woman's house for any reason after their betrothal until their wedding day. If necessary, the woman should live in another house where such separation could be guaranteed.

In the diocese of Nueva Caceres in southeastern Luzon (Bicol region) a series of ordinances condemning bridewealth and brideservice was issued. The pastoral letter of Isidro de Arévalo of 1746 compiled the ordinances and decrees issued by his predecessor Felipe de Molina in 1724, who in turn had

87 APD, 1/79, Pangasinan, tomo 9, doc. 7, fol. 171v.

88 AUST, Libros 27, fol. 157r.

cited Domingo de Valencia's ordinances of 1717.[89] Bishop Valencia referred to Bishop Andrés González's 1684 ordinance prohibiting and imposing fines on *servicio personal* and broken marriage promises owing to the inability to provide the marriage prestation.[90] He reasoned that if canonical marriages did not take place, cohabitation consequently increased. González had likewise prohibited the practice of gifting the mother. In addition, in a radical move subverting the age-old conception of brideprice, the bishop attempted to transform bridewealth into the European notion of *donatio propter nuptias*, which was to be given to the parents of the bride a few days before the wedding, with guarantors to ensure that the entire amount should be given to the couple upon marriage. The point of these rules was to prevent the bride's parents and their relatives from consuming the gifts and money from the groom, a scenario that had led more than one family to force their daughter into marriage "so that without freedom, they contract an act which needs to be very voluntary".[91] To enforce this new norm, aside from requiring that the gifts be exhibited, the bishop stipulated fines, part of which was to be awarded to the denouncer. The responsibility for implementing these rules fell to parish priests. So far, there is no evidence to indicate that this particular mandate was observed.

The Archbishop of Manila, Pedro de la Santísima Trinidad Martínez de Arizala, issued his own ordinance in 1751. He also castigated brideservice, devoting an entire section to it, in which he blamed the clergy for not being zealous enough in their efforts to eliminate the practice. He directed the parish priests to collaborate with the town elite and *alcaldes mayores* to exclude violators from the nomination lists for public office. He also targeted the parents, and not the men who complied with the required service to be able to win their brides, as the main culprits. As it would stain their honor, Martínez de Arizala thought this course of action could more effectively deter the *principales* from demanding brideservice. In this respect, he echoed the tenor of the original legal source from Guatemala found in the *Recopilación de las leyes de Indias*. With his determined stance, the Archbishop instructed the parish priests to notify him should such a measure prove ineffectual, in which case he would threaten deportation to Zamboanga in the far south of the Archipelago.[92]

---

89 AUST, Libros 27, fols. 179–260.

90 AUST, Libros 27, fols. 205r–v.

91 AUST, Libros 27, fols. 207v–208r.

92 Santísima Trinidad, *Carta pastoral*, 19–33.

6.2 *Enforcing Marriage Practices: Litigation over Broken Promises of Marriage*

The evidence about the implementation of these rules remains anecdotal. The Franciscan parish priest of the Tagalog town of Baras in the archdiocese of Manila, Casimiro Pitarque, remitted to the diocesan tribunal a case of an unfulfilled betrothal. In the testimonies gathered, the purported cause was Servando de los Santos' omission: he was unable to help finish building his future in-laws' house as an expected part of the brideservice. From Pitarque's point of view, the betrothed daughter was simply obeying her father in all this. Servando had rendered service indirectly by hiring laborers to work in the fields on his behalf and by providing provisions and construction materials. He claimed to have done that to avoid the penalties for violating the prohibition of *servicio personal*, for which Pitarque cited the relevant law from the *Recopilación de las leyes de Indias*, the 1751 pastoral letter of Archbishop Martínez de Arizala, and several orders of *alcaldes mayores*. Pitarque explained that in 1777 he himself had urged the local authorities to enforce the law strictly and since then a few violators had been punished. To encourage persons to confess violations, four years later an additional provision stipulated that in case of an aborted marriage, the person who owned up would not be punished. In a tone of resignation, the parish priest admitted that these practices were so deeply rooted that it was not enough to preach against them, "so it is necessary to accompany the bread of doctrine with the stick of chastisement".[93]

An initial analysis of the pronouncements of ecclesiastical authorities and the admonitions of clergymen vis-à-vis the concerns of litigants in lawsuits revolving around broken promises of marriage shows the gap between the ideal and the reality. On the one hand, the laws decried the moral consequences of the controverted marital prestations, conveyed as permanently detrimental to individual and family integrity and to canonical marriage. On the other, unfulfilled betrothals could in reality be threshed out with economic compensations and other forms of censure and satisfaction contemplated in canon law.[94] The person who reneged from the marriage promise without

93 AAM, Informaciones matrimoniales, 14.A.3, fold. 12 (a). The series labeled as 'Informaciones matrimoniales' contains various types of documents, not only pre-matrimonial information declaring that the contracting parties were free to marry. The bulk of the records consist of records of matrimonial cases brought before the ecclesiastical tribunal, and of them a good number revolved around broken marriage promises. Unfortunately, none of them include legal opinions and references to legislation considered in the formulation of verdicts and sentences.

94 Murillo Velarde, *Curso de derecho canónico*, lib. IV, tit. 1, De los esponsales y matrimonios, no. 7.

justifiable cause would be penalized: the giver lost the arrha and the receiver restituted double its value.[95] Thus the bulk of court proceedings consisted in establishing whether the litigants—or their parents—had mutually made that promise, especially when a third party was involved or the woman had become pregnant. Canon law admitted a wide range of signs of betrothal, open to local conventions and various circumstances, which were applicable to indigenous matrimonial culture.[96]

In the third quarter of the 18th century, *servicio personal* was still presented as evidence for the existence of a betrothal, which was binding in conscience, in ecclesiastical judicial proceedings in the archdiocese of Manila. In Ignacio Flores's pursuit of the fulfillment of his betrothal to Nicolasa Pagtachan, he mentioned the three years of service that he had rendered as proof. He concluded that Nicolasa had been forced to belie their engagement when her parents changed their mind, seeing the little advantage they could gain from having him as a son-in-law.[97] Brideservice was also presented as secondary evidence to the principal cause of litigation, when the complainant demanded restitution following a broken promise of marriage.[98] The witnesses from the community of the litigants took for granted that *servicio personal* as a matter of tradition was a true signifier of a marriage agreement.[99] Its absence could likewise be used as an argument as it was in the case of Gerónimo Bernabé who wished to suspend his daughter María's marriage to Manuel: "he [Manuel] had never been to the house of the person I represent, nor performed any personal service there, neither has the aforementioned man communicated by himself or through his elders about his aforementioned aspiration".[100] Thus, the lack of *servicio personal* signaled that no marriage had been agreed upon.

The tribunal did not accuse the litigants of violating the law against brideservice but adhered to the core issue of determining whether the betrothal existed in the first place or a just cause for breaking the marriage promise could be proven. Similarly, records show how traditional it was for the man to give foodstuff and other goods to the woman and her parents and for their household. These gifts would have been more akin to the *sponsalitia largitas*; there was an unspoken understanding that those tokens were traditional

95 Murillo Velarde, *Curso de derecho canónico*, lib. IV, tit. 1, De los esponsales y matrimonios, no. 9.

96 Murillo Velarde, *Curso de derecho canónico*, lib. IV, tit. 1, De los esponsales y matrimonios, no. 4.

97 AAM, Box 14.A.2, fold. 4.

98 AAM, Informaciones matrimoniales, 14.A.3, fold. 12 (b); 14.A.3, fold. 3.

99 AAM, Informaciones matrimoniales, 14.A.2, fold. 4; 14.A.3, fold. 13, fols. 7 and 9; 14.A.3, fold. 1.

100 AAM, Informaciones matrimoniales, 14.A.3 fold. 14.

manifestations of the man's abiding intention to pursue marriage.[101] If a party desisted from the marriage, the question of restitution of the gifts and compensation for brideservice came to the fore.

Juan Manuel Pérez, a *principal* of the town of Malate, a suburb of Manila, demanded that the wedding of his son take place after the stipulated period of *servicio personal*. Suspecting that the other party was going back on their word, Pérez presented a list of the expenses incurred by his son, consisting of gifts and farming needs such as a plow, seeds, laborers' wages, and rental fees for carabaos, and, at the end of the list, "the seven months, more or less, that my son worked in their house (priceless)".[102] Even then, the other party insisted on another year of service. A similar case was brought to the ecclesiastical court by Patricio Xavier, native of Taguig, a town east of Manila. The parents of Maria Candelaria refused his suit, but he claimed that the girl had already promised to marry him. To substantiate his demand, he presented a long list of items, mostly foodstuff and building materials, including details of the manual work he had rendered around the house. Many of the items had been given upon the request of his future in-laws, but the latter only admitted to having received some of the items, which they were willing to reimburse.[103] Unfortunately, none of the cases of the latter kind were resolved on record, nor are there notations in that regard, perhaps signaling that it was to be settled in the secular court or extrajudicially.

Maria Rita de Rivera resorted to the legislated prohibition of brideservice to liberate herself from Vicente Hernández, whom her father wanted her to marry. When witnesses testified that Vicente had been staying in their house, they were implying that he had rendered the customary brideservice. Maria Rita argued that he should be punished for having performed an unlawful act, thereby leaving her free to marry the man to whom she was truly engaged:

> Because it is the usual way of contracting betrothals among the natives to begin with personal service, both harmful and prohibited with many penalties, which Your Honor knows, and that its transgression favors my freedom's rights.[104]

Regarding broken marriage promises, the partnership between secular and ecclesiastical jurisdiction theoretically corresponded to a division in jurisdiction, with the demands for restitution and compensation being pursued before

101 AAM, Informaciones matrimoniales, 14.A.3, fold. 12 (b); 14.A.3, fold. 3.
102 AAM, 14.A.3, fold. 12 (b).
103 AAM, 14.A.3, fold. 3.
104 AAM, 14.A.3, fold. 4.

civil authorities such as the town *gobernadorcillo* in the first instance. However, on the ground, this jurisdictional division was not always as unambiguous.[105] The ecclesiastical court was principally concerned with establishing the veracity of promises and mutuality of consent, in which the material aspects played a central role, examining the litigants' willingness to honor betrothals and imposing the appropriate sentence for those who unjustifiably reneged, which included economic compensations for the wronged party. In accordance with canon law, the parties who reneged without just cause were admonished with a view to compelling them to proceed with marriage; in cases of firm refusal, the judge did not risk leading them into an unhappy marriage and settled the case by dispensing other forms of satisfactory justice. Censuring the reneging party was not considered an attempt against their freedom which they had already used irresponsibly; as Murillo Velarde affirmed, "such fear is not unjustly inflicted, but rather justly, and therefore is not harmful to marriage".[106] Thus, in the lawsuits concerning betrothals the basic prescriptions of canon law were applied regardless of the ethnicity of the litigants.

The handful of cases involving brideservice indicates that the repeated legal dispositions to stamp it out did not effect radical changes on the micro-level of villages and towns, even up to the latter half of the 18th century. Whether the 1782 case from Baras signaled the strengthening of legal force cannot be concluded in the absence of more cases. Moreover, at the turn of the 18th century, the persistence of the *bigay-kaya* and other gifts, with the same spending patterns associated with them, was still reported and repeatedly denounced by churchmen.[107]

6.3 *Instituting Tridentine Marriage through Ecclesiastical and Royal Regulation*

The colonial Church consolidated its pronouncements on the sacrament of matrimony in the first Provincial Council of Manila and the Synod of Calasiao in the province of Pangasinan in the suffragan diocese of Nueva Segovia. The first was held in 1771, almost two centuries after the creation of the ecclesiastical province, as part of the implementation of Charles III's 1769 decree to hold

---

105 AUST, Pangasinan 3, rollo 50, no. 14. The confusion in the realm of implementation was exemplified by a woman's appeal regarding a broken marriage promise and her demand for restitution of gifts, addressed to the *alcalde mayor* of the province of Pangasinan in northern Luzon. Having been first arraigned in her town, she was told afterwards by the *escribano* in another town that her case belonged to the ecclesiastical jurisdiction. She ended up subjected to public penance by the *vicar forane*.

106 Murillo Velarde, *Curso de derecho canónico*, lib. IV, tit. 1, De los esponsales y matrimonios, no. 7.

107 Martínez de Zuñiga, *Estadismo de las Islas Filipinas*, 163–164.

provincial councils in all Spanish territories.[108] Although promulgated in the Philippines, the conciliar decrees were never ratified, neither by the Spanish Crown nor by the Holy See. The synod was held two years after the Council. Like the Council, its decrees were published without approval of colonial civil authorities; thus, they were also not ratified. The conciliar decree on marriage recapitulated, among other aspects, the perceived status of the customs that ecclesiastical authorities wished to temper. The scenario presented, which relied heavily on pre-conciliar reports, did not vary much from the earlier observations recorded in the handbooks for clergy as well as in civil and ecclesiastical laws.[109] As Schafer Williams noted, the aforementioned decree gives "a picture of the conflict between immemorial Philippine practices and the Christian requirements".[110]

The first four canons under the decree on marriage dealt with *dote* and *servicio personal* (*servitium personale*). The Council acknowledged the "deep roots" of the tradition of brideservice. Although it was forbidden it had not been eradicated as the natives found ways to avoid it coming to the attention of parish priests. The Council was concerned with invalid marriages resulting from canonical impediments, particularly those arising from the groom's illicit relationships with the bride's sisters. It entrusted parish priests with the strict duty of eliminating *servicio personal* and investigating cases of violation; absent any canonical impediments, they were also to facilitate marriage for engaged couples to avoid delays and thereby prevent premarital relations and cohabitation. The Council also declared that the bride's parents, when proven culpable, should restitute to the groom whatever he had given them by way of service and imposed on them the penance of declaring their guilt for three days in church. Similarly, *pasusu*, the sum of money given to the bride's mother, was condemned with the corresponding penance and restitution.[111] The decree on the annual episcopal visitation determined that one of the matters of inquiry in relation to marriage was whether the traditional brideservice and gift-giving persisted.[112]

---

108 Schumacher, "The Manila Council of 1771", 120–124; Williams, "The First Provincial Council of Manila", 39–40, 46–47.

109 See the report of the Franciscan Fr. Maceyra (Pérez, "Informe del P. Francisco Antonio Maceyra"). For Augustinian reports, see Pérez, *Relaciones Agustinianas de las razas del norte de Luzon*, 249, cited in Sison, "The First Philippine Provincial Council", 48.

110 Williams, "The First Provincial Council of Manila", 45.

111 Bantigue, *The Provincial Council of Manila*, 121–122; Actio v, tit. ii, decr. 7, *De sacramento matrimonii,* cans. 1–4. According to the Council, *bigay-kaya* was a custom peculiar to Chinese mestizos. The extent to which the practice had become predominantly identified with that ethnic group has yet to be verified.

112 Bantigue, *The Provincial Council of Manila,* actio II, decr. 1, *De visitatione annua,* can. 5, 192.

The Synod of Calasiao approached the same issues in a more benign pastoral manner, emphasizing the sanctity of the sacrament of marriage for which the chastity of the bride was of key importance. Preaching and spiritual guidance were to be the principal means for explaining the doctrine on the sacrament. To avoid delaying marriages, the Synod instructed the natives and their parents to inform the parish priest of their engagement, after which the priest had to ensure that the couple be wedded within a month. While the Synod likewise recognized that the inability of the groom to provide the gift to the bride's mother and grandmother was a common cause of postponement of marriage, it did not recommend doing away with the practice; instead, it suggested a reasonable, more affordable sum of 20 pesos in silver or gold for wealthy individuals and 15 for the rest.[113]

The discourse on *dote* and *servicio personal* by colonial authorities and the resulting normative interventions ultimately aimed at instituting Tridentine marriage, which consisted of the exchange of matrimonial consent before the parish priest and witnesses. So as not to prolong the betrothal stage, couples were urged to marry any time of the liturgical year and leave the nuptial Masses for later in the periods allowed, that is, before Advent and after Epiphany and before Lent and after the end of the Easter octave. As further facilitation, the Archbishop of Manila Miguel García Serrano (1618–1629) authorized that in *visitas* (remote villages) and *rancherías* (hamlets) nuptial blessings might be given even during the prohibited period.[114] The deplored delays in weddings and cohabitation out of wedlock clearly ran contrary to the Church's endeavor to promote canonical marriage. In addition, since only Church marriage was considered legitimate, the colonial tribute lists were based on the canonical records: the number of tributaries and, among them, married couples.[115] Therefore, it was in the interest of secular authorities to have marital unions in order and duly documented. Another angle from which to view the discourse is that, prior to the Council of Trent, canon law had qualified that sexual relations

113 Smith, "The Acts of the Synod of Calasiao", 104–105. This translation does not mark the division into acts, titles, decrees, and canons. The sacrament of matrimony is the fifth section under the administration of sacraments, which in turn is the third main division after those on the Catholic Faith and Christian Doctrine and on Preaching the Word of God.

114 Ortiz, *Práctica del ministerio*, § 7, De la administracion del matrimonio, no. 72, 23. About Archbishop Serrano's decree, see the Franciscan *Ritual para la recta administracion de los Santos Sacramentos*, 130.

115 A tribute amounted to ten reales with an additional one real each for the celebration of Corpus Christi, patron saint of the pueblo, and Holy Week, and another real went to the municipality. Married couples paid the whole tribute as husband and wife; unmarried males (over 20) and females (over 25) living with their parents paid half.

after betrothal, assumed to be an expression of marital affection and intention to marry (*affectio maritalis*), resulted in marriage. Such intention—to prove the validity of marriage—could not be proven in the external forum although in the internal forum the truth could be established.[116] The Tridentine canonical form, by requiring that marriage be solemnized publicly, had sought to eradicate clandestine marriages to which the pre-Tridentine understanding of marriage applied.[117]

The next major intervention by civil authorities with regard to these issues came in the form of the Pragmática Sanción of 23 March 1776 and its extension, the *Real Cédula* of 7 April 1778, applied through the resolution (*Real Acuerdo*) of the *Audiencia* of Manila dated 21 January 1781.[118] Essentially the decree sought, on the one hand, to safeguard parental authority over their children's marriage—particularly to ensure equality of status—represented by their permission and, on the other, the children's freedom to marry in the face of unreasonable parental objection. Such parental opposition could derive from personal interests, particularly material advantages, resulting in forced marriages, thus undermining the sacramental meaning of matrimony. This rationale strongly resonated in the Philippines. Not only did the *Audiencia* exhort the clergy to dissuade native women from marrying "recent converts to Catholicism from among Negroes, Malabarese, and Chinese", who were perceived as potentially exerting harmful influence on families and communities, but it also reminded the clergy to uproot the practice of brideservice as a way of enforcing the aims of this new law: "to be avoided are the unchaperoned meetings of unmarried persons, the detestable interest of parents, and the evil results of ill-fated marriages and much prostitution".[119]

In his commentary on these laws, the Franciscan Pitarque clearly wrote from a pastoral perspective. With his years of experience as parish priest of towns east of Manila, in the present-day province of Rizal, he heartily agreed with the *Audiencia* and the king's intention to remove obstacles to marriage and to prevent forced marriage. He observed that women were more often victims of the latter, owing to the benefits received from the gifts and brideservice. Parents arranged their daughter's marriage without asking her opinion, while she in turn carried on a clandestine relationship with the man she

---

116 Murillo Velarde, *Curso de derecho canónico*, lib. 4, tit. 1, De los esponsales y matrimonios, no. 8.

117 Latasa, "Matrimonios clandestinos", 22–23.

118 APAF 147/1. This is a printed copy of the three concatenated laws. See Garcia, "Particular discipline on marriage", 13–14.

119 APAF 147/1, Real Acuerdo, Audiencia de Manila, 21 January 1781, no. 3.

loved and revealed it only shortly before the wedding. This kind of situation rarely led to a happy outcome: either litigation ensued, as the suitor who had rendered service demanded restitution, or the woman gave in to her parents' wishes but was unfaithful to her husband. Pitarque strongly defended the royal decree's provision for non-elite indigenous people, requiring only the consent of parents and elders in general, and in their absence, of the *doctrinero* or parish priest. It was more lenient relative to the rules for Spaniards and the indigenous elite, which stipulated a series of individuals with moral authority who could substitute for parents. He was wary of the self-interest of the woman's relatives who, because they enjoyed the gifts and service of another man, might withhold their permission for her to marry the man she preferred. In his zeal to defend ecclesiastical jurisdiction over marriage, Pitarque selectively focused on the provision that those who married without the required permission would suffer the penalty of ineligibility for public office, even if it pertained to their lineage, up to the fourth generation. He took it to mean that they did not need to settle their situation before the secular authority that the *Real Acuerdo* had actually stipulated. He insisted on the spirit of the law to reduce hindrances to legitimate marriage and, as corollary, to reduce occasions for illicit relationships and cohabitation.[120]

7 Conclusion

In the earliest Spanish accounts on indigenous society and culture, the term *dote* was used to denote the indigenous practice of *bugay/bigay-kaya*. European appreciation of the practice was essentially comparative, noting immediately that the indigenous custom was opposite to European usage; at the same time, like in Europe, it was the crucial transaction—involving the transfer of goods and services—in negotiating marriage. Another major difference was the destination and function of the *dote*. That it went to the parents, instead of serving the married couple directly, was key in introducing the language of purchase that eventually predominated. When the Jesuit authors from the period of contact began to compare the practice to that of other civilizations, they likened it to a commercial transaction and thereby implied the commodification of the bride. Nineteenth-century Filipino nationalists considered this perception derogatory and sought to defend their ancestors as civilized people who treated their women with respect and recognized their pivotal place in

120 AFIO, 52/32, fols. 2v and 4r.

kinship groups, thus explaining the cultural meaning of these normative practices not far from the findings of contemporary anthropology.[121]

Book 6, title 1, law 1 of the *Recopilación de las leyes de Indias* resonated with the aforementioned perspective: "Indians cannot sell their daughters into marriage".[122] In this law, Church prelates in the Philippines found the basic articulation of a concern they shared as guardians and promoters of Tridentine marriage. The Guatemaltecan social classes to which it referred proved congruent with those in the Philippines and a simple substitution of terms was made in the local versions, literally a case of legal translation. The various ordinances issued by civil and ecclesiastical authorities in the 18th century echoed the rhetoric of this law while elaborating on its damaging moral consequences. The customs in question were seen to foster canonical impediments to marriage and undermine Christian matrimonial values, particularly those concerning fidelity to one's spouse and sexual morality. The law consistently aimed at defending freedom of marriage, especially women's, as expressed in free consent which comprised the essence of marriage. The shared interest of public authorities in promoting canonical marriage as the only valid form reveals the perceived importance of the stabilizing function of marriage in the colonial order.

Civil and ecclesiastic rules and ordinances converged in the intention and efforts to eliminate those practices. Penalization fell mainly under secular jurisdiction, although its role in settling contentions about these material aspects of pre-matrimonial arrangements is yet to be more distinctly established given the lack of documentation. Additionally, while on the parish level the *doctrinero* and parish priest, in collaboration with indigenous community leaders, played a critical role in implementing the rules, questions remain as to which sets of factors affected their efficacy in different localities. The continuance of these indigenous marriage institutions points to different levels of enforcement, which in turn might have depended on the degree of understanding of the socioeconomic meaning of those practices and the limits of compromise.

In matrimonial litigation before ecclesiastical courts, the presence and importance of indigenous traditions was not lost on the ecclesiastical judges, and much less on the natives. On a fundamental level, they served as proof of willingness to marry. They were also presented as evidence of betrothal to accompany demands for the fulfillment of marriage promises, particularly on the part of the men who had invested time, labor, and material resources to

---

121 Paterno, *Los tagalog*, lib. 1, 35; lib. 2, 18; Rizal, *Sucesos de las Islas Filipinas*, 301, footnotes 1 and 5.

122 *Recopilación de las leyes de Indias*, 190.

ratify their commitment. In judicial proceedings, mention of actual practice of *bugay/bigay-kaya* was given freely as evidence and was not punished. In effect, native agency was able to integrate these indigenous practices into the new Catholic matrimonial order, cognizant of the similarity of functions with comparable Spanish institutions despite some divergence in meanings.

The consistent translation of *bugay/bigay-kaya* to *dote* was the solution Spanish magistrates and scholars found to make a customary practice that was at once alien and familiar fit within the Spanish socio-juridical framework. *Dote* was the accepted analogue between the 16th and 18th centuries, to which Paz's translation of *bugay/bigay-kaya* as *arras* seems to have been an isolated case. The conceptual clarification attempted by Paz to sort out the normative encounter appears to go against the grain of the prevailing juridical terminology in the Philippines. Considering the tenacity of indigenous matrimonial normativity, Bishop González's radical attempt to adapt the meaning and purpose of *dote* to its European usage seems quixotic. While the clergy's immersion in native communities afforded them a better understanding of local usages in the context of family dynamics, community values, and gender roles, their pastoral duty obliged them to negotiate between the regulated continuance of indigenous normative practices and the enforcement of canonical marriage. The public normative discourse altogether left out the sociocultural meanings either by choice or out of sheer lack of insight. The position that the Synod of Calasiao adopted, as early as the latter part of the 18th century, would seem to be the most understanding of the critical importance of *bugay/bigay-kaya* in establishing the interrelated spheres of marriage, status, and family alliances. It conceded to the strength of native institutions while seeking ways to mitigate the effects detrimental to canonical marriage. The Catholic matrimonial order in the colonial Philippines continually attempted to bridge the gap, to the extent possible, between Tridentine rules and doctrines and indigenous practices.

Bibliography

Manuscripts

Archdiocesan Archives of Manila (AAM), Informaciones matrimoniales, Box 14.A.2, fold. 4, Demanda puesta por Ygnacio Flores contra Nicolasa Pagtachan sobre palabra de Casamiento, 1760.

Archdiocesan Archives of Manila (AAM), Informaciones matrimoniales, Box 14.A.3, fold. 1, Demanda de Lucia Bernarda natural del Pueblo de Lumbang de la Provincia de la Laguna de Bay sobre esponsales con Alonso Estacio assimesmo natural y principal en dicho Pueblo, 1773.

Archdiocesan Archives of Manila (AAM), Informaciones matrimoniales, Box 14.A.3, fold. 3, Expediente seguido por Patricio Xavier natural del Pueblo de Taguic, sobre trato de casamiento que tiene contrahido con Maria Candelaria, 1775.

Archdiocesan Archives of Manila (AAM), Informaciones matrimoniales, Box 14.A.3, fold. 4, Vicente Hernandez contra Maria Rita de Rivera. Macabebe, Pampanga, 1777.

Archdiocesan Archives of Manila (AAM), Informaciones matrimoniales, Box 14.A.3, fold. 12 (a), Presentacion de Ygnacia de Sta Maria en que solicita se le ponga en livertad a su hija Maria de la Concepcion, que se halla depositada en las casas de las Recogidas por remision que hizo el Parroco del Pueblo de Baras Fr Casimiro Pitarque de su persona con motivo del trato de casamiento que con ella tiene celebrado con un nombrado Servando de los Santos, 1782.

Archdiocesan Archives of Manila (AAM), Informaciones matrimoniales, Box 14.A.3, fold. 12 (b), Presentacion de Juan Perez Principal del Pueblo de Malate sobre el Matrimonio que tiene pactado su hijo Florentino Prez con una nombrada Juliana, 1782.

Archdiocesan Archives of Manila (AAM), Informaciones matrimoniales, Box 14.A.3, fold. 13, Don Manuel Constantino contra Estevan de los Santos, 1783.

Archdiocesan Archives of Manila (AAM), Informaciones matrimoniales, Box 14.A.3, fold. 14, Expediente que sigue Geronimo Bernabe del Pueblo de Sta. Cruz de Malabon sobre la suspension del Matrimonio de su hija Maria Bernabe, 1784.

Archivo Franciscano Ibero-Oriental (AFIO), 88/40, Ordenanzas circuladas por el Alcalde mayor de Bulacan para el buen gobierno de los pueblos, 1733.

Archivo Franciscano Ibero-Oriental (AFIO), 52/32, Parecer sobre las dudas de Reales Cédulas y acuerdos en orden al casamiento de los indios, 1781.

Archivo Provincial de los Agustinos Filipinos (APAF), Real Acuerdo, Audiencia de Manila, 21 January 1781.

Archivo Provincial de los Dominicos (Avila) (APD), 1/79, Pangasinan 9, doc. 7, Asuntos civiles de alcaldes y de. los pueblos de Pangasinan, y Miscelanea de otros documentos, fols. 171r–171v.

Archivo de la Universidad de Santo Tomas (AUST), Libro 27, fols. 152r–159r, Dos pastorales del Ilmo. Sr. D. Fr. Miguel García.

Archivo de la Universidad de Santo Tomas (AUST), Libro 27, fols. 179–260, Pastoral del Sr. Arévalo, Obispo de Nueva Cáceres, sobre las ordenanzas y edictos en dicho obispado.

Archivo de la Universidad de Santo Tomas (AUST), Libros 60, fols. 133–134, Decreto del Gobernador prohibiendo que los indios casandos trabajen en casa de los padres de las novias.

Archivo de la Universidad de Santo Tomas (AUST), Pangasinan 3, rollo 50, no. 14, fols. 106r–109r, Quejas de un alcalde sobre intrusion en materias civiles por parte de los parrocos de Pangasinan.

Printed Sources

Alzina, Francisco Ignacio, *Una ethografía de los Indios Bisayas del Padre Alzina*, ed. Yepes, Victoria, Madrid 1996.

Chirino, Pedro, *Relacion de las Islas Filipinas y de lo que en ellas han trabajado los padres de la Compañia de Iesus*, Rome 1604: Estevan Paulino.

Colin, Francisco, *Labor evangelica, ministerios apostolicos de los obreros de la Compañia de Iesus, fundacion, y progressos de su Provincia en las islas Filipinas*, Madrid 1663: Ioseph Fernandez de Buendia.

Díaz, Casimiro, *Parrocho de Indios instruido idea de un perfecto pastor copiada de los SS. PP. Y Concilio. Con la resolución de las principales deudas que en la administracion de los Sacramentos se ofrecen à cerca de los Indios*, Manila 1745: Imprenta de la Compañía de Jesús.

Extracto de las Leyes del Fuero Juzgo de Juan de la Reguera Valdelomar, Madrid 1798: Imprenta de la viuda e hijo de Marín (facsimile, Madrid 2015).

Governors Corcuera (1642), Cruzat y Góngora (1696), and Raón (1768) (Comp.), "Ordinances of Good Government", in Blair, Emma H. and A. Robertson, James A. (eds.), *The Philippine Islands, 1493–1898*, vol. 50, Mandaluyong 1973, 191–264.

Landa, Fray Diego de, *Relación de las cosas de Yucatan*, ed. Prage, Christian, Mexico City 1959.

López Gregorio, *Las Siete Partidas*, vol. 2, Salamanca 1555: Andrea de Portonariis (facsimile, Madrid 2011).

Luarca, Miguel de, "Tratado de las Yslas Philipinas en que se contiene todas las islas y poblaçones que estan reduçidas al servicio de la Magestad real del rey don Phelipe, nuestro Señor", in Gorriz Abella, Jaume (ed.), *Filipinas antes de Filipinas. El archipiélago de San Lázaro en el siglo XVI*, Madrid 2010, 29–92.

Martínez de Arizala, Pedro de la Santísima Trinidad, *Carta pastoral*, Manila 1751.

Martínez de Zuñiga, Joaquín, *Estadismo de las Islas Filipinas, o mis viajes por este país*, vol. 1, ed. Retana, W. E., Madrid 1893.

Mentrida, Alonso de, *Diccionario de la lengua bisaya, hiligueina y haraya de la Isla de Panay*, Manila 1841: Imprenta de D. Manuel y de D. Felis Dayot.

Morga, Antonio de, *Sucesos de las Islas Filipinas*, ed. Perujo, Francisca, Mexico City 2007.

Murillo Velarde, Pedro, *Curso de derecho canónico hispano e indiano*, ed. Carrillo Cázares, Alberto, Zamora, Michoacán 2004.

Ortiz, Tomás, *Práctica del ministerio que siguen los Religiosos de N.P.S. san Augustin en Philippinas*, Manila 1731: Convento de Nuestra Señora de los Ángeles.

Paterno, Pedro Alejandro, *Los tagalog*, Madrid 1894.

Paz, Juan de, *Consultas y resoluciones varias theologicas, jurídicas, regulares, y morales*, Seville 1687: Thomas López de Haro.

Pérez Martín, Antonio (ed.), *Fuero Real de Alfonso el Sabio X*, Madrid 2015.

Recopilacion delas leyes destos reynos hecha por mandado... del Rey don Philippe segundo... : contienense... las leyes hechas hasta fin del año de mil y quinientos y sesenta y ocho, excepto las leyes de partida y del fuero y del estilo, y tambien van en el las visitas de las audiencias, Alcalá de Henares 1569: Andres de Angulo.

Recopilacion de leyes de los reynos de las Indias mandadas imprimir, y publicar por la magestad catolica del rey Don Carlos II nuestro señor: va dividida en quatro tomos, con el indice general, y al principio de cada tomo el indice especial de los titulos, que contiene, vol. 2, Madrid 1791: Viuda de D. Joaquin Ibarra (repr. Madrid 1998).

Río, Manuel del, *Instrucciones morales y religiosas para el govierno, direccion y acierto en la nuestros ministerios que deben observar todos los religiosos de esta nuestra Provincia del Santo Rosario de Filipinas del Orden de Predicadores,* Manila 1739: Imprenta de Santo Thomas.

Ritual para la recta administracion de los Santos Sacramentos y demas funciones Parochiales, Sampaloc (Manila) 1756: Imprenta del Convento de Nuestra Señora de Loreto.

Rizal, José, *Sucesos de las Islas Filipinas por el Doctor Antonio de Morga, obra publicada en Méjico el año de 1609 nuevamente sacada a luz y anotada por José Rizal,* Manila 1961.

Salazar, Vicente de, *Historia de la Provincia de el Santísimo Rosario de Filipinas, China y Tunking, de el Sagrado Orden de Predicadores. Tercera parte en que se tratan los sucessos de dicha Provincia desde el año de 1669 hasta el de 1700,* Manila 1742: Colegio de Santo Tomas.

San Antonio, Juan Francisco de, *Chronicas de la Apostolica Provincia de S. Gregorio de Religiosos Descalzos de N.S.P. S. Francisco en las Islas Philipinas, China, Japon. Parte primera,* Manila 1738: Imprenta de N. S. de Loreto.

San Antonio, Francisco, *Vocabulario tagalo. Tagalog-Spanish Dictionary,* ed. Postma, Antoon, Quezon City 2000.

Tovilla, Martín Alonso, *Relaciones histórico-descriptivas de la Verapaz, el Manche, Lacandon,* ed. Prage, Christian, Guatemala City 1960.

Literature

Anderson, Siwan, "The Economics of Dowry and Brideprice", in *Journal of Economic Perspectives* 21:4 (2007): 151–174.

Bantigue, Pedro, *Provincial Council of Manila of 1771* (PhD Dissertation), Washington 1957.

Birriel Salcedo, Margarita María, "Mujeres y matrimonio: Senetido y significación de las arras en la Corona de Castilla", in López Beltrán, María Teresa, Marion Reder Gadow and María Isabel del Val Valdivieso (eds.), *Historia y género: imágenes y vivencias de mujeres en España y América (siglos XV–XVIII),* Málaga 2007, 69–100.

Bossen, Laurel, "Toward a Theory of Marriage: The Economic Anthropology of Marriage Transactions", in *Ethnology* 27:2 (1988): 127–144.

Botticini, Maristella and Aloysius Siow, "Why Dowries?", in *The American Economic Review* 93:4 (2003): 1385–1398.

Camacho, Marya, "Mirando las cosas de cerca": Indigenous Marriage in the Philippines in the Light of Law and Legal Opinions (17th–18th Centuries)", in *The School of Salamanca: A Case of Global Knowledge Production,* Leiden 2021.

Cannell, Fenella, *Power and Intimacy in the Christian Philippines*, Quezon City 1999.

Costa, Horacio de la, "Review of Pedro N. Bantigue, *The Provincial Council of Manila of 1771*", in *Philippine Studies* 7:1 (1959): 120–124.

Donoso, Isaac (ed.), *Boxer Codex. A Modern Spanish Transcription and English Translation of Sixteenth-Century Exploration Accounts of East and Southeast Asia and the Pacific*, Quezon City 2016.

Evans-Pritchard, Edward E., "An Alternative Term for 'Bride-Price'", in *Man* 31 (1931): 36–39.

Garcia, Excelso, "Particular Discipline on Marriage in the Philippines during the Spanish Regime", in *Philippiniana Sacra* 8 (1973): 7–88.

Goody, Jack, "Bridewealth and Dowry in Africa and Eurasia", in Goody, Jack and S. J. Tambiah (eds.), *Bridewealth and Dowry*, Cambridge Papers in Social Anthropology, no. 7 (1973): 1–58.

Gonzalbo Aizpuru, Pilar, "Las cargas del matrimonio. Dotes y vida familiar en la Nueva España", in Gonzalbo Aizpuru, Pilar and Cecilia Rabell Romero (eds.), *Familia y vida privada en la historia de Iberoamérica*, Mexico City 1996, 207–226.

Hidalgo Nuchera, Patricio, *Los autos acordados de la Real Audiencia de las Islas Filipinas de 1598 y 1599*, Madrid 2012.

Javellana, René B., "The Jesuits and the Indigenous Peoples of the Philippines", in O'Malley, John, S.J., Gauvin Alexander Bailey, Steven J. Harris, and T. Frank Kennedy, S.J (eds.), *The Jesuits: Cultures, Sciences, and the Arts, 1540–1773*, Vol. 1, Toronto 1999, 418–438.

Junker, Laura Lee, *Raiding, Trading, and Feasting: The Political Economy of Philippine Chiefdoms*, Quezon City 2000.

Korth, Eugene H. and Della M. Flusche, "Dowry and Inheritance in Colonial Spanish America: Peninsular Law and Chilean Practice", in *The Americas* 43:4 (1987): 395–410.

Latasa, Pilar, "Matrimonios clandestinos y matrimonios secretos", *Diccionario Histórico de Derecho Canónico en Hispanoamérica y Filipinas*, Max Planck Institute for European Legal History Research Paper Series, No. 2019–11.

Mijancos Gurruchaga, Laliana, *La igualdad entre el varón y la mujer casada en el Derecho español, con especial atención al actual Código Civil de 1889. Aspectos doctrinales y filosófico jurídicos* (PhD Dissertation), Palma de Mallorca, 2014.

Owen Hughes, Diane, "Del precio de la novia a la dote en la Europa mediterránea", in *Arenal. Revista de Historia de las Mujeres* 8:2 (2001): 237–289.

Pérez, Lorenzo, "Fr. Juan de Plasencia y sus relaciones sobre las costumbres que los filipinos observaban en la tramitación de sus juicios civiles y criminales antes de la llegada de los españoles a Filipinas", in *Archivo Ibero-Americano* 40 (1920): 52–75.

Pérez, Lorenzo, "Informe del P. Francisco Antonio Maceyra sobre varios puntos de los que convendrá tratar en el Concilio provincial de Manila (Paquil, Febrero 1771)", in *Archivo Ibero-Americano* 30 (1928): 377–397.

Pérez, Ángel, *Relaciones Agustinianas de las razas del norte de Luzon, Parte décima, Informes que se remitieron al Señor arzobispo para el concilio de Manila sobre aniterías, supersticiones y otros abusos de los Indios por Fr. Sebastián Moreno y Fr. Eusebio Polo*, Manila 1904.

Phelan, John Leddy, *The Hispanization of the Philippines. Spanish Aims and Filipino Responses*, Madison (Wisconsin) 2011.

Rubiés, Joan-Pau, "The Spanish Contribution to the Ethnology of Asia in the Sixteenth and Seventeenth Centuries", in *Renaissance Studies* 17:3 (2003): 418–448.

Scott, William Henry, *Barangay: Sixteenth-Century Philippine Culture and Society*, Quezon City 2015.

Sison, Raphael Magno, *The First Philippine Provincial Council (1771). Its Controversies as Reflected in the Unpubished Documents of Its Preparatory Congregations* (PhD Dissertation), Rome 1979.

Smith, Philip F., "The Acts of the Synod of Calasiao, 1773", in *Philippiniana Sacra* 5:13 (1970): 65–107.

Tambiah, Stanley J., "*Bridewealth and Dowry* Revisited: The Position of Women in Sub-Saharan Africa and North India", in *Current Anthropology* 30:4 (1989): 413–435.

Testart, Alain, "Reconstructing Social and Cultural Evolution: The Case of Dowry in the Indo-European Area", in *Current Anthropology* 54:1 (2013): 23–50.

Vroklage, Bernard, "Bride Price or Dower", in *Anthropos* 47:1–2 (1952): 133–146.

Williams, Schafer, "The First Provincial Council of Manila, 1771", in *The Jurist* 13 (1955–56): 33–47.

CHAPTER 6

The Janus Face of Normativities in a Global Mirror: Viewing 16th-Century Marriage Practices in Japan from Christian and Japanese Traditions

Luisa Stella de Oliveira Coutinho Silva

1 Introduction

Since the 13th century, the Ashikaga clan governed Japan as shōguns (military rulers). During the rule of Ashikaga Yoshiharu, the 12th shōgun of the Muromachi period (1336–1573), Japan was amid the turmoil of a civil war. Due to the lack of political articulation, the effective power of the shōgun was diminishing considerably day by day. To complicate this scenario, something unique happened for the first time on Japanese soil: in 1543, Portuguese travelers arrived in the island of Tanegashima aboard Chinese junk ships, making the first contact between Japan and Europe.[1] Six years later, the first Jesuits in Japan, Francisco Xavier, Cosme de Torres, and Juan Fernández, landed in today's Kagoshima, at that time part of the Satsuma fief, and began the Christian mission in Japan. After these events, an increasing number of missionaries came to Japan, developed their evangelical mission, and attempted to forge alliances with daimyōs (local warlords) and shōguns.

From that moment, Christians began to document their life, their preaching, and their mission in Japan. Today, this corpus of sources can be found in different parts of the world in Jesuit, Franciscan, and Dominican archives. Descriptions about early Christian life in Japan can also be found in national archives around the world: in Tokyo, Madrid, Mexico City, Lisbon, Seville, and Manila, to name a few. This includes official correspondence with monarchs in Europe, histories of Japan, descriptions and letters, and instructions for the captains of the official trips from China to Japan.[2]

The same, however, cannot be said about Japanese sources about the Christians written in the same period. Many factors account for this imbalance, with the most significant one being the systematic persecution of Christians since

1 Igawa, "The encounter between Europe and Japan".

2 For more information on the jurisdiction of these captains, see Hesselink, "The Capitães Mores of the Japan Voyage: a group portrait".

DOI: 10.1163/9789004472839_007

FIGURE 6.1 Namban Folding Screen (Namban Byobu) (excerpt).
COURTESY OF THE MUSEO NACIONAL DE ARTE ANTIGA, PHOTOGRAPHED BY LUISA OLIVEIRA/JOSÉ PAULO RUAS; DIREÇÃO-GERAL DO PATRIMÓNIO CULTURAL / ARQUIVO DE DOCUMENTAÇÃO FOTOGRÁFICA (DGPC/ADF)

the 1580s in different parts of Japan and, later, in a more general and centralized manner, during the Tokugawa unification, when they had to hide and deny Jesus; professing the Christian faith and preaching became a life-threatening practice.[3]

This chain of events, that occurred in a place far from Europe immersed in a singular political context and the abovementioned inconsistencies regarding sources gathered from Japan and Europe, indicates the complexity involved in studying and writing about missionary history in Japan. Further, such an

3 On the persecution of Christians in Japan, see Ehalt (Chapter 8) in this volume.

approach is highly challenging as it requires not only multilingual expertise in Japanese, Chinese, Latin, Portuguese, Spanish, and Italian, but also some technical understanding of concepts and ideas from different traditions. Hence, interdisciplinary cooperation is necessary for opening new perspectives in the field. This is particularly true when one looks into intersectional perspectives that consider sexuality, religion, social and economic condition, and status as categories that can be studied in an interrelated manner through the lens of legal history.

Therefore, this chapter proposes that the detailed European descriptions about the life of the Japanese, found in archives in different parts of the world, cannot be studied without looking at what has been developed by Japanese historiographies and interpretations based on Japanese sources. This chapter thus aims to uncover the *prolegomena* to a legal history of the presence of the Christians in Japan from the 1540s to the 1630s, from the viewpoint of various normativities found in the practices of marriage among the Japanese.

In this sense, normativity and the making of legal history is understood beyond (and includes) the application of legal instruments commonly attributed to the period of analysis—not only normativities found in the works of missionaries, chroniclers, kings, and captains, but also those present in different Japanese sources and practices of daily life at the time. Taking advantage of methods of comparison developed by global and women's history, this paper compares this documentation in terms of the definitions and descriptions of marriage, its types and classifications, inheritance and kinship systems, divorce matters, and the role of women in society, as understood by missionaries as well as according to Japanese tradition, legal history, and sources.

This chapter is divided into three parts. First, it analyzes the missionaries' sources, particularly those of the Jesuits in Japan, concerning their discussions of Japanese marriage according to the law of nature. This part takes into consideration that religion is an important component of legal history in the early modern period, showing a complex interlayered combination of norms. Religion, manifold as it was, is a source of normative practices. The sources about Japan in the context of the Iberian empires are mostly the product of pragmatic practice and probabilistic thinking of the period; theologians, missionaries, and church officials had to find provisory and more probable solutions for questions about the daily life of Christians, sending letters to priests and theologians with pragmatic content relating to moral theology and canon law.[4]

4 For more on the pragmatic normative production, see Duve "Pragmatic Normative Literature and the Early Modern Iberian Empires in the 16th – 17th Centuries" and Tutino, *Uncertainty in Post-Reformation Catholicism*.

The idea of marriage according to the law of nature has been interpreted in various ways in the context of the Iberian empires and was largely discussed in the 16th century in this global arena as it involved the marriage of heathens.[5] Beyond Japanese marriage, theologians and scholars also wanted to know if the peoples of Africa, Asia, and America, who had been recently integrated into the realms of the Portuguese and Spanish empires, were aware of Christian marriage, because according to canon law, certain peoples did not know the natural institution of marriage, i.e., marriage with the intention of staying together forever and recognizing this as a bond that was only dissoluble by death, instead only participating in transient unions. This was important when validating a previous marriage after a heathen was baptized, so he or she would not live in sin. If the heathens' marriage was considered to have taken place according to the law of nature rather than canon law, it could be validated after their conversion to Christianity. Therefore, it was accepted that marriage could exist in other non-Christianized societies, however, only Christian marriage fulfilled the requirements of divine law. This issue was widely discussed in places like Brazil, China, Mexico City, and Rome.[6]

Second, this chapter introduces the norms of Japan in various periods—during the *Ritsuryō* state, the Nara (710–794) and Heian (794–1185) periods, the Kamakura Rule (1185–1333), the Muromachi period, and some of the Sengoku House Laws—as well as further interpretations of different Japanese sources concerning the same issues discussed by missionaries in the 16th and 17th centuries. This paper argues that to understand Japanese marriage and women's legal situation from the 14th century onwards, when women's status and their position in matrimony began to change drastically, it is important to look back throughout the history of Japan to draw a more complete picture of the situation by the time the Christians arrived. This is also crucial for interpreting the inconsistences of the Sengoku period[7] and highlighting further understandings of the beginning of the Edo period (1603–1868).

The idea to focus on the Christian and Japanese traditions stemmed from the lack of detailed research into the normative background of Japanese marriage according to legal-historical sources from Japan. In general, authors agree

5 For the discussion on the marriage of the heathens in colonial Brazil and the law of nature, see de Castelnau, "Le mariage des infidèles au XVIe siècle".

6 Cruz, *Espejo de los Conyuges;* Leite, *Monumenta Brasiliae.*

7 I will use the expression Sengoku period to refer to the years between the Ōnin wars and the siege of Osaka to emphasize the state of war in which Japan was immersed and the political forces and plurality of houses involved in this war. However, I am aware that the expression can be inaccurate due to the historical precision associated to the the Shokuhō period, for example.

that the familial and matrimonial organizations in 16th-century Japan were structured during the Taika reforms (645) and were reflected in the *Taihō* legal code. Jesús López Gay, an influential author on the history of Christianity in Japan, for example, used *Kirishitan* sources and stated that the *Yōrō* was the code that ruled Japan until this time, connecting these two periods without further explanations of what happened in between.[8] Following Gay, Haruko Ward emphasized that missionaries were "ignorant about the laws that were in operation in Japan [...], namely the *Taihō* legal code".[9] More recently, Hélène Vu Thanh mentioned the *Taihō* code in a footnote regarding the issue of divorce in her analysis of the topic within Jesuit sources.[10]

Pierre Souyri wrote a piece with a different association; he tried to understand Luís Fróis' second chapter about women, *Tratado em que se contêm muito sucinta e abreviadamente algumas contradições e diferenças de costumes entre a gente de Europa e esta província de Japão*, by looking at Japanese studies. To expand the understanding of divorce and repudiation in Fróis' *Tratado*, Souyri relied on a study by Takagi Tadashi on 'Medieval' Japan, mostly about the Kamakura shogunate and the Edo period. On the topic of women's liberty and economic independence in Medieval Japan (*Chūsei Nihon* or 中世日本), he used ethno-folkloric studies. The importance here is his agreement on the fact that practices from 'ancient' times in Japanese history still influenced the 'modernity'.[11] Importantly, consciously or not, these authors did not mention the laws, norms, and practices that existed between these periods, i.e., from the *Taihō* code until the laws of the Tokugawa shogunate.

8 López Gay, *El Matrimonio de los Japoneses*. López Gay uses in his analysis of the *Yōrō* code the translation made by Sansom in the beginning of the 20th century. This paper also relies on but is not limited to this translation. Recent developments in women's history have pushed forward another interpretation of the translation and adaptations of this code based on the study by Akiko, Ijuin, and Piggott, *Gender in the Japanese Administrative Code Part 1*.

9 Ward, *Women Religious Leaders in Japan's Christian Century*, 134.

10 Vu Thanh, quoting indirect sources about the *Taihō*, says: "In fact, according to the Taihō code from the 8th century, there are seven reasons why a husband may divorce his wife. In principle, a man could not repudiate his wife if she had always been obedient and faithful, or if she had nowhere to go for instance. In practice, the rules were not strictly observed and trivial motives could lead to repudiation". Vu Thanh. "Introducing Tridentine Marriage", 145.

11 Souyri, "Luís Fróis et l'histoire des femmes japonaises": "A côté des historiens, les ethno-folkloristes ont remarqué la persistance dans les campagnes japonaises jusqu'au debut du XXe siècle de praticques sociales heritées des temps ancient et qui n'ont disparu que sous l'influence répressive de la modernité. Des mots sortis tout droit de l'époque ancienne ou medièvale comme yobai ou utagaki renvoyaient il y a encore peu à une réalité quotidienne dans les zones recilées", 636.

By contrast, this chapter offers a new baseline for comparisons through the discourses and descriptions of the European and Japanese. It provides the reader with a more complex picture of the intertwined normativities present in the Christian Century in Japan, to use an expression coined by Charles Boxer. Thus, it demonstrates how a legal history based on Japanese norms can offer information about the description of European sources from the ecclesiastical sphere in the context of a global facet like the Iberian expansion. This chapter argues that although missionaries mentioned little about the Japanese legal tradition behind their descriptions of Japanese marriage, four topics can be highlighted in the sources, whether the documents were from missionaries or the Japanese: the ceremonies and formalities for celebrating marriage that mark the beginning of the act, the number of wives a man could have, the duration of the relationships or the willingness to stay together forever, and the connection between repudiation and divorce.

With this in mind, let us take advantage of the mythological image of Janus as a metaphor: although both faces share the same bust, they can never see each other, unless they use a mirror. But like all mirrors, it would only reflect, never really showing what exists in itself. In the same way, Japanese and Christians could not describe each other by looking into each other's eyes, but as they met, listened to each other's language and voices, and perceived each other's understandings of the world for the first time, the documents they left behind worked just like mirrors: the reports on what they saw were no more than the reproduction of an image because they did not know each other's language, culture, or normative tradition. Each one only exists today due to the description of the other. And, just like the bust of Janus, they cannot be separated.

2 The First Face in the Mirror: Japanese Marriage and the Pragmatic Requests of Missionaries in Japan

> "and when [the Japanese were] asked about their intentions, if engaged couples marry with the intention to cohabit until they are dead, almost everyone answered no, only for as long as they are happy".
>
> ALEXANDER VALLA[12]

12 "Y perguntando a elhos por sus intentiones, si determinan quando se casan de habitar ambos até la muerte, quasi todos responden que no, sino até quanto fueren contentes". *Documenta Indica* VII, 350.

A few years before the first Jesuit set foot in Japan, Captain Jorge Álvares was already sending Francis Xavier news about these 'new' lands.[13] According to Álvares, men had only one wife there, and honored and rich people had slaves to serve them. They had their own priests who were responsible for conducting marriages according to a ritual. However, these marriages appeared to be temporary: Japanese men had the habit of repudiating their wives if they considered them to be lazy or bad, often sending them back to their parents if they had children or simply killing them if they were childless. Álvares described women as white, of good proportions, and always worried about the honor of their husbands. In the same letter, he observed that women did all the work at home, like cooking and sewing, and they could go wherever they wanted without having to ask their husbands for authorization. Women were also very clean but lacked modesty: they used to wash all parts of their bodies with their hands, in front of whoever wanted to see. At the same time, he described women as very pious; they had their own house of religion and prayed, as the Portuguese did, using prayer beads. Therefore, women were not all the same: in contrast to the good women who were honored and chaste, there were others who were bad and cunning.

It did not take long for Xavier to see with his own eyes all the events and people that he read about while still in Malacca. In a letter he wrote from Cochin to the Jesuits in Europe, he noted that women had other roles in society beyond being a wife: *bomzas* [*sic.*], for instance, were religious nuns.[14] In 1557, less than a decade after Xavier's arrival in Japan, Gaspar Vilela, a Jesuit who received permission to preach Christianity from Ashikaga Yoshiteru, the 13th shōgun of the Ashikaga shogunate, described encountering an enormous group of Japanese converts who wanted to be married according to the Christian ritual. At the time, however, Vilela observed that only some of them would be introduced to Christian marriage because not all were as firm in their beliefs for this new faith as to enter into Christian wedlock and follow the Christian precepts.[15]

As mentioned above, the question about the validity of Japanese marriage circulated widely between Europe and Asia, as well as throughout Asia. In 1565, the priest Cosme de Torres wrote from Japan to the general priest of the Jesuit order in Rome musing on the intentions of the Japanese in getting married;

---

13 Carta de Jorge Álvares a Francisco de Xavier. Malaca, 1546/1547. *Documentos del Japón, 1547–1557*, 13, §21.

14 Carta de Francisco de Xavier a los jesuitas de Europa. Cochín, 29 de enero de 1552. *Documentos del Japón*, 1547–1557, 293, §5.

15 Carta de Gaspar Vilela a los jesuitas de Portugal. Hirado, 29 de octubre de 1557. *Documentos del Japón*, 1547–1557, 692–693, §50.

they did not seem to be 'internally' convinced of the eternal bond considering that they would separate due to any small incident and marry again with another person. Thus, missionaries needed some guidelines to be able to judge if they could consider such an act as marriage and what they should do in case one of the persons was a Christian.[16] Similarly, Melchior Carneiro, an apostolic administrator residing in Malacca, received questions or, more accurately, cases of conscience, from the missionaries about the marriage of the heathens in Japan.[17] In 1567, he argued that Japanese marriage was not true because they married with the intention of repudiation. It was important, however, that this intention was explicitly expressed in the act. Pragmatic questions from the priests in Japan also reached the capital of the *Estado da Índia*. Doubts were sent to Goa to be answered by the provincial of India, Antonio de Quadros, and Francisco Rodrigues, the rector of the *Colégio de São Paulo* in Goa.[18]

On November 9, 1567, the priest Alexander Valla wrote from Malacca to Francisco de Borja, the General of the Society of Jesus in Rome, complaining about the lack of formalities in the ceremony of marriage among the Japanese and asking for advice on what to do. Giving an example, he said that, upon marriage, wives would simply go to the husband's house and stay there for as long as the men wanted. When the men got tired of them, they could send them away and, if repudiated, the women could remarry. But if it was the woman who left the husband, she would need a document from her former husband to remarry.[19] Repudiation was thus seen by the missionaries as a common practice in Japan, frequent among both women and men, facilitated by the lack of ceremonies involved in the formation of Japanese marriage.[20]

16 "Tambem os casamentos entre os Japoens pareçe que não se obrigão interiormente porque por pequena cousa que pasa entre hum e outro se apartão e casase com outras, e asi dis o marido que não estara mais com sua molher que enquanto le agradar nem a molher con o marido". RASJ, Japonica Sinica, 6, fols. 4v–5r.

17 "Pergunta e reposta do Sr. Bispo D. Melchior Carneiro sobre os cazamentos dos gentios de Japam dada na era de 1567, em que pareçe foi eleito". BA, Jesuítas na Ásia, Série Miscelâneas, Cód. Ms. 49-VI-6, fol. 85.

18 "Preguntas hechas del Japón al P. Francisco Rodrigues, y al P. Antonio de Quadros, provincial de la India toda, que era entonces una sóla provincia". BA, Jesuítas na Ásia, Série Miscelâneas, Cód. Ms. 49-VI-6, fol. 85v.

19 *Documenta Indica* VII, 350.

20 "el padre de la mujer manda la hija a la casa del marido, con sus vestidos, y esto se hace sin ninguna ceremonia. Quieren dizir algunos que antigamente se hazían algunas ceremonias, mas se esto es ansí, no se sabe en certo. Y después del marido tener la muger, si le plaze, tiénela y si no, héchala fuera; y las mugeres tanbién, si no se contentan delhos, vanse de las casas de sus maridos. Y en esto ha esta diferencia que, quando los maridos echan las mugeres, puédense casar ellas libremente, com quien quisieren, mas quando elhas se apartan de los maridos, no se caasan, sina ver primero del marido hun escrito

In their requests for doctrinal clarification, the priests of Japan were mostly concerned about the lack of ceremonies. Could relationships be considered true marriages according to canon law in cases where almost no formalities were observed during the marriage ceremonies and where repudiation was so common? Since the practice of repudiation led to successive marriages, the question also arose as to which of the women was the true wife.[21] When these questions arrived in Goa, Quadros believed that Japanese men should choose the first wife and, if possible, always return to the first marriage.[22] Furthermore, the missionaries considered that incest taboos, i.e., the prohibitions of marrying close relatives, did not seem to be well known in this extreme part of Asia. Quadros, for example, struggled with the problems associated with prohibitions of consanguinity in Japanese marriage and, in 1565, asked the Superior General of the Society of Jesus to intervene before the Pope for a general concession of dispensation of power to marry the Japanese despite not meeting the canonical requirements.[23]

Considering that an answer from Rome could take years to arrive in Japan, missionaries kept sending questions to Goa in an attempt to find a solution for their pragmatic issues. A manuscript found in the Torre do Tombo in Lisbon, containing another series of questions sent to Francisco Rodrigues, excellently portrays the way the practices of those times were seen by the missionaries.[24] Among questions and answers, there are discussions of the sacraments of confession and communion, querying whether they could be ministered to Christians who lived in Japan with non-Christian women or to a Christian woman who lived with a husband who refused to convert. These questions dealt with the issue of *disparitas cultus* (disparity of worship), and Rodrigues answered

---

para se pudieren casar, y esto scrito no es sino para evitar algunas discórdias, y no para que sea necessario para el casamiento, porque algunas vezes también se casan sen estos". *Documenta Indica* VII, 348–350, §§6–8.

21 On the choice of a wife in case of more than one marriage and the applicability of the *Gaudemus in domino* in Japan, see: Wirbser, "A Law Too Strict? The Cultural Translation of Catholic Marriage in the Jesuit Mission to Japan".

22 BA, Jesuítas na Ásia, Série Miscelâneas, Cód. Ms. 49-VI-6, fol. 86v.

23 P. Antonius de Quadros S. I., Provincialis, P. Praeposito Generali S. I., Romam. Malaca 20 Novembris 1565. *Documenta Indica* VI, 496–497, §12.

24 ANTT, "Comentários do Padre Francisco Rodrigues Da Companhia De Jesus sobre os casos versados na Índia e suas partes com muitas outras resoluções mui importantes e necessárias aos confessores, com seu Index de todas as coisas que neste livro se contém. Resposta de alguns cazos que os padres de Japão Mandaram perguntar", Manuscritos da Livraria, nº 805, 112. This manuscript has been studied by Lobato, "Notas e Correcções para uma Edição Crítica do Ms. da Livraria N. 805 (IAN/TT)", Pinto and Pires, "The 'Resposta que alguns Padres de Japão mandaram perguntar': a clash of strategies?".

that sacraments should still be ministered in these cases, in order to encourage the conversion of the heathens. But if one partner still refused to convert to Christianity thereby pushing the other partner away from the doctrine of Christ, he advised that it was safer for them to separate or even remarry. In addition, he agreed that Japanese couples could marry at any time, including during Holy Week.

Rodrigues' comments also noted that virginity was treated differently when compared to Europe: according to the priests, virginity was not an important issue in Japan. Women who had been raped before would neither be considered dishonored, nor incur infamy or injury or lose a good marriage. Priests in Goa believed that this was irrelevant—it should still be treated as the deflowering of a corrupted woman if the woman was not a virgin before it happened. In describing adulterous men of heathen women, as was a common situation in Japan, the same rule was to be applied: the bond between them should never be broken. Finally, in the case of polygamous relations, it seemed that men promised to leave their many wives after baptism into Christianity, albeit without enthusiasm, which made the priests doubt their true intentions.

As the Visitor Alessandro Valignano arrived in Japan in 1579, Rome acquired greater importance in defining how to proceed in these cases. Valignano believed that only Rome should be the one to determine the nature of Japanese marriage. In his writings, he also observed and commented on the propension of the Japanese, as all heathens had, to sins and vices of the flesh. He observed that husbands and relatives killed not only adulterous women, but also the adulterer. Further, the Japanese had as many wives as they desired, although one was considered the principal. The husband could repudiate this principal wife at any time, through a divorce. No family would be offended by this; they would agree on it and even visit each other to talk, probably in reference to political arrangements between families.[25]

In 1582, Valignano went to Macau, where he attended many meetings to discuss the problems of the mission in Japan, which was now a Vice-Province. In one of these gatherings, he met Alonzo Sánchez, who was temporarily in Macau on a diplomatic mission sent by the governor of the Philippines. They discussed the marriage of the Japanese and Sánchez, a connoisseur of the situation of the mission in Mexico, Philippines, Macau, and (less in) Japan, stated that the marriage of the heathens could not be solved in different places using the same solution; different solutions should be chosen for each single situation.[26] The outcome of this meeting acknowledged that there was no such thing as a true concept of marriage among the Japanese.

---

25 Valignano, *Sumario de las Cosas de Japon*.

26 López Gay, *El Matrimonio de los Japoneses*.

A decade later, in 1592, the priests in Japan organized with Valignano the First Provincial Congregation of Japan in Nagasaki.[27] They decided that questions about Japanese marriage should be sent directly to Rome. For this purpose, Gil de la Mata was elected as the mission's Procurator and sent by Valignano to Rome, where he arrived in 1594 to report on the progress and difficulties of the Jesuits in Japan to the general of the Society of Jesus. Valignano was firm in his attempts to make direct contact with Rome avoiding the passage through Goa. He proposed two solutions to be taken to Rome by Mata. First, he asked the Pope to declare that Japanese marriages were not valid. Second, if the Pope was against this first solution, it was necessary to, at least, dissimulate Japanese marriage.[28]

Besides having to come back with a definitive solution from the Pope, Mata was also responsible for reporting these cases of the Japanese mission to universities in Europe. Therefore, before reaching Rome, he stayed in (what is today) Spain where he was in touch with priest Gabriel Vázquez, professor at the University of Alcalá, with whom he discussed the moral problems of the mission in Japan. Questioned about Japanese marriage, Vázquez answered that he did not believe in its validity, since the Japanese presupposed repudiation of the wives when getting married. Nevertheless, the solution was more complex than this,[29] thus, he considered it a special case compared to other heathen peoples.[30] Therefore, the distinction between those who could or could not follow Christian doctrine inside wedlock and the discussion about whether the Japanese could understand the responsibility and sacramentality of Christian marriage reached European universities.

---

27 The complete text of the discussions can be found in Valignano, *Adiciones del Sumario de Japon, Primeira Congregación de Japón*, Apendice III, 677.

28 On the concept and discussion of dissimulation, Zagorin says that "the practice of dissimulation as it has been rationalized and justified by theologians, casuists, philosophers, and political theorists [...] is a distinct and profoundly important historical phenomenon that is especially related to politics and, even more, to the persecution by states and churches of heretical and minority religious bodies and heterodox and dangerous ideas. In the case of those who are victims of either religious or intellectual intolerance, dissimulation is also associated with clandestinity, the maintenance of an underground existence, and esotericism. In this second form, it played a major role in the religious and intellectual life of Western Europe in the sixteenth and seventeenth centuries, not to speak of its antecedents in the Middle Ages and its persistence to a certain extent during the Enlightenment". See Zagorin, *Ways of Lying*, 2.

29 See "Respuestas del Padre Vazquez a varios casos, que de japon preguntaron los nuestros, los cuales truxo el Padre Gil de la Mata procurador de Japón. Difficiliores casus, quorum resolutio in japonia desideratur, et primo circa matrimonia", in López Gay, "Un Documento Inédito del P.G. Vázquez (1549–1604) sobre los Problemas Morales del Japón".

30 BA, Jesuítas na Ásia, Série Miscelâneas, Cód. Ms. 49-VI-6.

Mata came back to Japan in 1598 and died a year later in a shipwreck on his return to Europe as procurator of the Vice-Province of Japan. Before these events, he wrote his own treaty defending Japanese marriage, *De Japponiensum Matrimonio*, where he came to an understanding of it through three approaches. First, he acknowledged those young people who were forced to marry by their parents. Here, the marriage was clearly not valid. Second, he noted the marriages that happened according to the couple's wishes but could be dissolved at any time if they did not go well. Third, there were those agreed upon without any special intention of maintaining them. According to him, the Japanese were somewhat aware of the true idea of marriage. However, they had false ideas about its characterization. Furthermore, he was also interested in differentiating marriages from concubinates.[31]

Another document from 1585 written by Jesuit missionary Fróis, compared women from Japan and women from 'Europe' (*povos da Europa*). In his comparative treaty, Fróis argued that women from Europe took care of their honor and modesty, while Japanese women did not care about virginity, since they did not have honor, and freely showed their arms and breasts. While in Europe husband and wife shared the conjugal patrimony, which belonged to the couple, in Japan each one possessed it separately after the marriage. In Europe, men did not repudiate women; in Japan they did so whenever they wanted without women losing their honor or marriage because of it. On the contrary, sometimes women even repudiated men. Further, abortion, which was not so frequent in Europe, was common in Japan with some women having it done more than 20 times. The killing of children was also frequently committed even when maintaining the children was possible. While European women were enclosed at home and needed authorization from the husband to come and go, in Japan they were used to going wherever they wanted without the need for authorization. Even religious women in Japan, *Bikunin* (比丘尼ん), lived in open places (that looked like houses of prostitution), while in Europe they lived in confinement. Japanese women were also encouraged to receive education and they rode horses, just like men. Fróis also argued that in Europe, women cooked, and men were tailors, whereas in Japan it was the opposite.[32]

Recently discovered documents are making it possible to deepen the discussion of the application of even more complex norms according to the Council of Trent, held between 1545 and 1563, by the missionaries in Japan. Considering the importance of the new rules decided by the Council for the celebration and recognition of marriage, the discussion of their application is highly valuable

---

31 López Gay, *El Matrimonio de los Japoneses.*

32 Fróis, *Tratado em que se contem muito suscinta e abreviadamente algumas contradições e diferenças de costumes entre a gente de Europa e esta província de Japão*, cap. 2, 119–136.

for understanding marriage practices in Japan during the Christian Century.[33] Although since October 7, 1565, Pius V established the mandatory application of the Council in the 'Orient' with the papal brief *Pervenisse ad te litteras*,[34] it was difficult to maintain the mission in Japan and to follow the specific rites established in Trent because of the persecution of Christianity, which was systematically more organized since the 1580s. As it begins by addressing the lack of answers received from Rome, the *Cassos Resueltos en Goa pro los Padres de la Companhia cerca del ministério de Japon,* recently discovered in Manila,[35] proves that the priests in Japan were still caught up in these pragmatic problems facing the Japan mission.[36] This information proves that the theologians in Goa were indeed addressing these matters and that Rome was not sending answers.

The *Cassos* manuscript brings together the missionaries' struggles concerning controversial themes within their evangelization, such as usury, slavery, and idolatry. But, primarily, a huge part is dedicated to the validity of Japanese marriage. The priests argued that, despite the custom of repudiation, marriage among the Japanese was true and could not be dissolved. The consequence of this recognition was that the Japanese, after becoming Christians, could only have one wife, who they could choose, and were not allowed to take another. Even if they did not marry according to Trent, but according to the customs of the Gentiles (*costumbre de los gentiles*), the act would be considered not only a contract, but also a true marriage.

The document reveals yet more details. The Japanese had the custom of making strong promises of marriage among themselves and for their children which, according to ancient custom, as written in the document, or simple obligation, were kept although, at the time of the marriage, they no longer wished to keep them. Thus, marrying only to keep the promise, they repudiated the spouse one or two months after the marriage.

The priests in Goa insisted on the publication of the decisions of the Council with some guidance. First, during the sermons, the priests should emphasize the importance of the sacrament of marriage. Second, the priests should advise everyone to marry following the prescriptions of Rome, and those who were not married accordingly should nevertheless keep their marriages and never repudiate their wives. Third, the publication of the rules from Trent should be

33 Reynolds, How Marriage Became One of the Sacraments.

34 Magnino, *Pontificia Nipponica*, 7.

35 Ehalt, "Goa no Iezusukai Shingakusha to Nihon no Doreika Mondai" and Ehalt, "Casuística nos Trópicos".

36 "Aun que la verdadera resolucion de muchos cassos de Japon sea de esperar de Roma despues q fueron embiados a su Sanctidade [...]". AUST, Varios Tratados Manuscritos y Varias Consultas. Siglo XVII.

delayed by one month, and only after that could it be declared that married couples who did not follow the specific norm of marrying with a priest and testimonials would be treated as *amancebados* (cohabiting) and not married.

From these sources and the information they offer concerning the marriage practices of the Japanese, it can be highlighted that, although the Christian marriage procedure is clearly defined, someone can only infer, from these missionaries' observations, what Japanese marriage meant according to Japanese peoples' own sources and normative system. So, where and how can someone find another way to tell this story? To open new paths in this direction, the following section studies what it meant to marry according to the Japanese normative system, taking advantage of the fact that many Japanese sources from the period before the arrival of the Christians are known, which unfortunately is not the case for other places under influence of the Iberian empires in the early modern period.

3 The Other Face in the Mirror: Japanese Normativities

Japanese legal history is strongly influenced by the Chinese codes from the Sui and Tang dynasties. During the late 7th and early 8th centuries, under the influence of the Taika reforms, the Japanese 'state' compiled and promulgated the *Ritsu* and the *Ryō*, two books that contained a series of norms based on Chinese sources, also known as the *Ritsuryō*. These codes were in force for centuries and influenced centuries of legal production in Japan, determining the features of legal systems of different historical periods.

However, as will be discussed in this section, more recent historiographical studies, highly influenced by women's history, have shown that the letter of the law had little importance when analyzing what happened in people's daily lives—particularly regarding normative practices. This is not only due to previous Japanese normative practices, but also because of a long process of translation of and comments on the codes which took place in the centuries following the Taika reforms. Therefore, the production of normative knowledge in such contexts can be considered as an ongoing process that involved interpreters who added new features according to local practices and particular epistemic traditions.[37] This section explores how practices concerning Japanese marriage often went beyond the letter of the law, even after the promulgation of the *Ritsuryō*.

37 Duve "Pragmatic Normative Literature and the Early Modern Iberian Empires in the 16th – 17th Centuries".

3.1 *Marriage Norms in the Ritsuryō Tradition*

The *Ritsuryō* was divided in two books. The *Ritsu* was the code of criminal matters, including prohibitions and punishments; the *Ryō* prescribed administrative norms, functions of the department of state, and duties of officials. The first versions of these books have not survived, including that which was promulgated by emperor Tenji (Tenji-tennō) in 662. The version of the *Ritsuryō* we know today is the *Yōrō* code, enacted in 718 but promulgated in 757, which is an updated version of the Taihō code of 701.[38] These books remained in effect until they were formally abolished in the early Meiji period in the late 19th century.

The specific norms of the domestic sphere and household, the Law on Residence Units (*Ko* or 戸), were addressed in section 8 of the *Yōrō* code, and divided into 45 clauses.[39] A *Ko* consisted of a residence unit head (*Koshu* or 戸主) and 20 to 30 members while a group of 50 *Ko* would form a *Sato* (里). The term *Ko* has had many translations through time and there is still no scholarly consensus on its definition.[40] This section of the *Yōrō* code established the norms for household registers (*Koseki* or 戸籍), taxation of the population, and preparation of provincial population registries.[41] But, most importantly, this section also included norms regarding the organization, administration, and control of the *Ko*, the norms regarding marriage and family structure, and the regulation of the status of the people.

In the clauses of the *Yōrō* code there are various norms on household, as well as rules that regulated marriage, inheritance, divorce, and lineage. Marriage, according to the code, meant the wife moving to the husband's house. The term used for marriage in the *Ritsuryō* (clause 24) is *Konka* (婚家), referring to a man taking a wife (*Kon* 婚) and a woman entering her husband's

38 Inoue, *Ritsuryō*.

39 The *Yōrō* Laws on Residential Units are included in Inoue, *Ritsuryō*. Translation can be found in Sansom, *Early Japanese law and administration*, vols. 9 and 11. For a more detailed analysis, transcription, and precise translation, see Yoshie, Ijuin, and Piggott, *Gender in the Japanese Administrative Code Part 1*.

40 Yoshie, Ijuin, and Piggott highlight the definitions made by several scholars, such as Whitney Hall (*Ko* as natural communities and local residential groups inspired by the family organization), Conrad Totman (*Ko* as statutory households), and Carl Steenstrup (*Ko* as artificial extended families). However, they choose to "follow the consensus in recent research by avoiding such terms as 'household' and 'family', while emphasizing the statutory quality of this 'residence unit'". See Yoshie, Ijuin, and Piggott, *Gender in the Japanese Administrative Code Part 1*, 99.

41 Some of the records have survived and have been archived in the *Shōsōin* (正倉院), the storehouse located at the *Tōda-ji* in Nara (東大寺). They were included in the *Dai Nihon komonjo* (大日本古文) *shōsōin monjo*, vols. 1 and 24.

household (*Ka* 家). The norms compiled in the 7th and 8th centuries had a strict distinction between wives and concubines, specifying, among other things, that a man could have only one wife while placing no restriction on the number of concubines he could have.[42] The status of women concerning conjugal relations was particularly relevant for their social roles, as can be seen by the language and distinctions used in the period.[43] The notion of illicit sexual intercourse also found a place among these norms: if intercourse took place before the marriage, including all unions with concubines, the marriage was to be dissolved.[44] Divorce was only a possibility for ending relationships when initiated by the man, and only in certain circumstances.[45]

Beyond the letter of the law, there is still much more to discover about marriage practices in Japan under the influence of the *Ritsuryō*. Even though the *Yōrō* code became central for the newly created *Ritsuryō* state, it is not the only source for understanding the normative practices that influenced Japanese marriage and the constitution of the household. Sources for the legal history of *Ritsuryō* Japan also include, for example, commentaries on these laws, such as the *Ryō no Gige* (令義解) (833)[46] and the *Ryō no Shuge* (令集解),[47] both attempts to adapt Chinese laws to Japanese society, giving them meaning, significance, and applicability. Among these commentaries, it is also possible to include the Procedures of the Engi Era, the *Engi-Shiki* (延喜式), completed around 927. These are a collection of 50 volumes on norms and customs concerning how to better implement the codes from China in Japan, regarding essential regulations for carrying out the day-to-day details of civil and religious administration and requirements for holding office. They represent a body of regulations designed to supplement the administrative code that was drawn up in the early 8th century.[48]

---

42 Clause 23, for example, allowed inheritance to be shared between children from wives and children from concubines.

43 See Yoshie, Ijuin, and Piggott, *Gender in the Japanese Administrative Code Part 1*.

44 *Hossō shiyōshō*. The original text from the Ritsuryō regarding consensual sex or adultery, *Wakan* (和姦), and rape, *Gōkan* (強姦), has been lost, but some parts survived among quotes found in the *Hossō Shiyōshō* (法曹至要鈔), a legal commentary dating from the late-Heian or early-Kamakura periods. Also see Goodwin, *Selling Songs and Smiles*, and Goodwin, "Shadows of Transgression: Heian and Kamakura Constructions of Prostitution".

45 For example, according to Clause 28, if the wife did not bear a male child; if she had committed adultery or was promiscuous; if she disobeyed her parents-in-law; if she talked too much; if she stole something; if she was jealous; or if she had a serious disease.

46 "Ryō no Gige", in *Shintei zōho kokushi taikei,* XXII, 348–350.

47 "Ryō no Shuge", in *Shintei zōho kokushi taikei,* XXIV.

48 The first ten books were translated in *Engi-shiki*, books I–V and VI–X. Norito, the 8th book about the rituals, is also translated in *Norito.*

Other sources have also been taken into consideration by recent historiography, such as collections of poems like *Man'yōshū* (万葉集)[49] from the 8th century; archeological findings such as *Mokkan* (木簡)[50] and *Setsuwas* (説話); or tales of the period that recount the lives of the common people. The latter was an East Asian literary genre that consisted of myths, legends, folktales, and anecdotes, such as the *Nihon Ryōiki* (日本霊異記), written between 787 and 824.[51]

These sources and recent studies have highlighted that the norms of the *Ritsuryō* polity, in the Chinese format, were not strictly applied to Japan. Gradual transformations and adaptations from China took place in the archipelago, creating a system that better fit the social and economic situation of Japan. These discussions prove that the importation of the Chinese codes did not represent the mere implementation of foreign written laws, but rather were the object of scholarly discussions and social adaptations. Some specific themes illustrate these adaptations. Issues such as family and household, lineage patterns, inheritance, and divorce, as well as religion and the social role of nuns[52] and the sex trade[53] appear in these sources and provide a complementary way of understanding what happened in the period.

For example, the household statute, the *Koryō* (戸令), that survived in the *Ryō no Shūge* and *Ryō no Gige,* has references to marriage. Illicit sexual relations were difficult to prove in Japan because marriage usually began with voluntary sexual relations between the couple. In practice, the authorization to marry in Japan seemed to be up to the man and woman and, only then, were the parents consulted. Likewise, the residence unit (*Ko*), as it was organized in China, cannot be confused with a family group in Japan where, unlike China, different marriage arrangements were possible. Therefore, since the Nara period at the latest, wedding ceremonies were not clearly defined, and the easy possibility of a divorce made it even more difficult to clearly define the type of relation a couple had. Thus, marriage was not formalized by an elaborate ceremony, but rather by a fluid protocol that changed from one period to the next.[54]

49 Translation: *The Ten Thousand Leaves.*

50 Piggott, "Keeping Up with the Past. New Discoveries Enrich Our Views of History" and Piggott, "Mokkan. Wooden Documents from the Nara Period".

51 Translation: *Miraculous Stories from the Japanese Buddhist Tradition: The Nihon Ryōiki of the Monk Kyōkai.*

52 Meeks, "Buddhist Renunciation and the Female Life Cycle". In the *Yōrō* code, there was a special section with 27 clauses regulating Buddhist monks (*sō*) and nuns (*ni*). See *The Yōrō Ritsuryō Sōniryō. Laws on Monks and Nuns.*

53 Goodwin, *Selling Songs and Smiles.*

54 Wakita, "Marriage and Property in Premodern Japan from the Perspective of Women's History".

Related to the concept of *Ko*, it is important to discuss the *Ie* (家), another central and controversial institution in the history of Japan which has characterized the constitution of families. In the 7th century, since the residence was not yet an independent unit of production, the *Ie* could have at least three different meanings: a unit made up of a mother, father, and child; a unit of production including residence and storehouses (also called *Yake* or *Yaka* 宅[55]); or a patrilineage transmitted from father to son or heir, or, more controversially, from mother to sons and daughters. At this time, only the first option existed for commoners; but, in the late 8th century and early 9th century, some commoners were already creating households that were also units of production.[56]

This unstable definition is due to the fact that the *Ie* changed many times in Japanese history and was the outgrowth of an earlier institution, the *Uji* (氏), which dated to before the Taika reforms in the 7th century. Today, the word is still used in the Japanese language, though not in the same sense as it was used in the Sengoku, Edo, and Meiji periods, when it acquired its more modern features.[57]

For now, it is important to observe and understand how the *Ie* connected and influenced the inheritance systems of Japanese society and, hence, also the marriage system. In Japan during the period of the implementation of the

55 Before the codes, the Chinese character for *Ie* was read as *Yake* or *Yaka* and used to refer to a storehouse or similar structure. See Shiro, *Beyond Paradoxology*.

56 Yoshie, Ijuin, and Piggott, *Gender in the Japanese Administrative Code Part 1*.

57 The discussion of the *Uji* and the *Ie* deserves much more attention than is possible to address in this chapter. While McCullough writes that the *Uji* and the *Ie* in Heian times would mean a *Uji* closer to the concept of a clan (a patrilineal institution whose members bore a common name, worshipped common deities, had common properties, claimed on descendancy, and were buried together), the *Ie* is considered a co-residential family/household in which the female line is respected. Shiro Ishii deepens the discussion in his work. According to him, the thesis of Yoshida Takashi defended that the Japanese state sought to establish a ruling class (great noble families who had been granted *Ie*) of blood-lineage groups whose leadership would be unilaterally hereditary, passing from father to son, and this new type of blood-lineage group was given the name of *Ie* in imitation of the Chinese model. As a result, the way in which the word *Ie* was used also changed. It no longer referred to a building of a facility (the storehouse) but was used to allude to organization and blood-lineage groups, and the pronunciation *Ie* began to be used consistently for the reading of the kanji from this time. It would take another 200 years before the consolidation of the *Ie* as it was recognized in later periods of Japanese history. Ishii defends the thesis that the *Ie* is a group that existed to serve a higher-ranking ruler, ultimately, the emperor. A corollary to this is that the emperor had no *Ie* and no *Ie* name. The prototype for this *Ie* was the *sekkan-ke* forerunners and *Ie* of nobility that were formed after the 11th century and became a universal institution in Japanese society. See Shiro, *Beyond Paradoxology*.

Yōrō, it was not yet customary to inherit from a spouse. Instead, inheritance was typically passed on from parent to child or from one *Uji* head to the next. Women as well as men participated in this process; female holders of property frequently appear in records of land sales and purchases.[58] Thus, beyond the Chinese-influenced written law, other sources indicate that the management of the household until the late 8th and 9th centuries could be exercised either by a man or a woman, or even collaboratively.[59]

From this perspective, more historians are questioning the straightforward application of the *Ritsuryō* law, which foresaw patrilineal transmission of property and the house registry system required families to register in the name of the male head of the household.[60] This may have been only a fictional narrative overlaid on top of a still-matrilineal society or, at least, a society that allowed both male and female participation in household decisions. Therefore, scholars are increasingly concluding that the social systems of China and Japan were essentially different in various aspects. During the imperial governance (Asuka, Nara, and Heian periods) Japan did not have a patrilineal lineage like that in China, where patriarchal and patrilineal families were the rule. Instead, it is considered a bilateral or bilinear descent society, where both sides were important for the lineage because family structures and marriage types were much more fluid. Sons and daughters could claim lineage belonging to the father, the mother, or to both. But to understand the practice, one must look at the kind of marriage that was practiced in Japan in the 8th century.

3.2 *Household, Inheritance, and Marriage in Japanese Women's History*

Moving beyond the legalist approach to the codes, women's history in Japan has helped track the complexity of marriage arrangements and types, as well as details on the sexual behavior of the Japanese.[61] The political roles of women in the history of Japan have been questioned and new interpretations of the sources highlight a more complex scenario concerning how social and economic standings changed through time.

58 Yoshie, "Gender in Early Classical Japan".

59 Sekiguchi, analyzing the *Man'yōshu*, for instance, defended that the terms heirs and non-heirs were borrowed from China and existed only in the codes. In practice, the patrilineal succession had not been established yet. See Sekiguchi, "The Patriarchal Family Paradigm in Eighth-Century Japan".

60 Wakita, "Marriage and Property in Premodern Japan from the Perspective of Women's History".

61 In Japanese, women's history (*joseishi* or 女性史) and gender history (*jendāshi* ジェンダー史). For more, see Noriyo Hayakawa, "The Development of Women's History in Japan" and Hitomi, "Family, women, and gender in medieval society".

Although the *Yōrō* referred to the Chinese patriarchal organization—where a bride was brought to the family of the husband—there are indications that dispositions of the code were not wholly representative of how certain relations were practiced. This was already addressed by Asakawa in the early 20th century: "the custom, already outgrown by some people but still in evidence with many at the beginning of history, of the husband and his wives all living apart from one another".[62]

In the 1930s, Takamure Itsue began to trace the lines of the first modern aspect of women's history in Japan. She chose to focus on the changes undergone in the marriage system from uxorilocal to virilocal marriages, interpreting it as the major factor in the decline of women's status during what was considered by the historiography of the time as 'medieval' Japan. Her innovative ideas were based on the argument that marriage and family relations differed drastically from period to period, alongside which she developed a system based on three types of marriage: *Tsumadoikon* (妻問い婚), *Mukotorikon* (婿取り婚), and *Yometorikon* (嫁取り婚). The first, which prevailed until the late Nara period, was also known as duolocal or visiting marriage, in which the couple did not live together, but belonged to two different households, with the husband visiting the wife.[63] In the second, common in the Heian period, the husbands lived with their wives. In the third, standard during the Muromachi period, the wife was taken into the husband's family.

William McCullough's pioneer work in the 1960s on Japanese marriage institutions in the Heian period, although extremely focused on high-class women in Kyoto, suggested that marriage did not involve a clear move of the wife to the house of the husband. Many more manifold arrangements were possible at that time, revealing even more types of marital residential models. Duolocal residence, where husband and wife lived in separated residences, was as common as uxorilocal unions, when the man moved into the residence of the wife's parents, becoming part of her family; and even virilocal marriages, when the woman lived with the man's family, existed.[64] There were also neolocal marriages, when man and woman lived together apart from their in-laws. Strikingly, McCullough agreed with Takamure: he found no virilocal (or patrilocal) marriage in the 12th century. This affirmation means that the conjugal tie as

62 Asakawa, *The early institutional life of Japan*, 57.

63 This marriage was different from the one established in Clause 24 of the *Ritsuryō*. While the expression *konka* made explicit reference to Chinese virilocal marriage, the type of marriage where the wife moved to the husband's house, we can observe that this was not the general model practiced in Japan, where the term simply meant 'to marry'. See Yoshie, Ijuin, and Piggott, *Gender in the Japanese Administrative Code Part 1*.

64 McCullough, "Japanese Marriage Customs in the Heian Period".

forming an independent unit did not happen in Japan in the early centuries; family was not a coherent institution, which is why the legal category of *Onna*, the reading of the character 女 in Japanese for woman, did not imply any marital status, because a married woman could still be in the house of her family.

Wakita Haruko questioned Takamure's and McCullough's classifications in the 1990s, while also contesting another writer of women's history in Japan, Inoue Kiyoshi,[65] who only looked at women of the lower 'classes' who lacked status and property.[66] For Wakita, in the Nara and Heian periods women and men enjoyed relative equality in marriage, along with property rights and membership in the village communal organization, such as community religious rituals. Uxorilocal marriages predominated among aristocracy. But there were also duolocal marriages in the Heian period: the couple lived separately and children stayed with the wife.[67] Wakita proposed additional classifications for the different marital arrangements in the Heian period: the *Boshokon*, where the mother's wife's residence was central for the marriage; *Tsumadoikon*, where the husband visited the wife but lived in another place; *Mukotorikon*, where the son-in-law was adopted by the wife's family; *Shōseikon* (招婿婚), where the husband was invited to the wife's residence; *Yometorikon*, where the husband took the wife into his family; and *Dōkyo* (同居), when the couple lived together.

Therefore, women developed different roles in society beyond that of being 'merely' a wife. Women could exercise many social and economic roles in Nara and Heian Japan. For example, women of powerful families engaged in moneylending,[68] production and sale of sake and storage of rice, and, among those of yet higher status, managing productive enterprises in their independent residences, thus playing a major role in society.[69] Women performed the greater portion of work in the *Za* (座), commercial organizations like guilds, where knowledge was passed from mother to daughter. Among higher social positions, in the aristocratic world, men and women participated in state politics as officials, working together to support the emperor's private life. Aristocratic women worked at the courts and had their own economic independence, like ladies-in-waiting who served in powerful noble families. Serving at court was the most widespread social occupation for noblewomen, whose work entailed

---

65 Inoue, *Nihon joseishi*.

66 See Wakita, *Women in Medieval Japan. Motherhood, Household Management and Sexuality*.

67 Wakita, "Marriage and Property in Premodern Japan from the Perspective of Women's History".

68 See Gay, *The moneylenders of late medieval Kyoto*.

69 Wakita, "Marriage and Property in Premodern Japan from the Perspective of Women's History".

the political and economic aspects of the organizations of the great families. Women also worked as entertainers, artists, and prostitutes, occupations that have received some attention in research on sexualities and women's history in Japan.[70]

However, when the power of the emperor diminished due to the rise of the Kamakura shogunate, the complex family system changed again, this time to the new medieval *Ie* in Japan, described above. Moreover, the beginning of the 11th century is associated with the establishment of the *Ie* and the spread of the practice of *Yometori(kon)* marriages among commoners and the feudal classes. All institutions and occupations, including political and economic structures and agriculture, were based on the institution of the *Ie* which, in this period, changed to a patriarchal unit with one husband and one wife where the wife came to live with her husband.[71]

This change had to do with the manorial system of land control, the *Shōen* (荘園) and the *Sōryō* (少領) system. If in Heian Japan elite women's property rights were guaranteed in the form of land, residence, and movable goods, in the Kamakura shogunate land rights passed through a process of change because of the militarization of Japan and the rise of a warrior aristocracy. For example, vassal-lord relationships were based on the vassal's promise of civil, military, and financial obligations, with the lord in return pledging protection. Inheritance and kinship ties were transformed to strengthen the property by naming only one heir and to unify the family under the head of the house.[72]

Nevertheless, this process varied from family to family.[73] The practice of primogeniture was gradually adopted and can only be understood in the context of the land division system because the family unit was in control of the land and the production of goods and the warrior houses needed to find ways to perpetuate their lineage while, at the same time, guaranteeing the survival of its members. The oldest son received the largest share of the estate and exercised control over the property of all family members, aligning closer with the Chinese system of imperial organization.[74] As virilocal marriage became more

70 Wakita, *Women in Medieval Japan. Motherhood, Household Management and Sexuality* and Yoshie, Ijuin, and Piggott, *Gender in the Japanese Administrative Code: Laws on Officials in the Back Palace (1)*.

71 Wakita and Philips, "Women and the Creation of the 'Ie' in Japan".

72 Mass, *Lordship and Inheritance in Early Medieval Japan.*

73 Hitomi, "Family, women, and gender in medieval society" mentioned various cases of daughters and wives and widows that still inherit in the first half of the Kamakura shogunate.

74 This chapter dedicates little space to the changing system of division and ownership of land and the distribution and utilization of Japanese soil, but the issue is fundamental to understanding inheritance patterns since the Kamakura shogunate. For more on the

and more common, the warrior family unit based on the *Sōryō* system inflated the power of the head and his leadership over the extended family. Inheritance rules depended on the children the couple had.[75]

To secure the new regime, a new written norm was reinforced in the 13th century. The Formulary of Adjudications, *Jōei Shikimoku* (貞永式目) or *Goseibai Shikimoku* (御成敗式目), was the legal code of the Kamakura shogunate in Japan, promulgated by the third *shikken,* Hōjō Yasutoki, in 1232. This new law expected to create a new society for a new era, which was to be governed by the warrior class and their lords, the daimyōs. In this specific law, there were some articles that dealt with Japanese marriage and the modification and transformation of the inheritance system. In cases of serious crimes (treason, murder and maiming, dacoit, piracy, night attacks, robbery), the guilt of the husband was extended to the wife.[76]

In cases of divorce, whether the woman was a wife or concubine, after the husband filed for divorce, there was the possibility that the woman could retain the tenure of the fief of her former husband. If she had a virtuous record and was innocent of any fault, simply having been discarded by reason of the husband's preference for novelty, her fief could not be revoked. However, if the wife had been repudiated, it was possible that she might not retain the fief.[77]

Women could adopt heirs—a legal novelty introduced during this time. Although the spirit of previous laws did not allow adoption by females, the practice was well known and widespread in both cities and rural areas, again pointing to the little pragmatic effect the legal codes had. Thus, women who had no children of their own could adopt an heir and guarantee her line of succession.[78] The relevant article shows that the separation of the lines of succession between man and woman, husband and wife, was theoretically still in force by the beginning of the government of the Kamakura shogunate, but would not last until the end of the Kamakura *Bakufu* (or 幕府, another word for the rule of the shogunate). Furthermore, documents analyzed by Hitomi Tonomura show that women were not only adopting mothers as heirs but were also adoptees.[79]

---

subject, see Mass, *Lordship and inheritance in Early Medieval Japan* and Hitomi, "Re-envisioning Women in the Post-Kamakura Age".

75 Wakita, "Marriage and Property in Premodern Japan from the Perspective of Women's History".

76 Hall, *Japanese Feudal Law*, art. 11.

77 Hall, *Japanese Feudal Law*, 197, art. 21.

78 Hall, *Japanese Feudal Law*, art. 23.

79 Hitomi, "Family, women, and gender in medieval society". For the translation of other disputes and wills, see Mass, *Lordship and Inheritance in Early Medieval Japan.*

Widows who had succeeded in retaining the fief of their deceased husbands had to give up any personal projects and devote themselves to their husbands' legacy. If they disagreed and wished to marry again, the fief held by their late husband was to be granted to the husband's son.[80] This article was modified seven years later: it seems that some widows were transferring the late husband's land to their chosen heirs before marrying again. The *Bakufu* changed the article, limiting the alienation to be made at deathbed only.[81] This information implicitly indicates that, at this time, women were already inheriting from men.

Article 34 differentiates between women's sexual relations, such as rape and adultery: rape was a subcategory of *Kan*[82] or violation, while *Gōkan* (強姦) was illicit coercive violation. Adultery, *Wakan* (和姦), involved illicit and consensual violation.[83] This article is different from the one in the *Ritsuryō*, in which man and woman were considered equal in questions of adultery involving consensual relations. A man who committed adultery, regardless of whether the act was rape or not, would be deprived of half of his fief. If he had no assets, he would be exiled. However, although the norm differentiated rape from adultery, it foresaw only one punishment for both cases. A woman who committed adultery or was raped was to be deprived of her fief. If she had none, she would also be exiled.

These articles dealt with the administration of inheritance of the head of the *Ie*, the man, and the division of the property between the children and the wife. Each warrior family needed to maintain consistency and continuity in their specific jurisdiction and territory. Thus, now connected to the land and the protection of the warrior class and daimyōs, it was important to concentrate the lineage and inheritance in a single heir, disregarding brothers and sisters, in order to maintain the family and the *Ie*. The practical solution solidified over time: inheritance would be unitary, excluding younger siblings.

From this point on, women's property, which was clearly independent of the husband, was subordinated to the family unit and the man of the house. In addition, from the 10th and 11th centuries, women were gradually denied membership rights to local communal organizations (*Kyōdōtai*, 共同体) and

---

80 Hall, *Japanese Feudal Law*, art. 24.

81 Hitomi, "Family, women, and gender in medieval society".

82 The term most used for sexual violation is 姦 or 奸, usually pronounced *kan* in combination with other characters, but also read *midare*, *midasu*, and *okasu*. Another term for sexual violation is 淫 (pronounced *in*). In Heian sources, this is sometimes used to indicate licentiousness, rather than a specific offense, and is often applied to women. Entries from the 8th-century chronicle *Nihon shoki* show that both men and women could be punished for sexual violations. See Goodwin, *Selling Songs and Smiles*, 46.

83 Hall, *Japanese Feudal Law*, art. 34.

were prohibited from doing specific work, instead assuming auxiliary roles as the wives of community members.[84]

However, Wakita defends that *Yometori* marriages, typical in Japan from the 11th and 12th centuries, did not cause an absolute lowering in the status of women. While husbands took on a patriarchal position as head of household, the official wife was guaranteed social status and rights in a secure position.[85] Particularly among the marriages of commoners who had no assets, both partners would take up joint residency and have equal status. Again, Wakita points to the need of analyzing the sources according to status, nobility, social position, and gender.

According to her, women had responsibilities and, as official wives and mistresses of the house, they managed the *Ie* of the medieval period together with the husband. Although women were second in command, their authority was as strong as their husband's. The responsibilities of the wife of a warrior, for instance, were not only focused on the acquisition and preparation of food and clothing, but also involved managing the budget, selling tributary items, purchasing provisions, maintaining weapons and armors, and looking after subordinate members of the household, such as servants.

More recently, however, Hitomi Tonomura showed that by the second half of the Kamakura shogunate, the perpetuation of the *Ie* was conditioned to a vertical transmission of inheritance and lineage, rendering women peripheral; they were only reproductive vehicles and pieces to be exchanged in the forging of alliances.[86] As family organization and inheritance practices had changed by the end of the *Bakufu*, women publicly became vassals to their husbands and owed them a higher degree of obedience. Therefore, during the 14th century, women were excluded from membership in local organizations, marriages became exclusively virilocal, and women began, as a rule of thumb, to live with the husband's family to guarantee the maintenance of property and patrilineal lineage and inheritance.[87]

3.3 *Local Marriage Practices under the Laws of the* Daimyō

When the *Shōen* system began to dissolve between the 14th and 15th centuries and the warrior class gained power, conflicts with landowners increased. To complicate the scenario, in the second part of the 15th century, rival daimyōs

84 Wakita. "Marriage and Property in Premodern Japan from the Perspective of Women's History".

85 Wakita and Philips, "Women and the Creation of the 'Ie' in Japan".

86 Hitomi, "Family, women, and gender in medieval society" and Hitomi, "Re-envisioning Women in the Post-Kamakura Age".

87 Wakita, "Marriage and Property in Premodern Japan from the Perspective of Women's History".

began to fight wars, referred to as the Ōnin Wars, marking the beginning of a period of civil wars known in Japanese history as the warring state or the Sengoku period. Many of the so-called daimyō had their own laws regarding their own houses (*Ie*) and domain (*Ryōgoku,* 領国), legitimately recognized by the *Bakufu* and restricted to the boundaries of each daimyō domain, making laws more decentralized and diverse.[88]

This is the context of the arrival of the Christians: a complex system inherited from China, coexisting with different local applications of the law and under the influence of different interpretations of Buddhism and Confucian ideals. Once the daimyōs exercised a position of authority, they took a firm stand on enforcing their laws. The jurisdictions, application of justice, and resolution of conflicts took a more local shape, enough for the Portuguese Álvares to say that, in Japan, "Anyone could do justice in his own house".[89] In the same way, comparing the Japanese with the people of Europe (*gente da Europa*), Fróis would also agree that in Europe only those with jurisdiction over the other could punish with death but in Japan anyone could apply the capital punishment within his own domain, reinforcing that each daimyō applied justice himself.[90]

By the time the missionaries arrived in Japan, there were many codes in force, such as the *Imagawa kana mokuroku tsuika* (1553), of the daimyō Imagawa Yoshimoto; the *Jinkaishū* (1536), from the daimyō Date Tanemune; *Kōshū hatto no shidai* (1547), from the daimyō Takeda Harunobu; and the Asakura House Law and Hōjō House Law. Documents from these houses have a lot of potential for shedding light on the Japanese's relationship with the Christians and how law was developed in the period.

For the current purpose and analysis, the House Law of Takeda Shingen, a daimyō who actively fought for the unification of Japan, will be looked at. Article 4 established that marriages should happen inside the domain; any man who married a person from outside the province would create causes for great disturbance, as he may agree to take possession of his wife's estate (*Sōryō*) and send his "retainers" to serve her family. Therefore, these marriages were strictly forbidden, putting Shingen's vassals at risk of possible severe reprimands if they disobeyed.[91]

---

88 Shizuo and Collcutt, "The development of Sengoku Law".

89 "Quada hum pode en sua casa fazer justiça", in Carta de Jorge Álvares a Francisco de Xavier. Malaca, 1546/1547. *Documentos del Japón*, 13.

90 Fróis, *Tratado em que se contem muito suscinta e abreviadamente algumas contradictões e diferenças.*

91 Satō and Ikeuchi, *Chūsei hōsei shiryōshu. Buke kahō.* Partial translation to English in: Lu, *Japan. A Documentary History;* and a complete translation to German in Röhl, "Das Gesetz Takeda Shingen's".

Looking now at the *Chōsokabe* House Law, from the family of Chosokabe Motochika, there is an attempt to establish heavier penalties for moral matters. According to article 33, illicit relations with another man's wife would be punished with the execution of both parties. Unless the guilty pair killed themselves, revenge was permitted, but unnatural cruelty would constitute a crime. If the husband failed to kill the man, or if he was away at the time the offense became known, the people of the village could kill the offender.[92] Furthermore, this code also stated that if there was no man in the house, no males were allowed to set foot in the house, not even priests. In the outside domain, when a man was not present, a woman was not to visit Buddhist temples or Shintō shrines or go sightseeing.

Regarding marriage practices, whether one's status was high or low, matters of marriage would not be addressed if the understanding of both families had not yet been reached. But if the one planning to marry was a samurai who received over 100 *Koku* (石), a Japanese unit of volume, it was strictly prohibited to arrange a marriage without the lord's approval. If the matter involved economic issues, inheritance practices changed too, depending on the lord (article 85). In addition, it was strictly forbidden to decide succession matters privately (article 82).[93]

Further, in the Code of Conduct of Odawara, a fief ruled by Hōjō Soun, maidservants were reported as negligent and stupid in their household affairs. Also, whether of high or low status, women were to be controlled and have their affairs supervised, on account of their innate negligence.[94]

Consequently, the definitions of sexual behavior and its misconducts followed the new structure molded by inheritance, household organization, and marriage norms during the Sengoku period. Inserted in the complex system of land ownership that cannot be classified as private or public, with their own hierarchical system, the *Bakufu* came to favor male heirs over partible inheritance, choosing to limit women's rights to inherit and transmit their goods. Virilocal marriages were preferred during this time, coming closer to what was established centuries before by the Chinese codes, unlikely in practice before then.[95] The norms about marriage should also be applied locally: they must follow each domain's rules, although scholars agree that generally it became for the public to reinforce political alliances. "Even among the warrior class,

92 Satō and Ikeuchi, *Chūsei hōsei shiryōshu. Buke kahō.* trans. English in Jansen, "Tosa in the Sixteenth Century".

93 Lu, *Japan. A Documentary History.*

94 Steenstrup, "Hōjō Sōun's Twenty-One Articles". See articles 18 and 20.

95 Hitomi, "Re-envisioning Women in the Post-Kamakura Age".

however, the institution of publicly visible marriage ceremonies evolved slowly until the sixteenth century when the warlords (*daimyō*) demonstratively asserted their material strength in their unambiguously patrilocal marriage practice".[96]

But the decisive blow against women's property was given by Nobunaga, Hideyoshi, and Tokugawa when the commercial guilds known as *Za* were overridden and women lost even their commercial rights; commerce and industry were subsumed within the patriarchal framework. In the 16th century, the right to hold commercial properties passed to men. By the early Edo period, patriarchal authority and control of village households were firmly established. Female merchants disappeared and women were forbidden to brew sake or even enter a brewery. Women's work and general activities were enclosed within the rule of the *Ie* as they became men's helpmates. A dominant feature of the *Ie* system was that while a wife's work was performed in support of her husband, the results of the labor were considered his achievement.

Finally, in 1603, Tokugawa Ieyasu unified Japan under a new, much more centralized shogunate, which lasted until 1868. During the Tokugawa rule, as the Japanese became more familiar with Confucian ideals, it became common to treat one's wife harshly. Even though missionaries had been expelled from Japan, the persecution of hidden Christians continued. However, in Europe, Japanese marriage was still under discussion, even at the end of the 17th century, while Europeans, especially the Portuguese, were still waiting for Japan to again open its borders to foreigners.[97]

4 The Bust: The Janus Face of Marriage in 16th-Century Japan

This paper uses a more systematic approach to the missionaries' sources on Japanese marriage by adding a legal historical perspective and using Japanese sources from periods before the arrival of the Christians in Japan. While some scholars already acknowledged the importance of looking at legal sources from different historical periods before the Tokugawa shogunate to understand missionaries' descriptions of Japan in the 16th and 17th centuries, a systematic approach to the missionaries' and Japanese sources was still lacking.

---

96 Hitomi, "Re-envisioning Women in the Post-Kamakura Age", 153.

97 In 1669, the Holy Office was still solving questions that were proposed about the marriage of the Japanese. "Dubia et resolutiones de matrimonio Iaponensium. Congreagatio S. Officii habita die XVII iulii MDCLXIX", in Magnino, *Pontificia Nipponica*, 173–174.

Such an approach, applied to the marriage of the Japanese, proved that there was much more to be said beyond the Jesuit descriptions in the sources. The long-term perspective on marriage according to Japanese history connected to Christian sources shows that there is no common idea of sacramentality, salvation, or redemption in marriage according to Japanese traditions; there is also no strict preoccupation with its ceremonies and performance for the whole of Japan. In different periods of the history of Japan, married couples did not necessarily live together, children could be raised by mothers and their families, and inheritance and lineage came from mothers, fathers, or both.

Therefore, four themes stand out from this discussion about Japanese marriage that are determinants for its characterization, both in Japanese legal traditions and in the Christian world: the ceremony of the marriage, its formalities, and the types of relationships involved; the number of wives a man could have; the duration of the relationships or the willingness to stay together forever; and the connection between repudiation and divorce. These topics demonstrate that while Christians were discussing whether the Japanese could understand true marriage according to Christian precepts, the Japanese themselves had different models of marriage according to complex and multilayered legal traditions that need to be understood according to their historical context. In the end, missionaries did not indicate knowledge of what was behind the issues they were discussing regarding Japanese practices and norms and, seen together, the different sources indicate that marriage was not the same all the time in all places. This affirmation is especially true if someone takes into consideration processes of changing norms throughout the centuries in Japanese legal history, culminating in the variety of local norms based on the daimyōs houses' norms.

Regarding the first theme, the following reflects on the missionaries' descriptions about the lack of ceremonies according to their standards. Looking at Japanese norms, one can observe that ceremonies were predicated on Japanese practices beyond the law of the *Ritsuryō* state, such as the consent of the families, the possibilities for annulling promises of marriage, and the limits of age. Further, sources from the Heian, Kamakura, and Muromachi periods do not emphasize an exact act marking the start of the marriage. Since the Sengoku period, marriages tended to be more political between houses, becoming more public in comparison with the private practices from the periods before, when the families' arrangements counted more for themselves. Of course, this clearly points to virilocal marriage, although the lack of ceremonies at this point could also indicate a difference of social conditions in Japanese society—the higher the social position someone belonged to, the more goods he or she would have to share and the more political alliances to make.

In terms of the missionaries' descriptions, some of them generalized these ceremonies saying that the Japanese followed a ritual according to their monks, while others said that there were no ceremonies at all and that women used to just move to their husband's houses. Instead of simply looking at Japanese marriage as lacking ceremonies, both sources complexify the debate showing that there is no uniformity that the missionaries' sources could prove. Further, although the debate on types of historical marriage in Japan still exists, Christian sources add another layer of complexities to the period and description. If they usually proved that the prevalent model of the time involved the wife going to the house of the husband, reinforcing recent interpretations of virilocal marriages typical of the Sengoku period (which ironically resembles the norms of the *Yōrō* code), other descriptions showed that, in fact, even in the 16th century, women had separated patrimony, as Fróis described, contradicting the transformations that happened during the rise of the warrior class and daimyōs. This points to the conclusion that the procedure for the marriage could be much more fluid than imagined.

Regarding the second theme concerning the number of wives, polygamy, which was rejected by the Christians, was legal in Japan since the *Ritsuryō* state. However, there was a hierarchical distinction between a principal wife and 'secondary' wives, which was clearly practiced among Japanese people. But, again, this is not an undisputed statement according to the missionaries. Some Jesuits mentioned the Japanese having as many wives as they wanted and others mentioned a man with one wife only, which was more convenient in case Jesuits had to solve which wife was the most important. This is particularly structural considering the changing tradition linked to the rise of the samurais and daimyōs in Japan. In early periods, the number of wives in Japanese marriages was never a problem, as the inheritance system was more flexible. However, the rising of the shogunates brought changes involving owning land and its division concerning inheritance rights which would become complicated in situations involving more than one partner.

The third theme, on the duration of relationships in Japan, was also reported by the missionaries as not relevant in constituting a valid marriage among the Japanese. Jesuits repeatedly mentioned the temporary nature of unions and how short they could be; sometimes marriages lasted only some months. This finding was essential to the characterization of the Christian marriage which could only be true if the couple intended to stay together forever. In their sources, there is repetitive information on how the Japanese did not want to stay eternally united and that repudiation, our next topic, was in their thoughts since before the marriage began as a possibility they could resort to when one of the spouses did not want to stay in the union. Indeed, the stability of the relations was not relevant for the marriage. This can be inferred by the possibility of marrying and remarrying during many centuries in Japan, which was negotiated by the families, as well as the possibility of sending women away. In fact, for the Japanese, family relationships were not a permanent institution throughout the historical periods and, as such, the willingness to stay together forever could not be understood as the core concept for the union as this was as difficult for them to grasp as the notion of an inner will.

Finally, the fourth theme, repudiation, is important because the many different ways of getting a divorce were common in Japan since the *Ritsuryō* state, although the process was different for a man and for a woman, particularly for remarrying. The *Yōrō* code itself and the practices since the Nara period seemed to be congruent on this matter. But in the Sengoku period, divorcing would not have been possible in some houses' laws without the lord's authorization, pointing to the political consequences of such a decision. This points to the necessity of a deeper analysis of possibly contrasting information between practices and norms established by the unstable governance in this period. Jesuits, from their side, observed in their reports that, after being repudiated, women were sent back to their parents' houses. Others tried to find reasons for the repudiation and separation, distinguishing a good and a bad woman, or stating general descriptions, such as separation for a small incident. Again, there are indications in the sources that divorce was a very well-known institution for the Japanese and was commonly practiced throughout the centuries. In Europe, although divorce was also possible under some circumstances in the ecclesiastical jurisdiction, to the Jesuits the Japanese conditions seemed to be much more trivial and flexible than those of the Europeans.

5 Conclusions

As the missionaries did not have a complex idea about the true intentions of the Japanese because of the conditions of the mission, the differences of the cultures that met for the first time, and the difficulties caused by misunderstandings due to language, it is perhaps only now possible to take a closer look at the descriptions of the missionaries according to a legal history perspective that incorporates Japanese sources. Scholars insisted on writing the history of the Christian Century in Japan using only missionaries' sources, even when they were trying to decipher the (inner) motivations of the converted Japanese.

Therefore, this chapter insists, first, that scholars should interpret this period of Japanese and Iberian histories using the most sources possible in a connected way, overcoming the tendency to rely only on Christian ones.

Second, a specific legal historical approach can offer tools for an even more complex interpretation of the sources. Third, recent developments in women's history in Japan can contribute to the development of a women's legal history based on normativities as a methodological tool to read legal history beyond written laws and closer to practices. This proposal, defended in this paper, can complexify specific institutions and behaviors in the Christian Century in Japan, help to understand the discrepancy among missionaries' descriptions, and question a static view on Japanese normativities by highlighting the difference in practices in various places of Japan in the 16th and 17th centuries.

As this initial analysis shows, this research requires much more development considering that there is a complexity that can only be understood if legal history is viewed not as a single process of reading written laws, but as a complex process always in the making that includes practices, norms, principles, discourses and rules that vary according to places, institutions, and conflicts connected to a global world. This is true in different stages at this point: in deepening the application of the *Ritsuryō* based on other sources and in the necessity to go further in the study of normativities through the Nara, Heian, Kamakura, Muromachi, and Sengoku periods. For this last one, it is now imperative that the house laws of daimyōs, who were politically and religiously closer to the missionaries, are studied in order to problematize a more explicit relation between local governance and the Japan mission. This could help to connect the documents from the houses of the Sengoku period to the specific relations they had with Christians and explore in depth the Christian Japanese that changed the practices of religious rituals in Japan.

Bibliography

Manuscripts

Archivo de la Universidad de Santo Tomas (AUST), Manila. Varios Tratados Manuscritos y Varias Consultas. Siglo XVII, 1–427.

Arquivo Nacional da Torre do Tombo (ANTT), Lisboa, Comentários do Padre Francisco Rodrigues Da Companhia De Jesus sobre os casos versados na Índia e suas partes com muitas outras resoluções mui importantes e necessárias aos confessores, com seu Index de todas as coisas que neste livro se contém. Resposta de alguns cazos que os padres de Japão Mandaram perguntar, Manuscritos da Livraria, no. 805 (Codex 805).

Biblioteca da Ajuda (BA), Lisboa, Jesuítas na Ásia, Série Miscelâneas, Cód. Ms. 49-VI-6.

Hossō shiyōshō, 1662, digitalized by Waseda University. See: http://www.wul.waseda.ac.jp/kotenseki/html/wa03/wa03_02482/index.html (last accessed 04.18.2021).

Roman Archives of the Society of Jesus (RASJ), Rome, Japonica Sinica, 6, 4v–5r.

Printed Sources

Documenta Indica VI (1563–1566), edited by Wicki, Josef, Rome 1948.
Documenta Indica VII (1566–1569), edited by Wicki, Joseph, Rome 1962.
Documentos del Japón, 1547–1557, Monumenta Historica Societatis Iesu, editados y anotados por Juan Ruiz-de-Medina, Rome 1990.
Fróis, Luís, *Tratado em que se contem muito suscinta e abreviadamente algumas contradictões e diferenças de custumes antre a gente de Europa e esta Provincia de Japão*, Tokyo 1955.
The Laws of the Muromachi Bakufu. Kemmu Shikimoku (1336) & Muromachi Bakufu Tsuikahō. trans. Kenneth A. Grossberg and Kanamoto Nobuhisa, Tōkyō 1981.
Leite, Serafim, *Monumenta Brasiliae*, tomo 1, Rome 1956.
López Gay, Jesus, *El Matrimonio de los Japoneses: Problema y Soluciones según un ms. inédito de Gil de la Mata*, Rome 1964.
López Gay, Jesus, "Un Documento Inédito del P.G. Vázquez (1549–1604) sobre los Problemas Morales del Japón", in *Monumenta Nipponica* 16:1–2 (1960): 118–160.
Magnino, Leo, *Pontificia Nipponica. Le relazioni tra la Santa Sede e il Giappone attraverso i documenti pontifici. Parte prima* (s. *XVI–XVII*), Rome 1947.
Miraculous Stories from the Japanese Buddhist Tradition. The Nihon Ryōiki of the Monk Kyōkai, trans. and edited Kyoko Motomochi, Nakamura, London 1973.
Philippi, Donald, *Norito: A translation of the ancient Japanese rituals prayers*, New Jersey 1990.
Röhl, Wilhelm, "Das Gesetz Takeda Shingen's", in *Oriens Extremus* 6:2 (1959): 210–235.
Shintei zōho kokushi taikei, XXII, Tōkyō 1939, "Ryō no Gige".
Shintei zōho kokushi taikei, XXIV, Tōkyō 1966, "Ryō no Shuge".
Steenstrup, Carl, "Hōjō Sōun's Twenty-One Articles: The Code of Conduct of the Odawara Hōjō", in *Monumenta Nipponica* 29:3 (1974): 283–303.
Valignano, Alejandro, *Sumario de las Cosas de Japon (1592)*, Tokyo 1954.
Valignano, Alejandro, *Adiciones del Sumario de Japon (1583)*, Tokyo 1954.
Vera Cruz, Antonio de la, *Espejo de los Conyuges* (1556), trans. Carolina Ponce Hernández, México 2007.
Yoshie, Akiko, Ijuin, Yōko and Piggott, Joan, 日本令にみるジェンダーその(1)戸令, *Gender in the Japanese Administrative Code Part 1: Laws on Residence Units*, Ritsuryō Translation project, USC Project for Premodern Japan Studies.
Yoshie, Akiko, Ijuin, Yōko and Piggott, Joan, 日本令にみるジェンダーその(2)後宮職員令(上), *Gender in the Japanese Administrative Code: Laws on Officials in the Back Palace(1)*, Ritsuryō Translation project, USC Project for Premodern Japan Studies.

Literature

Asakawa, Kenichi, *The early institutional life of Japan*, Tokyo 1903.
Boxer, Charles Ralph, *The Christian Century in Japan. 1549–1650*, Manchester 1993.

Castelnau, Charlotte de, "Le mariage des infidèles au XVIe siècle : doutes missionnaires et autorité pontificale", in: *Mélanges de l'Ecole française de Rome. Italie et Méditerranée*, tome 121, no. (2009), Administrer les sacrements em Europe et au Nouveau Monde : la curie romaine et les dubia circa sacramenta, 95–121.

Duve, Thomas, "Pragmatic Normative Literature and the Early Modern Iberian Empires in the 16th – 17th Centuries, in Duve, Thomas, Otto Danwerth (eds.), *Knowledge of the pragmatici: Legal and Moral Theological Literature and the Formation of Early Modern Ibero-America*, vol. 1, Leiden 2020.

Ehalt, Rômulo da Silva, "Goa no Iezusukai Shingakusha to Nihon no Doreika Mondai", in: *Kirishitan Bunka Kenkyukai Kaiho*, 154, Kirishitan Bunka Kenkyuka (2019): 1–14.

Ehalt, Rômulo da Silva, "Casuística nos Trópicos: a pragmática teológico-moral de Francisco Rodrigues na Ásia portuguesa (séculos XVI e XVII)", in *Revista de História da Sociedade e da Cultura* 19 (2019): 399–418.

Engi-shiki: Procedures of the Engi era, trans. Felicia Gressit Bock, books I–V, Tōkyō 1970.

Engi-shiki: Procedures of the Engi era, trans. Felicia Gressit Bock, books VI–X, Tōkyō 1972.

Gay, Suzanne Marie, *The moneylenders of late medieval Kyoto*, Honolulu 2001.

Goodwin, Janet, *Selling Songs and Smiles. The Sex Trade in Heian and Kamakura Japan*, Honolulu 2007.

Goodwin, Janet, "Shadows of Transgression: Heian and Kamakura constructions of Prostitution", in *Monumenta Nipponica* 55:3 (2000): 327–368.

Hall, John Carrey, *Japanese Feudal Law. Studies in Japanese Law and Government*. Washington 1979.

Hayakawa, Noriyo, "The Development of Women's History in Japan", in: Offen, Karen, Pierson, Ruth Roach, Rendall, Jane (eds.), *Writing Women's History: International Perspectives*, Basingstoke 1991.

Hesselink, Reinier, "The Capitães Mores of the Japan Voyage: a group portrait", in *International Journal of Asian Studies* 9:1 (2012): 1–41.

Hideo Lavy, Ian, *The Ten Thousand Leaves*. A Translation of the Man'Yōshū, Japan's Premier Anthology of Classical Poetry, Princeton 1981.

Igawa, Kenji, "The encounter between Europe and Japan", in: *Acta Asiatica. Bulletin of the Institute of Eastern Culture*, Intercultural Contact in Medieval Japan 13 (2012): 77–94.

Inoue, Mitsusada, *Ritsuryō*, Nihon shisō taikei 3, Tōkyō 1976.

Inoue, Kiyoshi, *Nihon joseishi* 1, Kyōtō 1952.

Ishii Shiro, *Beyond Paradoxology. Searching for the logic of Japanese History*, Tōkyō 2007.

Jansen, Marius B., "Tosa in the Sixteenth Century: The 100 Article Code of Chosokabe Motochika", in Hall, John Whitney, Jansen, Marius B. (eds.), *Studies in the Institutional History of Early Modern Japan*, Princeton 2015.

Katsumata, Shizuo and Collcutt, Martin, “The development of Sengoku Law”, in Hall, John Whitney, Nagahara, Keiji and Yamamura, Kōzō (eds.), *Japan Before Tokugawa*, Princeton 1981.

Lobato, Manuel, “Notas e Correcções para uma Edição Crítica do Ms. da Livraria N. 805 (IAN/TT), a Propósito da Publicação de um Tratado do Pe. Manuel de Carvalho SJ”, in *Anais de História de Além-Mar* 3 (2002): 389–408.

Lu, David J., *Japan. A Documentary History. Volume 1. The dawn of history to the late Tokugawa Period*, London 2010.

Mass, Jeffrey, *Lordship and Inheritance in Early Medieval Japan. A Study Of The Kamakura Sōryō System*, Stanford 1989.

Mccullough, William H., “Japanese Marriage Customs in the Heian Period”, in *Harvard Journal of Asiatic Studies* 27 (1967): 103–167.

Meeks, Lori, “Buddhist Renunciation and the Female Life Cycle: Understanding Nunhood in Heian and Kamakura Japan”, in *Harvard Journal of Asiatic Studies* 70:1 (2010): 1–59.

Piggott, Joan, “Keeping Up With the Past. New Discoveries Enrich Our Views of History”, in *Monumenta Nipponica* 38:3 (1983): 313–319.

Piggott, Joan, “Mokkan. Wooden Documents from the Nara Period”, in *Monumenta Nipponica* 45:4 (1990): 449–470.

Piggott, Joan, *The Yōrō Ritsuryō Sōniryō. Laws on Monks and Nuns,* Ritsuryō Translation project, USC Project for Premodern Japan Studies, Los Angeles, http://www.uscppjs.org/ritsury-translation-project (last accessed 04.18.2021).

Pinto, Ana Fernandes, and Pires, Silvana Remédio, “The ‘Resposta que alguns Padres de Japão mandaram perguntar’: a clash of strategies?”, in *Bulletin of Portuguese/Japanese Studies* 10–11 (2005): 9–60.

Reynolds, Philip, *How Marriage Became One of the Sacraments. The Sacramental Theology of Marriage from its Medieval Origins to the Council of Trent*, Cambridge 2016.

Sansom, George Bailey, “Early Japanese law and administration”, in *Transactions of the Asiatic Society of Japan* 2, vol. 9 and *Transactions of the Asiatic Society of Japan* 2, vol. 11, Tokyo 1932–1933.

Satō, Shin’ichi and Ikeuchi, Yoshisuke, *Chūsei hōsei shiryōshu, Buke kahō*, Tōkyō 1965.

Satō, Shin’ichi and Ikeuchi, Yoshisuke, *Chūsei hōsei shiryōshu, Muromachi Bakufu hō*, vol. 2. Tōkyō 1969.

Sekiguchi, Hiroko, “The Patriarchal Family Paradigm in Eighth-Century Japan”, in Ko, Dorothy, Haboush, JaHyun Kim, and Piggott, Joan R. (eds.), *Women and Confucian Cultures in Premodern China, Korea, and Japan*, Berkeley 2003, 27–46.

Souyri, Pierre F., “Luís Fróis et l’histoire des femmes japonaises”, in Carneiro, Roberto and Matos, Artur Teodoro de (eds.), *O Século Cristão do Japão: Actas do Colóquio Internacional Comemorativo dos 450 Anos de Amizade Portugal-Japão, 1543–1993 (Lisboa, 2 a 5 de Novembro de 1993)*, Lisboa 1994, 630–644.

Tonomura, Hitomi, "Family, women, and gender in medieval society", in: Friday, Karl (ed.), *Routledge Handbook of Premodern Japanese History*, London 2017, 275–295.

Tonomura, Hitomi, "Re-envisioning Women in the Post-Kamakura Age", in: Mass, Jeffrey (ed.), *The Origins of Japan's Medieval World. Courtiers, Clerics, Warriors, and Peasants in Fourteenth Century*, California 1997.

Tutino, Stefania, *Uncertainty in Post-Reformation Catholicism. A History of Probabilism*, Oxford 2017.

Vu Thanh, Hélène, "Introducing Tridentine Marriage: The Jesuits' Strategy in Japan (Sixteenth and Seventeenth Centuries)", in *Rechtsgeschichte – Legal History* 27 (2019): 143–151.

Wakita, Haruko and Gay, Suzanne, "Marriage and Property in Premodern Japan from the Perspective of Women's History", in *The Journal of Japanese Studies* 10:1 (1984): 73–99.

Wakita, Haruko and Philips, David, "Women and the Creation of the "Ie" in Japan: an Overview from the Medieval Period to the Present", *U. S. – Japan Women's Journal* 4 (1993): 83–105.

Wakita, Haruko, *Women in Medieval Japan. Motherhood, Household Management and Sexuality*, trans. Alison Tokita, Victoria 2006.

Ward, Haruko Nawata, *Women Religious Leaders in Japan's Christian Century, 1549–1650*, London and New York 2016.

Wirbser, Rouven, "A Law Too Strict? The Cultural Translation of Catholic Marriage in the Jesuit Mission to Japan", *Translating Catechisms, Translating Cultures*, Leiden, The Netherlands 2017.

Yoshie, Akiko, "Gender in Early Classical Japan. Marriage, Leadership, and Political Status in Village and Palace", *Monumenta Nipponica* 60:4 (2005): 437–479.

Zagorin, Perez, *Ways of Lying: Dissimulation, Persecution and Conformity in Early Modern Europe*, Cambridge, Massachusetts 1990.

CHAPTER 7

On *Gentilidade* as a Religious Offence: A Specificity of the Portuguese Inquisition in Asia?

Miguel Rodrigues Lourenço

1 Introduction

The transfer of the Iberian Inquisitions to the overseas territories of Portugal and Spain in 1560 and 1569–71 impacted the functioning of these tribunals in ways that were by no means superficial—to the extent that this institution was challenged by problems that it had not anticipated and for which it was only minimally prepared. Despite being an institution that was intended to be uniform in its organization and procedures, in African, American, and Asian contexts, the Inquisition was forced to adjust its models of surveillance as they were practiced in the Iberian Peninsula.

The territories where the Crown—and by extension, the Holy Office—claimed jurisdiction encompassed large geographies that contrasted with the Iberian/European background that provided the social and religious matrix on which the jurisprudence practiced by the inquisitorial courts was based. Modern Inquisitions were heirs to a centuries-old process of adapting, employing, and defining the vocabulary relating to transgression and orthodoxy. Drawing from different social settings of Greek-Roman society, early Christian authors employed terms such as "sect", "heresy", or "superstition" to structure the basic discourse on faith and religion.[1] The theological sophistication that ensued from the need to differentiate Christian orthodoxy from other groups claiming doctrinal authority also fostered a heresiological discourse that named, classified, and defined religious dissention to the point that it resulted in the production of handbooks on heresies, while Roman courts were making use of their own terminology to address charges of religious dissention.[2] Thus, the

1 See Le Boulluec, *La notion d'hérésie*; Sachot, "Religio/superstitio", 355–394; Boulhol, "*Secta*: de la ligne de conduite au groupe hétérodoxe", 5–33; Humfress, "Roman law, forensic argument and the formation of Christian Orthodoxy", 125–147.

2 McClure, "Handbooks against heresy in the West", 186–197; Humfress, "Roman law, forensic argument and the formation of Christian Orthodoxy", 131–142; Humfress, Orthodoxy and the Courts in Late Antiquity, esp. chapter 9, Heresy and the Courts, 243–268.

DOI: 10.1163/9789004472839_008

Portuguese and Spanish Inquisitions inherited a theological and legal tradition that bequeathed to each of their individual courts not only an organized classification of the typologies of offences, but also paradigms of the specific behaviors or practices that indicated them. In these predetermined formats of delinquent behavior lay the conviction that the Holy Office could uniformly pass judgment on any offences to religion in any Christian (Catholic) society. In light of this, the non-European religious background with which the bishops (in the American domains of the Habsburgs) and inquisitors (of the Portuguese tribunals) were confronted was not a problem in itself. Every behavior with possible implications against the Catholic faith was liable to translation into available categories of offence, being framed and judged accordingly, regardless of the fact that attitudes perceived as religious could stem from long-standing local, non-European traditions.[3]

The debate on the miserable condition of the Indians and their rusticity and ignorance, which was the basis for King Philip II's decision to exclude them from inquisitorial jurisdiction, did not alter this fundamental assumption.[4] The behaviors of the converted Indians—now under the jurisdiction of the Episcopal courts—continued to be framed in a grid of offences that classified them as "idolatry", "superstition", etc.[5] In Portugal and its domains, despite the fact that there were no noticeable cases of capital punishment of neophytes, as occurred in New Spain,[6] the debate on the nature of the Indians was still present in some institutional choices of the Crown.[7] Nevertheless, Africans, Amerindians, and Asians remained under the jurisdiction of the Inquisition and the argument about the rusticity and ignorance of the Indians was applied

3 In her discussion of the formation of Christian orthodoxy, Humfress emphasized how Roman courts had pre-existing legal categories in order to lawfully create a jurisdictional space under which offences against orthodoxy could be judged. Humfress, "Roman law, forensic argument and the formation of Christian Orthodoxy", 131–142.

4 Castañeda Delgado, "La condición miserable del indio y sus privilegios", 245–335; Alberro, *Inquisición y Sociedad en México*, 21–22; Zaballa Beascoechea, "Del viejo al nuevo mundo", 28–34; Lara Cisneros, *¿Ignorancia invencible?*, 67–91.

5 Zaballa Beascoechea, "Visitadores, extirpadores y 'tratados de idolatrías'", 258–280; Traslosheros, "Los indios, la Inquisición y los tribunales eclesiásticos en Nueva España", 47–74; Lara Cisneros, *¿Ignorancia invencible?*, 91–117; Bernand and Gruzinski, *De la idolatría*, 129–171.

6 Bruno Feitler recently pointed out how little is known about the re-entry of apostates into the Catholic society in the *Estado da Índia*, beyond the fact that it involved a form of public penance. Feitler, "The Portuguese Inquisition and Colonial Expansion", 114; Mendonça, *Conversions and Citizenry*, 298.

7 Cardim, "Os povos indígenas e as instâncias de justiça na América portuguesa e espanhola", 33–38, 44–45, 52–55.

to inquisitorial praxis, as recently demonstrated by Maria Leônia Chaves de Resende.[8] Thus, in Portuguese courts that held jurisdiction over territories with a remarkable number—often the majority—of converted inhabitants, such as Lisbon and Goa, the same principle was applied, meaning that a transgressive behavior could be translated into a crime codified in law. However, in Goa, host to the only Portuguese court of the Holy Office ever to be established in a colonial territory—and with exclusively non-European territories under its jurisdiction—the inquisitors conducted trials for offences which they labeled *gentilidade*, of which a direct equivalent in Portuguese- or Spanish-American colonial territories is absent.

This chapter analyzes the emergence of *gentilidade* as a category of religious offence and discusses its uniqueness in the context of the Portuguese inquisitorial system. First, the discussion focuses on how this term, which was specifically used to signify the cultural-religious context of "*Gentiles*" (non-Christian, non-Jewish, and non-Muslim populations), came to be employed as a category of religious misconduct by the Holy Office in Goa. Special emphasis is given to the inquisitors' different understandings of the reality they ended up labeling *gentilidade*. It is important to note here that the use of the words 'Gentile(s)' and 'Gentilic' throughout this chapter, when speaking about the populations listed above, reflects identities as they were recognized through such terminology at the time.

Second, this chapter analyzes the Goa Inquisition's procedures to determine precisely what kind of behavior could fall under the label *gentilidade* and in what way it differed from other categories of transgression. Finally, a comparison between the offence that the inquisitors in Goa came to refer to as *gentilidade* and behaviors stemming from a non-Christian context in Brazil in the 1590s is established. By focusing on the inquisitorial trial records from the *Santidade* movement of the previous decade, I will highlight the criteria according to which *gentilidade*—as understood in Goa—can be considered exceptional in the context of the Portuguese Inquisition.

2 Lexical Entanglements: The Problem of *Gentilidade* in the Goa Inquisition

Established in 1560, the Goa Inquisition was not far away, either in space or time, from the universe of *gentilidade*. Located on Tiswadi island, the court

8 Resende, "'Da ignorância e rusticidade': os indígenas e a Inquisição na América portuguesa (séculos XVI–XIX)", 101–110.

functioned in the city that constituted the center of the political and administrative power of the *Estado da Índia*.[9] This territorial base that the Portuguese had conquered in 1510 would only be expanded in 1543 with the incorporation of the territories of Salcete and Bardez. The original nucleus of Tiswadi (with the smaller islands of Divar, Chorão, and Juá) alongside the new provinces formed what became known as the 'Old Conquests'. In this highly porous space, the *terra firme* as it appears in documents, was to become a constant concern for the Portuguese authorities and the Inquisition itself. The hardening of Portuguese religious policy from 1540 onwards on the island of Tiswadi (extending to the provinces of Salcete and Bardez in the decades that followed), as well as the periodic renewal of repressive measures against the 'Gentilic' customs over the centuries, stimulated the crossing of Christians of local origin (*novamente convertidos*; *cristãos da terra*) to the territories of the sultanate of Bijapur, in search of spaces where they could continue to celebrate their rituals. Indeed, when the Inquisition was established in Goa, not only was *gentilidade* far from being eradicated, but Portuguese domains were not impervious to its influence.[10]

'*Gentilidad*(*e*)' is a familiar term in the Portuguese and Spanish languages. Still, it is worth looking at what Iberian *Tesoros*, *Vocabularios*, and *Diccionarios* indicate. Although Sebastián de Covarrubias used the term *gentilidad* in his 1611 *Tesoro*, there is no specific entry for it; s. v. "Gentiles", he informs us that these are "the idolaters who had no knowledge of a true God, and worshipped false Gods, and hence *gentilidad*, paganism".[11] The *Diccionario* of the Real Academia Española refers to *gentilidad* as the false religion of the *Gentiles* or idolaters or, alternatively, the whole and aggregate of the *Gentiles*.[12] In this volume, we also find the word *gentilismo* which is presented simply as being the same as *gentilidad*. In Raphael Bluteau's *Vocabulario Portuguez e Latino*, *gentilidade* is simultaneously "A False Religion of the Gentiles" and "The time, or the place, in which formerly there were & still today are gentiles". In this same *Vocabulario* we also find *gentilismo*, whose meaning is presented to us as

9 On the origins of the Inquisition of Goa see Cunha, *A Inquisição no Estado da Índia*, and Paiva, "The Inquisition Tribunal in Goa: Why and for What Purpose?", 565–593.

10 Xavier, *A invenção de Goa*, 122, 130–131, 170–171. For the notions of "novamente convertido" and "cristão da terra" see also Xavier, "De *converso* a *novamente convertido*" and "Conversos and Novamente Convertidos".

11 Covarrubias Orozco, *Tesoro de la lengua castellana, o española*, 434: "[…] los idolatras que no tuuieron conocimiento de vn verdadero Dios, y adoraron falsos dioses, y de alli gentilidad, el paganismo".

12 DRAE, 1734, vol. 4, s. v. *Gentilidad*: "La falsa Religión de los Gentíles o Idólatras; el conjunto y agregado de los Gentíles".

"Religion, doctrine, & rites of the *Gentilidade*".[13] These very succinct definitions seem to admit the rank of "religion" to the whole of the cults and venerations of the Gentiles. This choice of words is far from casual, as it corresponds to the definition of religion found in the *Diccionario* of the *Real Academia Española*: "Improperly and abusively, it is also called the worship and veneration that some Nations pay to their false Gods".[14] There are, therefore, two prevailing definitions for '*gentilidad*(*e*)': on the one hand, that of false religion; on the other hand, that of the collective human reality that underlies the term.

Early Christians employed the term "Gentiles" as a marker of religious differentiation for every person that did not profess the revealed faith of the God of Abraham in any of its forms (Jewish or Christian), usually connoting idolatry.[15] During the Middle Ages, this basic distinction remained in effect, even as Muslims (*Saraceni* or *Mahometanos*) were integrated into the taxonomy of unbelievers. Authors such as Alan of Lille (†1202), Thomas Aquinas (†1274), and Albert the Great (†1280) tended to integrate them in the broader notion of Gentiles or *paganos* (pagans), all the while recognizing a distinction to them.[16] On a Hans Burgkmair engraving from 1508 representing the Triumphant Church, that served as title page for Johannes Stammler's *Dialogus de diversarum gencium sectis et mundi religionibus*, among the defeated "sects" or "religions" (depicted as women, carrying broken standards, on whose feet lie deposed shields) "Gentilitas" appears separately from "Saracenathur" and "Machometus" (Muslims).[17] Thus, in this pictorial narrative, "Gentilitas" has equal status to the rest of the expressions of religious infidelity.

Since the 16th century, missionary experiences in America and Asia have played an important role in diversifying the traditional narrative focus on and definition of Gentiles and *gentilitas*, from its historical sense linked to the Greek-Roman culture to the universe of the peoples that the Europeans contacted during their expansionist endeavors. The former is still the meaning employed by Martín de Azpilcueta when he contrasted the "*legisladores de la gentilidad*" (legislators from the *gentilidad*) with the ones from the "*Christiandad*".[18] Juan de Solórzano Pereira in his *Politica Indiana* retains both notions:

13 VPL, 1713, vol. 4, s. v. Gentilidade and Gentilismo: "Religião, doutrina, & ritos da Gentilidade".

14 DRAE, 1737, vol. 5, s. v. Religion: "Impropriamente y por abuso, se llama tambien el culto y veneración que tributan algunas Naciones a sus falsos Dioses".

15 Rubiés, "The concept of a Gentile Civilization in Missionary discourse and its European reception", 118–119.

16 Congar, "'Gentilis' et 'Iudaeus' au moyen âge", 223–224; Evans, *Alain of Lille*, 127–129; George-Tvrtković, "Deficient Sacraments or Unifying Rites", 107–108.

17 Stammler, *Dialogus de diversarum gencium sectis et mundi religionibus*.

18 Azpilcueta, *Manual de Confessores y Penitentes*, 462.

as a side note to his dedication to King Philip IV he specified that Jupiter was "the greatest of all the planets and of the gods of the *Gentilidad*", while later mentioning the "time of [the American Indians'] infidelity, or *gentilidad*".[19] In both examples *gentilidad* seems to be a reality separated by time, i.e., before and after conversion. However, insofar as Solórzano Pereira used the term to encompass the customs, rites, ceremonies, and experiences of the Gentiles, he was responsible for conferring a presentness to it, one that it likely did not enjoy in the centuries prior to the European expansion.[20]

The status of infidelity ascribed to the socio-religious setting of the Indians should constitute an indicator of where in the hierarchy of crimes under the jurisdiction of the Holy Office the crime *gentilidade* could be located. From the identification of the term as sect and false religion, it could be inferred that a crime of *gentilidade* would suggest a case of heresy and/or apostasy. Therefore, it would be logical to find it referenced in certain inquisitorial documentation such as the inquisitors' manuals—not necessarily Eimeric's *Directorium* but, more generally, the handbooks that the inquisitors had at their disposal to guide them in their interrogations for each offence.[21]

Regrettably, the archive of the Goa Inquisition was almost entirely destroyed in the 19th century, with only a collection of nine volumes surviving, composed mostly of correspondence and provisions from the Portuguese inquisitor general.[22] As an alternative, a comparison with the Inquisition of Lisbon could be made to overcome such gaps. This court also had jurisdiction over a district comprised of vast areas where a large part of the population had recently converted to Christianity and/or had borders that were very permeable to the context of *gentilidade* such as Brazil or Angola. However, when looking at the handbooks that guided the inquisitors of Lisbon in their procedural work, there is no mention of this kind of offence.[23] Presumably, in terms of transgression of the rules of law, *gentilidade* was not a reality that imposed itself on the

---

19 Solórzano Pereira, *Politica Indiana*, "Dedicatoria", fn k; lib. 2, cap. XIV, 137.

20 Rubiés, "The concept of a Gentile Civilization in Missionary discourse and its European reception", 113–155.

21 Surviving handbooks of the Inquisition of Lisbon evince that each tribunal—likely at the request of the inquisitors—prepared guidelines on how to proceed during the interrogations. Those guidelines were, often, structured by typologies of offences. See, for instance, ANTT, *Tribunal do Santo Ofício, Inquisição de Lisboa*, liv. 73, 75, and 76.

22 Feitler, "O Secreto do tribunal indiano da Inquisição portuguesa", 48–50.

23 In 2009, Célia Tavares had already noticed that what she called "gentilismo" was absent from yet a different type of document, the *Regimentos* (instructions prepared by the inquisitor general and the deputies of the General Council) of the Portuguese Inquisition. Tavares, "A Inquisição e a Companhia de Jesus diante do 'Gentilismo'", 4.

Lisbon court to the point of generating specific guidelines to be used in judicial sessions. This is all the more remarkable because the trials conducted by this court included a large number of cases against natives of Brazil and Angola who converted to Catholicism, where the mention of Gentilic ceremonies is expressly recorded.

It is very likely that this textual silence shown in Lisbon, did not occur in Goa. Although the original trial records were lost, a *Reportorio* (directory) of cases tried between 1561 and 1623 survived. This invaluable document prepared by the *promotor* (prosecutor) of the Goa Inquisition, João Delgado Figueira, provides very succinct information about each case tried by the court during this period: name of offender, birthplace, socio-religious category, locations to which they were socially bound (by marriage, residence, or function),[24] name of spouse (if applicable), occupation, description of offence, sentence, and typology of offence.[25] The inquisitors also sent lists of *autos-da-fé* to Lisbon—similar to the *relaciones de causas* (trial reports) sent from the different tribunals to the Supreme Council in Madrid. However laconic they may be, these types of documents provide ample evidence of trials conducted on charges of *gentilidade*. Sadly, these lists are inconsecutive, so that an assertion regarding the Goa Inquisition's procedures for the entirety of its activities is not possible.

It is, precisely, in the *Reportorio* that we first acknowledge the ample use of the category *gentilidade* to classify a type of religious offence, whose definition is not provided by the document. The emergence of this category in the early 1620s has not been the object of debate so far. Rather, it was the diversity of offences tried by the court that the inquisitors grouped together under "gentilismo" or "gentilidades" that attracted the attention of scholars. Maria de Jesus dos Mártires Lopes stated that such charges "comprise[d] the various Hindu rites committed by Christians".[26] These terms, which Lopes recognized as judicial categories current in the 18th century, came to be used, in recent years, as

---

24 Not to be confused with the place of arrest by the Inquisition. This type of information in the *Reportorio* indicates the formal place of social affiliation, usually preceded by the statements of "morador em" (resident at), "casado em" (married in: the phrasing in Portuguese indicates the place where the actual marriage took place, which is not necessarily the place where the defendant and his/her spouse reside) or "gancar em" (gaunkar in). For a discussion of this category used by João Delgado Figueira in his *Reportorio*, see Lourenço, "Macau, porto seguro para os cristãos-novos?", 479–480.

25 *Reportorio Geral de tres mil oitocentos processos, que sam todos os despachados neste Sancto Officio de Goa, & mais partes da India*. BNP, Cód. 203. On this document, see Tavim, "Um inquisidor inquirido"; Feitler, "João Delgado Figueira e o *Reportorio* da Inquisição de Goa"; Silva, *Inquisição e Mestiçagem Cultural no Estado da Índia (1560–1623)*.

26 According to the author, these included demonic pacts, to invoke or make offerings to the idols, to perform superstitious ceremonies, to work in the construction of temples, to

broad epistemological categories in their own right, irrespective of the specific charges brought against the defendants[27]. Nevertheless, the question was raised by Bruno Feitler when he pointed out the difficulty of understanding exactly what was characterized as *gentilidades* due to the loss of the Goa Inquisition trial records.[28] Authors such as Ricardo Ventura, who also employed the plural form *gentilidades*, introduced an operative distinction between charges of heresy and apostasy that involved the frequency of "Gentile ceremonies" associated with rites of passage, on the one hand, and demonic pacts, associated with popular healing, divinatory, protective, and agrarian rites, on the other.[29]

Charles Amiel especially emphasized Hinduism as the common denominator of these offences. The author has simultaneously employed the terms "Hinduism" or "crypto-Hinduism" to refer to this impressive volume of cases which, in the *Reportorio*, constituted 44% of the total.[30] Significantly, he never once mentioned the term *gentilidade*, which means that he incorporated this category under the larger notion of "crypto-Hinduism".[31] The dilution of *gentilidade*

---

cultivate the rice fields of Hindus, as well as "cases of reverting to *gentilismo*". Lopes, "A Inquisição de Goa na primeira metade de Setecentos", 129.

27 In her thorough analysis of the *Reportorio*, Luiza Tonon da Silva identified the following categories: divinations, to worship the devil, to worship *pagodes*, witchcraft, to consult sorcerers, to consult *pagodes*, sorcery, *gentilidades*, idolatry, to idolize the devil with sorceresses, to summon the devil, oblations, covenant with the devil, sacrifice, sacrifice to the devil, sacrifice to *pagodes*, to become a Gentile, superstition, treasure, and visionary. Silva, *Inquisição e Mestiçagem Cultural no Estado da Índia (1560–1623)*, 74. In the context of Portuguese presence in Asia, *pagode* simultaneously means temple and idol. Dalgado, *Glossário Luso-Asiático*, 129–133; Henn, "Shrines of Goa", 2–3.

28 José Alberto Tavim also pointed out that the Inquisition distinguished *gentilismo* from other realities considered as belonging to the scope of demonic cults. Feitler, "A Inquisição de Goa e os nativos", 109; Tavim, "'O culto ao diabo' na Inquisição de Goa, segundo o *Reportório* de João Delgado Figueira (1623)", 274.

29 Ventura, *Conversão e conversabilidade*, vol. 1, 290–296. Silva also singled out the summaries in the *Reportorio* that in her understanding presupposed apostasy for the Holy Office. She registered 52 occurrences of behaviors described as "to become a gentile" ("se fazer gentio") and "to rebaptize" ("se rebaptizar") which would constitute such an offence. Silva, *Inquisição e Mestiçagem Cultural no Estado da Índia*, 98.

30 Amiel, "L'Inquisition de Goa", 240. Recently, Luiza Tonon da Silva must have used an analysis grid similar to that of Amiel, since she obtained the same value for a typology of crimes that she called *gentilidades*. Silva, *Inquisição e Mestiçagem Cultural no Estado da Índia (1560–1623)*, 74.

31 There is a logic for doing so; on the one hand, the *Reportorio* registers an impressive number of cases regarding prisoners from local populations accused of *gentilidade* and other types of offences. On the other hand, the importance that the cases of Judaism and the standardized figure of the "crypto-Jew" as a paradigm of infidelity to the divine majesty have had in the historiography of the Inquisition generated an analytical paradigm that scholars felt could be transposed to other behaviors that would imply an adherence to

into *gentilidades* or "crypto-Hinduism" evinces the choice to reunite the diversity of local rites under one category of religious offence in historiography. However, in doing so, it disregards the reasoning behind these classifications, of which *gentilidade*—in its singular form—was an intentional one.

If we keep to the classifications actually employed in the *Reportorio* we may notice a change in the institutional attitudes of the court regarding the behavior that Figueira labeled *gentilidade* over the first 62 years of inquisitorial activity in Goa (see Chart 7.1).

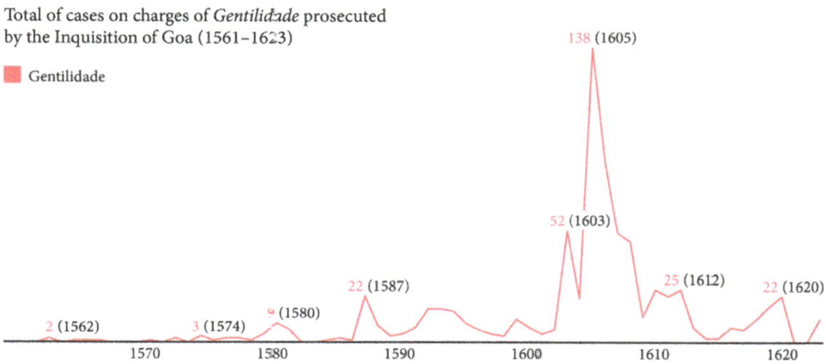

CHART 7.1 Total number of cases tried on charges of "*Gentilidade*" prosecuted by the Inquisition of Goa (1561–1623)[32]

The data represented in Chart 7.1 does not linearly represent the number of cases regarding offences of *gentilidade* tried by the Holy Office of Goa. Of the 745 cases reported here, 8.4% of them are double or triple offences, i.e., the charge of *gentilidade* occurs alongside others, such as sacrifice, sodomy, sorcery, rebaptism, perjury (*falsario*), or preventing the expansion of Christianity and the righteous ministry of the Holy Office. In Chart 7.2, double and triple offences have been excluded, thereby including only single offences, and the evolution of offences of *gentilidade* to those of Judaism and "Moor" (a category used in the *Reportorio* to denote adherence to Islam or performing its practices) was compared. As can be seen, offences of *gentilidade* began to increase from the mid-1580s, at a time when Inquisitor Rui Sodrinho de Mesquita declared the court's inability to uncover new cases of Judaism: "*o judaísmo stá*

other systems of beliefs: Amiel, for example, also uses the term "crypto-Mahometism" to mean the inquisitorial category of "mouro" (Moor) or "to become a Moor". Ahmed Boucharb had already employed the similar term "crypto-Muslims" in the late 1980s to refer to the populations forcibly baptized from Islam into Catholicism in Portugal. Boucharb, *Les crypto-musulmans d'origine marocaine et la société portugaise au seizième siècle*.

32 *Reportorio Geral de tres mil oitocentos processos, que sam todos os despachados neste Sancto Officio de Goa*, BNP, Códice 203.

quieto", he wrote to the Inquisitor General of Portugal in 1587.[33] The rise of charges labeled "Moor" had even preceded those of *gentilidade* at this time. Francisco Bethencourt points out that the power to classify heresies represented, for the Holy Office, a space of statutory affirmation in society by revalidating its position in determining the boundaries of orthodoxy.[34] The gradual growth of charges of "Moor" and *gentilidade* after 1585 perhaps represents the adjustment of the tribunal to its new reality, where its social relevance could no longer be dependent upon cases of Judaism, as well as the hardening of the ecclesiastical stance on Gentilic rites and ceremonies following the 1579 revolt of Salcete's inhabitants and the execution of five Jesuits in the village of Cuncolim in 1583.[35] Particularly in the beginning of the 17th century, there were moments in the procedural rhythm of the Goa Inquisition, especially between 1603 and 1607, when charges of *gentilidade* sometimes represented more than half of the cases. It does not seem likely that the inquisitorial handbooks used in Goa—unfortunately, lost forever—kept the same silence on this kind of offence as the ones in Lisbon.

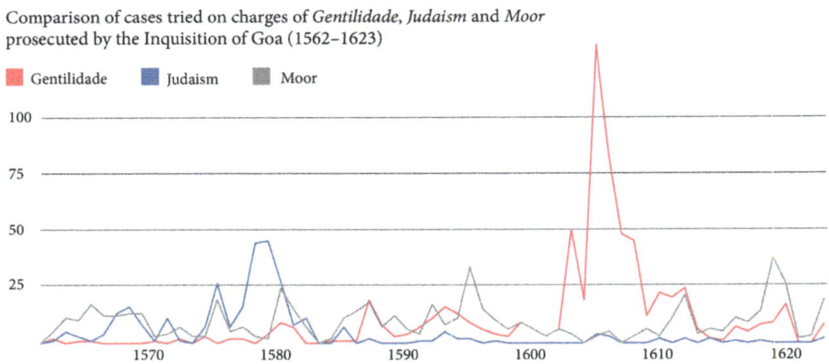

CHART 7.2 Cases tried on charges of "Gentilidade", "Judaism", and "Moor" prosecuted by the Inquisition of Goa (1561–1623)[36]

33 Letter from Rui Sodrinho de Mesquita, Inquisitor of Goa, to the Archduke Albert of Austria, Inquisitor General of Portugal, December 2, 1587, Goa; Baião, *A Inquisição de Goa*, vol. 2, 119.

34 Bethencourt, *História das Inquisições*, 262.

35 On the context of the tensions felt in Salcete in the 1570s and early 1580s, see Aranha, *Il Cristianesimo Latino*, 146–162.

36 *Reportorio Geral de tres mil oitocentos processos, que sam todos os despachados neste Sancto Officio de Goa*, BNP, Códice 203. This chart indicates only the cases where the defendants were not subjected to a second or third accusation.

The fact that the Portuguese employed the terms *gentilismo* and *gentilidade* to refer to religions beyond Judaism and Islam also raises difficulties when trying to achieve a definition of *gentilidade* as a religious offence.[37] If it is taken to be an equivalent to "crypto-Hinduism", how should charges against defendants that lived in locations far from Hindu contexts be interpreted?[38] At the same time, is it not possible for those who converted from the Gentiles of Brazil or Angola to also have committed crimes of *gentilidade* from the point of view of an inquisitor?

Considering the absence of the handbooks used in Goa, and without being able to benefit from the diverse array of the original proceedings followed by this court, the task of defining *gentilidade* as a behavior under the jurisdiction of the Holy Office is a challenging one. The identification of *gentilidade* with one of the most used categories of offence in Spanish America, that of idolatry, poses a methodological problem. The fact that the Goa Inquisition and its activities remained a marginalized subject until the early 2000s explains why *gentilidade* as a judicial category was never truly addressed on its own terms. In recent years, scholars who addressed the Inquisition of Goa's actions against religious offences stemming from local customs showed a preference for analyzing the issue from the point of view of idolatry.[39] This epistemological framework is, of course, in accordance with both theological, missionary, and legal discourse of the time, insofar as it meant diverting worship—which was due to God alone—to things or false Gods.[40] However, when looking at the categories used in the *Reportorio*, it is noteworthy that idolatry is practically absent from Figueira's choices of classification, something that is quite puzzling if one considers the abundance in which idolatry is mentioned in missionary reports to refer to the local population's ritual practices. According

37 This paper will also not address the issue on the reified character of Hinduism nor the appropriateness of referring to local populations' beliefs under Portuguese rule as "Hinduism". The Portuguese employed terms such as *gentilismo* and *gentilidade* to refer to the beliefs and rituals of non-Muslims and non-Jews and it is this conceptual framework that will be analyzed here. See, on the epistemological difference between *Gentilismo* and Hinduism, Rubiés, "Reassessing the 'Discovery of Hinduism'", 114–119.

38 In 1591, Constantino Farinha, a merchant living in Macau, China, was tried on charges of *gentilidade*. Since it is known that Farinha lived in Siam for a part of his life, Buddhism rather than Hinduism seems to be the obvious background for the practices tried by the Inquisition. *Reportorio* [...], fol. 220r; Lourenço, *A Articulação da Periferia*, 155.

39 Xavier, *A Invenção de Goa*, 326; Marcocci, *A Consciência de um Império*, 391. For Burkardt, in Goa the concept of idolatry came to be equated with that of superstition on account of the association between the practices of Gentiles of India and the superstitions of ancient paganism. Burkardt, "Superstizione".

40 For a broad analysis of the term, see Barbu, "'Idolatry' and Religious Diversity", 39–50.

to the *Reportorio*, there is but one case unequivocally identified as idolatry (curiously pertaining to an Old Christian, a Portuguese person from Lisbon, for making a solemn oath before the idols); one case of an Armenian "idolizing the devil with spells", which has no classification; and one case of a man born in Goa (although it is not known whether he was an Old Christian or a *cristão da terra*) idolizing the *pagodes* and making offerings to them, which Figueira classified as "sacrifices".[41]

The issue of classification of religious offences by the Goa Inquisition grows ever more complex if we consider other sources that refer to the defendant's actions. In a list of defendants tried in 1609 and 1610, the inquisitors of Goa prepared a summary of their offences and the resolutions of the court to send to the higher inquisitorial authorities in Lisbon. This is a most unique list, not only because it is the oldest surviving document of this type, but also because it is the only one that was prepared during the period covered by the *Reportorio*. This provides an extraordinary opportunity to compare the choices of classification employed by the compilers of the list with Figueira's.[42] And, as it turns out, the 1609–10 list provides no less than six cases explicitly described as "offences of idolatry", all of which were described by Figueira as cases of *gentilidade* in 1623.[43]

As can be seen from these examples, not only is there a diversity in deviant behavior that does not come together in unequivocal criminal categories, but also the ministers of the Holy Office themselves did not display the same preferences regarding the classification of the same offences over a very short span of time. The divergence between the categories employed by the inquisitors of 1609–10 and Figueira in 1623 reveals how much the Portuguese legal, missionary, and inquisitorial context of dealing with or repressing *gentilismo* or *gentilidade* imposed itself in different ways on the intellectual attitudes of the Holy Office's members on the subject (some of whom had recently arrived from Europe). This presents an additional difficulty when trying to understand what exactly constituted a crime of *gentilidade*.

---

41 *Reportorio* [...], fols. 194v, 293v, 583r. The term *cristão da terra* literally translates to "Christian of the land", i.e., a person indigenous to the territory, or Asia broadly speaking, converted to Catholicism.

42 By the time Figueira began his work as prosecutor of the Inquisition of Goa in late 1617, both inquisitors that were in office in 1609–1610, Jorge Ferreira and Gonçalo da Silva, had ceased their functions in the court.

43 List of individuals tried by the Inquisition of Goa in the year 1609 and 1610, undated. ANTT, *Tribunal do Santo Ofício, Conselho Geral do Santo Ofício*, liv. 369, fols. 23v, 26v–27. The cases specifically referred to as offences of idolatry are those of João de Figueiredo (regarding a previous trial), Filipe Rodrigues, Pêro de Oliveira, Domingos Fernandes, Domingos da Cunha, and Simão Furtado.

3 Constructing '*actos de gentilidade*' as a Religious Offence

It is possible to find a concrete example of the methodological difficulties regarding the definition of this concept in one of the few surviving recorded procedures against a *cristão da terra*. In 1592, Francisco Rangel, a *gaunkar*[44] of Corlim, was accused of and sentenced for *gentilidade*. In 1603 he was again brought before the Inquisition. According to the *Reportorio*, the same verdict of *gentilidade* was passed on both occasions.[45] In his second trial, Rangel was accused of having sacrificed rams to a *pagode* (which here must be understood as a deity/idol) or—as it appears in another testimony against him—to a *diabo* (devil), to ensure the protection of the *várzea* (rice field) they were planting.[46] Rangel confessed to having done this along with other *gancares* because it was the condition imposed by Domingos de Mesquita, a recently elected *camotim*—responsible for the vigilance of the *valados* (dykes/sluice gates) with which the *várzeas* were fenced so that saltwater could not enter.[47]

From the interrogation and accusation, it is clear that Rangel was being questioned on the possibility of having made a demonic pact, because the inquisitor asked him if he believed that the *pagode* or *diabo* had the power to protect the *várzea* and if he was aware that it was a sin to kill the rams for the sake of the devil.[48] Afterwards, the inquisitor asked him the following question, which warrants being reproduced in full:

> Asked if he, the defendant, believed in the *Pagode* Rauelanato [Ravalnath] as he did the first time he was tried by this Board, he said that since that time he no longer believed in said *Pagode*, nor in any other of the Gentiles, because he knew very well that everything was wind [*sic.*, hollow].[49]

---

44 A *gancar* (*gaunkar*) was the male member of the *vangad* (clan) who, after coming of age (c. 12–18 years old) belonged to the councils of the rural communities (*gaunkari*). See Souza, *Goa Medieval*, 60; Dalgado, *Glossário Luso-Asiático*, vol. 1, 416–417; and Xavier (Chapter 2) in this volume.

45 *Reportorio* […], fols. 316r, 327v.

46 Procedures against Francisco Rangel by the Inquisition of Goa, 1603–1605. ANTT, *Tribunal do Santo Ofício, Inquisição de Lisboa*, no. 8916, fols. 2r–6v.

47 Procedures against Francisco Rangel by the Inquisition of Goa, 1603–1605. ANTT, *Tribunal do Santo Ofício, Inquisição de Lisboa*, no. 8916, fol. 11r. Dalgado, *Glossário Luso-Asiático*, vol. 1, 192–193.

48 Procedures against Francisco Rangel by the Inquisition of Goa, 1603–1605. ANTT, *Tribunal do Santo Ofício, Inquisição de Lisboa*, no. 8916, fol. 14r.

49 Procedures against Francisco Rangel by the Inquisition of Goa, 1603–1605. ANTT, *Tribunal do Santo Ofício, Inquisição de Lisboa*, no. 8916, fol. 14r.

Later, pressed to declare his *tenção* (intention; will) in making the sacrifices and *sumbaias* (reverential greetings)[50] to the *pagode* (in this case, an idol) and whether he ever believed it was God, Rangel said that it was customary to offer a ram to the *pagode* in his village, but that he never saw it as God nor did he believe in it after he was reconciled with the Catholic faith. If he had committed such acts, he stressed, it was because he feared that the devils/*pagodes* might come and destroy the fence and the *novidade* (new crops). Furthermore, he emphasized that he did not entrust (*encomendava*) himself to the *pagode* in his house nor did he practice Gentilic ceremonies.[51]

But, above all, what the Inquisition could not prove in this case was the coincidence between the charges of 1592 and those of 1603, which would suggest a case of *relapsia* (relapse) and a second accusation of *gentilidade*. As a result, the majority of the Goa Inquisition's board determined that the acts were not heretical and differed from the previous ones and that evidence was insufficient to suggest a second incidence of the same offences.[52] Nevertheless, one dissenting voice argued that the defendant should be delivered to the secular authorities for execution due to him relapsing. Deputy Fr. Domingos da Trindade opposed the prevailing opinion that Rangel's poor indoctrination, natural inclination, communication with the Gentiles of the surrounding areas, and material interest of *cristãos da terra* in the new crops should excuse the presumption of ill will (*má vontade*) on his part. On the contrary, the fact that Rangel had committed many different acts for many years was proof of his ill will, Trindade argued.[53] The deputy's understanding was that insofar as Rangel committed the offences with ill will, thus, aware of his wrongdoing, he should be tried as a relapse. It was due to this disagreement that a copy of the trial records was sent to the General Council of the Holy Office in Portugal for analysis, hence its existence today. The Council replied in 1605, validating the decision of the majority of the board.[54] As pointed out by Giuseppe Marcocci, the

50 From the Malay *sembahyang*, composed from the root words *sembah* (worship) and *yang* (divinity). The Portuguese in Asia used the word as a synonym of "courtesy", signifying the reverential greetings and honors bestowed on a person or an idol. See Wilkinson, s.v. "sembahyang", 405; Dalgado, *Glossário Luso-Asiático*, vol. 2, "Sumbaia, zumbaia", 326–328.

51 Procedures against Francisco Rangel by the Inquisition of Goa, 1603–1605. ANTT, *Tribunal do Santo Ofício, Inquisição de Lisboa*, no. 8916, fols. 21r–21v.

52 Procedures against Francisco Rangel by the Inquisition of Goa, 1603–1605. ANTT, *Tribunal do Santo Ofício, Inquisição de Lisboa*, no. 8916, fol. 22.

53 Procedures against Francisco Rangel by the Inquisition of Goa, 1603–1605. ANTT, *Tribunal do Santo Ofício, Inquisição de Lisboa*, no. 8916, fols. 22r–22v.

54 Procedures against Francisco Rangel by the Inquisition of Goa, 1603–1605. ANTT, *Tribunal do Santo Ofício, Inquisição de Lisboa*, no. 8916, fol. 23. See, also Marcocci and Paiva, *História da Inquisição Portuguesa*, 115.

issue in such cases "was how to find a common opinion on the exact boundary between rites and customs with religious meaning, and those without".[55]

So, even though the records of the first trial of Rangel were lost, it seems clear that the accusation of *gentilidade*, as registered by the *Reportorio*, implied the identification of a given supernatural being with a deity or, to be more exact, with an equivalent to God—something that presupposed belief in a divine being and the act of "entrusting oneself" to it or, if we follow an 18th-century definition, "giving oneself and resigning oneself into the hands of another, and trusting in their protection and will".[56] It was this trust and belief in the divine otherness that, for the Inquisition, constituted a crime with a whole range of other consequences.

As can be seen, in addition to the diversity of practices that appear to signify the same offence, an analysis of the actions of the Holy Office of Goa is also made difficult by the choices of the compiler at the time of categorization. For instance, although Figueira categorized both offences committed by Rangel as *gentilidade*, it should be noted that the inquisitors' ruling of 1603 makes no mention of this term. The issue here concerns what can be defined as *gentilidade*. If we consider that officers employed in the service of the Holy Office shared a common lexicon necessary to the administration of justice according to a rule of law, the differences of categorization in 1610 and 1623 should reflect qualitative changes in the understanding of the phenomena. Precisely, in order to comprehend these changes, it must first be determined which features in the offenders' behaviors justified being classified under the category *gentilidade*, as well as the reasoning behind it according to inquisitorial procedures.

When, in the early 1580s, the inquisitors of Goa and the General Council of the Holy Office began to appreciate in greater depth the *cristãos da terra*'s propensity to revert to the practice of Gentilic rituals, this problem was addressed alongside the broader issue of apostasy in the territories surrounding Goa, Bardez, and Salcete.[57] In 1584, the deputies of the General Council clarified to

55 Marcocci, "Rites and Inquisition", 151.

56 DRAE, 1732, t. 3, s. v. Encomendarse: "entregarse y resignarse en mano de otro, y fiarse de su amparo y voluntad".

57 In 1579, an ecclesiastical conference (*junta*) which brought together the Bishop of Cochin (acting as governor of the Goa archbishopric and elected Archbishop), the prelates of the Dominicans and the Franciscans, and other members of their orders (the Jesuits provided a resolution at another time) issued a resolution against sanctioning certain rites and ceremonies to the non-Christianized populations of Salcete. The conference reached a resolution that did not meet the expectations of either side, despite the undergoing revolt of Salcete's inhabitants. Ultimately, this decision received the support of the new monarch, Philip I (II of Spain) who, in 1581, prohibited the existence of *pagodes* and Gentile

the Goa Inquisition the appropriate procedure to follow in cases where Portuguese, *mestiços*, and *cristãos da terra* "went to the Moors or to the Gentiles and there joined their sects and then came back to the Holy Office to reconcile themselves, confessing how they departed from the faith of our Lord Jesus Christ and believed in the said sects".[58] In the same document, "to change to their sects" is equivalent to being a renegade or having committed infidelity. Accordingly, the inquisitors were told to investigate the causes for which the defendants committed "Moor or Gentile acts" (*autos de mouro ou gentio*), i.e., analyze their "will" (*tenção*).[59]

As can be appreciated, the type of crime under discussion involves an act of infidelity against the divine majesty which presupposes a rupture of belief in the Catholic faith, expressed by adherence to an alternative—and therefore false and erroneous—doctrine. For the purposes of inquisitorial justice, this change or transition can be objectively identified in the public behavior of the defendant, from their choice of attire (to dress in the manner of a "Moor" or a Gentile) to the performance of certain rites and rituals. Determining the intention behind these exterior acts is, therefore, paramount to proving infidelity.

---

and Muslim public rites and ceremonies in his territories. The matter had been a concern of the First Provincial Council of Goa (1567), but not of the Second Provincial Council (1575), who did not issue any decrees on the rites of the Gentiles. In 1585, however, the first decrees of the Third Provincial Council concerning conversion readily addressed the problems arising from idolatry. The 1579 resolution appears to have been based on the anonymous allegation of "a Friar of much zeal" whose identity we ignore. This allegation was incorporated into Francisco de Sousa's *Oriente Conquistado a Jesu Christo* in 1710. The author, however, misplaces the year of the *junta*, wrongfully stating that it took place in 1576. The 1579 letter of the inquisitor Bartolomeu da Fonseca confirms that the *junta* took place during that year. See: "Sententia superiorum ecclesiasticorum Indiæ et consultorum de liceitate rituum ethnicorum", April 9, 1579, in Goa, in *DI*, vol. 11 (1970), 562–569; Charter of King Philip I of Portugal, of 25 February 1581, in Elvas, in *O Livro do 'Pai dos Cristãos'*, 69; Letter of Bartolomeu da Fonseca, Inquisitor of Goa, to Cardinal Henrique, King of Portugal and Inquisitor General, December 1, 1579, in Goa, in Baião, *A Inquisição de Goa*, vol. 2, 78–79; Francisco de Sousa, *Oriente Conquistado*, vol. 2, 136–143. The anonymous allegation was analyzed in detail by Paolo Aranha in *Il Cristianesimo Latino*, 146–151; For a general appreciation of the Provincial Councils' decrees on the matter of conversion see, Aranha, *Il Cristianesimo Latino*, 164–170; Faria, "Os concílios provinciais de Goa", 233–237. See also Faria chapter (Chapter 4) in this volume.

58 Reply from the General Council of the Holy Office to the memorandum by André Fernandes, acting inquisitor of Goa, undated (c. March 1584). ANTT, *Tribunal do Santo Ofício, Conselho Geral do Santo Ofício*, liv. 311, fol. 91r.

59 Reply from the General Council of the Holy Office to the memorandum by André Fernandes, acting inquisitor of Goa, undated (c. March 1584). ANTT, *Tribunal do Santo Ofício, Conselho Geral do Santo Ofício*, liv. 311, fol. 91r.

This much is clear from a 16th-century trial record that has fortunately survived. Lopo Álvares was tried on charges of *gentilidade* in 1594, according to the *Reportorio*.[60] His trial record was copied by order of Inquisitor António de Barros and sent to the General Council of the Holy Office for analysis.[61] Álvares was a *cristão da terra* who had been baptized just two years before. The inquisitor suspected apostasy due to his absence from Catholic territory a mere three months after baptism, as well as to his change of attire. Thus, his interrogation was aimed at ascertaining that possibility. In his first session, Barros admonished Álvares to provide a complete confession of his offences, confirming whether "he shared the belief of the law of the Gentiles".[62] He further inquired whether he believed that the Gentiles could be saved if they followed the "law of their sect",[63] as well as if when entering a *pagode* (temple) he removed his shoes "in the manner of the Gentiles", if he prayed and did any "*sumbaia*",[64] or if he venerated any *pagode* (idol).[65] Álvares denied having ever done so, stating on more than one occasion that if he "wished to become Gentile again he would have taken up caste".[66] His response, which referred to a process of purification well-known to Portuguese ecclesiastical authorities and regarded as apostasy, reveals the consensus between the two people involved in the interrogation—that the practices and rituals mentioned by Barros were binding to the "law of the Gentiles" and that to embrace them was to break away from Catholicism. Ultimately, the Inquisition could only prove that Álvares wore a turban or a pagri (*touca*) and a tunic (*túnica*) among Muslims and Gentiles,

60 *Reportorio* [...], fol. 453v.

61 Procedures against Lopo Álvares by the Inquisition of Goa, 1594. ANTT, *Tribunal do Santo Ofício, Inquisição de Lisboa*, no. 12738, fol. 1r. Silva describes the case in detail. See Silva, *Inquisição e Mestiçagem Cultural no Estado da Índia (1560–1623)*, 146–153.

62 Procedures against Lopo Álvares by the Inquisition of Goa, 1594. ANTT, *Tribunal do Santo Ofício, Inquisição de Lisboa*, no. 12738, fol. 3v.

63 Procedures against Lopo Álvares by the Inquisition of Goa, 1594. ANTT, *Tribunal do Santo Ofício, Inquisição de Lisboa*, no. 12738, fol. 4r.

64 Procedures against Lopo Álvares by the Inquisition of Goa, 1594. ANTT, *Tribunal do Santo Ofício, Inquisição de Lisboa*, no. 12738, fol. 4r.

65 Procedures against Lopo Álvares by the Inquisition of Goa, 1594. ANTT, *Tribunal do Santo Ofício, Inquisição de Lisboa*, no. 12738, fol. 4v.

66 Procedures against Lopo Álvares by the Inquisition of Goa, 1594. ANTT, *Tribunal do Santo Ofício, Inquisição de Lisboa*, no. 12738, fol. 4r. Ines Županov and R. Po-Chia Hsia employed the less literal but more accurate translation of "return to caste" when analyzing the official declaration of the Third Ecclesiastical Council of Goa that described how new converts left Catholic territory to perform ceremonies and consume foul drinks to purify themselves from the food they ate as Catholics. Županov and Hsia, "Reception of Hinduism and Buddhism", 577; Third Ecclesiastical Council of Goa, 1585, Decree 7, *Archivo Portuguez Oriental*, fasc. 4 (1862), 125–126. See, also Faria, "De réus a colaboradores", 171–172.

disregarded Friday fasts, and washed his body in the fashion of the Gentiles while living among them.[67] Figueira's choice to catalogue this case as one of *gentilidade* was thus not based on the offences that the Inquisition was able to prove according to behavior, but on the presumed charges and general direction of the interrogation.

Despite the apparently straightforward identification between *gentilidade* and apostasy ("to become a Gentile"[68]), the unique social and ritual features that the Goa Inquisition had to pass judgment on made legal communication inside the different organisms of the Portuguese inquisitorial system difficult. In 1596, the General Council of the Holy Office revealed its lack of expertise in interpreting cases involving rites and ceremonies specific to Asia. In that year, its deputies requested the inquisitors of Goa to clarify the usage of some "peculiar terms such as 'to take up caste' or 'make sumbaia' and other similar ones" so that they could be understood in Lisbon.[69] The request reveals the conceptual distance between the Holy Office of Goa and the General Council, to the extent that lexical specificity could prevent a sound comprehension of the offenders' behaviors. Nevertheless, the need for clarification was of paramount importance for the correct exercise of inquisitorial justice because, as will be shown, according to the inquisitors' understanding, "Gentile acts" played a concrete role in expressing devotion to deities of the *gentilidade*. It was, therefore, against specific "Gentile acts" that the intention of a defendant should be scrutinized.

By 1606, the inquisitors of Goa were referring to the offences perpetrated by the *cristãos da terra* as "acts of *gentilidade*", meaning a form of behavior originating in that particular context.[70] In the following year, those very same inquisitors—the ones who later developed the 1610 list—spoke of such actions as the result of idolatry.[71] As discussed, this document categorized as

67 Procedures against Lopo Álvares by the Inquisition of Goa, 1594. ANTT, *Tribunal do Santo Ofício, Inquisição de Lisboa*, no. 12738, fols. 6r–6v.

68 This expression ("se fazer gentio") appears in several of the *Reportorio*'s summaries regarding offences by *gentilidade*. The earliest use of this expression on the *Reportorio* occurred in the record of one António of Gujarati origin who had been baptized in adulthood. He was tried in 1586 by Inquisitor Rui Sodrinho de Mesquita precisely "for becoming a Gentile". *Reportorio* [...], fol. 114r.

69 Ruling of the General Council of the Holy Office regarding the list of individuals sentenced by the Goa Inquisition in 1594, [March 16] 1596. ANTT, *Tribunal do Santo Ofício, Conselho Geral do Santo Ofício*, liv. 100, fol. 78. See Faria, "De réus a colaboradores", 169.

70 Letter from the inquisitors of Goa to D. Pedro de Castilho, Inquisitor General of Portugal, December 20, 1606, Goa. Baião, *A Inquisição de Goa*, vol. 2, 343.

71 Letter from the inquisitors of Goa to D. Pedro de Castilho, Inquisitor General of Portugal, December 24, 1607, Goa. Baião, *A Inquisição de Goa*, vol. 2, 355.

idolatry what Figueira labeled *gentilidade*, which means that, in a very short span of time, the same institution listed the same behavior under two different categories of offence. Moreover, the list mentions a variety of other individuals whose offences were not described in the same manner. Aside from idolatry, the inquisitors registered offences that included the performance of reverential greetings to idols, as well as keeping with the superstitions of the Gentiles, and turning into a Gentile.[72] What is interesting here is that, while Figueira predominantly labeled many of these offences as *gentilidade*, he also chose different categories (such as "sacrifices" or "offerings to the *pagodes*") to label offences that were considered identical for the compilers of the 1610 list. A systematic study of Figueira's categorization of offences has yet to be undertaken by scholars but, without being able to access the actual records, what prompted him to resort to different classifications for the same types of behavior may never be fully ascertained. Nevertheless, what seems to be certain is that, by 1623, the prosecutor understood that a variety of actions could fall under the label *gentilidade*, as long as the defendants could be questioned on their will.

An incident that occurred in the 18th century illustrates in a perceptible way the fine line between *gentilidade* and other behaviors that fell outside this category. In 1736, the Viceroy of India wrote a letter to the King of Portugal referring to a dispute between the chancellor of the *Estado da Índia* and the Inquisition of Goa. Following the publication of an edict by the inquisitors that prohibited a wide range of practices carried out by local Christians, the chancellor protested before the viceroy, claiming that the inquisitors had overstepped their jurisdiction. The viceroy then proceeded to inform the king that the decision regarding the edict had been coordinated between himself and the Goa Inquisition. His letter summarizes what, in essence, was the crux of the matter in relation to the Gentilic customs:

> The Board of the Holy Office represented to me, through one of its inquisitors, that it had determined to publish an Edict against many customs, which were observed in all these lands, *derived from gentilidade*, of which experience had shown many to be *idolatrous*; and although in most

72 These included "to make *sumbaia*" as unto an idol, to claim to be an idol and to accept reverence for it, "to make *sumbaia*" to an idol, to make offerings to an idol, to keep the Gentilic superstitions, to go to the house of an idol and ask for his favor, to make donations to the idols, to become a Gentile and use their attire, as well as to break from the Catholic faith and adhere to the "sect" of the Gentiles. List of individuals tried by the Inquisition of Goa in the year 1609 and 1610, undated. ANTT, *Tribunal do Santo Ofício, Conselho Geral do Santo Ofício*, liv. 369, fols. 20, 27–28, 30v–31v, 33v–34v, 35v.

> people who practiced them there was no intention (*espirito*) *of infidelity*, in many others, especially in the humblest people, their observance was always with regard to *gentilismo*; because of this the Board [of the Inquisition] did not doubt that it had jurisdiction to prohibit them, but seeing as there were many that had been allowed for a long time, and in some, who seemed *merely political*, [to the point that] there was no suspicion of its inconveniences, except amongst the Ministers of the same Board, who had examined them, it seemed to him [the inquisitor] not only that their prohibition required my approval, but also that once the prohibition was published by the Edict of the inquisitors, that I validate it with a charter.[73]

If we read the document carefully, we can see that the Inquisition is walking on quicksand. The simple fact that it needed to consult the viceroy's opinion on this matter suggests that these were a variety of behaviors that had not been regarded as having a necessarily religious value. What seems to be at stake is precisely whether it is possible to separate the "political", i.e. non-religious, side of these traditions from their Gentile context and, consequently, from their apparent devotional meaning. For all intents and purposes, this meant that the practice of such customs had to be scrutinized by the court and clarified in terms of the notion or opinion that the supposed perpetrator held about it.[74] As is transparently evident from the letter, the inquisitors' main concern was how many of these customs might lead to adherence to a belief, law, or sect, in short, to *gentilidade* or *gentilismo*, or, as the text says, to an attitude of infidelity towards the divine majesty of God. Irrespective of the many kinds of customs "derived from *gentilidade*", the text reveals that what separated a religious offence perpetrated with a "spirit of infidelity" from other types of crimes was notion, opinion, and belief.[75]

As suggested by the trial of Rangel, as well as other entries in the *Reportorio*, the crime of *gentilidade* certainly concealed a diversity of ceremonial or ritual realities. In fact, it is very possible that underneath this classification lay many of the social or cultural circumstances mentioned in Rangel's trial alongside an unequal expression of the intentions, opinions, or notions declared by the

73 Letter from Pedro Mascarenhas, Viceroy of India, to D. João v, King of Portugal, December 29, 1736, Goa. Rivara, *Ensaio Historico da Lingua Concani*, 368. Emphasis added.

74 The issue of the awareness of crime on the part of converted populations is addressed in the context of New Spain, *inter alia*, in Lara Cisneros, *¿Ignorancia invencible?*, 83 et seq.

75 Leaning on Erving Goffman, Pierre Bourdieu, and Michel Foucault, Rowena Robinson provides another analysis of this edict, seeing in it an instrument of deculturation aimed at creating attitudes of internalized discipline that would detach the individuals from their local ('pagan') background. Robinson, "Taboo or Veiled Consent?", 2427–2428.

defendants over the course of their interrogation. As noted by Délio de Mendonça, relapses cannot be reduced to "deliberate, planned and uncommon happenings".[76] All this diversity in attitudes, intentions, or group pressures eventually came to the fore when facing the Inquisition, molding testimonies in unexpected ways, particularly when faced with linguistic adversities, as Rangel was, having his session conducted with recourse to an interpreter.[77]

What does seem clear is that in the inquisitors' eyes *gentilidade* suggested a crime that presupposed the return, precisely, to that homonymous universe, to a community or system of beliefs parallel to Catholicism, which placed that transgression alongside the crimes of heresy and apostasy, such as those of Judaism, "Moor" or "Lutheran". This is evident from the notion of *tomar casta* in Álvares' trial as something that was equal to "becoming Gentile again". It is also suggested in a questionnaire sent by the inquisitors of Goa to which the General Council of the Holy Office replied in 1636. In this document, in which the judges expressed 25 doubts about the court's procedures, the first question addressed what they said was *estilo* (custom) in Goa "not to accuse the *cristãos da terra* based on *tenção*, [even when it was] certified by witnesses or by [the defendants'] confessions of Gentilic rites and ceremonies".[78] The inquisitors had realized that, by subjecting these defendants to torture, they had obtained confessions attesting to "the will, and belief with all the circumstances, required by law".[79] As such, owing to the "quality of the ceremonies and rites" and to the "propensity to follow the Gentile sect in everything", the inquisitors felt assured of the veracity of the confessions.

The language used in this question is of no minor importance, as it frames the typology of offence under consideration. On the one hand, the emphasis given to *tenção* and *crença* (belief) is significant, since they are precisely the

76 Mendonça, *Conversions and Citizenry*, 298. For a critique of rationalized and materialistic understandings of conversion under Portuguese rule, see Aranha, "Early Modern Asian Catholicism and European Colonialism", 289–291.

77 The issue of the credibility of inquisitorial testimonies has been the object of much debate, especially among scholars focusing on the religiosity of New Christians. The achievements of this debate have yet to be applied to the extant testimonies of the *cristãos da terra*. See H. P. Salomon, "Les procès de l'Inquisition Portugaise"; Eberenz and De la Torre, *Conversaciones estrechamente vigiladas*.

78 Questions addressed to the General Council of the Holy Office by the inquisitors of Goa, answered in 1636. BNRJ, *Inquisição de Goa*, 25,1,004, no. 43, fol. 106r. We know from a similar reply in 1634 from the Inquisitor General Francisco de Castro that the question had already been posed to the inquisitorial authorities in Lisbon. See Marcocci, "Rites and Inquisition", 145.

79 Questions addressed to the General Council of the Holy Office by the inquisitors of Goa, answered in 1636. BNRJ, *Inquisição de Goa*, 25,1,004, no. 043, fol. 106r.

criteria that allow a crime to be considered heretical.[80] Similarly, the reference to sect is not by chance. In the judicial context of the Holy Office, the word sect is used to refer to a variety of collectives that profess the same belief system (in accordance, moreover, with its common meaning).[81] Among those who belong to sects are Luther's followers, the "Mohammedans", the *alumbrados*, the sorcerers, the Freemasons, and the idolaters.[82] The inquisitors themselves did not fail to mention in their letter to the viceroy, when they sent him the edict, that the actions included therein were "the same as those of the Gentilic sect".[83] Therefore, the Gentiles, too, could be framed among the groups known as sects.

"Rites" and "ceremonies" were also objective criteria for warranting a charge of *gentilidade*. However, as we have seen from Rangel's case, the diversity of ceremonies held in a local context from which to infer such an offence could—and indeed did—generate differences of understanding within the Goa court. It was therefore important to attend to the "quality" of the rite or ceremony.

80 Nicolau Eimeric (†1399) stated in his *Directorium inquisitorum* that belief (*credentia*) in error and obstinacy of will (*voluntas*) were the two conditions required to classify someone as a heretic: "quod de tali errore credendo, habeat pertinaciam in voluntate". The role of choice (*electio*) and consent (*assensus*) had already been emphasized by Aquinas in order to determine partial or full withdrawal from Christ. In the 17th century, theologians such as Tomás Sánchez (1610) inherited the notion that heresy implied a voluntary and conscious adherence to an error when he discussed how will, obstinacy (*pertinacia*), and consent (*assensus*) were necessary to define someone as heretic: "Est error intellectus voluntarius, contra aliquem fidei veritatem, cum pertinacia assertus ab eo, qui fidem recipit. Dicitur error intellectus, id est, assensus falsus intellectus". Aquinas, *Summa Theologiæ*, II–II, quæst. 11, art. 1; Eimeric, *Directorium Inquisitorum*, part 2, quæst. 32, 319; Sánchez, *Opus Morale*, lib. 2, c. 7, no. 1, 110.

81 The entry "secte" in the *Encyclopedie* of Diderot and D'Alembert, signed by D.J. (Chevalier Louis de Jaucourt), recognizes the more neutral nature of the word inasmuch as it refers to a group following opinions or maxims originating from a particular person, be it "docteur ou maître particulier". However, he emphasized its proximity to the Greek word αἵρεσις, underlining the tendency to designate heresies as sects and heretics as sectarians. The prevailing sense is thus one of false opinion. Viewed at https://artflsrv03.uchicago.edu/philologic4/encyclopedie1117/navigate/14/4801/ (January 12, 2020).

82 In 1728 and 1729, several individuals from São João da Pesqueira, Ranhados, Poço do Canto, and Souto de Penedono, in the district of the Coimbra Inquisition were charged with idolatry, following their contact with Fr. António Guilherme Hebre de Loureiro. Their sentences explicitly mention their acceptance of the "infernais, e abominaueis erros, e diabolica çeita que comessou á leuantar o Padre Antonio Guilherme Hebre de Loureiro". Procedures against Luísa da Fonseca by the Inquisition of Coimbra, 1728. ANTT, *Tribunal do Santo Ofício, Inquisição de Coimbra*, no. 7339.

83 Letter from the inquisitors of Goa to Pedro Mascarenhas, Viceroy of India, April 18, 1736, Goa. Rivara, *Ensaio Historico da Lingua Concani*, 369.

Not every practice could warrant an accusation that implied adherence to the *secta gentilica*, but only, as is understood from the 1636 document, those ceremonies and rites that are *protestativas* (declarative) of the sect, like *sumbaias*: "which involve the greatest act of worship of the *pagodes*, which among the Gentiles are sacrifices of fire, blood, or any other, because they intend to give them honor and veneration as to God; aside from these there are many other superstitions and rites, which do not induce so effective a presumption, in which the ancient custom can be preserved, like going to the houses of the *pagodes*, without making them *sumbaias*, attending their feasts and dances, and others of this quality."[84]

This text provides the criteria by which an inquisitor should determine an accusation on the grounds of *gentilidade*: Only those acts that manifested "worship", "honor and veneration as to God" to the *pagodes*, specifically, *sumbaias* and sacrifices. These were the acts that, as we read from the response of the General Council, were considered "*protestativos e indicativos violentamente da sua secta*", that is, as emphatically revealing a statement and indication of adhering to a belief system centered around the idols.[85] Significantly, during the trial of Álvares, Barros asked him if he had embraced some of these practices.

The dividing line separating acts that denote adherence to another belief organized in a sect from those that did not was thus adapted to the Asian universe from the legal conceptions of heresy and from the judicial procedures destined to try it, systematized for the Portuguese Inquisition through the *Regimentos* of 1552 and 1613. According to the 1636 document, this delimitation had been the practice of the Goa court since the end of the 16th century and beginning of the 17th century. It was this legal framework that Figueira had in mind when he grouped the diversity of ritual declarative behaviors originating in the context of *gentilidade* under one same category of offence bearing the same name.[86] Either his choice of category was already part of the inquisitorial

84 Questions addressed to the General Council of the Holy Office by the inquisitors of Goa, answered in 1636. BNRJ, *Inquisição de Goa*, 25,1,004 no. 43, fols. 106r–106v.

85 Questions addressed to the General Council of the Holy Office by the inquisitors of Goa, answered in 1636. BNRJ, *Inquisição de Goa*, 25,1,004 no. 43, fol. 106r.

86 It is possible that the hard stance he took in 1619 against the "Gentilic features" adopted by Roberto Nobili, SJ, in the Madurai mission, which Figueira considered declarative *ipsius gentilitatis* may have favored the adoption of *gentilidade* as the general category of offence for actions that involved embracing the "false religion" of the Gentiles. On the discussions held in Goa on this matter, see Tavares, "Inquisição ao avesso", 20–21; Marcocci and Paiva, *História da Inquisição Portuguesa*, 214–215; Marcocci, "Rites and Inquisition", 155–161.

lexicon practiced in Goa, or it came to generate consensus in subsequent years, since the term *gentilidade* was eventually adopted as a category of offence in the lists of *autos-da-fé* during the second half of the 17th century and the 18th century.[87]

The General Council's decision to accuse the "Indios" when the rites they performed were "of this quality and nature",[88] equated, in practice and in spite of the style recently followed in the Goa Inquisition, the offence of *gentilidade* with that of heresy, which meant that the inquisitors should follow the manner of proceeding accordingly. Some decades later, in 1659, when the inquisitors Paulo Castelino de Freitas and Fr. Lucas da Cruz, OP, sent a new consultation to the General Council regarding a "*cristão da terra* detained on charges of *gentilidade*", the use of language did not vary.[89] The basis for forming such charges were still "declarative (*protestativas*) ceremonies" and the confession of regarding the "*pagode* as God". The problem that the inquisitors were addressing was whether a case with these characteristics, in which the defendant claimed to have hope of being saved "in the faith of Christ", constituted formal or material heresy, with implications to the degree of punishment. The debate again focused on the will and level of pertinacity necessary to attest to the defendant's malice and rejection of Christian doctrine. Freitas thought it inconceivable that someone who confessed rites and declarative ceremonies and performed them to the *pagodes*, recognizing them as God, could simultaneously hope to be saved in Christ.[90]

---

87 In 1616, the inquisitors still referred to the actions of one Salcete-born man, João Martins, as idolatry, whereas Figueira labeled his offence as one of *gentilidade* in 1623. However, the oldest extant *auto-da-fé* list after the one of 1609–1610 already refers to several individuals brought on charges of *gentilidade*. The category does not seem to have remained in effect for the entirety of the court's activity for, in 1766, the plural *gentilidades* was employed in the *auto-da-fé* list. Only a thorough examination of the extant correspondence could help determine the semantic variations of this category over time, which is outside the scope of this study. Letter from the inquisitors of Goa to Fernão Martins Mascarenhas, Inquisitor General of Portugal, December 23, 1616, Goa. Baião, *A Inquisição de Goa*, vol. 2, 547; List of individuals that took part in the *auto-da-fé* of the Goa Inquisition of April 3–4, 1650. ANTT, *Tribunal do Santo Ofício, Conselho Geral do Santo Ofício*, maço 33, no. 1; List of individuals that took part in the *auto-da-fé* of the Goa Inquisition of September 21, 1766. ANTT, *Tribunal do Santo Ofício, Conselho Geral do Santo Ofício*, maço 31, no. 13.

88 Questions addressed to the General Council of the Holy Office by the inquisitors of Goa, answered in 1636. BNRJ, *Inquisição de Goa*, 25,1,004 no. 43, fol. 106r.

89 Letter by Paulo Castelino de Freitas and Fr. Lucas da Cruz, OP, inquisitors of Goa, to Diogo Velho, secretary of the General Council of the Holy Office, February 6, 1659, Goa. BNRJ, *Inquisição de Goa*, 25,1,006 no. 34, fol. 48r.

90 Letter by Paulo Castelino de Freitas and Fr. Lucas da Cruz, OP, inquisitors of Goa, to Diogo Velho, secretary of the General Council of the Holy Office, February 6, 1659, Goa. BNRJ, *Inquisição de Goa*, 25,1,006 no.34, fol. 48v.

The opinion of this inquisitor, subsequently validated by the General Council of the Holy Office, nevertheless illustrates a recurrent tension within the Goa Inquisition. As can be seen from subsequent consultations and appeals sent to Lisbon, the local devotional setting of Portuguese domains divided inquisitors over the value that should be attributed to the presumption that the practice of rituals and ceremonies identified as Gentilic implied adherence to the "sect of the Gentiles". For example, in 1726, the prosecutor filed an appeal against the court's sentence in the case of one Joana, protesting that the inquisitors did not want to examine the defendant as to the intention with which she had committed the offences she was accused of. In the prosecutor's opinion, her actions, even if strictly not heretical, could give rise to doubts, considering that she was a commoner and a daughter of Gentiles who professed the same sect, and that she lived in the Northern lands where "similar mistakes with withdrawal from faith are frequent, and almost customary".[91] Furthermore, he stated that:

> since the errors and rites of this *gentilidade*, and of those who follow them, consist of gifts to the *pagodes* with withdrawal [*apartamento*] from faith as is always seen in this court, and even if this fact is not judged as heretic, obviously one sees the great suspicion that results from it; and even if the act is not declarative [*protestativo*] of a sect, *saltem*, it is indicative.[92]

The inquisitors, it should be said, rejected the prosecutor's appeal, alleging that the defendant confessed to the offences of which she had been accused. They believed that the *cristãos da terra* performed "said ceremonies, and others of the same quality, without any malice, nor more foundation than for simplicity, and because their forefathers used to do so, from which, *ad plurimum*, can result a slight presumption of [the defendants] performing them with belief in idols, and gentile sect".[93]

---

91 Procedures against Joana "Curumbim" by the Inquisition of Goa, 1726. ANTT, *Tribunal do Santo Ofício, Inquisição de Lisboa*, no. 17048, fol. 19r.

92 Procedures against Joana "Curumbim" by the Inquisition of Goa, 1726. ANTT, *Tribunal do Santo Ofício, Inquisição de Lisboa*, no. 17048, fol. 20: "como os erros, e ritos desta gentilidade, e dos que o seguem são offertas aos pagodes com appartamento da fe como sempre se está uendo esta Verdade neste Tribunal, e quando este facto se não julgue por heretico euidentemente Se Vé a grande Suspeita, que delle resulta; e ainda que o acto não he protestatiuo de Seita saltem hè indicatiuo; e basta para poder ser accusada ad indagandam Veritatem".

93 Procedures against Joana "Curumbim" by the Inquisition of Goa, 1726. ANTT, *Tribunal do Santo Ofício, Inquisição de Lisboa*, no. 17048, fol. 22v: "[…] as ditas cerimonias, e outras da mesma qualidade, sem malicia algũa, nem mais fundamento, que por simplicidade, e

The difference of opinions between the prosecutor and the inquisitors demonstrates the existence of distinct sensitivities within the Holy Office of Goa, something that had already occurred in the 1659 consultation. On that occasion, Fr. Lucas da Cruz argued that those who expected only material goods from the *pagodes* should not be accused of formal heresy, but only material. He added that among the errors of the *cristãos da terra* was the fact that they had many gods to take care of their houses, the rice fields, or the sea.[94] By insinuating, with these examples, a space of material but not spiritual expectations, Cruz intended to remove the stigma of formal condemnation for *gentilidade* from several of the ritual behaviors displayed by local Christianity. The different understandings of what might indicate presumption of adherence to the "Gentile sect", and therefore wavering from faith, were also present in the dispute between the prosecutor and the inquisitors of Goa in 1726—a dispute which was decided in favor of the former.[95]

---

porque seus antepacados assim o costumauão faser, do que ad plurimum pode resultar hũa leue presumpcão de as poderem faser com crença nos J[d]ollos, e Seita gentilica".

94 Letter from Paulo Castelino de Freitas and Fr. Lucas da Cruz, OP, inquisitors of Goa, to Diogo Velho, secretary of the General Council of the Holy Office, February 6, 1659, Goa. BNRJ, *Inquisição de Goa*, 25,1,006 no. 34, fols. 49r–49v.

95 It is worth noting that in the judicial practice of the Holy Office of Goa, the matter of *gentilidade* has been discussed as a form of heresy and not directly regarding what it could formally mean as apostasy. Resuming the juridical debate that preceded him, Francisco Suárez (†1617) pointed out that Christians who turned (*transiens*) to Judaism or Paganism committed an act of apostasy because they fully rejected faith in Christ. In the inquisitorial praxis, however, the notion of infidelity in the assessment of guilt prevails, as can be seen from the prosecutor's opinion in Joana's case. In referring to the practice of Gentilic ceremonies, he stated that those who exercised them should be considered infidels "ac [p]er conseque<n>s hæreticus" in accordance with the provisions of Boniface VIII's *Liber Sextus*, which in 1298 collected the decretals subsequent to Pope Gregory IX in a single volume. There it was stipulated that the procedure against those who went back to observing the Jewish rites should be the same used against the heretics ("Contra christianos, qui ad ritum transierint vel redierint Iudæorum (...) tanquam contra hæreticos (...) procedendum"). Eimeric reflects the spirit of this legislation in the title *De Apostatis*, stating that those who apostatized "a fide etiam et ab Ecclesia totaliter deuiant. Et tales hæretici, immo infideles habendi sunt". *Sextus liber*, lib. 5, tit. *De hæreticis*, c. 13; Eimeric, *Directorium Inquisitorum*, part. 2, quæst. 49, art. 4, 364; Suárez, *Opus de triplice virtute theologica. De fide*, part. 2, disp. 16, sect. 5, art. 3, col. 591; Procedures against Joana "Curumbim" by the Inquisition of Goa, 1726. ANTT, *Tribunal do Santo Ofício, Inquisição de Lisboa*, no. 17048, fols. 19v–20r; Letter from the General Council of the Holy Office to the inquisitors of Goa, 13 April 1728, in Western Lisbon. ANTT, *Tribunal do Santo Ofício, Conselho Geral do Santo Ofício*, liv. 102, fol. 139r.

4 The Offence of *Gentilidade*: A Specificity of Goa?

Fifteen years into the creation of the Inquisition of Goa, the matter of how to treat the newly converted gained broader proportions. From 1576 onwards, different inquisitor generals strived to negotiate a papal exception for the newly converted, something that had very likely to do with the many occurrences involving the return to local practices in Goa. Although the *Reportorio* does not indicate many charges of *gentilidade* at this time, the matter was addressed in the 1576 letter written by Cardinal Henrique to the inquisitor in Goa, in which he ordered that the cases of relapses be suspended until further notice.[96] This is indicative of the greater relevance that this type of crime was acquiring in the activity of this court. The papal grace that allowed absolution for repeated offenders on charges of heresy was only obtained in 1599, thus preventing the imposition of the capital sentence on the newly converted.[97]

At that time, accusations on grounds of *gentilidade* were on the rise in Goa, as shown in Chart 7.2, above. A comparison with Brazil should be made in this regard; the years when *gentilidade* proceedings began to increase in the Inquisition of Goa were also years in which Gentilic ceremonies were under scrutiny by another court, namely that of Lisbon, through the visit (*visitação*) led by Heitor Furtado de Mendonça to the captaincies of Bahia (1591–1593) and Pernambuco (1593–1595) in Brazil. In particular, it was during his long stay in Salvador that H. F. de Mendonça came into contact with the phenomenon mentioned in documents as *Santidade*, a movement of indigenous origin deeply penetrated with contents from the Catholic religious and devotional world. Between c. 1580 and 1586—the year in which it was suppressed—the movement brought together natives of the *sertão* (hinterland), Christianized Amerindians, *mestizos*, Africans, and even Europeans.[98] According to the testimonies collected by H. F. de Mendonça, the unlawful behaviors practiced in this context suggest a parallelism with the Asian setting: genuflections and idol worship, reverence in the manner of the "*gentios*", Gentile ceremonies and adorations, etc.

---

96 Letter from Cardinal Henrique, Inquisitor General of Portugal, to Bartolomeu da Fonseca, inquisitor of Goa, February 15, 1576. Baião, *A Inquisição de Goa*, vol. 1, 298; Marcocci, "A fé de um império", 87, fn. 77.

97 On this brief, see Marcocci, "A fé de um império", 86–88; Marcocci and Paiva, *História da Inquisição Portuguesa*, 113–115.

98 Calasans, *Fernão Cabral de Ataíde e a Santidade de Jaguaripe*; Vainfas, *A heresia dos índios*, 141; Metcalf, "Millenarian Slaves?".

Recently, Jamille Cardoso argued that H. F. de Mendonça qualified the offences of those involved in the *Santidade* movement as heresy.[99] I found no documentary evidence to sustain this hypothesis, since none of the cases relating to the *Santidade* expressly refers to a category of crime within which to frame the proceedings. In fact, neither the rulings (*acórdãos*) of the vote of the board of the visit, nor the trial sentences, present indicators that describe the movement as heretical or a heresy.[100] To the contrary, the *Santidade* is consensually designated as *abusão* and *erronia*, often together, terms sometimes qualified with the adjective Gentilic. This is, therefore, a lexical frame closer to superstition than to heresy. If, in rhetoric, *abusão* is the improper or abusive use of one word to designate another, in this context it should be understood as "superstitions of those who abuse or misuse various things, [that] by their nature [are] disproportionate to the intended objective", and also "common error".[101] According to Bluteau, on the other hand, *erronia* means "error", "opinion", "maxim", "wrongful imagination", which is a "*palavra do vulgo*", i.e., a word used by the common folk.[102]

These same meanings, moreover, are found in the Jesuit documents that refer to the movement prior to the inquisitorial visit and are therefore independent of it. Both the *Informação do Brasil e de suas capitanias* of 1584 and the Annual Letter from the Brazilian mission of 1585, published in Rome two years later, coincide with a framework in the field of superstition. The *Informação do Brasil*, written before the suppression of the *Santidade*, does not refer to a specific movement, but to the frequent mobilizations of Amerindians by "sorcerers", characterized as charlatans creating an "invention (*invenção*) from which he thinks he will profit".[103] The terms most commonly used in this document are "inventions" and "lies". Its author suggests that the Amerindians were

---

99 Cardoso, *Ecos de Liberdade*, 138.

100 The only circumstances in which the term heresy was mentioned in the judicial sentences of those who adhered to the *Santidade* movement was when the defendants were also prosecuted for not respecting the precepts of not eating meat during Lent, something that, in the inquisitorial processology, was considered as an "heretical fault". Pantaleão Ribeiro's testimony contains the statement that followers of *Santidade* spoke in the Holy Trinity with "heretical errors". However, this statement is isolated and was not included in the final sentence despite the very close proximity between the narratives of the testimonies and those of the sentences. Procedures against Pantaleão Ribeiro by the Inquisition of Lisbon, 1591. ANTT, *Tribunal do Santo Ofício, Inquisição de Lisboa*, no. 11036, fol. 15.

101 VPL, 1712, s. v. "abusão": "superstiçoens dos que abusão, ou usão mal de varias cousas, por sua natureza desproporcionadas para o fim, que intentão"; Moraes (1789) s. v. "abusão": "Erro vulgar".

102 VPL, 1713, s. v. "erronia": "Erro. Opinião, maxima, imaginação errada".

103 Anchieta, *Cartas, Informações, Fragmentos Historicos e Sermões*, 331.

even aware of the inherent falsehood of these sorcerers' actions,[104] and he concludes by saying that they had many "other *agouros* (omens) and *abusões*", the latter being the same word that was extensively repeated in the inquisitorial proceedings.[105] In turn, the Annual Letter of 1585 refers precisely to the phenomenon that became known as *Santidade* and assumes its hybrid character of indigenous origin impregnated with Christian contents. In this document, *Santidade* is simultaneously a "superstition" (*nouum inter Indios superstitionis genus est ortum*) and a "ridiculous" "madness" (*Ad hanc vel superstitionem uel amentiam adiungitur illa non minus ridicula*).[106]

The consensus on how to define *Santidade* in the trial records of the inquisitorial visit should thus express not only the memory of the events among the population, but also a memory formatted into a terminology of its own, a process in which the Society of Jesus itself must have participated. As Ronaldo Vainfas recalled, the indoctrination of the Indians who adhered to *Santidade* was largely a responsibility of the Society of Jesus.[107] A possible intention to attenuate a close connotation between the movement and heresy in the description of events should not be overlooked.[108] These elements suggest that, in transposing the characterization of the movement into his own legal, inquisitorial framework, H. F. de Mendonça did not steer away from the crystallized portrayal of *Santidade* in Bahian society. In fact, he continually alluded to the movement as *abusão*, *erronia*, and even idolatry, in absolute conformity with the statements of the confessants, denouncers, and defendants, not to mention Governor Teles Barreto himself.[109] On the contrary, the use of the term sect, which tends to be more closely associated with the notion of heresy, is almost absent from the testimonies and was on no occasion included by the board of the visit, either in their decisions or in the judicial sentences.[110]

---

104 Anchieta, *Cartas, Informações, Fragmentos Historicos e Sermões*, 331.

105 Anchieta, *Cartas, Informações, Fragmentos Historicos e Sermões*, 331–332.

106 *Annuæ Litteræ Societatis Iesv Anni 1585*, 133–134.

107 Vainfas, *A heresia dos índios*, 150–151.

108 Conversely, Vainfas sees in some aspects of the 1585 Annual Letter elements that point to framing the *Santidade* movement as heresy, such as having books of their own. See Vainfas, *A heresia dos índios*, 208–209.

109 Certificate by Manuel Teles Barreto, governor of Brazil, August 8, 1586, in Procedures against Fernão Cabral de Ataíde by the Inquisition of Lisbon, 1591–1593. ANTT, *Tribunal do Santo Ofício, Inquisição de Lisboa*, no. 17065, fol. 171r.

110 A characteristic of the trial records from the inquisitorial visit to Brazil is the overlapping of narratives of the deponents (their testimonies) and those attributed to the visitor or to the inquisitorial board (interrogations, decisions, and judicial sentences). The record of the testimonies was copied almost *ipsis litteris* into the text of the judicial sentences, making it very hard to ascertain and outline the autonomy of each narrative recorded

For the purposes of judgment, perhaps the adoption of a term of its own was not necessary, due to the presumption of heresy identified in different forms of superstition, of which idolatry was one.[111] However, the language used to characterize the movement in the inquisitorial documentation steers away from a direct identification as heresy, as can be appreciated from the way ritual practices are referred to. The testimonies refer to what is practiced in *Santidade* as *despropósitos* (nonsense), *invenção*, *imperfeições* (imperfections), and the counterfeiting of Church customs—terms that largely point to errors in the exterior forms of cult, i.e., to ritual practices and not to doctrine.[112] As a result, they place the movement in opposition to an organized belief system, because no law or doctrine was attributed to it. For example, when asked about "what substance and what law was that of the *abusão* so-called *Santidade*", Pantaleão Ribeiro replied that:

> a Brazilian Christian named Antonio, who was raised in the villages of conversion, fled into the *sertão* and there invented this *erronia* called *Santidade*, which in itself has no order, no certainty, no rule, but to howl and honk, having no god in particular, [...] and speak in the most holy Trinity, with no purpose, and heretical errors, so that they live like this without any significance.[113]

Although, as Ribeiro's testimony proves, there were those among the residents of Bahia who used the image of heresy to characterize the movement, it was not the predominant representation and other elements prevailed.[114] In *Santidade*, its lack of intellectual depth, its Gentile origin, and its distorted understanding

---

during the visit. In light of this, it is interesting to note the absence of terms such as heresy and sect from the judicial sentences. The term sect was used by Fernão Cabral de Ataíde to address the *Santidade* movement, and H. F. de Mendonça even inquired why he invited that "sect of idolatry" into his property, but that is as far as he went, and he did not use the term again. Procedures against Fernão Cabral de Ataíde by the Inquisition of Lisbon, 1591–1593. ANTT, *Tribunal do Santo Ofício, Inquisição de Lisboa*, no. 17065, fols. 168v–169v.

111 Paiva, *Bruxaria e Superstição*, 56–59; Lara Cisneros, *¿Ignorancia invencible?*, 91–112.

112 Jean-Baptiste Thiers, collecting and systematizing the production that preceded him, wrote in 1679 that superstition was the domain of cults and undue practices, whether by defect, excess, content or form, or latria: "Si bien que l'on est veritablement Superstitieux lorsque l'on ne donne pas à Dieu ce qui luy appartient; lorsque l'on donne à la creature plus qui'il ne faut; lorsque l'on donne au Createur autre chose qu'il ne demande, & d'une autre maniere qu'il ne demande; lorsque l'on rend à tout autre qu'à Dieu un culte de latrie". In listing the different forms of superstition, the author makes use of the terms *abus*, and *excés*. Thiers, *Traité des Superstitions selon l'Écriture Sainte*, 4–5.

113 Procedures against Pantaleão Ribeiro by the Inquisition of Lisbon, 1591. ANTT, *Tribunal do Santo Ofício, Inquisição de Lisboa*, no. 11036, fols. 14v–15r.

114 The wide range of perceptions about the movement, from superstition to heresy, had already been noted by Ronaldo Vainfas. See Vainfas, *A heresia dos índios*, 172.

of the contents of the Christian message all may have contributed to blurring the characteristics more strongly associated with the heretic: the understanding (contrary doctrinal formulation) and the will (pertinacity in remaining in error).[115] The prevalence of a vocabulary that highlighted the absurd and imperfect nature of the practices of *Santidade* attests, as such, to a greater proximity to the semantic field of superstition than to that of formal heresy.[116]

In Brazil, therefore, there prevailed the notion that the Gentilic *humus* that nurtured the *Santidade* had generated an idolatrous practice which, perhaps due to the Christian elements that constituted it, did not involve a doctrine or law that could be considered indigenous to Brazil's *gentilismo*, contrary to what was happening in Asia.

The confession of Pêro Bastardo—a Portuguese man who lived in the hinterland of Raribe (Sergipe)—to living according to the "Gentilic way" can help us understand the dissociation between the Gentilic practices of Brazil and a charge of *gentilidade*. Asked by H. F. de Mendonça what the belief or law of the *gentilidade* of the Raribe Indians was and whether they worshipped idols or *pagodes*, he answered that:

> the Gentiles among whom he lived have no idols, nor *pagodes*, nor law, nor belief, nor faith; and that they believe only in what their sorcerers, their preachers, say to them, which is a thousand things without purpose, for example, when there are thunderstorms and storms, they say that what it means is that god commands them to sow and plant.[117]

Bastardo's opinion undoubtedly replicated the understanding shared by many about the Amerindians of Brazil. As early as 1549, when the Jesuit mission began, Father Manuel da Nóbrega, in a much-quoted passage, said that they were "people who have no knowledge of God, or idols".[118] This same idea is reproduced in the *Informação do Brasil*, which states that they "adore no creature as God—only the thunder do they believe is God—but they do not grant

115 See above, fn. 52.

116 Célia Tavares classifies the movement as "a very interesting type of *gentilismo*". If we take *gentilismo* to mean the action of withdrawing from faith and adhering to the "sect of the Gentiles", then the equivalence with the judicial category of *gentilidade* as used in Goa seems ill adjusted in light of the Christian contents of *Santidade*, pointed out in several of the testimonies. Tavares, "A Inquisição e a Companhia de Jesus diante do 'Gentilismo'", 6.

117 Procedures against Pêro Bastardo by the Inquisition of Lisbon, 1594. ANTT, *Tribunal do Santo Ofício, Inquisição de Lisboa*, no. 13180, fols. 3r–3v.

118 Letter from Father Manuel da Nóbrega, SJ, to Father Simão Rodrigues, SJ, [April 10?] 1549, Bahia. Leite, *Cartas do Brasil e mais escritos do P. Manuel da Nóbrega*, 21.

it any honor, nor do they commonly have idols, nor *sortes* (fortune telling), nor communication with the Devil, although they are afraid of him".[119]

It is possible that the absence of religious attitudes translatable into a system of beliefs—consisting of "law", "doctrine", and "sect"—disqualified, in the inquisitorial judgment, Gentilic practices as deserving of a specific legal framework, similar to what occurred at that time in Goa. The decision about Bastardo's sentence, which had nothing to do with the *Santidade* movement but concerned only the assumption of Gentilic customs in the hinterland of Raribe, stated that the defendant "confessed to his Gentilic offences", asserting that "he was never a Gentile in his mind nor did he leave the faith". However, it is not clear from the procedures whether the suspicion which rested on him resulted in an apostasy offence or whether "having their *gentilidade* [of Brazil's Indians]"[120] gained, in the visitor's mind, the same kind of significance as a particular type of offence as was happening in Goa. The matter did not escape the attentive eye of Vainfas, who stressed on numerous occasions that H. F. de Mendonça was not prepared to appreciate the Gentilic elements mentioned in the confessions he had received, and that he found it difficult to classify them into pre-existing categories.[121] However, the trials conducted during the visit were covered by the exceptional procedural circumstances established by a period of grace (*tempo da graça*) of one month, during which those who spontaneously appeared before the visitor to confess their faults were promised lenient treatment and exemption from the confiscation of assets. As such, trials such as those of Bastardo did not lead to thorough interrogations regarding the "Gentilic faults" that the visitor attributed to him because he confessed during the period of grace. The same applies to the cases of Lázaro da Cunha, who was questioned about whether he believed he could save himself "in that *gentilidade*" (of the Gentiles of Raribe), or that of Iria Álvares, who, having adhered to *Santidade* but not been put in a position to worship idols, was prosecuted for believing in the *abusão* and *erronia* and for having participated in other ceremonies, without it being possible to assess whether this particularity deserved specific considerations on the part of the visitor.[122]

---

119 Anchieta, *Cartas, Informações, Fragmentos Historicos e Sermões*, 331.

120 Procedures against Pêro Bastardo by the Inquisition of Lisbon, 1594. ANTT, *Tribunal do Santo Ofício, Inquisição de Lisboa*, no. 13180, fols. 11v–12r.

121 Vainfas, *A heresia dos índios*, 1995, reprint 2010, 168, 171, 181. As mentioned, this was not something unique to H. F. de Mendonça. The General Council of the Holy Office at Lisbon was also puzzled by the information conveyed by the inquisitors of Goa, requesting clarifications on what the realities they were describing actually meant. See, above, p. 224.

122 Procedures against Lázaro da Cunha and Iria Álvares by the Inquisition of Lisbon, 1592–1593 and 1595. ANTT, *Tribunal do Santo Ofício, Inquisição de Lisboa*, no. 11068 and 1335, respectively.

We cannot determine that, at the end of the 16th century, *gentilidade* already formed a category of offence that had been sufficiently discussed and publicized as such to the other inquisitorial courts, such as Lisbon. What is known, as demonstrated above, is that the Inquisition exhibited, since the end of the 1570s, special attention to the newly converted, even dispatching two commissions to the bishops of Brazil and China in 1579 to proceed locally against the newly converted, avoiding the inconvenience of a costly displacement of defendants to Lisbon and Goa.[123] However, it is difficult to determine whether the lack of prosecution on grounds of *gentilidade* in Brazil's 16th-century procedures derived from want of normalization of the term or from the fact that, in this period, the Holy Office did not recognize an autonomous law or doctrine that could be identified as a sect in Brazil's *gentilidade*. While inquisitorial perceptions of *gentilismo* and *gentilidade* in the Atlantic World have yet to receive broad treatment by scholars, preliminary analysis of later trial records relating to Brazil or Angola that involved Gentilic practices did not evolve into formal accusations of *gentilidade*, as was the case in Asia, but rather into accusations of idolatry or demonic pact.[124]

5 Final Remarks

In Asia, the recognition of a specific religious offence was likely the result of a court functioning in a completely non-European setting, on an island where direct contact with *gentilidade* was to be had by the simple act of crossing a river. In the 1590s, the Holy Office itself must have begun to find it difficult to assert the relevance of its activity via the European population sector, particularly

123 Lourenço, "Bispo da China e Inquisidor Apostólico".

124 Indeed, an accusation on *gentilidade* seems to be absent from the choices of categorization as is the case in the procedures against João Pereira da Cunha, who was a captain in the fort of Ambaca (Angola) (Procedures against João Pereira da Cunha by the Inquisition of Lisbon, 1749–1766. ANTT, *Tribunal do Santo Ofício, Inquisição de Lisboa*, no. 9691). As for Brazil, later cases studied by James Wadsworth such as the Jurema Cult in Paraíba and the *batuque* controversy in Pernambuco—both in the 18th century—seem to make use of a lexicon associated to the Indian's religious world such as "invention" and "diabolical witchcraft", as well as idolatry. In both cases we may find mentions of Indians and slaves from Angola adoring "smoke […] instead of God" or "false divinities". However, the types of offence associated with such beliefs were either divinations or "a sort of idolatry". Letter from José Ferreira Passo [to the Lisbon Inquisition], February 12, 1759, Paraíba. ANTT, *Tribunal do Santo Ofício, Inquisição de Lisboa*, maço 40, doc. 79; Requirement by Alexandre Jansen Moller, prossecutor of the Lisbon Inquisition, to the inquisitors [undated, c. 1779, Lisbon]. ANTT, *Tribunal do Santo Ofício, Inquisição de Lisboa*, no. 4740, fol. 3; Wadsworth, "*Jurema* and *Batuque*", 144. See also Resende, "Da ignorância e rusticidade", 97 et seq.; Marcocci and Paiva, *História da Inquisição Portuguesa*, 323–324.

through the offences of Judaism or Lutheranism, which had dropped to insignificant levels since the early 1580s. If we focus on the types of crime that imply adherence to another belief system, the comparison of the evolution of the cases followed by the Goa Inquisition in this period shows an increase in the trials of "Moor" and *gentilidade*. The renewal of the court's social function, of its legitimation in the *Estado da Índia*, was achieved by reorienting its repressive activity towards other types of crime. This shift meant, in the court's relationship with its immediate surroundings, the creation or the reinforcement of a new type of crime classification, that of *gentilidade*, but above all, of a new profile of delinquent: the *cristão da terra*.

It was these types of defendants that, from the 1580s until the definitive abolition of the Goa Inquisition, constituted the majority of the culprits prosecuted by the court. The cases of *gentilidade* became a recurrent feature in the lists of *autos-da-fé*. Convictions on *gentilidade* multiplied amid what can be perceived as an underlying uneasiness inside the Inquisition of Goa between its ministers. The ever-resurging question of the inherent value of the ceremonies and practices of the local populations divided inquisitors on where to draw the line of apostasy and heresy with regards to the diversity of behaviors of local Christians. The lack of preparation that Vainfas noticed in H. F. de Mendonça may have been due to the overwhelming challenges posed by the colonial world and faced by the visitor's notions or classifications of religious dissent. If that were the case, his attitude would not have differed from that of his colleagues in Goa, who faced similar challenges about where in the legal framework at their disposal they should place each misconduct. For them, the line that separated *gentilidade* from other crimes zigzagged between *sumbaias*, *pagodes*, ceremonies, sacrifices, and other circumstances of local life in the 'Old Conquests' or the 'Northern Province,' depending on the reaches of each defendant's intent (*tenção*). This line, however, was not fixed and likely depended on the personalities and education of each inquisitor and prosecutor and on the circumstances of the court's activities.

The edict of 1736, by discriminating against a whole panoply of practices previously considered as "political" or "non-declarative" of adherence to the "sect of the Gentiles", likely reinforced a tendency amongst the ministers of the Inquisition to perceive in each case that involved *gentilidades* a potential case of apostasy—an offence that was equivalent to that of heresy for the purposes of judicial procedure. In itself, the choice to claim broader jurisdiction over local customs is indicative of the accumulated pressure felt by different generations of inquisitors in dealing with their entourage and the frustration over not being able to overcome what they perceived as the shortcomings of mission and Inquisition.

Although a network of commissioners of the Holy Office was established in Brazil, the territory never had a functioning court. As such, the issue of the faith of the converted populations remained ever distant from the Inquisition of Lisbon's priorities, unlike in Goa. Here, the Inquisition operated in an entirely colonial territory surrounded by a majority of newly converted Catholics and their descendants. The interaction with the universe of *gentilidade* was an insurmountable reality, which had furthermore been intensified by decades of intense extirpation of idolatry campaigns and hostile policies towards local customs by Portuguese authorities. The emergence of a crime called, by the inquisitors, by the same name as the environment in which local beliefs originated, thus reflects the great difference between the Holy Office of Goa and the other Portuguese inquisitorial courts. Unlike Brazil and Angola, which were too far away from Lisbon and its inquisitors' eyes, the reality of individuals who were continuously crossing the river to the *terra firme* and apostatizing or performing the ceremonies and rituals of *gentilidade* was a matter directly witnessed and widely discussed by the ecclesiastical authorities residing in Goa. While the Inquisition in Lisbon remained, in essence, a European inquisitorial tribunal, Goa became a truly Asian one, particularly after trials on Judaism there dwindled. The emergence of a category whose name was taken from the term that defined the socio-religious otherness of the Gentiles testifies to the extent that the colonial context imposed itself on the court's activities. *Gentilidade*, re-signified by the Inquisition of Goa as a category of religious offence for apostatizing to the "sect of the Gentiles", became the legal expression of this reality.

Acknowledgements

This study was conducted as part of the project "Religiosidad nativa, idolatría e instituciones eclesiásticas en los mundos ibéricos, época moderna". Proyecto PAPIIT IG400619. Universidad Autónoma de México (UNAM). I wish to thank Gerardo Lara Cisneros for his attentive observations, as well as Manuel Bastias Saavedra and the two anonymous reviewers. I am also indebted to Ana Santos Pereira, Andrea Cicerchia, Dale Menezes, Jessica J. Fowler, João Eleutério, Paolo Aranha, Roger Lee de Jesus, and Susana Bastos Mateus.

Bibliography

Manuscripts

Arquivo Nacional Torre do Tombo (ANTT), *Tribunal do Santo Ofício, Conselho Geral do Santo Ofício,* Reply of the General Council of the Holy Office to the memorandum by André Fernandes, acting inquisitor of Goa, undated (c. March 1584), liv. 311, fols. 91r–92v.

Arquivo Nacional Torre do Tombo (ANTT), *Tribunal do Santo Ofício, Conselho Geral do Santo Ofício,* Ruling of the General Council of the Holy Office regarding the list of individuals sentenced by the Goa Inquisition in 1594, [March 16] 1596, liv. 100, fols. 78r–78v.

Arquivo Nacional Torre do Tombo (ANTT), *Tribunal do Santo Ofício, Conselho Geral do Santo Ofício,* List of individuals tried by the Inquisition of Goa in the year 1609 and 1610, undated, liv. 369, fols. 20r–39r.

Arquivo Nacional Torre do Tombo (ANTT), *Tribunal do Santo Ofício, Conselho Geral do Santo Ofício,* List of individuals that took part in the "auto-da-fé" of the Goa Inquisition of April 3–4, 1650, maço 33, no. 1.

Arquivo Nacional Torre do Tombo (ANTT), *Tribunal do Santo Ofício, Conselho Geral do Santo Ofício,* Letter from the General Council of the Holy Office to the inquisitors of Goa, April 13, 1728, Western Lisbon, liv. 102, fols. 136v–143v.

Arquivo Nacional Torre do Tombo (ANTT), *Tribunal do Santo Ofício, Conselho Geral do Santo Ofício,* List of individuals that took part in the "auto-da-fé" of the Goa Inquisition of September 21, 1766, maço 31, no. 13.

Arquivo Nacional Torre do Tombo (ANTT), *Tribunal do Santo Ofício, Inquisição de Coimbra,* Procedures against Luísa da Fonseca by the Inquisition of Coimbra, 1728, no. 7339.

Arquivo Nacional Torre do Tombo (ANTT), *Tribunal do Santo Ofício, Inquisição de Lisboa,* Procedures against Pantaleão Ribeiro by the Inquisition of Lisbon, 1591, no. 11036.

Arquivo Nacional Torre do Tombo (ANTT), *Tribunal do Santo Ofício, Inquisição de Lisboa,* Procedures against Fernão Cabral de Ataíde by the Inquisition of Lisbon, 1591–1593, no. 17065.

Arquivo Nacional Torre do Tombo (ANTT), *Tribunal do Santo Ofício, Inquisição de Lisboa,* Procedures against Lázaro da Cunha by the Inquisition of Lisbon, 1592–1593, no. 11068.

Arquivo Nacional Torre do Tombo (ANTT), *Tribunal do Santo Ofício, Inquisição de Lisboa,* Procedures against Lopo Álvares by the Inquisition of Goa, 1594, no. 12738.

Arquivo Nacional Torre do Tombo (ANTT), *Tribunal do Santo Ofício, Inquisição de Lisboa,* Procedures against Pêro Bastardo by the Inquisition of Lisbon, 1594, no. 13180.

Arquivo Nacional/Torre do Tombo (ANTT), *Tribunal do Santo Ofício, Inquisição de Lisboa,* Procedures against Iria Álvares by the Inquisition of Lisbon, 1595, no. 1335.

Arquivo Nacional Torre do Tombo (ANTT), *Tribunal do Santo Ofício, Inquisição de Lisboa,* Procedures against Francisco Rangel by the Inquisition of Goa, 1603–1605, no. 8916.

Arquivo Nacional Torre do Tombo (ANTT), *Tribunal do Santo Ofício, Inquisição de Lisboa,* Procedures against Joana "Curumbim" by the Inquisition of Goa, 1726, no. 17048.
Arquivo Nacional Torre do Tombo (ANTT), *Tribunal do Santo Ofício, Inquisição de Lisboa,* Procedures against João Pereira da Cunha by the Inquisition of Lisbon, 1749–1766, no. 9691.
Arquivo Nacional Torre do Tombo (ANTT), *Tribunal do Santo Ofício, Inquisição de Lisboa,* maço 40, doc. 79, Letter from José Ferreira Passo [to the Lisbon Inquisition], February 12, 1759, Paraíba.
Arquivo Nacional Torre do Tombo (ANTT), *Tribunal do Santo Ofício, Inquisição de Lisboa,* Requirement by Alexandre Jansen Moller, prossecutor of the Lisbon Inquisition, to the inquisitors [undated, c. 1779, Lisbon], no. 4740.

Printed Sources

Aquinas, Thomas, *Summa Theologiæ.* Online: https://aquinas.cc/la/en/~ST.I (January 27, 2021).
Annuæ Litteræ Societatis Iesv Anni MDLXXXV. Ad Patres, et Fratres eiusdem Societatis, Rome 1587: Collegio eiusdem Societatis.
Archivo Portuguez Oriental, fasc. 4, Nova Goa 1862, Third Ecclesiastical Council of Goa, 1585, 109–184.
Azpilcueta, Martín de, *Manval de Confessores y Penitentes, que clara & brevemente contiene, la vniuersal y particular decision de qvasi todas las dudas, que en las confessiones suelen ocurrir de los pecados, absoluciones, restituciones, censuras, & irregularidades,* Salamanca 1556: En casa de Andrea de Portonarijs.
Bluteau, Raphael, *Vocabulario portuguez e latino, aulico, anatomico, architectonico, bellico, botanico, brasilico, comico, critico, chimico, dogmatico, dialectico, dendrologico, ecclesiastico, etymologico, economico, florifero, forense, fructifero* [...], Coimbra 1712–1728.
Boniface VIII, *Sextus liber. Sexti libri argumentum multis signatum sillabis: Quis capita quater centum, quadraginta octo dabis,* Paris 1510: Jean Chappuis.
Covarrubias Orozco, Sebastián de, *Tesoro de la lengua castellana, o española,* Madrid 1611: Luis Sanchez, impressor del Rey.
Eimeric, Nicolau and Francisco Peña, *Directorium Inquisitorium* [...], Venice 1607: apud Marcum Antonium Zalterium.
Leite, Serafim (ed.), *Cartas do Brasil e mais escritos do P. Manuel da Nóbrega,* Coimbra 1955.
Real Academia Española (RAE), *Diccionario de la Lengua Castellana: en que se explica el verdadero sentido de las voces* [...], Madrid 1726–1739.
Rivara, Joaquim Heliodoro da Cunha, *Ensaio Historico da Lingua Concani,* Nova Goa 1858: Impr. Nacional.

Silva, Antonio de Moraes, *Diccionario da lingua portugueza composto pelo padre D. Raphael Bluteau, reformado, e accrescentado por* [...], Lisbon 1789: Na Officina de Simão Thaddeo Ferreira.

Solórzano Pereira, Juan de, *Politica Indiana*, Madrid 1647: En la Officina de Diego Díaz de la Carrera.

Sousa, Francisco de, *Oriente Conquistado a Jesu Christo pelos Padres da Companhia de Jesus da Provincia de Goa*, vol. 2, Lisbon 1710: Na Officina de Valentim da Costa Deslandes.

Stammler, Johannes, *Dialogus de diversarum gencium sectis et mundi religionibus*, Augsburg 1508: Per Erhardum Oglin & Ieorgi Nadler.

Suárez, Francisco, *Opus de triplice virtute theologica. De fide, Spe, et Charitate*, Paris 1621: Typis Edmundi Martini.

Thiers, Jean-Baptiste, *Traité des Superstitions selon l'Écriture Sainte, les Décrets des Conciles et les Sentiments des Saintes Péres et des Theologiens*, Paris 1679: Antoine Dezallier.

Literature

Amiel, Charles, "L'Inquisition de Goa", in Borromeo, Agostino (ed.), *L'Inquisizione. Atti del Simposio internazionale, 29–31 ottobre 1998*, Vatican City 2003, 229–250.

Amiel, Charles, "Goa", in Prosperi, Adriano, Vincenzo Lavenia and John Tedeschi (eds.), *Dizionario Storico dell'Inquisizione*, vol. 2, Pisa 2010, 716–718.

Anchieta, José de, SJ, *Cartas, Informações, Fragmentos Historicos e Sermões*, Rio de Janeiro 1933.

Aranha, Paolo, "Early Modern Asian Catholicism and European Colonialism: Dominance, Hegemony and Native Agency in the Portuguese *Estado da Índia*", in Koschorke, Klaus, Adrian Hermann (eds.), *Polycentric Structures in the History of World Christianity*, Wiesbaden 2014, 285–306.

Aranha, Paolo, *Il Cristianesimo Latino in India nel XVI Secolo*, Milan 2006.

Baião, António, *A Inquisição de Goa. Correspondência dos Inquisidores de Goa (1569–1630)*, vol. 2, Coimbra 1930.

Baião, António, *A Inquisição de Goa. Tentativa de história da sua origem, estabelecimento, evolução e extinção (Introdução à correspondência dos Inquisidores da Índia. 1560–1630)*, vol. 1, Lisbon 1945.

Barbu, Daniel, "'Idolatry' and Religious Diversity: Thinking about the Other in Early Modern Europe", in *Asdiwal. Revue Genevoise d'Anthropolgie et d'Histoire des Religions* 9 (2014): 39–50.

Bernand, Carmen and Serge Gruzinski, *De la idolatría. Una arqueología de las ciencias religiosas*, Mexico 1988 (repr. Mexico 2018).

Bethencourt, Francisco, *História das Inquisições. Portugal, Espanha e Itália*, [s.l.] 1994.

Boucharb, Ahmed, *Les crypto-musulmans d'origine marocaine et la société portugaise au XVIe siècle* (PhD Thesis), 3 vols., Montpellier 1987.

Boulhol, Pascal, "*Secta*: de la ligne de conduite au groupe hétérodoxe, Évolution sémantique jusqu'au début du Moyen Âge", *Revue de l'histoire des religions* 219:1 (2002): 5–33.

Burkardt, Albrecht, "Superstizione", in Prosperi, Adriano et al. (eds.), *Dizionario Storico dell'Inquisizione*, vol. 3, Pisa 2010, 1549–1551.

Calasans, José, *Fernão Cabral de Ataíde e a Santidade de Jaguaripe*, Madrid 1952 (repr. Salvador 2011).

Cardim, Pedro, "Os povos indígenas e as instâncias de justiça na América portuguesa e espanhola", in Domingues, Angela et al. (eds.), *Os Indígenas e as Justiças no Mundo Ibero-Americano (Sécs. XVI–XIX)*, Lisbon 2019, 29–84.

Cardoso, Jamille Oliveira Santos Bastos, *Ecos de Liberdade: a Santidade de Jaguaripe entre os alcances e limites da colonização cristã (1580–1595)* (MA thesis), Salvador 2015.

Castañeda Delgado, Paulino, "La condición miserable del indio y sus privilegios", in *Anuario de Estudios Americanos* 28 (1971): 245–335.

Congar, Yves, "'Gentilis' et 'Iudaeus' au moyen âge", in *Recherches de théologie ancienne et médiévale* 36 (1969): 222–225.

Cunha, Ana Cannas da, *A Inquisição no Estado da Índia. Origens (1539–1560)*, Lisbon 1995.

Dalgado, Sebastião Rodolfo, *Glossário Luso-Asiático*, vol. 1, Coimbra 1919.

Dalgado, Sebastião Rodolfo, *Glossário Luso-Asiático*, vol. 2, Coimbra 1921.

Eberenz, Rolf and Mariela de la Torre, *Conversaciones estrechamente vigiladas: Interacción coloquial y español oral en las actas inquisitoriales de los siglos XV a XVII*, Zaragoza 2003.

Evans, G. R., *Alain of Lille. The Frontiers of Theology in the Later Twelfth Century*, Cambridge 1983.

Faria, Patricia Souza de, "De réus a colaboradores: Nativos convertidos ao catolicismo diante do tribunal da Inquisição de Goa", in *Revista Brasileira de História das Religiões* 3:8 (2010), 165–182.

Faria, Patricia Souza de, "Os concílios provinciais de Goa: reflexões sobre o impacto da 'Reforma Tridentina' no centro do império asiático português (1567–1606)", in *Topoi*, 14:27 (2013): 218–238.

Feitler, Bruno, "A Inquisição de Goa e os nativos: achegas às originalidades da ação inquisitorial no oriente", in Furtado, Júnia Ferreira et al. (eds.), *Justiça, governo e bem comum na administração dos impérios ibéricos de Antigo Regime (séculos XV–XVIII)*, Curitiba 2017, 95–116.

Feitler, Bruno, "João Delgado Figueira e o *Reportorio* da Inquisição de Goa: Uma base de dados. Problemas metodológicos", in *Anais de História de Além-Mar* 13 (2012): 531–537.

Feitler, Bruno, "O Secreto do tribunal indiano da Inquisição portuguesa: entre Goa, Lisboa e Rio de Janeiro", in *Revista de fontes* 5:9 (2018): 36–50.

Feitler, Bruno, "The Portuguese Inquisition and Colonial Expansion. The 'Honor' of Being Tried by the Holy Office", in Del Valle, Ivonne et al. (eds.), *Iberian Empires and Roots of Globalization*, Nashville 2020, 105–130.

George-Tvrtković, Rita, "Deficient Sacraments or Unifying Rites? Alan of Lille, Nicholas of Cusa, and Riccoldo da Montecroce on Muslim and Jewish Praxis", in Levy, Ian Christopher, Rita George-Tvrtković and Donald F. Duclow (ed.), *Nicholas of Cusa and Islam. Polemic and Dialogue in the Late Middle Ages*, Boston 2014, 105–122.

Henn, Alexander, "Shrines of Goa: Iconographic Formation and Popular Appeal", in *South Asia Multidisciplinary Academic Journal*, no. 18 (2018): 1–17.

Humfress, Caroline, "Roman law, forensic argument and the formation of Christian Orthodoxy (III–VI centuries)", in Elm, Susanna, Éric Rebillard and Antonella Romano (eds.), *Orthodoxie, Christianisme, Histoire*, Rome 2001, 125–147.

Humfress, Caroline, *Orthodoxy and the Courts in Late Antiquity*, Oxford 2007.

Lara Cisneros, Gerardo, *¿Ignorancia invencible? Superstición e idolatría ante el provisorato de Indios y Chinos del Arzobispado de México em el siglo XVIII*, Mexico 2014.

Le Boulluec, Alain, *La notion d'héresie dans la littérature grecque. IIe–IIIe siècles*, 2 vols. Paris 1985.

Lopes, Maria de Jesus dos Mártires, "A Inquisição de Goa na primeira metade de Setecentos", *Mare Liberum*, no. 15 (1998): 107–136.

Lourenço, Miguel Rodrigues, *A Articulação da Periferia. Macau e a Inquisição de Goa (c. 1582–c. 1650)*, Lisbon; Macau 2016.

Lourenço, Miguel Rodrigues, "Bispo da China e Inquisidor Apostólico. D. Leonardo de Sá e os inícios da representação inquisitorial em Macau", in *Revista de Cultura*, no. 48 (2014): 49–67.

Lourenço, Miguel Rodrigues, "Macau, porto seguro para os cristãos-novos? Problemas e métodos sobre a periferia da Inquisição de Goa", in *Cadernos de Estudos Sefarditas*, no. 10/11 (2011): 451–500.

Marcocci, Giuseppe, "A fé de um império: a inquisição no mundo português de Quinhentos", in *Revista de História*, no. 164 (2011): 65–100.

Marcocci, Giuseppe, *A Consciência de um império. Portugal e o seu mundo (sécs. XV–XVII)*, Coimbra 2012.

Marcocci, Giuseppe, "Rites and Inquisition: Ethnographies of Error in Portuguese India (1560–1625)", in Županov, Ines G, and Pierre Antonie Fabre (ed.), *The Rites Controversies in the Early Modern World*, Leiden; Boston 2018, 145–164.

Marcocci, Giuseppe and José Pedro Paiva, *História da Inquisição Portuguesa. 1536–1821*, Lisboa 2013.

McClure, Judith, "Handbooks against heresy in the West, from the late fourth to the late sixth centuries", *The Journal of Theological Studies* 30, no. 1 (1979): 186–197.

Mendonça, Délio de, *Conversions and Citizenry. Goa under Portugal 1510–1610*, New Delhi 2002.

Metcalf, Alida C., "Millenarian Slaves? The Santidade de Jaguaripe and Slave Resistance in the Americas", in *The American Historical Review* 104:5 (1999): 1531–1559.

Nogueira, Eduardo Borges de Carvalho, *Pagodes do Diabo. Sociedade e religião hindu na Goa portuguesa* (*c. 1510– c. 1560*) (MA Thesis), Niterói 2012.

Wicki, José, *O Livro do "Pai dos Cristãos"*, Lisbon 1969.

Paiva, José Pedro, *Bruxaria e superstição num país sem "caça às bruxas". 1600–1774*, 2nd ed., Lisbon 2002.

Paiva, José Pedro, "The Inquisition Tribunal in Goa: Why and for What Purpose?", in *Journal of Early Modern History* 21:6 (2017): 565–593.

Resende, Maria Leônia Chaves de (2019), "'Da ignorância e rusticidade': os indígenas e a Inquisição na América portuguesa (séculos XVI–XIX)", in Domingues, Ângela et al. (eds.), *Os Indígenas e as Justiças no Mundo Ibero-Americano* (*Sécs. XVI–XIX*), Lisbon 2019, 87–126.

Robinson, Rowena, "Taboo or Veiled Consent? Goan Inquisitorial Edict of 1736", in *Economic and Political Weekly* 35:27 (2000): 2423–2431.

Rubiés, Joan-Pau, "Reassessing the 'Discovery of Hinduism': Jesuit Discourse on Gentile Idolatry and the European Republic of Letters", in Amaladass, Anand and Ines G. Županov (dir.), *Intercultural Encounter and the Jesuit Mission in South Asia* (*16th–18th Centuries*), Bangalore 2014, 113–155.

Rubiés, Joan-Pau, "The Concept of a Gentile Civilization in Missionary Discourse and its European Rception. Mexico, Peru and China in the *Repúblicas del Mundo* by Jerónimo Román (1575–1595)", in Castelnau-l'Estoile, Charlotte de, Marie-Lucie Copete, Aliocha Maldavsky and Ines G. Županov (dir.), *Missions d'Évangelisation et Circulation des Savoirs*, Madrid 2011, 311–350.

Sachot, Maurice, "'Religio/superstitio'. Historique d'une subversion et d'un retournement", *Revue de l'histoire des religions* 208:4 (1991): 355–394.

Salomon, H. P., "Les procès de l'Inquisition Portugaise comme documents littéraires, ou du bon usage du fonds inquisitorial de la Torre do Tombo", *Estudos Portugueses: Homenagem a António José Saraiva*, Lisbon 1990, 151–164.

Sánchez, Tomás, SJ, *Opus Morale in Præcepta Decalogi*, Venice 1623.

Silva, Luiza Tonon da, *Inquisição e Mestiçagem Cultural no Estado da Índia* (*1560–1623*) (MA Thesis), Niterói 2018.

Solange, Alberro, *Inquisición y Sociedad en México, 1571–1700*, Mexico 1988 (repr. Mexico 2004).

Souza, Teotónio R. de, *Goa Medieval. A cidade e o interior no século XVII*, Lisboa 1994.

Tavares, Célia Cristina da Silva, "A Inquisição e a Companhia de Jesus diante do 'Gentilismo'", in *ANPUH – XXV Simpósio Nacional de História. Anais*, Fortaleza 2009, 1–9.

Tavares, Célia Cristina da Silva, "Inquisição ao avesso: a trajetória de um inquisidor a partir dos registros da Visitação ao Tribunal de Goa", in *Topoi* 10:19 (2009): 17–30.

Tavim, José Alberto Rodrigues da Silva, "'O culto ao diabo' na Inquisição de Goa, segundo o *Reportório* de João Delgado Figueira (1623)", in *Anais de História de Além-Mar*, no. 17 (2016): 271–302.

Tavim, José Alberto Rodrigues da Silva (1997), "Um inquisidor inquirido: João Delgado Figueira e o seu *Reportorio*, no contexto da "documentação sobre a Inquisição de Goa"", in *Leituras: Revista da Biblioteca Nacional*, no. 1 (1997): 183–193.

Traslosheros, Jorge, "Los indios, la Inquisición y los tribunales eclesiásticos en Nueva España. Definición jurisdiccional y justo proceso, 1571–c.1750", in Traslosheros, Jorge and Ana de Zaballa Beascoechea (eds.), *Los indios ante los foros de justicia religiosa en la Hispanoamérica virreinal*, Mexico 2010, 47–74.

Vainfas, Ronaldo, *A heresia dos índios. Catolicismo e rebeldia no Brasil colonial*, São Paulo 1995 (repr. São Paulo 2010).

Ventura, Ricardo Nuno de Jesus, *Conversão e conversabilidade. Discursos da missão e do gentio na documentação do Padroado Português do Oriente (séculos XVI e XVII)* (PhD Thesis), 2 vols., Lisbon 2011.

Wadsworth, James, "*Jurema* and *Batuque*: Indians, Africans, and the Inquisition in Colonial Northeastern Brazil", in *History of Religions* 46:2 (November 2006): 140–162.

Wicki, Ioseph, S.I. (ed.), *Documenta Indica*, vol. 11, Rome 1970.

Wilkinson, R. J., *A Malay-English Dictionary*, part 1, Singapore 1901.

Xavier, Ângela Barreto, "De converso a novamente convertido. Identidade política e alteridade no Reino e no Império", in *Cultura. Revista de História e Teoria das Ideias*, no. 22 (2006): 245–274.

Xavier, Ângela Barreto, *A invenção de Goa. Poder imperial e conversões culturais nos séculos XVI e XVII*, Lisboa 2008.

Xavier, Ângela Barreto, "Conversos and Novamente Convertidos: Law, Religion and Identity in the Portuguese Kingdom and Empire", in *Journal of Early Modern History* 15:3 (2011): 255–287.

Zaballa Beascoechea, Ana de, "Visitadores, extirpadores y 'tratados de idolatrías'", in Saranyana, Josep Ignasi (ed.), *Teología en América Latina, I – Desde los orígenes a la Guerra de Sucesión (1493–1715)*, Madrid 1999, 258–280.

Zaballa Beascoechea, Ana de, "Del viejo al nuevo mundo: novedades jurisdiccionales en los tribunales eclesiásticos ordinarios en Nueva España", in Traslosheros, Jorge and Ana de Zaballa Beascoechea (eds.), *Los indios ante los foros de justicia religiosa en la Hispanoamérica virreinal*, México 2010, 17–46.

Županov, Ines and R. Po-Chia Hsia, "Reception of Hinduism and Buddhism", in R. Po-Chia Hsia (ed.), *The Cambridge History of Christianity*, vol. 6 [*Reform and Expansion*], Cambridge 2007, 577–597.

CHAPTER 8

Theology in the Dark: The Missionary Casuistry of Japan Jesuits and Dominicans during the Tokugawa Persecution (1616–1622)

Rômulo da Silva Ehalt

1 Introduction

> About 18 years ago [...], a devil entered the body of a heathen and publicly declared he had come from England, and he had come to Japan to teach the devils of Japan how to persecute Christians. [...] since then this poor Church of Japan has been put to shame, and all those who protected the priests and their neighbors were executed and had their possessions taken away; not only those who sheltered and harbored [the missionaries] in their homes, but also ten neighbors of the house where they were harbored suffered the same punishment. [...] the door to that country is closed so tightly that it seems that, if this harsh persecution continues for long, everything will be lost.[1]

From his cubicle in Macau in 1622, the Portuguese Jesuit Afonso de Lucena (1551–1623) reminisced about his time in Japan. He had arrived there in 1578, about 30 years after Francis Xavier (1506–1552) and his companions started the mission. According to his account, the situation had worsened when a "possessed" English merchant, William Adams (1564–1620), arrived in Japan in the year 1600. Adams successfully became close to the new rulers of the country, the Tokugawa clan. In Lucena's estimation, that was the spark which started the persecution against Jesuits, Dominicans, Franciscans, Augustinians, and Christians in general in the archipelago.[2] The result was a decree in 1614 that expelled the missionaries: sixty-five priests, mendicant friars, and brothers embarked on three vessels to Macau, while 23 others took a ship to Manila.[3]

1 Lucena, *De algumas cousas*, ed. Schütte, 284. All translations are mine except when noted.
2 Concerning the political influence and land owned by Japan Jesuits in this period, see my text "From Tenants to Landlords". For an overview on William Adams and the Japanese, see Katō, "Aspects of Early Anglo-Japanese Relations", 31–59.
3 Shimizu et al. (eds.), *Kinsei Nagasaki*, 100–101; Schütte, *Introductio*, 200.

© RÔMULO DA SILVA EHALT, 2022 | DOI: 10.1163/9789004472839_009

Despite the order, 47 missionaries decided to stay. Living in hiding meant that the clergy no longer had a fixed residence. Those coming from Macau to Japan had to use Japanese vessels, given the strict vigilance over foreign ships imposed by local authorities, as well as to avoid Dutch and English merchants eager to denounce concealed missionaries.[4] Once in the country, they had to quickly learn the art of disguise. While Japanese Jesuits could easily pass as laymen, that was not an option for their European peers. Although they could dress up as merchants in Nagasaki and other areas where foreigners were not an uncommon sight, non-Japanese missionaries needed to disguise themselves as commoners whenever wandering into regions farther removed from the port.[5] In a letter to his brother, the Dominican Angel Ferrer Orsucci wrote that the priests used to dress like Spaniards, with a sword tied to the waist, long beards but no tonsure—a style that would later earn them the moniker "barbones" or big beards.[6] Besides their attempts to blend in, missionaries also depended on the good will of Japanese Christians ready to risk their own lives to give them shelter as this act was considered a crime immediately after the expulsion decree.[7] Once authorities began actively looking for hidden missionaries, the danger quickly escalated. In 1617, the Tokugawa *Bakufu* started collecting oaths in which signatories declared that they would not aid missionaries.[8] The punishment represented being stripped of one's wealth and being sentenced to death. Moreover, the offender's family and up to nine neighbors could face the same fate.[9] These severe restrictions turned what had been a question of survival into the most pressing moral challenge of the late 1610s. How could missionaries justify the risk they imposed on Japanese Christians?

In 1620, missionaries of the Jesuit administrative unit known as the Province of Japan submitted a questionnaire of 61 items to their counterparts in Macau. The Dominicans in Japan followed suit in 1621, with a similar—but much shorter—list of eight questions sent to the former rector of the *Colegio de Santo Tomás* in Manila. Both consultations dealt with the series of problems created by the oaths imposed on Christians in Japan. By focusing on these documents, this chapter explores the production of norms or rules for local

4 Ajuda, 49-V-7, fol. 173; JapSin 37, fols. 156–156v.

5 Schütte, *Monumenta Historica Japoniae* (hereafter MHJ), 793–794.

6 Anon., *Lettere edificante*, 38–39; Boxer and Cummins, "The Dominican mission in Japan", 41; Odstrčilík, "Between Languages", 121.

7 Orfanel, *Historia Eclesiastica*, cap. LIX, fols. 115v–116; JapSin 58, fol. 293.

8 *Bakufu*, literally "tent office", was the name given to the shogunate in Japan.

9 JapSin 17, fol. 287. However, as noted by Alvarez-Taladriz, this was not a juridical innovation, since it was customary in Japan to kill and confiscate the wealth of those who hid someone who had been ordered to be arrested. Alvarez-Taladriz, "Fuentes Europeas", 414.

Christian communities in Japan and the use of moral theology in the process. The objective is to analyze both consultations as pieces of the dialogue here understood as missionary casuistry. This dialogue relied both on personal experience and theological authorities, while also considering circumstances imposed locally, with the ultimate aim of negotiating norms and confession guidelines with superiors outside of Japan. Considering the operations of both the Jesuits and the Dominicans in Japan, this chapter presents an in-depth appreciation of local conditions that determined the production of casuistry for the issue of the oaths imposed by the Tokugawa *Bakufu* on Christians in the late 1610s and early 1620s Japan.

2 Norm-Making through Missionary Casuistry

Done by Jesuits and Dominicans in Japan during the persecution, wearing the attire of locals when in the land of infidels was an issue with a long history. By the early 17th century, names such as the Dominican Domingo Bañez, as well as Jesuits Juan Azor and Tomás Sánchez, were among the most authoritative voices invoked by missionaries in Japan—and other regions—when justifying the adoption of non-Christian clothes.[10] Similar issues were the object of the science known at the time as 'cases of conscience': a field dedicated to analyzing instances where a person had to make a correct moral choice between two or more possible courses of action. Doubts (*dubia*) concerning the moral acceptability of the available alternatives made great prudence necessary when considering what advice should be given by a priest to the individual facing the dilemma.[11] As the Council of Trent put forward efforts to standardize liturgy and dogma, the increase in the number of situations met in missionary frontiers and colonial societies that could not be solved by classic medieval *summas*, or other materials available to priests and confessors abroad, led to a complex process of reformulation of the confessional practice during the 16th century that resulted in "high casuistry".[12]

---

10 Particularly useful for missionaries were the following passages: Bañez, *Scholastica commentaria in secundam secundae*, q. 3, a. 3; Azor, *Institutionum moralium*, vol. 1, lib. 8, c. 27, q. 4; Sánchez, *Opus Morale in Praecepta Decalogi*, vol. 1, lib. 2, c. 4, no. 16 and no. 20. But Japan Jesuits met severe criticism, both internal and external, when they decided to imitate Buddhist monks and wear their robes. On this issue: Brockey, "Authority, Poverty, Vanity", 185–195; Prosperi, "The missionary", 172–176; Alberts, *Conflict and Conversion*, 96.

11 Tutino, *Uncertainty in Post-Reformation Catholicism*, 9.

12 Schüssler, *The Debate on Probable Opinions*, 125–126.

In areas of missionary activity and in colonial societies, problems such as inheritance, matrimony, the ownership of enslaved individuals, usury, idolatry, vows, penance, and how to administer and understand other sacraments, precepts, and dogmas comprised the bulk of issues that casuistry dealt with.[13] In the study of the colonial enterprise led by the Portuguese Crown, the documental corpus of opinions and debates produced in colonial and missionary contexts has been collectively referred to by Giuseppe Marcocci as missionary casuistry, which he understands to be the vast system of integrated knowledge that allowed the emergence of a unified Portuguese empire.[14]

As in Europe, casuists outside the 'Old World' resorted to classic scholastic theologians and summists, as well as civil and canon lawyers.[15] However, in this context, a different notion of casuistry may be helpful; in a classic dictionary of philosophy, casuistry is defined both as the study of cases of conscience, as well as a "method of solving conflicts of obligations by applying general principles of ethics, religion, and moral theology to particular and concrete cases of human conduct".[16] By taking casuistry as a dynamic science, rather than the accumulated archival set of questions, opinions, and responses, it is possible to imagine how casuists worked in colleges in Goa, Mexico, Macau, Lima, Malacca, Salvador, and Bahia. In these institutions, professors of cases of conscience were more than coaches to confessors; they were active producers of a theological discourse aimed at addressing the issues met in colonial societies—those under legal jurisdiction of the colonial empires—and in missionary frontiers—beyond the limits of colonial enterprises.

Take the example of Lopo de Abreu (1547–1606), a Portuguese Jesuit who taught for more than two and a half decades in Asia. When he wrote his *indipeta* (petition for the Indies) letter in 1575, his plan was to leave Europe and work as a missionary in India or, if possible, in Japan. However, he ultimately became an established professor in Jesuit colleges in India. The highpoint of his career was his *summa*; written in the early 17th century, it was met with wide acceptance in Asia but harsh criticism in Europe. Despite its critics, the work was later translated into Latin and could still be found in use in various Catholic colleges and churches throughout Asia until the end of the century.[17] Casuists such as Abreu were part of an army of theological and legal polymaths

13 Wicki, "Problemas morais no Oriente Português", 257–258.

14 Marcocci, *L'invenzione di un impero*, 124; Marcocci, "Conscience and Empire", 487–488.

15 Schüssler, *The Debate on Probable Opinions*, 217.

16 Rolbiecki, "Casuistry", 46. See also the discussion in Jonsen and Toulmin, *The Abuse of Casuistry*, 11–16.

17 See my upcoming article on Abreu's *Suma de Moral* and its Latin translation, Vicente Álvares's *Summa Lusitana*.

established in educational institutions outside of Europe, capable of resorting to rules and principles not derived from the accumulated volume of opinions and responses to previous questions, but rather from moral theology and civil and canon law. Their role, which still needs to be better understood, seemed to be that of an intermediary between tensions arising from the work and needs of missionaries and the projects and demands from superiors in Europe. As for the sources of casuistry itself, Rudolf Schüssler reminds us that even though there were no clear guidelines for how to apply these principles, judgements and discussions were at the core of casuistry and how it viewed moral dilemmas.[18] In Asia, Abreu was just one from a list of little known casuists such as Francisco Rodrigues, António de Quadros, Gomes Vaz, Manuel de Carvalho, Domingos do Espírito Santo, Paulo da Trindade, Sebastião da Maya, Domingo González, Andrés Lopez, Arcadio do Rozário, and Juan de Paz, whose work and achievements the field is only beginning to grasp.[19]

By changing the definition of casuistry and considering the field in which it was used, missionary casuistry can be understood as the study of cases of conscience that arose from problems met in missionary settings, beyond the relative stability guaranteed by colonial dominance in certain cities, such as Goa, Malacca, Macau, or Manila. But it was more than that; in fact, it was a discourse formed by reports on the actions of missionaries and elaborated upon by theologians in colonial colleges, with the aim of negotiating with hierarchically superior authorities the validity of ad hoc decisions taken in the missions. Thus, the body of sources where missionary casuistry can be found involves, primarily, consultations from colonial or missionary settings addressed to superiors in these same areas or in Europe.

For that reason, missionary casuistry carried considerable political weight. The aim of solving moral problems in the missions involved much more than simply resolving dilemmas. It was indeed part of a political dialogue and negotiation between priests of the same order but in different hierarchical categories. Although it could be part of the job, it was not the ultimate goal of casuists to organize the jurisprudence of confessional issues and their solutions. Instead, their work was aimed at solving political and hierarchical conflicts between missionaries and their organizational units—provinces, vice-provinces, and so on—and superiors in Europe or other areas. Accordingly, missionary casuistry was a border-crossing science and discourse, oriented toward solving problems that arose in different local conditions. It was thus instrumental in exchanges

18 Schüssler, *The Debate on Probable Opinions*, 126.

19 Ehalt, "Casuística nos Trópicos", 399–418; McManus, "Limited-Term Servitude in Early Modern Nagasaki".

between missions in areas such as Japan, China, India, Brazil, Mexico, Peru, North America, and Africa, and hierarchically superior centers of power in Rome, Goa, Macau, Manila, and others. In addition, it formed the basis upon which inquiries were made concerning how to deal with issues met on the missionary front in order to avert unwanted attention from critics. The unity of this discourse was made possible because of a common language, shared by all involved parties, comprised of moral theology, as well as civil and canon law. Upon mastering these three corpora, casuists could then engage in missionary casuistry and the negotiations that ensued. Scholarship on Christian missions in early modern Japan has, for the most part, left aside the role of moral theology and casuistry in the relations between missionaries in the East and superiors overseas, thus overlooking how important mastering this linguistic and political code was.[20]

In the negotiation process between missionary peripheries and centers, Jesuits and Dominicans in Japan created numerous moral guidelines for Christian communities in the country, namely foreign residents and Japanese Christians. These groups were enmeshed in a complex set of different normativities and subjected to various authorities simultaneously, such as local legislations like *Bakufu* decrees, regional codes, and city or village ordinances; Portuguese royal officials; and the authority of various administrative entities and divisions in Japanese cities like ward administrators, city officials, *Bakufu* officials, and regional officials. Amidst this complex entanglement of different hierarchies and authorities, missionaries used missionary casuistry to influence the behavior of the faithful in Japan through the establishment of moral guidelines for Japanese Christians. In creating liturgical rules for those who wanted to lead a pious life, they also addressed issues that concerned Christian morals and canon law but were not regulated by Japanese legislation: trading practices, marriage, and slave trade and ownership, for example. In practice, these rules were regularly repeated by the members of these brotherhoods, forming constant reminders of what was to be expected from a Christian.[21]

Ultimately, missionary casuistry was significant because it gave authoritative normative value to local experiential reasoning. In the process of negotiating courses of action within Jesuit and Dominican ranks, missionaries put

20 For the case of Japan, exceptions include but are not restricted to the following: Ahn, *Kirishitan Jidai no Kon'in Mondai*; Asami, *Kirishitan Jidai no Gūzō Sūhai*; Takase, "Kirishitan Fukyō ni okeru Usura"; López Gay, *El Matrimonio de los Japoneses*; Pinto and Pires, "The 'Resposta que alguns Padres de Japão'"; Ehalt, *Jesuits and the Problem of Slavery*; Ehalt, "Goa no Iezusukai"; Vu Thanh, "Introducing Tridentine Marriage".

21 See, for instance, the rules of the Confraria de Jesus. Murakami, "Kirishitan Kenkyū no Kaiko", 14.

their own ad hoc decisions to the test. Under the enormous pressures put upon them by the intensification of the persecution in Japan in the early 17th century, their use of theology spoke to the need to obtain further support and recognition abroad, while at the same time it served as a tool for regulating Christian life during the persecution.

3 The Underground Church

Luís Yakichi (c. 1592–1622), his wife Lúcia (?–1622), and their sons André (c. 1615–1622) and Francisco (c. 1620–1622), were a Japanese Christian family living in Nagasaki. Behind their house, they had built a small chapel where they used to receive and hide missionaries.[22] Despite their poverty, they would also let the space be used by other hiding Christians who wanted to confess whenever there was a priest there. Besides harboring missionaries, Luís Yakichi used to accompany them whenever they had to walk the streets seeking new refuge or places to hold mass. His dedication to the priests made him leave his home from time to time to travel with the missionaries in the Nagasaki region. Eventually, Luís Yakichi was arrested for trying to free the Flemish Dominican friar Lodewijk Frarijn or Luis Flores (c. 1563–1622) from the prison in Ōmura and was executed along with his family and seven other Christians on October 2, 1622.[23]

Following the expulsion of all missionaries in 1614, the Japanese Catholics and their pastors went underground. Like Luís Yakichi, numerous Christians helped hide missionaries during the persecution, a condition which European and Japanese alike referred to as *hissoku* (*fisocu* in Jesuit documents), i.e., "to be hiding, or enclosed, secluded, not going public".[24] This led to two different outcomes. First, many Christians were executed for harboring missionaries. In 1622, when Luís Yakichi's family was killed, a total of 132 people had been executed in Japan due to the persecution.[25] Out of 115 lay people, at least 64 were directly or indirectly related to the sheltering of priests.[26] Second, priests

22 According to the 1615 annual letter from Japan, the number of small, private chapels had grown to such an extent in the city that there were "more churches now in Nagasaki than ever before". JapSin 58, fol. 293v.

23 Ruiz-de-Medina, *Martirológio*, 473–475; *Japón* 2, fols. 46–50.

24 Anon., *Vocabulario*, fol. 95v. *Hissoku* was also the name of a punishment given to *bushi*, monks, and Shintō priests. It was a form of house arrest that would normally last for 30 or 50 days. See Fujii, *Oshioki*, 230–231.

25 Boxer and Cummins, "The Dominican Mission in Japan", 20.

26 Ruiz-de-Medina, *Martirologio*, 435–478. There were 17 missionaries executed that year. Gonoi, *Tokugawa Shoki*, 186.

had to clandestinely recreate the way they administered the sacraments, held masses, and performed all the necessary liturgies required for the maintenance of Christian communities. In 1619, the Jesuit priest Francisco Vieira (1555–1619), Visitor of the Jesuit Province of Japan between mid-1618 and October of 1619, reported the situation in the following words:

> We now have no house, no college, no residence, no parish in the villages that here are called *inacas*, nor any public church, because we do not have even a palm of land to call ours where we could stay without being discovered. Now we go from Christian house to Christian house, hiding, taking along our equipment and all necessary materials to hold mass, and in these Christian houses we erect a small altar, and while we are there hiding for one or two days, or a week, or a month, we hold mass, hear confessions, give communion to the Christians, and give sermons, and teach the Christians, and exhort them to persevere in the faith, and baptize those who have newly converted. All this we do in hiding, and perform the rest of the exercises as we used to do before in the churches when we had peace, in such a way that we are like a walking army with portable altars, helping the faithful with our ministries.[27]

Despite Vieira's rather optimistic view of the missionaries' activities under such circumstances, reality was in fact quite grim. In a report written the previous year, another Jesuit explained that all that priests could do was wait to be killed either by the sword or on a cross.[28] In 1614 and 1615, two military campaigns known collectively as the Siege of Ōsaka eliminated the last traces of the old opposition from the Toyotomi clan and consolidated the authority of the shōgun Tokugawa Hidetada (1579–1632). In September 1616, Hidetada turned his attention back to the religious problem and determined that local warlords—daimyō—were to have no Christians among their retainers. This led to a wide-spread prohibition against the presence of Christians.[29] However, aware of the inseparable relation between religion and trade, Hidetada tried to ensure the continuity of the commerce with European merchants. Portuguese and Spanish ships were restricted to Nagasaki, a city under direct shōgun

27 JapSin 17, fol. 195. Similar arguments were made by Vieira in a 1617 letter. See Brockey, *Journey to the East*, 69.

28 JapSin 17, fol. 177.

29 Jesuit sources suggest that there were about 500,000 Japanese Christians in congregations and brotherhoods under the Society of Jesus' sponsorship prior to the expulsion of 1614, while in 1618 the number had fallen to about 300,000. See Schütte, *Introductio*, 433.

authority, while Dutch and English vessels were instructed to harbor in Hirado, a small trading port ruled by the Matsura clan on the northwestern portion of Kyūshū.[30] Missionaries, who up to that point had enjoyed an apparent tacit consent, at least in Nagasaki, now faced increasing pressure. In 1616, a small vessel (*galeota*) coming from Macau carried four missionaries: one Franciscan, one Dominican, and two Jesuits. While the two priests of the Society of Jesus left the ship before it docked in Nagasaki and managed to enter the city on a Japanese boat, the two mendicant friars tried to disembark disguised as merchants. Upon being alerted of their presence on the ship, the Nagasaki authorities stopped the friars and made them return to Macau on the same vessel, creating a public display of the changes in the policy toward missionaries.[31]

Amidst the chaos that ensued due to the growing persecution, lay brotherhoods played a fundamental role in arranging secure shelters for missionaries. These organizations first appeared in Japan in the 1550s as charitable confraternities following the model of the Portuguese *Misericórdias* and native Buddhist lay organizations.[32] Lay brotherhoods, known as *confrarias* in Portuguese, *cofradías* in Spanish, or *kumi* in Japanese, organized under different parishes or by the initiative of missionaries, were established at various times in Japan as a direct response to persecution.[33] That explains why they first appeared after 1587, when Toyotomi Hideyoshi signed an unenforced decree expelling missionaries from the country.[34] By the early 17th century, there were numerous such organizations in Japan. After the 1614 expulsion of missionaries, they became instrumental in keeping Christian communities together and addressing the difficulties that arose from the absence of priests. Although brotherhoods could not perform sacraments that needed the participation

30 Yamamoto, *Tokugawa Hidetada*, 141–144.

31 This seems to have been a different ship from the usual great ship from Macau to Nagasaki, given that financial disputes involving that year's *Capitão-Mor*, João Serrão da Cunha, prevented his vessel from leaving Macau. JapSin 58, fol. 411; Boxer, *The Great Ship from Amacon*, 89; Gonoi, *Tokugawa Shoki*, 195.

32 For more on the Portuguese *Misericórdias*, see Sá, *As Misericórdias Portuguesas*, Sá, *História Breve das Misericórdias*, and Kawamura, *Kirishitan Shinto Soshiki no Tanjō to Henyō*.

33 That was also the impression Japan Jesuits had at the time. In the 1615 annual letter from Japan, Mateus de Couros comments on the direct correlation between persecution and the resurgence of brotherhoods. JapSin 58, fol. 286v.

34 Historians Ebisawa Arimichi, Kawamura Shinzō, and Reinier Hesselink have put forward different classifications of brotherhoods according to distinct criteria, although they mostly agree on the functions these organizations had under the Tokugawa persecution. See Ebisawa, *Kirishitan no Dan'atsu*, 125, 132; Kawamura, *Making Christian*, 41–55, 119, 134; Hesselink, "104 Voices", 247–248. For an overview of lay brotherhoods in Japan, see Costa, "The Misericórdias", 67–79; and Costa, "The Brotherhoods", 67–84.

of ordained clergy, such as marriage, confession, and confirmation, they were fundamental for communities in observing the liturgical calendar, holding masses, and performing baptisms.

Some brotherhoods comprised wide networks of Christian communities organized under elder men and women as spiritual leaders. The better documented example of a brotherhood is that of the Jesuit *Confraria de Nossa Senhora da Assunção* or *Santa Mariya no Onkumi*, named after the day upon which Xavier arrived in Japan. According to the records written in 1618 by Jerónimo Rodrigues in Macau, the organization gathered, under the auspices of the Society of Jesus, numerous Christian lay leaders, dividing them into a plethora of minor, major, and universal brotherhoods: minor organizations had about 50 male members plus their wives and servants; above them, major brotherhoods gathered minor organizations and had about 500 to 600 members; lastly, universal brotherhoods gathered all the major organizations from a single district.[35] Most of these brotherhoods owed allegiance to a single religious order or were run by priests from a given order. Nevertheless, in many cases, that did not mean brotherhoods would deny aid to missionaries of orders different to that of their sponsors. Christians would help missionaries by performing various tasks such as delivering messages or letters, offering them food and shelter, transporting them by sea or land, and searching for new places to hide. Not only that, brotherhoods also created spaces for praying and gatherings, like the chapel behind Luís Yakichi's house, some of which even housed relics obtained from the sites of martyrdoms. For example, Manuel Murayama (1596–1620), one of the sons of the disgraced Nagasaki magistrate António Murayama Tōan (1562–1619), who was executed in 1619 for harboring priests, preserved five martyrs' bodies in his house as well as 80 fingers from Christians killed because of their faith, all collected by servants of the family from various martyrdom sites.[36]

Because of the difficulty faced by priests in visiting and administering the sacraments to Japanese Christians, brotherhoods assumed most of the liturgical duties that could be performed without priests. In order to maintain some degree of uniformity in the different underground churches, they were often regulated by sets of rules written by the missionaries, which could allow them to perform some rituals, including communal prayer.[37] Some of the extant

35 JapSin 59, fol. 165a. This structure resembles the organization implemented by China Jesuits for their missions. Particularly valuable is the comparison drawn by Brockey between lay groups and parishes. Brockey, *Journey to the East*, 329–330.

36 After his own martyrdom on July 24, 1620 in Nagasaki, when he was beheaded alongside two brothers and a nephew, all relics were bequeathed to Dominican and Franciscan friars. Ruiz-de-Medina, *Martirologio*, 425.

37 Liam Matthew Brockey wrote about this for the case of China. See Brockey, *Journey to the East*, 100, 339.

statutes include those for brotherhoods such as the abovementioned Jesuit *Confraria de Nossa Senhora da Assunção* or *Santa Mariya no Onkumi*, the Jesuit *Confraria de Santa Maria* or *Santa Mariya no Kumi*, the Jesuit *Confraria de Jesus* or *Zezusu no Kumi*, the Dominican *Cofradia del Nombre de Jesus* or *Zezusu no Mina no Onkumi*, and the Franciscan *Sesuta-kō*.[38] Generally, there were no rules expressly defining the sheltering of missionaries as an obligation, but a Jesuit proposal sent in the early 1620s to Rome suggested that plenary indulgences should be given to those that harbored or helped missionaries to find shelter in Japan.[39]

It is unclear whether members of Japanese brotherhoods ever clashed with each other, but the competition between mendicant orders and Jesuits for the allegiance of these organizations was evident. Furthermore, the existence of numerous brotherhoods, each associated with a different order, led to much suspicion regarding the validity of their practices. Mateus de Couros, Jesuit Provincial of Japan between 1617 and 1621, was highly suspicious of non-Jesuit organizations. In a 1619 letter, Couros denounced Franciscan brotherhoods for "accepting some [men] who are in reality living away from their real wives and having affairs with other women, absolving many to whom we have denied absolution", as well as "making preachers out of ignorant and secular young men, who spread numerous and grave errors, often heresies". He also accused friars of founding brotherhoods with the sole intention of "taking from our hands all the Christian communities we have spent so many years creating".[40]

In 1617, Japan Jesuits tried to prove locals' preference for priests and brothers of the Society of Jesus. They submitted a bundle of 75 affidavits signed by 755 Japanese lay leaders, collected from all over the southern island of Kyūshū to the northeastern region of Tōhoku. Swearing allegiance to the Society of Jesus' missionaries and certifying the priests' commitment to each community, the documents were certified by the Jesuit Provincial.[41]

Dominicans, who had been in the Nagasaki area since 1609, adopted a similar strategy a few years later. Between 1621 and 1622, friar Diego Collado (c. 1587–1641) personally traveled and gathered the signatures of numerous lay

---

38 JapSin 59, fols. 165–173; Murakami, "Kirishitan Kenkyū no Kaiko", 10–15; Schütte, "Futatsu no Komonjo", 135–147; Los Angeles [Rueda], *Virgen S. Mariano*, 195–225; Nawata-Ward, *Women Religious Leaders*, 338–344; Kawamura, *Making Christian*, 133; Kawamura, *Kirishitan Shinto Soshiki*, 296–383; Delgado García, *El Beato Francisco de Morales*, 39–44.

39 Gonoi, *Tokugawa Shoki*, 195; Ramos, "Renier sa foi", 196; JapSin 22, fol. 258v.

40 MHJ, 817. Couros could be referring to the case of the *Confraria da Cruz*, founded by the secular priest Francisco António Murayama (?–1615). After the priest's death in the Siege of Ōsaka, the organization was overtaken by the Dominicans and merged with the Dominican *Cofradia del Santo Nombre de Jesus*. Delgado García, *El Beato Francisco de Morales*, 40.

41 Kawamura, *Making Christian*, 201–207; Matsuda, *Kinsei Shoki Nihon*, 1022–1145.

leaders of the various *Cofradías del Rosário*, although only a handful of these documents survive.[42] The collection of letters, as well as two sets of rules of Jesuit brotherhoods and other papers, were taken by Collado to Madrid in order to discredit the Society of Jesus and end their monopoly in Japan.[43] But while the signatories of the Jesuit documents put their names under a short and very standardized text, the *Rosário* brotherhood's letters revealed a lot more about their commitment to the priests.[44]

In December 1621, 18 members of the Shimabara *Rosário* signed a document stating their willingness to shelter missionaries from whichever religious order.[45] An early 1622 letter from the six elders of the *Rosário* of the village of Chijiwa revealed that the Jesuit Giacomo Antonio Giannone had exhorted them to leave the *Rosário* and join Jesuit brotherhoods.[46] In March of the following year it was the turn of the 104 elders of the Nagasaki counterpart of the same brotherhood to sign a similar document. According to the Nagasaki brothers and sisters, the offering of rewards for missionaries by the city's authorities had led many people to search for the priests. These people entered houses forcefully, searching neighborhoods for missionaries. For that reason, the brotherhood worked "to provide [the missionaries] with places to stay and other necessities, each according to his or her individual capacity and circumstances".[47] Moreover, the document explained that, because of the dedication of the Dominicans, most of them had been arrested, unlike what was happening to the Jesuits at the time. A couple of months later, the Ōmura *Rosário* brotherhood issued a similar statement. Signed by 77 members residing in areas surrounding Nagasaki, it declared that 25 of the *Rosário* members had been executed for aiding missionaries of all orders, meeting their martyrdoms "with true joy". However, it extensively praised the Dominican missionaries, who were, according to the letter, "sleeping in the fields and making mountains their home" in order to tend to the Christian community.[48] As evidence

42 However, a better understanding is needed regarding what influence the long tradition of the Rosary brotherhoods had in the Japanese organizations in comparison to those created by Jesuit initiative. Klötter, *The Language of the Sangleys*, 38–42; Menegon, *Ancestors, Virgins, & Friars*, 57–58.

43 Doñas, "Órdenes Religiosas en Japón", 55.

44 On the Collado papers, see Matsuda, *Kinsei Shoki Nihon*, 1146–1276.

45 Matsuda, *Kinsei Shoki Nihon*, 1169.

46 Matsuda, *Kinsei Shoki Nihon*, 1171.

47 Matsuda, *Kinsei Shoki Nihon*, 1173. See also, Hesselink, "104 voices", 267–269; Boxer and Cummins, "The Dominican mission in Japan", 22.

48 Matsuda, *Kinsei Shoki Nihon*, 1184–1185. Twenty-four Christians were executed in the Ōmura region between 1617 and early 1622, that is to say, since the persecution against Christians helping missionaries increased and the Ōmura *Rosário* letter was penned.

of their dedication, the letter mentions that most Dominicans in Japan at the time were in prison.

Although there were probably other *Rosário* letters such as these, the large discrepancy between the number of signatories of the Jesuit papers and the Dominican papers reveal that while the mendicants had gained a strong foothold in Nagasaki since the start of the persecution, Jesuits maintained their influence on local Christian communities elsewhere. The existence of a network of Christians spread throughout Japan guaranteed to missionaries of all orders in Japan at this time a safety net of allies in their constant search for refuge and sustainment.

4 The Jesuit Consultation of 1620

In the late 1610s and early 1620s, Japan Jesuits faced competition with the non-Jesuit orders for the hearts and souls of Japanese Christians and were also confronted with internal disputes. Created in 1549 with the arrival of Xavier to the archipelago, the Jesuit mission in Japan was elevated to Vice-Province in 1583 and Province in 1611.[49] In October of 1614, a few weeks before the *Bakufu* expelled them from the country, the missionaries gathered on Japanese soil for the final Jesuit Provincial Congregation.[50] After that, radical changes brought by the expulsion made any kind of gathering virtually impossible in Japan.

Internally, members of the Jesuit Province of Japan were divided by the East China Sea. By September of 1620, there were 28 priests and brothers of the Province in Japan, 70 in Macau, and 21 spread through Cochinchina, India, and Malacca. Distance created a lot of suspicion between those in the archipelago

This number, however, includes those who were not associated with Dominican but with Jesuit brotherhoods, thus it is necessary to take the "25 martyrs" affirmation with a pinch of salt. See Ruiz-de-Medina, *Martirologio*, 375–376, 378, 392, 398–401, 422, 432–435.

49 Initially, the mission of Japan and the Vice-Province of Japan were subordinated to the Province of India, created in 1552 and split into Province of Goa and Province of Malabar or Cochin in 1605. Hélène Vu Thanh, "Principles of Missionary Geography in Jesuit Spirituality and their Implementation in Japan (16th–17th centuries)", *Bulletin of Portuguese/Japanese Studies* 18/19 (2009), 178; Maria de Lurdes Ponce Edra de Aboim Sales, *Do Malabar às Molucas: os Jesuítas e a Província do Malabar (1601–1693)*, doctoral dissertation, Universidade Nova de Lisboa (2015), 17.

50 Congr. 55, fols. 270–279b. The first congregation was held in 1592, while the third took place in 1598. Both were organized under extraordinary circumstances, given that Japan was not a Jesuit province at the time.

and those in Macau.[51] In October of 1620, the Jesuit priest Cristóvão Ferreira (c. 1580–1650) alerted the Superior General Claudio Acquaviva about a purported scheme by China Jesuits to celebrate a congregation of the Province of Japan in the *Colégio da Madre de Deus* of Macau. According to him, their plan was to hold a vote in the congregation and make decisions without the participation of the elders of Japan.[52] The Provincial of Japan, Couros, was also vehemently against holding the congregation in Macau. Sharing most of Ferreira's sentiment toward China Jesuits, Couros feared he could not trust those who had passed from the Vice-Province of China to his province. He also believed that since the number of Jesuits in Macau who had taken the fourth vow was not sufficient and they had little to no experience of Japan, a congregation without the presence of the provincial would not be able to properly address the needs of the missionaries.[53] The grave crisis of trust between Japan Jesuits on the background of the 1620 consultation was worsened by their disputes with China Jesuits. The Vice-Province of China, first created in 1615 by Acquaviva and established *de facto* in 1619, relied on the help of a number of Christian Mandarins but was mainly supported by the finances of the Province of Japan which, in turn, depended on the profits from their participation in the Nagasaki-Macau trade.[54] Eventually, the congregation was delayed until 1623, when it was held in Macau.

Despite all difficulties, a handful of Jesuit elders of the Province of Japan gathered at the *Colégio da Madre de Deus* in Macau on July 8, 1620 to analyze the list of 61 questions collected from their colleagues in Japan.[55] Visitor Vieira was probably the one responsible for taking the questionnaire to China.[56] The consultation was held without Couros—and possibly without his consent—nor any of the provincial's consultants or any of the rectors in Japan. According to Ferreira, the meeting was endorsed by consultants of the visitor, who claimed to be consultants of the Province of Japan (*consultores da província*),

51 JapSin 25, fol. 125; JapSin 37, fol. 156; Ajuda, 49-V-7, fols. 183–186v, 191–194, Schütte, *Introductio*, 238.

52 JapSin 17, fol. 263.

53 JapSin 37, fols. 190v–191. The fourth vow of obedience to the pope taken by Jesuit priests was, and still is, a particular feature of the Society of Jesus. For the historical genesis and context of the vow, see O'Malley, "The Fourth Vow in Its Ignatian Context".

54 Brockey, *Journey to the East*, 58, 64–66, 73, 437.

55 Ajuda, 49-VI-6, fols. 120–153, "*Perguntas q[ue] os P[adr]es de Japam fizeram no tempo da perseguição aos P[adr]es de Macao, com Reposta destes a ellas*". There is also a Latin version bearing a Portuguese title: "*Repostas* [sic] *de alguãs duuidas q[ue] no tempo da perseguição de Jappão se mandarão perguntar a Macao no anno de 1620*". Vanves, GBro 94, fols. 5–20.

56 JapSin 17, fol. 248.

a title that the priest denounced as inaccurate, since Vieira had died soon after coming back to Macau.[57]

The list presented numerous possible answers to the questions it contained, suggesting the goal was to check the validity of decisions that had already been taken in Japan. In general, there were no clear categories dividing the questions, but the focus was mainly on liturgy, confessions, social obligations of Japanese Christians, their participation in martyrdoms, public oaths, and the external use of non-Christian signs. The assembly, following previous examples of similar consultations, resorted to a number of theological authorities to support their claims. There were, of course, references to classic authorities such as Silvestro Mazzolini, Angelus Prierias, and Martín de Azpilcueta, but there were also citations from more recent manuals such as those by Thomás Sanchez, Luis de Molina, and Juan de Azor.[58] Interestingly, there were also a couple of references to the *Suma de Moral*, the theology textbook written by Lopo de Abreu, mentioned earlier. His textbook on cases of conscience in India appeared in at least two catalogues of Jesuit libraries in Macau in the first half of the 17th century.[59] While most issues presented did not have precedents in previous consultations and congregations, the consultants took the opportunity to review the problem of the confession of the sick, an issue that had been debated by the second and third Congregations of Japan, in 1592 and 1614.[60]

Most of the questions referred to specific problems faced by Christians and the clergy in Japan during the persecution. For instance, how could missionaries perform mass without candles made of bee's wax, or without proper assistants? Could an arrested priest celebrate mass without a fire? Or by himself, while in hiding?[61] There was also plenty of uncertainty regarding the confessions of arrested Christians—could they accept written confessions, or displays of contrition via hand gestures, or could they hastily hear confessions before a martyrdom?[62] There were also numerous doubts about what made one a martyr; should a Christian who threw themselves into the fire during an execution of others be considered a martyr?[63] What about Christians who were arrested for various crimes and refused to apostatize in exchange for their

57 JapSin 17, fols. 255, 263v.

58 In a probable reference to the second or even third volume of the manual, Jerónimo de Angelis wrote that Azor's *Institutionum moralium* arrived in Macau in 1619. JapSin 34, fol. 40.

59 Recent scholarship on these libraries include Golvers, "The Library Catalogue" and "Circulation and Reception".

60 Ajuda, 49-VI-6, fols. 126v–128.

61 Ajuda, 49-VI-6, fols. 120–122v.

62 Ajuda, 49-VI-6, fols. 122v–125v.

63 Ajuda, 49-VI-6, fols. 138v–139.

pardon?[64] Could a Christian who did not want to disclose their finances to the authorities, in order to protect properties and other Christians, be considered a martyr?[65] There were yet several questions dealing with difficulties faced by Japanese Christians who needed to hide their faith and abide by orders from heathen lords, which could lead them to commit hurtful actions toward other Christians. For example, could they help destroy churches? Could they help tie up imprisoned fellow Christians in preparation for their martyrdom? Could they provide firewood for the martyrs' fires?[66] Could they listen to Buddhist sermons when ordered to by their lords? Could they take Christian prisoners to be executed and help by throwing their bodies into the sea? How should the Christians who helped burn two families in 1613 in Arima be treated?[67] These very concrete situations show how Christians in Japan were torn between social obligations to Japanese lords, their allegiance to the numerous Christian brotherhoods, and faithfully following the doctrines of their faith.

There are a number of topics questioning actions taken by Japanese converts to hide their faith by portraying themselves as non-Christians. For instance, there is mention of the custom of hanging an *ofuda*, a slip of paper or tablet placed at the entrance of a house that could indicate, among other things, that its residents were affiliated to a Buddhist temple or a Shintō shrine—were Christians allowed to hang *ofuda* in their houses?[68] Of course, the problem was more than hiding one's Christian faith behind a Buddhist or Shintō tablet.

64 Ajuda, 49-VI-6, fol. 139.

65 Ajuda, 49-VI-6, fols. 132v–133.

66 According to the Dutch observer Ryan Gysbertsz: "When anyone is to be burnt, it is given out and publicly proclaimed on the evening before, that each House which lies near the place where the burning is to take place, must bring 2, 3, 4 or 5 faggots of firewood, more or less, according as to whether there are many or few persons to be burnt". Boxer, *A True Description*, 74.

67 The dramatic martyrdom of the Hayashida family and Taketomi Kan'emon Leo and his son, Taketomi Dan'emon Paulo, was considered the first in which Christians were burnt at the stake in Japan. See Anesaki, *A Concordance*, 31; Ruiz-de-Medina, *Martirologio*, 325–326.

68 Ajuda, 49-VI-6, fols. 129–129v; Ramos, "Renier sa foi", 192. I thank Martin Nogueira Ramos for clarifying the reference to the *ofuda* in the document. Letters from the period indicate that the word *fuda* (without the honorific *o-*) could also refer to the *kōsatsu*, tablets posted in public spaces to inform the population of government determinations and legislation, although this is unrelated to the context here. See MHJ, 905. The use of the *ofuda* in Nagasaki seems to be connected with the resurgence of Shinto beliefs in previously Christian areas of the region such as the Ōmura fief. See Kudamatsu, *Kirishitan Denraichi no Jinja*, 254–263. The increasing use of these tablets and leaflets made Collado discuss their acceptability in his confessor's manual, published in 1632. Hino (ed.), *Koryaado Zangeroku*, 20, 156, 266–267.

Jesuits considered the use of the *ofuda* to be a public denial of their faith, an act condemned by Azor and Sánchez.[69]

Effectively, these two authors guide most of the discussions regarding the confession of the faith. A precept directly linked to the first of the Ten Commandments, the obligation to confess the Christian faith, was discussed by Thomas Aquinas (ST II-II, q. 3, a. 2), who considered it necessary for the salvation of the soul and concluded that to not confess one's faith was a mortal sin. After Aquinas, numerous theologians discussed the circumstances that could allow a Christian to avoid this obligation.[70] In India, Abreu considered that tyranny could be reason enough to allow Christians to avoid the obligation of the precept, although he did not permit the use of non-Christian symbols to hide one's faith.[71] Here, like the Jesuits in Macau, Abreu also referred to Azor's and Sanchéz's conclusions, indicating the circumstances they listed allowing, for instance, the use of clothes or languages to hide one's faith when in pagan or heretic regions.[72] In the end, the Japanese policy that forced Christians to sign oaths stating that they would not shelter missionaries, was at least partially viewed in Macau as an issue of faith confession.

In early 1617, the shōgun Tokugawa Hidetada decided that all Christians helping or harboring priests in Japan would be executed along with the missionaries. According to Gonoi Takashi, the purpose was to put into practice the September 18, 1616 "Decree Against the Christian Religion" (*Bateren Shūmon Goseikin*), which sought to continue the *Bakufu*'s anti-Christian policy after the death of Tokugawa Ieyasu (1543–1616) by restating his prohibition against the presence of Christians in Japan.[73] Effectively, between the enactment of the decision and October of 1617, when that year's Portuguese ship left Nagasaki for Macau, one Franciscan friar, one Jesuit priest, one Augustinian friar, and one Dominican friar, as well as at least six lay assistants, were executed. The first execution of Japanese Christians who aided missionaries happened

69 Azor, *Intitutionum moralium*, vol. 1, lib. 8, cap. 27, q. 1; Sánchez, *Opus Morale in Praecepta Decalogi*, vol. 1, lib. 2, cap. 4.

70 See, for instance, Mazzolini, *Summa Silvestrina*, verbo Fides, q. 5; Angelus, *Summa Angelica*, verbo Fides, no. 8.

71 BC, TF-HS 79, fols. 26–28.

72 Azor, *Intitutionum moralium*, vol. 1, lib. 8, cap. 27, q. 4; Sánchez, *Opus Morale in Praecepta Decalogi*, vol. 1, lib. 2, cap. 4, n. 20. Similar rules regarding clothing were still valid among hidden Christians as late as the late 18th century, when Japanese authorities seized numerous documents describing these regulations. See Ramos, *La foi des ancêtres*, 74; Anesaki, *Kirishitan Shūmon*, 233–234.

73 Gonoi, *Tokugawa Shoki*, 196–197. There are numerous transcriptions of this decree. See, for example, Shimizu et al. (eds.), *Kinsei Nagasaki*, 113–114.

on October 1, 1617. Gaspar Ueda Hikojirō (?–1617) and André Yoshida (?–1617), who had harbored the Dominican friar Alonso de Navarrete and the Augustinian friar Fernando Ayala, were decapitated in a small island at the entrance of the Bay of Nagasaki.[74] However, while the friars were killed in Ōmura, the area where they were found, those who had helped them were purposefully transported to and executed in Nagasaki.[75] The beheading made clear to the residents of the city what would happen to those who dared to shelter missionaries.

The following year, the new Nagasaki Governor (*bugyō*), Hasegawa Fujimasa (?–1630), also known by the alias Gonroku, started the rigorous enforcement of the decree.[76] If in February of that year the Jesuit Visitor Vieira wrote that the persecution was against "the shepherds, not the sheep", by the end of the year things had changed entirely.[77] In 1618 alone, at least 12 people were executed for sheltering missionaries. Two sailors, one Nagasaki *otona*, or ward administrator, and their families—including seven children—were killed on November 25.[78]

The pressure grew exponentially after January of 1619, when Domingos Jorge, a Portuguese resident of the Bunchi-machi ward of Nagasaki, was arrested, along with a number of neighbors and members of his brotherhood, for harboring the Jesuit priest Carlo Spinola.[79] The realization that foreign residents were also helping missionaries led Gonroku to force all citizens of Nagasaki, Japanese and foreign, to abide by and sign, on January 22/23, 1619, a public oath swearing they would harbor no missionary in their house.[80] To extend the policy to foreign residents was nothing out of the ordinary—in early 17th-century Japan, the notion of nation or people (*kokumin*) included all those who resided in Japan and were subjected to the authority of the shogunate.[81]

---

74 Ruiz-de-Medina, *Martirologio*, 373–374; JapSin 17, fol. 104v.

75 Gonoi, *Tokugawa Shoki*, 195.

76 On Gonroku's past, see Hesselink, *Dream*, 174–175.

77 JapSin 17, fols. 238–238v.

78 Ruiz-de-Medina, *Martirologio*, 395–397. The Nagasaki *otona* were responsible for one ward or street (*chō*) each.

79 JapSin 59, fol. 175v. Domingos Jorge was burnt to death on November 18, 1619. His wife and four-year-old son were killed later that year in the Great Martyrdom of Nagasaki. Ruiz-de-Medina, *Martirologio*, 418 and 459. When Spinola was arrested, the Jesuit Visitor Vieira and his companion, priest Ferreira, were staying at a house in the same neighborhood where the arrest took place, forcing them to flee in the middle of the night. JapSin 17, fol. 238v. Since Spinola and another Jesuit who was also arrested the same night, Ambrósio Fernandes, were both *procuradores* of the Province of Japan, numerous Jesuit accounting books were forfeited and lost to Nagasaki authorities on that occasion. JapSin 38, fol. 49.

80 See Amaro, *Kōshi Nagasaki*, 170. Alvarez-Taladriz, "Fuentes Europeas", 414.

81 The place of residence was key to determining allegiance, belonging, and subjection. See Matsui, "Jendaa kara Miru", 95.

According to Vieira, Nagasaki officials would arrest anyone slightly foreign-looking that they could find on the city streets at night. However, he also suggested that the anti-Christian sentiment of Nagasaki authorities was only a smoke cloud to fool *Bakufu* authorities in Edo. According to Vieira, Gonroku tried negotiating with Japanese Christian *otona* so they would surrender all hidden missionaries in order to avoid the destruction of Nagasaki and its population. Certainly, Vieira's view credits the Christian tenacity of the Japanese *otona* for deepening the antagonism toward the tyrannical rule of the *Bakufu*, represented by the *bugyō* and his officials in Nagasaki, thus reinforcing the idea of profound opposition between the long-suffering Christian community and the Japanese central authorities. Since the *otona* denied handing missionaries over to the authorities, Gonroku decided to make all citizens sign the oath. This transformed Nagasaki into the perfect setting for martyrdoms because the clear opposition between tyrannical rule and Christian perseverance turned all executions into acts of defiance and resistance. According to Vieira, 30 silver bars, which had been publicly displayed in Nagasaki in Kurusu-machi (the "ward of the Cross") as a reward for the capture of thieves, were now also offered to anyone who reported priests or friars.[82] Here, Jacinto Orfanell, the Dominican chronicler who later became a martyr himself, pointed out the irony that the official responsible for keeping the silver was a Japanese Christian member of a lay brotherhood. In Orfanell's narrative, the official recused himself, thus becoming another heroic figure of Japanese Christianity.[83]

The issue of the oath imposed by Japanese authorities in Nagasaki was mentioned a few times during the 1620 debate in Macau, albeit indirectly. For instance, the questionnaire addressed the problem of arrested converts who were put in jail for reading spiritual books to their communities—an activity often promoted by lay brotherhoods—and had the opportunity to sign an oath denying help to missionaries in exchange for their freedom.[84] On the one hand, to sign such papers would be the equivalent of consenting to the very act of persecution, while refusing to sign, on the other hand, could elevate the spirits of those to whom the arrested Christian read spiritual books in the first place.[85] In fact, the questionnaire also explained that such oaths included a

82 Kataoka Yakichi highlights that it was not until 1633 that rewards would be offered for the capture of brothers, while rewards for the capture of apostates who had returned to the Christian faith were offered starting in 1682. Kataoka, "Hakugaika no Kirishitan", 9.

83 Ajuda, 49-IV-60, fols. 80–80v; JapSin 17, fol. 238v; Hesselink, *Dream*, 178; Orfanel, *Historia Eclesiastica*, cap. LIX, fol. 115v; Gonoi, *Tokugawa Shoki*, 197–198; Alvarez-Taladriz, "Fuentes Europeas", 414. Vieira evaluated the 30 bars were worth more than 120 *cruzados*. JapSin 17, fol. 238v.

84 Gonroku had imposed a prohibition against the reading of Christian books at the same time he started enforcing the no-harboring policy. See Ajuda, 49-IV-60, fol. 80.

85 Ajuda, 49-VI-6, fol. 148.

provision stating that those who signed it would also refuse to teach the Christian doctrine.[86] Notably, the consultation referred to the specific situation of Christians already imprisoned for breaking the law—reading spiritual books and disseminating the Christian faith—but failed to address the larger issue of Christians being forced to sign these oaths in the first place.

The questionnaire also points to an interesting fact: the widespread implementation of these oaths against the harboring and aid of missionaries in Japan. This meant that Japanese Christians traveling from one place to another were constantly asked about their faith. More specifically, the questionnaire asked whether Christians ought to respond honestly when inquired by innkeepers about their religious affiliations. Jesuits debated whether Christians could use ambiguity or amphibology to avoid constantly putting their lives at risk. Coined by Martín de Azpilcueta, this rhetorical tool turned out to be a valuable device in a number of situations.[87] Japan Jesuits, convinced of the value of amphibology and supported by Azor and Sánchez's arguments, justified its use in Japan, as long as the innkeeper and any other person questioning the Christian were not official authorities. Thus, the consultation concluded that Japanese Christians could answer ambiguously in order to protect themselves in these situations.[88]

Since there were numerous Christians in the Nagasaki administration, there were also some who faced difficulties following orders that directly threatened converts. The questionnaire described that when Gonroku started the oath policy, there were Christians directly involved with collecting signatures.[89] Called *yokome*, these were the officials responsible for announcing legal decisions to the population in Nagasaki and guaranteeing the observance of laws.[90] Since the policy promoted apostasy, Jesuits in Macau severely condemned the participation of Christian officers in this process.

---

86 Ajuda, 49-VI-6, fol. 140v.

87 Perez Zagorin, *Ways of Lying*, 170–171.

88 Ajuda, 49-VI-6, fols. 143–143v. By the late 18th century, Japanese Christians considered that, even though they were obliged to confess their faith in the past, that was no longer the case during the harsh persecution of the Edo period. See Anesaki, *Kirishitan Shūmon*, 86, 230–232.

89 Ajuda, 49-VI-6, fols. 140v–141.

90 It seems they were subjected to the same hierarchy of the *metsuke* or "inspector", who were directly subjected to the *Bakufu*, although they often came from local *bushi* families. The *yokome* and the *metsuke* played a fundamental role in the legislative and executive process in the region. Yasutaka, *Kinsei Nagasaki*, 74–75; Ōmura-shishi (ed.), *Shin'hen Ōmura*, 176–179. The 1620 consultation also suggests that the *yokome* were in charge of guarding condemned Christians on their way to their martyrdom. Ajuda, 49-VI-6, fol. 136v.

In the end, the 1620 consultation did not overtly endorse the signing of the oaths imposed by authorities. The particular circumstances surrounding the missionaries and their allies during the persecution guaranteed them a vast network of Christians, including economic and politically powerful individuals, that were willing to help. However, the implementation of the oath policy by Gonroku in 1618 severely curtailed the choices of missionaries in Japan, leading many to seek the help of poor people living in small huts.[91]

Despite the executions of citizens harboring missionaries between 1617 and 1620, Japan Jesuits were confident that they would have no trouble finding shelter whenever they traveled into the countryside. It seems this was particularly true in areas inhabited by generations of Christians, such as Nagasaki, Shimabara, or Amakusa. Provincial Couros felt there was no shortage of Christians willing to risk their lives to support the priests around the port city.[92] However, most Japanese Christians who opened their doors to the missionaries were poor. Jesuits believed, and rightly so, that only those who had no real estate or revenues dared to risk their lives to protect the clergy, since they had nothing material to lose if caught.[93] Other foreigners in Japan were also aware of these difficulties. A Dutch account of the period speaks of missionaries had to hide in holes in the ground under floorboards, covered by mats and planks, or in small spaces inside walls and, when the persecution grew stronger, they had to resort to hiding in lepers' huts.[94]

5 Dominican *casos de conciencia* between Nagasaki and Manila

While Jesuits could count on an expansive network of Christian communities, Dominicans were in a much more perilous situation. Though a part of the influential Province of Our Lady of the Most Holy Rosary in the Philippines, which enjoyed wide support from the Spanish administrators, their numbers in Japan dwindled in comparison to those of the Jesuits: by mid-1621, there were 25 Jesuit priests versus eight Dominican friars in Japan. Even worse for the friars, out of these eight, six were imprisoned, with a seventh, José de San

91 As did Ferreira in Kyūshū in the 1620s, when "moving in the shadows between huts on that island's remote mountains". Brockey, *The Visitor*, 388.

92 MHJ, 793.

93 MHJ, 833.

94 Boxer, *A True Description*, 78, 84.

Jacinto Salvanés, captured later that year, thus leaving the controversial Collado the only Dominican not in a jail cell in Japan.[95]

Among those arrested was a key figure of the Dominicans in Japan: the superior of the mission, Francisco de Morales (1567–1622). He arrived in 1602 at the southernmost area of the island of Kyūshū, in the fief of Satsuma. Under the Shimazu rule, Morales and the other Dominicans preached and built churches until May of 1609, when they were expelled and forced to flee to Nagasaki.[96] There, Morales managed to gain the support of the powerful Murayama clan and build the Santo Domingo church in July of 1609. Five years later, when the *Bakufu* ordered the expulsion of the missionaries, he tricked the authorities by embarking on a ship that left Nagasaki but returned immediately after. That marked the start of a period of five years during which Morales hid in the house of André Murayama Tokuan (?–1619), son of António Murayama Tōan, magistrate (*daikan*) of the outer wards of Nagasaki between 1602 and 1616.[97] According to Reinier Hesselink, an informant pointed out to officials that the house of a cloth dryer was likely holding a hidden missionary. A raid in the night between March 14/15, 1619 led to the arrest of another Spanish Dominican, friar Alonso de Mena (1578–1622). Under torture, Mena's servant betrayed "the information that there was another friar hiding in the residence of Tōan's eldest son, Tokuan. The same day, Morales [...] was seized at the Murayama residence".[98] By this time, Morales was among the senior missionaries of the country. He had participated in about two decades of missionary work in Satsuma and Nagasaki, he spoke the language, and he had as much knowledge about the Japanese as did any Jesuit at the time.[99]

On September 10, 1622, Morales' life was interrupted: he had been sentenced with 24 other missionaries, as well as 30 laymen and women, to be decapitated and burnt to death in what became known as the Great Martyrdom of Nagasaki.[100] However, between his arrest and tragic end, Morales kept up his correspondence with fellow Dominicans in Nagasaki and Manila.[101] Using materials

95 Boxer and Cummins, "The Dominican mission in Japan", 71. On Diego Collado, see Tronu, "The Rivalry", 25–39; Doñas, "Órdenes Religiosas en Japón", 51–92.

96 Aduarte and González, *Tomo Primero de la Historia*, 326.

97 Boxer and Cummins, "The Dominican mission in Japan", 13–14.

98 Hesselink, *Dream*, 179.

99 Boxer and Cummins, "The Dominican mission in Japan", 17.

100 Ruiz-de-Medina, *Martirologio*, 443–464. Andrew Ross argues that, until 1622, Christians were executed through various methods (decapitation, burning, etc.) by different local rulers, but that year Hidetada initiated a massive campaign to suppress Christianity. See Ross, *A Vision Betrayed*, 82.

101 See, for instance, his five letters written from prison in Anon., *Lettera edificanti*, 7–16.

such as smuggled pens, ink, and a cheap type of tissue paper, the so-called *hanagami* (literally, *nose-paper*), the friar also wrote theological opinions.[102] With this improvised stationery, Morales managed to send his opinions to Domingo González (1574–1647), rector of the *Colegio de Santo Tomás* in Manila between 1612 and 1616 and a famed theologian in the Philippines.[103]

González was well acquainted with the doctrinal problems of Christianity in Japan. His papers included at least one long discussion on martyrdoms in the country, which was probably written in this period.[104] In addition, it is believed he had previously visited the country.[105] In June of 1621, almost a year after the Jesuit consultation in Macau, González reviewed a series of eight issues submitted from Japan. Although much shorter than the Japanese consultation, topics included, for example, the participation of Christians in the destruction of churches, sales of gunpowder and foodstuffs to the Dutch, and marriages between Spaniards or Portuguese men and Japanese women in Japan. The fourth question on the list referred to the problem of harboring missionaries. More importantly, González transcribed an opinion sent from prison by Morales.[106]

The text begins with González's summary of the issue. According to him, Nagasaki authorities were aware that missionaries were hiding in the city and demanded the oaths to appease pressures from the *Bakufu*. This echoes the explanation of Jesuit Visitor Vieira, described above, regarding the anti-Christian sentiment of Gonroku toward the Christians of the city, according to whom the governor himself was not against the believers, but merely following orders.[107] González describes Gonroku, by contrast, as an unwilling enforcer of the law, who wanted to avoid any responsibility for any missionaries found in Nagasaki. As for the Christian population, González thought that they had no real intention of abiding by the terms of the imposed oaths and claimed that Christians signed the documents solely out of instinct for self-preservation. According to González, these unspoken circumstances led some Christians to

102 Boxer and Cummins, "The Dominican mission in Japan", 49.

103 González would be rector again three more times, between 1626 and 1633, 1639 and 1641, and 1643 and 1645. See Aduarte and González, *Tomo Primero de la Historia*, 147–158.

104 APSR, Miscelanea 1, fols. 52–96 and Consultas 2, fols. 320v–327v; Ehalt, "Goa no Iezusukai", 1–14.

105 Boxer and Cummins, "The Dominican mission in Japan", 71.

106 See the "Cassos Resueltos por el Padre Fray Domingo Gonçalez Rector de Collegio de Sto Thomas Para Iapon", Consultas 2, fols. 317–320.

107 JapSin 17, fol. 238v. Boxer wrote: "The humane character of Hasegawa Gonroku […] is fully attested by other contemporary sources both Catholic and Protestant". Boxer, *A True Description*, 130.

believe that they could sign said oaths with a clear conscience, while others argued that taking the oaths could not be condoned since the policy itself was motivated by hatred against the Christian faith (*odium fidei*). The Dominican agreed, however, that the actions of authorities such as Gonroku should be condemned by the Church, even though their ignorance of the dogma could eventually safeguard their consciences. Yet, the most important issue was not the actions of Japanese authorities, but whether Christians themselves should be allowed to take the oath. Here, González referred to a "very knowledgeable and prudent" opinion on the subject submitted by Morales from prison, which he then reproduced.[108]

Morales had recognized that the ideal course of action would be to denounce the Christians who took the oaths imposed by the Japanese authorities and to celebrate as martyrs those who had lost their lives refusing to do so. Nevertheless, he believed that it was not up to missionaries to force believers to choose martyrdom.[109] For the imprisoned theologian, the threat of harm or death was enough to allow believers to sign the pledges without actually being obliged to follow its terms. He recognized the oaths as contracts that created a natural obligation (*estoy obligado de iure nat*[*ura*]*li sub* [*poena peccati*] *mortali*), but because the oaths themselves were unjust (*iniuste*), Morales argued that the tyrannical nature at the origin of the pledges, and especially the threat of capital punishment, were sufficient reasons for considering them void.[110] Morales was certainly aware of the theories concerning the voidability of contracts of the time, which is exemplified in works such as Leonardus Lessius' (1554–1623) *De iustitia et iure* (1605).[111]

For Morales, the oath could only be taken if there was no sincere intention on the part of the Christian individual to abide by it, and solely when they had been threatened with death or loss of possessions. Their real intention on taking the oaths should be to avoid further angering the tyrant ruler of Japan—i.e., the shōgun Hidetada. That was, according to him, the common opinion of many experienced and learned priests of Japan, although it is unclear whether he included Jesuits in the same lot.[112] Japanese Christians themselves shared the same understanding, as shown by an anonymous confession from this period where the believer declared that by signing the "useless and empty"

---

108 Consultas 2, fol. 317v.

109 Consultas 2, fol. 318v.

110 Consultas 2, fol. 318.

111 For more on Lessius, see Wim Decock, *Theologians and Contract Law: The Moral Transformation of the Ius Commune (ca. 1500–1650)*, 261–263.

112 Consultas 2, fol. 318v.

oath he was not committing a sin nor "signing any real oath, but merely something serving to fool the pagan official".[113]

The distinction between intention and action used by Morales suggests he had Thomas de Vio's (Cajetan's) understanding of promise (*promissio*) in mind, according to which one could say—or, in this case, sign under—the words "I will do" without necessarily assuming a binding promise, unless the one promising was "motivated by a true *animus promittendi* [the intention to assume a compromise]".[114] This lack of obligation behind promises, implicit in the act of taking the oath imposed by Nagasaki authorities, was what Morales used to redirect the intentions behind the action itself and argue in favor of the morality of the Christian community's self-defense strategy.

Taking the oath was not an invitation for Japanese and foreign Christians in Nagasaki to sin. Considering Aquinas' division of scandals into active and passive, Morales explained that there was no active scandal, given that Christians were taking the pledges just as priests would have advised them to. As for passive scandals, he asked the addressee of his letter—González—to verify if there was any adequate theological rule for the case of Japan that would be accepted.[115] Considering scandals among non-Christians, though, he affirmed that the taking of the oath was seen not as a rejection of the faith or of the priests, but rather as an ingenious artifice or action—a *saikaku*—taken by the believers out of prudence. Much worse than signing the oath would be, in his words, to betray where missionaries were hiding, for that was "the work of Judas" ("pues és officio de Judas"). Moreover, he defended that missionaries were not supposed to criticize or denounce a Christian for refusing to give shelter to one of them, as they were not abiding by the oath but simply seeking to preserve their own lives.[116]

The theologian believed that the main reason behind Christians choosing to take the oath was what decided if their actions were morally acceptable. Morales understood that their intention was to avoid violating a decree from the shōgun ("el mandado de la Tenca") and being sent into exile, as well as safeguarding not only their own lives but also those of their neighbors. In fact, Morales explained that those who took the oath, in their own right (*utitur jure suo*), were also protecting all those in their own *jūningumi*.[117] The *jūningumi*

113 Hesselink, "104 Voices", 254.

114 Decock, *Theologians and Contract Law*, 180.

115 Consultas 2, fol. 318v. See *Summa Theologiae* IIa-IIae, q. 43, a. 2.

116 Consultas 2, fol. 319. There had been at least one case of a Christian (Lino Sashikata Tōemon) who was killed at home in 1619 by officials of the daimyō of Ōmura for refusing to sign the oath. His wife and kids were spared, though, and handed over to another household. See Ruiz-de-Medina, *Martirologio*, 399.

117 Consultas 2, fol. 318v.

("ten-person group") was a collective of ten households organized under a leader, the *kumigashira*. Common all over Japan since the early 17th century, these groups were responsible for collecting taxes and organizing festivals and religious ceremonies, as well as neighborhood surveillance.[118] Besides their civil obligations, the whole *jūningumi* was held responsible for crimes committed by any member of the group. These were the ten neighbors referred to by the Jesuit Lucena in the excerpt at the beginning of this chapter.[119] It has been argued that, in the fall of 1621, the system was replaced in Nagasaki by the *goningumi* ("five-person group") in order to facilitate the identification of hidden missionaries.[120] But there are still references to *jūningumi* in the city as late as 1633 among Japanese sources, which suggests that at least during this 13-year period there was a mixed system of five- and ten-person groups in different areas of Nagasaki.[121] Furthermore, from the point of view of Japanese authorities, executing a whole *jūningumi* meant a drastic reduction in revenue from tax collection. Thus, the change in 1621 could also have been motivated by financial reasons in an attempt to avoid the loss of fiscal revenues, similar to the measures taken by the authorities of the neighboring fief of Arima around the same time.[122]

---

118 Irimoto, "Jūningumi no Seiritsu", 163–200, especially 171; Yasutaka, *Kinsei Nagasaki*, 332.

119 Japanese sources put the beginning of the *jūningumi* in Nagasaki as 1618, although Léon Pagès wrote that when André Yoshida (?–1617) and Gaspar Ueda Hikojirō (?–1617) were arrested for harboring priests, the August 21, 1617 arrest order against them included the imprisoning of all the heads of neighboring houses, who, according to Pagès, "had been associated in groups of ten for many years". Pagès also understood that the 1616 anti-Christian decree would punish the "five closest neighbors" of those harboring priests, although he does not provide his source. Irimoto, "Jūningumi no Seiritsu", 171, 190. Pagès, *Histoire 1*, 338, 369–370; Ruiz-de-Medina, *Martirologio*, 373–374.

120 Hesselink, "104 Voices", 247; Hesselink, *Dream*, 188.

121 Irimoto, "Jūningumi no Seiritsu", 190–191. Referring to a 1628 martyrdom, Ryan Gysbertsz describes that "five householders" were punished along with the person harboring a priest. Boxer, *A True Description*, 84. Finding the geographical limits of this mixed system would considerably help to identify what areas authorities considered to be more problematic in Nagasaki.

122 Furthermore, it was common to have *jūningumi* in the cities and *goningumi* in smaller villages. Irimoto, *Goningumi to Kinsei Sonraku*, 30–32. Returning to Morales' opinions, the threat of executing a whole *jūningumi* was far from empty: as the Dominican was writing from prison, all members of a Nagasaki *jūningumi* were beheaded on November 27, 1619 after priests were found in their neighborhood. Additionally, at least seven members of the same *jūningumi* from the Nagasaki outer ward of Hama-no-machi along with five of their relatives were executed with Morales in the 1622 Great Martyrdom of Nagasaki. Ruiz-de-Medina, *Martirologio*, 419–422, 445–446, 458, 461–464; Pagès, *Histoire 1*, 369–370. For more on the martyrdom of Antonio Coreia from Hama-no-Machi, see Hesselink, *Dream*, 196–201.

Morales also believed that, if the oaths were not taken, the shōgun could coerce all Christians in a locality to apostatize. The relation between both measures—forced apostasies and the punishment against the *goningumi* or *jūningumi*—is clear, for instance, in a letter written by Gonroku to a local official on December 15, 1618, in which he mentioned orders from the shōgun to forcefully convert every single Christian of Nagasaki to Buddhism and confirmed his intentions to continue tracking any missionaries hidden in the city.[123] These two goals characterized the *Bakufu*'s policy toward the Christian population of Nagasaki in this period, and their success depended largely on the collection of oaths taken by the city's residents.

Accepting the imposition of the local government and taking the oaths meant, for Morales, not only protecting the various *jūningumi* of the city from undeserved punishment but of the Christian community as a whole. He argued that, if priests were to advise against the oaths, more fervent Christians would be put in harm's way. In general, a reduction in the numbers of Christians in Japan, particularly the more devout believers, would mean that missionaries would have fewer places to hide and the whole community would be jeopardized by the weakening of local lay brotherhoods.[124]

6 Conclusion

Days after the September 1622 martyrdom of Nagasaki, Christians were still lurking around the execution site in search of relics. Leading a defiant group of believers, a Christian woman called Ines was caught—perhaps not unexpectedly—by the guards of Gonroku. After being tied to a post and tortured, she begged to be killed like the priests, since not only was she a Christian, but she had also harbored missionaries herself.[125] Ines' pleas illustrate that Japanese Christians were aware that giving shelter to missionaries was one of the main reasons behind the martyrdom of lay believers. After all, at least 19 of the 30 Japanese Christians executed in the Great Martyrdom of Nagasaki were directly or indirectly related to the harboring of priests.[126]

---

123 Shimizu et al. (eds.), *Kinsei Nagasaki*, 120. Effectively, on December 13, 1618, Gonroku conducted a thorough search for hidden missionaries and forced all residents to sign new oaths. Hesselink, "104 Voices", 246.

124 Consultas 2, fols. 318v–319.

125 Pardo San Francisco, *Relación Verdadera*, fols. 44v–45.

126 Ruiz-de-Medina, *Martirologio*, 443–464. That was also the perception of a Dutch observer at the time. See Boxer, *A True Description*, 73.

But while the open persecution of priests and friars terrorized missionaries and Japanese Christians alike, subtle changes influenced their prospects, too. Shadowed by dramatic events such as the Great Martyrdom of Nagasaki, the year of 1622 marked the return of Miyajiri Santō Dayū, an *oshi* or guide specialized in taking pilgrims to the Grand Shrine of Ise, who had been absent from the region of Ōmura and Nagasaki since at least 1574.[127] The reemergence of the traditional Shintō guide after a hiatus of 48 years marked both the beginning of a return to previous beliefs and the resurgence of a more socially acceptable religious option for the local population. Shintō shrines popped up in Nagasaki during this period—seven in the 1620s, two in the 1630s, and seven more in the 1640s.[128] Of course, the rhythm of construction of Shintō shrines pales in comparison to the more than 30 Buddhist temples opened between 1620 and 1650.[129] As the Nagasaki landscape and its surroundings changed, Christians and missionaries gradually lost their safe havens while being killed off. The *Bakufu*'s persecution tested the faith and tenacity of numerous converts and, amidst apostasies and the arrest and execution of numerous laymen and women, missionaries were hunted down.

With the increasing pressure placed on them by the oaths, Jesuits and Dominicans struggled, each in their own way, to find appropriate solutions. On the one hand, the Society of Jesus dealt with the consequences of the policy by treating the oaths as issues of confession of the faith. Insofar as they avoided bringing the very topic of oath-taking to the debate, thus imposing its tacit acceptance to the addressees of their consultation, they placed focus on the circumstances that allowed the alleviation of the obligations imposed by the precept. On the other hand, Dominicans had a much more direct approach to the topic, highlighting the contractual nature of oaths and questioning their voidability. By and by, in their negotiations with superiors in Rome and Manila, both Jesuits and Dominicans agreed that the tyrannical nature of the Japanese rule was enough to both invalidate the oaths and allow Christians to refuse to answer when their faith was questioned by other Japanese people.

The hierarchical organization of both orders was crucial to the decision-making process as well as to the way moral issues were addressed in Japan. The Jesuits' rigid structure often demanded the holding of meetings where issues were compiled into consultations sent to external authorities,

---

127 Kudamatsu, *Kirishitan Denraichi*, 275; Kudamatsu, *Nagasaki no Ise Shinkō*, 34–35.

128 Almost half of the Shinto shrines in Nagasaki can be traced back to the early Edo period. Kudamatsu, *Kirishitan Denraichi*, 274–276.

129 Hesselink, *Dream*, 187.

be they in Macau, Goa, Rome, or various Jesuit universities and colleges across Europe. At the same time, however, Jesuit brotherhoods functioned as enforcers of norms determined locally and later confirmed outside of Japan. Dominicans, however, worked differently. First, the 1621 Dominican document refers to much fewer problems—only eight questions—than the 61 questions of the Jesuit questionnaire. The difference certainly arose from the way the consultations were formulated, since the Dominican process involved only two interlocutors, while the Jesuit consultation was the central piece of a negotiation process between those in Macau and their superiors in Rome. In the end, the small size of the Dominican mission in Japan allowed them to engage in personal dialogues when addressing more problematic issues—which included, for example, the difficult topic of marriage in Japan.[130] As a result, deep theological issues were discussed in private correspondence.

The issue of the oaths imposed by the *Bakufu* was a matter of life and death in the late 1610s and early 1620s in Japan. Possibly due to its importance, González and Morales had well-defined roles in their discussion: While the arrested theologian offered his experience of Japan, the Dominican in Manila confirmed the validity of Morales' decisions. However, González did not concern himself with citing a *summa*, manual, or treatise, despite the imprisoned friar's request for authoritative arguments. His role, as he understood it, was to accept and reproduce the authority of Morales' experience, at least in regard to the oath issue. In fact, the source suggests that there was an ongoing debate between both friars. Ultimately, the way Jesuits and Dominicans organized their theological debates spoke to how each order understood the dynamics of normative production and community administration.

Jesuit priests and Dominican friars alike understood Japanese Christianity as in its infancy.[131] Moreover, it was subjected to what they perceived as an almost prototypical tyrannical rule that worked in *odium fidei*, harshly persecuting the country's Christians and clergy. Under these circumstances, Japanese Christianity could be said to be doomed to be perfect; its desperate situation formed the ideal example of religious tenacity for Christians in other areas. This allowed for unorthodox responses to a variety of different norms,

130 Consultas 2, fols. 317–317v. See also the discussion by Coutinho Silva (Chapter 6) in this volume.

131 The González-Morales debate clearly refers to the *infancia ecclesie*, that is to say, the primitive state, that characterized Japan in this period. Consultas 2, fol. 317v. The topic is recurrent in numerous documents of the period. Jesuits made these observations since the early days of the mission and there are numerous references to Rome in Jesuit literature in Japan. See McManus, "Imperial History without Provincial Loyalty?".

from confessional guidelines to local political decisions, that had to be greatly improvised at times. Thus, in the government of Christian consciences during the period of persecution in Japan, theological authorities were overshadowed by local experiences, individual initiatives, communal expectations, hierarchical tensions, and extraordinary conditions.

Acknowledgements

I would like to thank the Japan Society for the Promotion of Science for the funding for this research (JSPS International Research Fellowship, P19015), and the anonymous reviewers for their comments. I am also grateful for the help provided by Ryan D. Crewe (University of Colorado Denver), who kindly offered me the Dominican documents from Manila used in this chapter. For suggestions and corrections on various stages of writing, I extend my gratitude to Ishizaki Takahiko (Hitachi-no-kuni Sōshagū, Ishioka, Japan), Manuel Bastias Saavedra (mplhlt, Frankfurt am Main), and Regalado Trota Jose (University of Santo Tomas, Manila). I am especially grateful to Liam Matthew Brockey (Michigan State University) and Martin Nogueira Ramos (École Française d'Extrême Orient, Kyoto) for sharing their thoughts on this article. Japanese names are noted in the order commonly used in Japan (family name followed by given name, without a comma between), including Japanese scholars (as in Matsuda Kiichi). The names of Japanese Christians are noted with the Christian name first, followed by family name and Japanese given name, whenever available (as in Bartolomeu Ōmura Sumitada).

Bibliography

Manuscripts

Archives jésuites en France, Vanves, France, Brotier Collection (GBro), 94.

Archivo de la Universidad de Santo Tomás, Central Library, Manila, Philippines

Archivo de la Província del Santíssimo Rosário (APSR): *Consultas* 2, *Japón* 2, *Miscelanea*, vol. 1.

Archivum Historicum Societatis Iesu, Rome, Italy, *Japonica-Sinica* (JapSin), 16, 17, 22, 25, 34, 37, 38, 58, 59.

Biblioteca do Palácio Nacional da Ajuda, Lisbon, Portugal, *Jesuítas na Ásia* (Ajuda), 49-IV-60, 49-V-7, 49-VI-6.

Tilburg University Library, Tilburg, Netherlands, Brabant Collection (BC), TF-HS 79.

Printed Sources

Aduarte, Diego de, and González, Domingo, *Tomo Primero de la Historia de la Provincia del Santo Rosario de Filipinas, Japon, y China, de la sagrada orden de Predicadores*, Zaragoza 1693: Domingo Gascon.

Aquinas, Thomas, *Summa Theologiae*.

Anon., *Lettere edificanti scritte dai frati predicatori martirizzati nel Giappone ed inseriti nel catalogo de beati dal regnante sommo pontefice Pio IX raccolte e pubblicate per fare seguito al commentario istorico già edito di loro vita e martirio*, Rome 1868: Bernardo Morini.

Anon., *Vocabulário da Lingoa de Iapam com adeclaração em Portugues, feito por alguns padres, e irmãos da Companhia de IESV*, Nagasaki 1603: Collegio de Iapam da Companhia de Iesus.

Azor, Juan, *Institutionum moralium, in quibus vniuersae quaestiones ad conscientizam rectè, aut prauè factorum pertinentes, breuiter tractantur*, Pars Prima, Rome 1600: Luigi Zanetti.

Bañez, Domingo, *Scholastica commentaria in secundam secundae angelici doctoris D. Thomae, Quibus, quœ ad Fidem, Spem, & Charitatem spectant, clarissimè explicantur*, Venice 1587: Altobello Salicati.

Carletti, Angelo, *Summa Angelica de casibus conscientialibus*, Venice 1578: Egidio Regazola.

Los Angeles [Rueda], Juan de, *Virgen S. Mariano Tattoqi Rosario no xuguiôto, vonajiqu Iesus no Mina no Cofradiani ataru riacuno qirocu*, Binondoc (Philippines) 1622.

Mazzolini, Silvestro, *Summa Sylvestrinae quae Summa Summarum mérito nuncupatur*, Lyon 1551: Jacobo Giunta.

Orfanel, Jacinto, *Historia Eclesiastica de los Sucessos de la Christandad de Iapon, desde el año de 1602, que entro en el la Orden de Predicadores, hasta el de 1620, compuesta por el Padre Fray Iacinto Orfanel, de la misma Orden, y Ministro antiguo del Santo Evangelio en aquel Reyno, Y añadida hasta el fin del año de 1622 por el Padre Fray Diego Collado, Vicario Provincial de la dicha Orden en el dicho Reyno*, Madrid 1633: la viuda de Alonso Martin.

Pardo San Francisco, Diego de, *Relación Verdadera, y Breve de la Persecución, y Martirios que padecieron por la confession de nuestra Santa Fee Catholica en Iapón, quinze Religiosos de la Prouincia de S. Gregorio, de los Descalços del Orden de nuestro Seraphico P. San Francisco de las Islas Philipinas. Aonde tambien se trata de otros muchos Martires Religiones, y seculares de diferentes estados. Todos los quales padecieron en Iapon desde el año de 1613 hasta el de 1624, la qual escriuio, y embiô a la dicha Prouincia Fray Diego de San Francisco Predicador de la misma Prouincia, y Comissario del Iapon*, Manila 1625: Thomas Pimpin.

Sánchez, Tomás, *Opus Morale in Praecepta Decalogi*, Madrid 1613: Luis Sánchez and Juan Hasrey.

Literature

Ahn Jung Won, *Kirishitan Jidai no Kon'in Mondai*, Tokyo 2012.

Alberts, Tara, *Conflict & Conversion: Catholicism in Southeast Asia, 1500–1700*, Oxford 2013.

Alvarez-Taladriz, Jose Luis, "Fuentes Europeas sobre Murayama Toan (1562–1619), II-Murayama Toan Antonio, según Bernardino de Avila Girón", in *Kōbe Gaidai Ronsō* 17 (1966): 395–418.

Amaro, Bébio Vieira, *Kōshi Nagasaki ni okeru Kirishitan Shisetsu ni Kansuru Kenkyū* [Research on Christian Structures in the port-city of Nagasaki], (PhD Thesis), Tokyo 2016.

Anesaki, Masaharu, *A Concordance to the History of Kirishitan Missions* (*Catholic Missions in Japan in the Sixteenth and Seventeenth Centuries*), Tokyo 1930.

Asami Masakazu, *Kirishitan Jidai no Gūzō Sūhai*, Tokyo 2009.

Boxer, Charles Ralph, *A true description of the mighty kingdoms of Japan and Siam by François Caron and Joos Schouten*, London 1935.

Boxer, Charles Ralph, *The Great Ship from Amacon—Annals of Macao and the Old Japan Trade, 1555–1640*, Lisbon 1963.

Brockey, Liam Matthew, "Authority, poverty, and vanity: Jesuit missionaries and the use of silk in Early Modern East Asia", in *Anais de História de Além-Mar* XVII (2016): 179–222.

Brockey, Liam Matthew, *A Journey to the East: The Jesuit Mission to China, 1579–1724*, Cambridge (US) and London (UK) 2007.

Brockey, Liam Matthew, *The Visitor: André Palmeiro and the Jesuits in Asia*, Cambridge (US) and London (UK) 2014.

Costa, João Paulo Oliveira e, "The Brotherhoods (Confrarias) and Lay Support for the Early Christian Church in Japan", in *Japanese Journal of Religious Studies* 34:1 (2007): 67–84.

Costa, João Paulo Oliveira e, "The Misericórdias among Japanese Christian Communities in the 16th and 17th Centuries", in *Bulletin of Portuguese-Japanese Studies* 5 (2002): 67–79.

Decock, Wim, *Theologians and Contract Law: The Moral Transformation of the Ius Commune* (*ca. 1500–1650*), Leiden 2012.

Delgado García, José, *El Beato Francisco de Morales OP mártir del Japón* (*1567–1622*) *Su personalidad histórica y misionera*, Madrid 1985.

Doñas, António, "Órdenes Religiosas en Japón: Diego Collado y el Memorial de 1631", in *Liburna* 13 (2018): 51–92.

Ebisawa Arimichi, *Kirishitan no Dan'atsu to Teikō* [Persecution and Resistance of the Kirishitan], Tokyo 1981.

Ehalt, Rômulo da Silva, "Casuística nos Trópicos: a pragmática teológico-moral de Francisco Rodrigues na Ásia portuguesa (séculos XVI e XVII)", *Revista de História da Sociedade e da Cultura* 19 (2019): 399–418.

Ehalt, Rômulo da Silva, "From Tenants to Landlords: Jesuits and Land Ownership in Japan (1552–1614)", in Županov, Ines G. and Vu Thanh, Hélène (eds.), *Conquering New Markets: Trade Routes, Conversion and Mission during the First Globalization (16th–18th c.)*, Leiden and Boston 2021.

Ehalt, Rômulo da Silva, "Goa no Iezusukai no Shingakusha to Nihon no Doreika Mondai" [Jesuit Theologians of Goa and the Problem of Enslavement in Japan], in *Kirishitan Bunka Kenkyūkai Kaihō* 154 (2019): 1–14.

Ehalt, Rômulo da Silva, *Jesuits and the Problem of Slavery in Early Modern Japan* (PhD Thesis), Tokyo 2017.

Fernandes Pinto, Ana and Pires, Silvana Remédio, "The 'Resposta que alguns Padres de Japão mandaram perguntar': a clash of strategies?", in *Bulletin of Portuguese-Japanese Studies* 10/11 (2005): 9–60.

Fujii Yoshio, *Oshioki—Edo Jidai no Tsumi to Batsu* [Punishment: Crime and Punishment in the Edo Period], Tokyo 1983.

Golvers, Noël, "Circulation and Reception of Portuguese Books in the 17th/18th Century Jesuit Mission of China, mainly in Three Bishop's Collections (Diogo Valente, Polycarpo de Sousa and Alexandre de Gouveia)", in Berbara, Maria and Enenkel, Karl A.E. (eds.), *Portuguese Humanism and the Republic of Letters*, Leiden and Boston 2012, 243–264.

Golvers, Noël, "The Library Catalogue of Diogo Valente's Book Collection in Macao (1633): A Philological and Bibliographical Analysis", in *Bulletin of Portuguese-Japanese Studies* 13 (2006): 7–43.

Gonoi Takashi, *Tokugawa Shoki Kirishitan-shi Kenkyū, Hoteiban* [Research on Kirishitan History in the Early Tokugawa Period, Revised version], Tokyo 1992.

Hesselink, Reinier H., "104 Voices from Christian Nagasaki – Document of the Rosario Brotherhood of Nagasaki with the Signatures of Its Members (February 1622): An Analysis and Translation", in *Monumenta Nipponica* 70:2 (2015): 237–283.

Hesselink, Reinier H., "The Capitães Mores of the Japan Voyage: a Group Portrait", in *International Journal of Asian Studies* 9:1 (2012): 1–41.

Hesselink, Reinier H., *The Dream of Christian Nagasaki: World Trade and the Clash of Cultures, 1560–1640*, Jefferson (US) 2016.

Hino Hiroshi (ed.), *Koryaado Zangeroku—Kirishitan Jidai Nihonjin Shinto no Nikusei* [Collado's Confession Manual: The Voice of Japanese Believers during the Kirishitan Period], Tokyo 2016.

Irimoto Masuo, "Jūningumi no Seiritsu" [The Establishment of the Ten-People Group System], in Kitajima Masamoto (ed.), *Kinsei no Shihai Taisei to Shakai Kōzō* [Early Modern Control Organization and Social Structure], Tokyo 1983, 163–200.

Irimoto Masuo, *Goningumi to Kinsei Sonraku—Rentai Sekininsei no Rekishi* [The Five-People Group and The Early Modern Village: The History of Collective Responsibility], Tokyo 2009.

Jonsen, Albert R. and Toulmin, Stephen, *The Abuse of Casuistry*: A History of Moral Reasoning, Berkeley, Los Angeles and London 1988.

Kataoka Yakichi, "Hakugaika no Kirishitan: Nagasaki ni okeru Yadonushi no Gyōseki wo Chushin to shite" [Kirishitan under Persecution: The Work of Hosts in Nagasaki], in *Kirishitan Bunka Kenkyūkai Kaihō* 6:4 (1963): 7–14.

Katō, Eiichi, "Aspects of Early Anglo-Japanese Relations", in Nish, Ian and Kibata, Yoichi (eds.), *The History of Anglo-Japanese Relations, 1600–2000: Volume I: The Political-Diplomatic Dimension, 1600–1930*, London and New York 2000, 31–59.

Kawamura, Shinzō, *Kirishitan Shinto Soshiki no Tanjō to Henyō: Confraria kara Konfurariya he* [The Birth and Changes of Christian Lay Organizations: From Confraria to Konfurariya], Tokyo 2003.

Kawamura Shinzō, *Making Christian Lay Communities during the "Christian Century" in Japan: A Case Study of Takata District in Bungo* (PhD Thesis), Washington DC 1999.

Klötter, Henning, *The Language of the Sangleys: A Chinese Vernacular in Missionary Sources of the Seventeenth Century*, Leiden 2011.

Kudamatsu Kazunori, *Kirishitan Denraichi no Jinja to Shinkō-Hizen-no-kuni Ōmura-ryō no Baai* [Shrines and Belief in Areas of Christian Missions: the case of the Ōmura fief of Hizen], Ōmura (Japan) 2008.

Kudamatsu Kazunori, *Nagasaki no Ise Shinkō—Oshi wo meguru Ise to Nishi-Hizen to no Nettowaaku* [The Ise Belief in Nagasaki: The Network of Guides Between Ise and East Hizen], Nagasaki 2018.

López Gay, Jesús, *El Matrimonio de los Japoneses: Problema, y soluciones según um ms. inédito de Gil de la Mata, S.J. (1547–1599)*, Rome 1964.

Lucena, Afonso de, *De algumas cousas que ainda se alembra o Pe Afonso de Lucena que pertencem à Christandade de Ōmura*, ed. Schütte, Josef Franz, Rome 1972.

Marcocci, Giuseppe, "Conscience and Empire: Politics and Moral Theology in the Early Modern Portuguese World", *JEMH* 18 (2014): 473–494.

Marcocci, *L'invenzione di un impero: Politica e cultura nel mondo portoghese (1450–1600)*, Rome 2011.

Matsuda Kiichi, *Kinsei Shoki Nihon Kankei Nanban Shiryō no Kenkyū* [Research on Nanban Sources Related to Early Modern Japan], Tokyo 1981.

Matsui Yōko, "Jendaa kara Miru Kinsei Nihon no Taigai Kankei" [Japan's Early Modern Foreign Relations as Seen from Issues of Gender], in Arano Yasunori (ed.), *Nihon no Taigai Kankei 6—Kinsei-teki Sekai no Seijuku* [Japan's Foreign Relations 6: The Maturity of the Early Modern World], Tokyo 2010, 93–121.

McManus, Stuart, "Imperial History without Provincial Loyalty? Reading Roman History in Renaissance Japan", *KNOW: A Journal on the Formation of Knowledge* 3:1 (2019): 123–157.

McManus, Stuart, "Limited-Term Servitude in Early Modern Nagasaki: Slavery and Contract Law in Gomes Vaz's *De mancipiis Indicis* (1610)", *Bulletin of Portuguese-Japanese Studies*, (2018).

Menegon, Eugenio, *Ancestors, Virgins, & Friars: Christianity as a Local Religion in Late Imperial China*, Cambridge (US) and London (UK) 2009.
Miyazaki Masakatsu, "Esutādo da India to Kapitan Mōru sei: Sekaishi Kyōiku ni okeru Daikōkai Jidai he no Ikkōsatsu" [Estado da Índia and the Capitão-Mor System: Reflections on the Great Navigations in the Teaching of World History], in *Tsukuba Daigaku Fuzoku Kōtō Gakkō Kenkyū Kiyō* 30 (1989): 7–24.
Murakami Naojirō, "Kirishitan Kenkyū no Kaiko" [Recollections of Kirishitan Research], in *Kirishitan Kenkyū* 1 (1942): 1–42.
Nawata-Ward, Haruko, *Women Religious Leaders in Japan's Christian Century, 1549–1650*, Surrey (UK) 2009.
O'Malley, John W., "The Fourth Vow in Its Ignatian Context: A historical context", in *Studies in the Spirituality of Jesuits* XV, 1 (1983): 1–59.
Odstrčilík, Jan, "Between Languages, Genres and Cultures: Diego Collado's Linguistic Works", in *medieval worlds* 11 (2020): 117–151.
Ōmura-shishi Hensan Iinkai (ed.), *Shin'hen Ōmura-shishi 3, Kinsei-hen* [New History of the City of Ōmura 2, Early Modern], Ōmura (Japan) 2015.
Pagès, Léon, *Histoire de la religion chrétienne au Japon, depuis 1598 jusqu'à 1651, comprenant les faits relatifs aux deux cent cinq martyrs béatifiés le 7 juillet 1867*, 1, Paris 1869.
Prosperi, Adriano, "The missionary", in Villari, Rosario (ed.), *Baroque Personae*, Chicago and London 1991, 160–194.
Ramos, Martin Nogueira, "Renier sa foi sans perdre son âme. Les catholiques japonais au début de la proscription (XVIIe s.)", in *Cahiers d'études des cultures ibériques et latinoaméricaines* 5 (2019): 177–202.
Ramos, Martin Nogueira, *La foi des ancêtres: Chrétiens cachés et catholiques dans la société villageoise japonaise XVIIe–XIXe siècles*, Paris 2019.
Rolbiecki, John J., "Casuistry", in Dagobert Runes (ed.), *Dictionary of Philosophy*, New York 1971, 46.
Ross, Andrew C., *A Vision Betrayed: The Jesuits in Japan and China, 1542–1742*, Edinburgh 1994.
Ruiz-de-Medina, Juan, *El Martirologio del Japón 1558–1873*, Rome 1999.
Sá, Isabel dos Guimarães, *As Misericórdias Portuguesas de D. Manuel I a Pombal*, Lisbon 2001.
Sá, Isabel dos Guimarães, *História Breve das Misericórdias Portuguesas (1498–2000)*, Coimbra 2008.
Sales, Maria de Lurdes Ponce Edra de Aboim, *Do Malabar às Molucas: os Jesuítas e a Província do Malabar (1601–1693)* (PhD Thesis), Lisbon 2015.
Schütte, Josef Franz, "Futatsu no Komonjo ni Arawaretaru Nihon Shoki Kirishitan Jidai ni Okeru 'Santa Maria no Onkumi' no Soshiki ni tsuite" [On the structure of the Santa Maria no Onkumi during the early Kirishitan period of Japan as seen in two documents], in *Kirishitan Kenkyū* 2 (1944): 135–47.

Schüssler, Rudolf, *The Debate on Probable Opinions in the Scholastic Tradition*, Leiden 2019.

Schütte, Josef Franz, *Introductio ad Historiam Societatis Jesu in Japonia 1549–1650*, Rome 1968.

Schütte, Josef Franz, *Monumenta Historica Japoniae I: Textus Catalogorum Japoniae Aliaeque de Personis Domibusque S.J. in Japonia, Informationes et Relationes, 1549–1654*, Rome 1975.

Shimizu Kōichi, Kisaki Hiromi, Yanagida Mitsuhiro and Ujie Takeshi (eds.), *Kinsei Nagasaki Hōsei Shiryōshū 1* [Legal Documents of Early Modern Nagasaki], Tokyo 2014.

Takase Kōichirō, "Kirishitan Fukyō ni okeru Usura Chōshū no Mondai ni tsuite" [On the problem of collecting usury against the background of the Christian mission] in *Shigaku* [History] 60.4 (1991): 25(429)–57(461).

Tronu, Carla, "The Rivalry between the Society of Jesus and the Mendicant Orders in Early Modern Nagasaki", in *Agora: Journal of International Center for Regional Studies* 12 (2015): 25–39.

Tutino, Stefania, *Uncertainty in Post-Reformation Catholicism: A History of Probabilism*, Oxford 2018.

Vu Thanh, Hélène, "Introducing Tridentine Marriage: The Jesuits' Strategy in Japan (Sixteenth and Seventeenth Centuries)", *Rechtsgeschichte - Legal History* 27 (2019): 143–151.

Vu Thanh, Hélène, "Principles of Missionary Geography in Jesuit Spirituality and their Implementation in Japan (16th–17th centuries)", in *Bulletin of Portuguese/Japanese Studies* 18/19 (2009): 175–191.

Wicki, Josef, "Problemas morais no Oriente Português do século XVI", in *O Centro de Estudos Históricos Ultramarinos e as Comemorações Henriquinas*, Lisbon 1961, 257–263.

Yamamoto Hirofumi, *Tokugawa Hidetada*, Tokyo 2020.

Yasutaka Hiroaki, *Kinsei Nagasaki Shihōseido no Kenkyū* [Research on the History of the Legal System of Early Modern Nagasaki], Kyoto 2010.

Zagorin, Perez, *Ways of Lying: Dissimulation, Persecution, and Conformity in Early Modern Europe*, Cambridge (US) and London (UK) 1990.

CHAPTER 9

Finding Norms for the Chinese Mission: The Hat Controversy in the Canton Conference of 1667/1668

Marina Torres Trimállez

1 Introduction

In 1676, the Dominican friar Domingo Fernández de Navarrete (onward Navarrete), OP (1619–1689) showed his admiration for the Chinese empire by describing the beauty and mystery of the emperor's crown, 冕冠 *mianguan*. In his *Tratados historicos, politicos, ethicos y religiosos de la monarchia de China,* he claimed to have seen with his own eyes its round and tall shape in some temples.[1] Navarrete explained that the quantity of tassels—a total of 12 pearls dangled from the crown—marked the emperor's status as 天子 *tianzi*—Son of Heaven—and he described their symbolism thus:

> Four of them over the eyes, which signify that the Emperor's eyes must be shut that he may not see litigants before him; and that he will neither favor the rich, nor pity the poor […]. Four strings of pearls fall over the ears […] that the judges ears are to be stop'd to the entreaties of great ones, and to the tears of the suitors, and he must only give ear to Reason, Law, and Justice. The last four strings hang behind, to express with how much Judgement, Foresight, Premeditation, and Staidness princes ought to weigh their resolutions, and how they are to be vers'd in the affairs of the Government.[2]

The Chinese imperial crown was the visual representation of a set of social norms and values admired by the missionary Navarrete, those corresponding to a well-organized society driven by values of good governance exercised by

1 This headgear fell out of use during the Qing dynasty but was used in earlier periods. Hector, "Chinese Bead Curtains, Past and Present", 42.

2 Fernández de Navarrete, *Tratados históricos*, trat. I, cap. IX, 22. English translation available at https://babel.hathitrust.org/cgi/pt?id=uc2.ark:/13960/t2n58tf55&view=1up&seq=9 (Last-accessed 04.18.2021).

DOI: 10.1163/9789004472839_010

the emperor as its highest authority.[3] In parallel, in his description the missionary recognized the importance of the headgear as an instrument of political communication. Head ornaments served in China to affirm social status and construct a hierarchy. [4] As Eugenio Menegon has pointed out, they were of great importance not only for sacred groups, but also for commoners and Chinese degree-holders. Their specific cap marked their position, since headgear was also associated with legal privileges.[5] The same applied in early modern Europe. Navarrete himself was a vassal of King Philip IV of Spain (1605–1665) who in 1621 used the wording "Count-Duke Olivares, cover yourself" as he conferred Gaspar de Guzmán y Pimentel (1587–1645) the title of grandee, considered at the time to be the highest dignity of nobility.[6] From that point onwards, the count-duke, as the king's favorite, was allowed to cover his head in the presence of the sovereign. This was a social honor given to only a few since it was mandatory for vassals to show their respect and subordination by uncovering their heads.

As these two examples demonstrate, sumptuary laws were equally important in both Chinese and Spanish early modern traditions. However, there was an important distinction between their external signs regarding headgear that would be the origin of future dissensions among Europeans who traveled to China: contrary to its meaning in Europe, in China it was considered impolite and disrespectful to speak to a superior without wearing a hat.

In their evangelization work in China, European missionaries faced this contradiction and were forced to set up a discussion to decide which tradition to follow when celebrating Christian rituals in China, including mass and confession. In this chapter, the topic of the Chinese hat will serve as an example when exploring missionaries' agency both in regulating their praxis in the

3 This explanation derives from The Analects of Confucius and the obligation of proper ritualistic behaviors: 非禮勿視，非禮勿聽，非禮勿言，非禮勿動 *fei li wushi, feli wu ting, feli li wu yan, feli li wu dong*: "Do not look if it is inappropriate; do not listen if it is inappropriate, do not speak if it is inappropriate, and do not act if it is inappropriate". Translation in Lee, *Warp and Weft. Chinese Language and Culture*, 190–191.

4 Dorothy Ko explains about late imperial China: "Correct attire—headdress, dress, and shoes—was the quintessential expression of civility, culture, and humanity, all being ramifications of *wen* [...]. The inherent links among clothing, the civilizing process, and politics are highlighted in the Book of Changes: 'The Yellow Emperor, Yao, and Shun allowed the upper and lower garments to hang down, and the world was in order.' [...] Getting dressed was thus at once a cultural act, one that distinguished humans from beasts, and a political act". Ko, "The Body as attire", 12.

5 Menegon, "Deliver us from Evil", 35 fn. 70.

6 Elliot, *The Count-Duke of Olivares*, 45.

missionary field and, consequently, to produce new norms regarding the use of head coverings.

The chapter is divided into three main parts. The first section briefly introduces the sources and the previous studies regarding the regulation of head coverings in the mission. The second section is devoted to the analysis of the Canton Conference of 1668 in which missionaries reached specific agreements regarding head coverings. The third section explores the different sources of authority mobilized by missionaries in their discourses in defense of their position. This analysis allows an evaluation of the importance of local conditions in these processes of creation of norms and to study missionaries in their roles as lawmakers. Accordingly, it will be possible to investigate how their European background interacted with Chinese realities. Moreover, the Chinese case of the regulation of hats will add new elements of debate to the current discussions regarding the construction of legal traditions during the process of European expansion.

2 Sources and Debates

Traditionally, in the field of Christianity in China, most studies on legislative activity have focused on the actions of the Papacy and the offices of the Holy See in direct relation to the well-known Chinese Rites Controversy.[7] The magnitude of the dispute involved eight popes and the Emperor 康熙 Kangxi (1654–1722).[8] Therefore, their consecutive interventions, through decrees, bulls, and legations, have drawn the attention of historians since studies of the missions began until today.[9] When descending from the central institutions to

---

7 Following Claudia von Collani's definition, the Rites Controversy was a series of debates among different parties "about the participation of Christians in certain non-Christian religious or secular rites and ceremonies in Asia (China, Japan, India, Indochina). Connected with the rites controversy was the accommodation of missionaries to local cultures and the question of an indigenous terminology and to what extent new Christians had to use Western sacramentals and observe the European canon law". Relevant problems were the translation of the term God and Chinese ritual practices of honoring family ancestors and Confucius. The latter were considered civic and not religious cults by some, while others took the opposite view considering these actions incompatible with Christian orthodoxy and therefore superstitious. Collani, "The Jesuit Rites Controversy", 891. See also Pavone, "Riti Cinesi", 1324–1329.

8 For the history of the Rites Controversy, see Minamiki, *The Chinese Rites*; Mungello, *Curious Land*; Cummins, *A Question of Rites*; Collani, "The Jesuits Rites", 891–917.

9 Among many other authors, see, for example: Di Fiore, *La legazione Mezzabarba*, 1989; Rule and Collani and Hughes, *The Acta Pekinensia*, 2015, reprint 2019; Gong Yingya, "The Edict of toleration", 178–182.

the mission field, one finds that, in the last years, scholars have also devoted their efforts to the study of the role of the Jesuit visitors, as illustrated by the cases of Alessandro Valignano, SJ (1539–1606) and André Palmeiro, SJ (1569–1635). Their duty to inspect and judge missionary policies in Asia also involved drawing up rules for missionary life that have been evaluated by scholars, too. [10] When discussing normativity in Asia, another aspect has also played an important role in the historiography of the last decade: casuistry. Theologians identified, discussed, and settled moral principles based on the evaluation of particular 'cases of conscience'.[11] In the missions, missionaries found numerous doubtful cases when evangelizing. Specialists such us Giovanni Pizzorusso, Charlotte de Castelnau-L'Estoile, and Giuseppe Marcocci, among others, have therefore analyzed the missionaries' correspondence that gives testimony to the continuous consultations posed by them as well as the resolutions provided by the authorities including the congregations from the *Propaganda Fide* in Rome and the higher ecclesiastical authorities within the orders.[12]

Considering that in the studies of casuistry and the papal and visitors' actions, norms were produced by central authorities, it is easy to assume that norms in the mission field were also thought up and systematically imposed by central institutions.[13] This may have been influenced by the archival selection: in studies of the mission, there has been a tendency to focus on the European archives of the highest entities instead of the local archives of the orders.[14] But it was also because resolutions, opinions, and enquiries are usually found in the archives as part of theological compilations labeled as "miscellaneous" which means reviewing sources requires a great effort. Apart from the fact that historiography has focused its attention on these cases, there are two other reasons that could explain this widespread connotation of norms as a product of central authorities. First, we naturally assume that in the *ancien régime* those in the lower stratum turned to superiors for decision making and there

10 Brockey, *The Visitor*, 2014; Schute, *Valignano's Mission*. See also Metzler, "Mezzi e modi", 38–50.

11 For a general examination of the method of casuistry in the early modern period, see Prodi (ed.), *Disciplina dell'anima*; Prodi, *Una storia della justicia*.

12 The analysis of the dubia circa sacramenta is a well-known example of this. See, among others, Pizzorusso, Charlotte de Castelanu-L'Estoile, and Broggio (eds.), "Administrer les sacrements"; or Marcocci, *A consciencia de um império*, 2013.

13 For a perspective on casuistry in the missionary field, see also Ehalt (Chapter 8) in this volume.

14 Archives such as the *Propaganda Fide* historical archives, Ajuda Library, and the Vatican Library have been historically visited more. The Jesuits and the Archives of the House of the Superior General (ARSI) were an exception because of their fourth vow of special obedience to the pope.

is general agreement on the fact that matters of relevance should be resolved by those higher in the hierarchy.[15] Second, Chinese missions were not part of lands conquered by Europeans. Consequently, the subsidiary nature of the missions, with respect to the Portuguese and Spanish empires, is added to the previously mentioned predominant European-centered-state perspective on legal history.[16] Although these assertions have been recently put into question by specialists, there is still a need to study local practices to write about legal history from a global perspective.[17]

With this in mind, this chapter uses the example of head coverings in China, in which the initial resolution of a norm takes place in the missionary field by the missionaries themselves. For this purpose, this chapter mainly focuses on two manuscripts that have so far received little scholarly attention, which are preserved in the archives of the Santo Tomás Convent (Avila, Spain), where the majority of documents regarding the Province of the Holy Rosary of the Dominican Order—concerning the Philippines, Japan, China, Formosa, and Tonkin—are stored.[18] The first manuscript is entitled *Respuestas a unas objeciones de las cortesías de los bonetes de China &ª firmado por varios PP. en la reclusión de Canton* (*incluido el VP. Fr. Antonio de Sta. María*) (hereinafter *Respuestas*) and the second is called *Dudase si en China es conveniente que asistan los cristianos a la misa cubierta la cabeza* (hereinafter *Dudas*).[19] These manuscripts are especially valuable because they were part of what has come to be known as the Canton Conference, a series of discussions held by the

---

15 As pointed out by Ehalt (Chapter 8), in this volume, citing Josef Wicki (1961): "estos casos [de consciência] envolviam temas como comércio, direitos de herança, matrimônios e otros, exigindo 'imediata e segura solução, […] mas que pelas graves consequências não podiam nem deviam ser resolvidas por un simples missionário". Ehalt, "Casuística nos Trópicos", 500.

16 For a reflection on the idea of law in the Iberian empires see Bastias Saavedra (Chapter 1) in this volume.

17 See also, Cardim, Herzog, Ruiz Ibáñez et al., *Polycentric Monarchies*; Duve, "What is global legal history?", 1–43; Bastias Saavedra, "Diversity as Paradox", 1–17; Duve, "Pragmatic Normative Literature".

18 I have considered both documents separately given their contents and titles. Nevertheless, the box in which they are preserved contains an index in which both documents come under the same reference: "Respuesta del P. Navarrete a ciertas objeciones sobre el uso de los bonetes". Sección Ritos Chinos 035. Tomo 3. Tratados misceláneos (1637, 1669, 1717). Carpeta 6, fols. 324v–342v. The handwriting would indicate that these are copies of original documents, probably from the 18th century.

19 "Dudase si en China .." is a second manuscript version that is also printed in the *Controversias* written by Navarrete, published in 1679. Navarrete, *Controversias,* Trat. 4, fols. 222r–227r. Anna Busquets included a description of this manuscript in her PhD dissertation about him. Busquets, *Los Tratados Históricos*, 279.

missionaries between 1667 and 1668 in Guangzhou, China. In the history of the Chinese mission, it is a rare example of a regulated discussion to look for agreements. Moreover, the importance of these meetings also comes from the fact that this was the first time the three main religious orders working in China—Jesuits, Franciscans, and Dominicans—are found together discussing the issues that most concern them.[20]

The analysis of the hat controversy not only allows a bottom-up approach, but also consists of an element often overlooked in the scholarship. Specialists have historically tended to focus on the regulation of more controversial aspects, such as the practices of ancestor worship and sacrifice to Confucius, which were central issues debated as part of the Rites Controversy.[21] Recent studies on the sacrament of marriage in the missions have opened new lines of research into the regulation of Christian rituals.[22] Yet, the question of the hat was not a direct and obvious attack on Christian orthodoxy, as were cases of marriage and concubinage. Therefore, the hat regulation provides us with a less controversial aspect in which it is easier to find elements that highlight processes of consensus within the missionaries' policies that had been neglected because of a preponderant understanding of the mission as involving quarrels between missionaries merely because of their different orders or nations.

Further, the issue of the hat did not produce much documentation because missionaries quickly chose to adapt their European custom to Chinese etiquette. Soon after their arrival in China, missionaries became aware of its intricate sumptuary laws. For this reason, in 1613, Father Nicolò Longobardo, SJ (1559–1654), superior of the Chinese mission, sent Father Nicolas Trigault, SJ (1557–1628) to Rome to negotiate several questions regarding the Chinese liturgy, including the issue of head coverings.[23] With the support of Cardinal Roberto Bellarmino, SJ (1542–1621), the most prestigious theologist in Rome at the time, Trigault requested permission from the Holy See to wear head coverings during mass.[24] In response, Pope Paolo V (1552–1621), in the brief *Romanae*

20 Metzler, *Die Synoden*, 11–21.

21 Standaert, *The interweaving*.

22 Collani, "Mission and Matrimony", 11–31; Catto, "La monogamia nella poligamia", 7–22. See also Meynard, "Could Chinese Vegetarians be Baptized? Part 1", 75–145; Meynard, Could Chinese Vegetarians be Baptized? Part 2", 285–341.

23 Jesuits also requested permission to translate the Holy Scriptures into classical Chinese, as well as authorization for future Chinese priests to celebrate mass, recite the breviary, and administer the sacraments in classical Chinese. For more on the Trigault trip to Rome, see Lamalle, "La propagande du P. Nicolas Trigault en faveur des missions de Chine (1616)", 46–120; Seah, "The 1670 Chinese Missal", 86–120.

24 Entitled *De Missa celebranda tecto capite*. Seah, "The 1670 Chinese Missal", 93–94. Transcriptions of the petition and decrees by the Holy Office can be found in Bontinck, *La Lutte Autour*, 405–411.

FIGURE 9.1 Reproduction of a 祭巾 Jijin. Domus Serapahica project.
COURTESY OF MR. HO LONG FRANCESCO LI

Sedis Antistes, granted that the Chinese could wear hats, unlike in Europe, and missionaries were permitted to wear head coverings during the Divine Office, the so-called 祭巾 *Jijin* (Figure 9.1).[25]

25 Its transcription can be found in Bontinck, *La Lutte Autour*, 411–412. Giulio Aleni (1582–1649) gives a well-known description of this special hat in his 彌撒祭義 *Misa jiyi*: "It has a square top, a round bottom, and four faces. To the top of each face an embroidered square panel is fixed, with three strings hanging from each top corner. One corner faces the front, and from the back hang two long ribbons". Translation by Gregory Dipippo in http://www.newliturgicalmovement.org/2018/08/the-chinese-sacrificial-hat-and.html (last accessed 05.25.2020). 巾 Jin (soft hat) was an everyday type of headwear that marked the person's affiliation to the church. The character 祭 refers to the action of offering a sacrifice. Zorkina, "Taoist garments in Rituals and Monastic Life", 163. See also Motoh, "Orphan(ed) Scroll", 139–159.

Paolo v's allowance of head coverings during Christian rituals continued for over 300 years. On July 31, 1673, Pope Clement x (1590–1676) once more confirmed permission to celebrate mass *coperto capite* (with the head covered). And, only in 1924, the use of the *Jijin* head covering was eventually abolished in the First Chinese Council held in Shanghai.[26] As a result, the impression given is that the question of head coverings was a more static and less disputed phenomenon compared to other questions of the Church in China. Nevertheless, the preservation of the *Respuestas* and *Dudas* manuscripts reveals that, behind this apparent agreement, there was in fact an ongoing passionate debate between missionaries on the wearing and not wearing of a hat, even if this had little resonance in the Roman central quarters compared to other more controversial matters.

There are also other reasons that the use of a Chinese sacrificial hat and permission to appear covered during mass and all sacred rituals have not yet received detailed attention. For example, as a liturgical element, the use of the hat has been more typically associated with the history of clothing, fashion, and material culture.[27] And, even from that point of view, it has been difficult for scholars to reconstruct these realities, particularly due to the lack of consistent implementation of the Catholic missionary enterprise in Asia, the periodical persecutions faced by missionaries, and the natural degradation of cultural materials over time. Recent contributions have begun to redress such gaps in the literature.[28]

---

26 Bontinck, *La Lutte Autour*, 387–388. See also *Concilium Sinense, ed. Primum Concilium Sinense anno 1924 a die 14 maii ad diem 12 iunii in ecclesia S. Ignatii de Zi-Ka-Wei celebratum: acta, decretal et normaa, vota, etc.*

27 The habit was one of the central elements of the missionaries' identity. Accusations of not respecting the vow of poverty by using silk garments and luxurious ceremonial dresses and hats were common in Asian missions. See Zampol, "Purple Silk and Black Cotton", 136–155; Menegon, "The habit that hides the monk", 30–49.

28 Sanfilippo, "L'abito fa il missionario", 610–620; Hsia, "From Buddhist Garb", 143–154; Brockey, "Authority poverty, and vanity", 179–222; Menegon, "The habit that hides the monk", 45–46; Amsler, *Jesuits and Matriarchs*, 13–31; Zampol, "Purple Silk and Black Cotton", 137–155.

To which the classical works of Bontinck, CICM, *La lutte autor de la liturgie chinoise*; López Gay, *La liturgia en la misión del Japón*; and Margiotti, OFM, *Il cattolicesimo nello Shansi,* should be added. Previous studies have focused on clothing and bodily practices, especially regarding dress code, as representations and external signs of the adaptability or non-adaptability of Catholic missionaries to non-European contexts. This adaptability, according to Menegon, has been studied from different perspectives including the classical accommodation approach, the paradigm of the Baroque "dissimulation", and the more general framework of the dialogue of cultures. Menegon, "The habit that hides the monk", 45–46.

The manuscripts under discussion here present a different perspective: the discussion about the regulation of the use of head coverings during Christian rituals. This chapter, first, studies the legal mechanisms used by missionaries to regulate their practice beyond their superiors. Second, it analyzes how different sources of authority were drawn upon to justify the use of Church or Chinese custom in the celebration of mass and confessions in the Chinese context. Read in conjunction, the two selected manuscripts of 1668 offer a picture of the different positions and argumentations adopted by missionaries when discussing the regulation of the use of hats in the Chinese mission. After these documents were written, missionaries continued to submit further statements on the issue. However, this chapter focuses only on the initial argumentations at the beginning of the controversy. This decision responds to the objective of understanding the discourses surrounding and the process of creation of the norm about head coverings. The intention is not to reconstruct how the question of the hat was dealt with by Catholics and the subsequent decisions made by all the participants over time, nor is the focus on the results of the missionaries' debates with the objective of understanding their degree of adaptation to Chinese culture. On the contrary, by moving away from that classical dichotomy, this chapter reflects on the complexity of the transcultural experiences undergone by missionaries in China and how these affected their normative practices, thus illustrating the normative pluralism that characterized the early modern period.

3 Head Coverings in the Canton Conference of 1667/1668

This section discusses how the question of head coverings was discussed in the Canton Conference of 1667/1668. The first part (3.1) shows how broader guidelines for the discussion and definition of norms were laid out by the missionaries, revealing some preestablished mechanisms for the revision and collective authorization of norms at the local level. The second part of this section (3.2) explores how the norms regarding head coverings were decided and certified, revealing that decisions by higher or more prestigious authorities did not necessarily end the discussion but could in fact lead to further debate. The *Dudas* and the *Respuestas* are a reflection of these ongoing conflicts of norms.

3.1 *Rules for Finding Rules for the Chinese Mission: The Canton Conference of 1667/1668*

The manuscripts under discussion here were produced in the last months of 1668. 53 years had passed since the Pauline brief had allowed the use of head coverings in the Chinese missions, after which many things changed. Trigault had returned to China in the 1610s, while the Chinese mission had been elevated to the status of Vice-Province in 1618 although it remained under the jurisdiction of the Japan Province. At that time, Jesuits kept monopoly of the missions in China and operated legally within the Portuguese *Padroado* by which the Church delegated the administration of the local churches to Portuguese monarchs. In the first years of the mission, they chose to adopt the Buddhist identity but later made the decision to change to the Confucian literati fashion and grew their hair long.[29] In 1621, they issued a compendium of rules for the new Vice-Province in which they also included instructions about hair. That same year "some of Nicolas Trigault's recruits slipped into China from Macau 'in literati costumes, with long beards, hair grown out and tied on their heads in Chinese fashion'."[30]

In 1633, Pope Urban VIII (1568–1644) issued the bull *Ex debito pastoralis* and opened China and Japan to missionaries of other orders and societies. The first Dominicans arrived in 1631, followed by the Franciscans in 1633. These were major changes not only because the mission was restructured, but also because the presence of different orders made the controversy over Chinese Rites public when the Dominican Juan Bautista Morales, OP (1597–1664) brought the question to Rome.[31] Furthermore, in 1622, Rome had created the Sacred Congregation for the Propagation of the Faith, known as the *Propaganda Fide*.[32] This institution sought to strengthen Rome's position within the Spanish *Patronato* and the Portuguese *Padroado* in order to restore the spiritual char-

29 This change has usually been attributed to Matteo Ricci at the suggestion of the Chinese literatus, 瞿太素 *Qu Taisu* (1549–1611). See, for instance, Menegon, "The habit that hides the monk", 33. Mathew Brockey, on the contrary, proves that this transformation was begun eight years earlier by Alessandro Valignano (1539–1606). Brockey, "Authority, poverty, and vanity", 202, 204.

30 Brockey, *Journey to the East*, 78. The Jesuit Visitor, André Palmeiro, SJ (1569–1635) also wrote a separate report on clothing to control excesses in 1628. Brockey, *The Visitor*, 252–253. See also Menegon, "The habit that hides the monk", 33, 45–46.

31 He submitted to *Propaganda* 17 propositions and as a result Pope Innocent X (1574–1655) condemned the Chinese Rites on September 12, 1645. Jesuits reacted by sending Martino Martini, SJ (1614–1661) to present the case in *Propaganda*. The Holy Office judged that the ceremonies could be allowed to the Chinese Christians given their civil and political character. Finally, Pope Alexander VII confirmed it by a decree on March 23, 1656. Minamiki, *The Chinese Rites controversy*, 25–32.

32 Established by Pope Gregory XV (1554–1623), it was responsible, in the name of the Pope, for promoting the spread of the Catholic faith and directing the life of the Church in the mission lands. Also, in parts of the world which had not yet been Christianized, there was a lack of regular ecclesiastical hierarchy or it was at an early stage of development. Dowd, *Rome in Australia*, 43.

acter of missionary work. Consequently, after 1620, the Chinese mission was formed of members of diverse religious orders, of different nationalities, and working under various privileges and institutional dependencies.[33]

The situation was complicated further when considering that the missionaries were primarily dependent on the local imperial power to carry out their work of evangelization. The 1650s and 1660s were turbulent times in China. The transition from the Ming to the Qing dynasty involved a long period of internal conflict including war and destruction, epidemics, and famines.[34] In addition, missionaries needed approval from the rulers of the new dynasty. To gain the favor of the new Emperor 順治 Shunzhi (1638–1661) they offered their technology and services, acting as scientists and diplomats, and adopted without reservation the new Qing robes and their official hats with rank buttons.[35]

Under the following emperor, Emperor Kangxi, Christianity experienced considerable growth, benefited particularly by the crucial positions achieved by the Jesuits in the imperial Astronomical Bureau (欽天監 *Qintianjian*), with Adam Schall von Bell, SJ (1592–1666) in the forefront.[36] In 1661, the Emperor died unexpectedly, and a new period of persecutions began. During the Oboi regency (1661–1669), 楊光先 Yang Guangxian (1597–1669), a Confucian scholar allied to the Muslim Astronomers, delivered a series of accusations against Schall, among others, blaming the Jesuits for the dissemination of pernicious doctrines and accusing them of falsifying the calendar and conspiracy against the state. In 1665, this conflict resulted in the proscription of Christianity, the imprisonment of Schall, and the confiscation of the missionaries' properties.[37] In addition, all missionaries were expelled to Guangzhou with the exception of

33 See Mensaert, "L'etablissement de la hiérarchie", 369–466; Pizzorusso, "Per servitio della Sacra Congregatione", 201–227.

34 For the causes of the fall of the Ming dynasty and the Manchu conquest of China, see Wakeman, *The Great Enterprise*; Struve, *The Qing Formation*. See also Chan, "Late Ming Society and the Jesuit Missionaries", 153–172.

35 Menegon, "The habit that hides the monk", 41–42. As the Dominican friar Alcober wrote in a letter in 1733 to his cousin: "La figura mía exterior es muy extraña, porque aquí no llevamos hábito. Vamos vestidos a la tártara, barba larga, rapada la cabeza como un galeote. Lo demás del vestido no cuento, porque no lo has de poder entender". González, *Historia de las misiones*, 204–205 fn. 22.

36 On the missionaries' role in producing calendars in the late Ming and early Qing dynasties, see Li (Chapter 10) in this volume.

37 In addition to Schall von Bell (1606–1682), Verbiest, SJ (1623–1688), and Magalhães, SJ (1610–1677) remained. On May 18, 1665, five Christian officials in the Astronomical Bureau were sentenced to death. Alden, *The Making of an Enterprise*, 145–146. See also Jami, *Revisiting the Calendar Case*, 459–477.

those who remained at court and a group of Dominicans that continued their apostolate underground in the regions of Fujian and Jiangnan.[38]

For several reasons, the period of the missionaries' house arrest in Guangzhou, from March 25, 1666 until September of 1671, was particularly relevant for the Catholic enterprise. First, it was a time in which Chinese Christians assumed greater leadership in the administration of the Church's activities due to the absence of the missionaries.[39] Second, members of the three orders lived together in the Jesuit residence of Guangzhou and used their time to work on writing Christian liturgical books in Chinese and translating the main Confucian texts into Latin.[40] Third, as this chapter highlights, missionaries undertook the difficult task of seeking agreement on the question of the Chinese Rites and created a set of norms that, in some cases, remained.

It was during this five-year house arrest in the Pearl River Delta when the *Respuestas* and the *Dudas* were written, as part of the Canton Conference which lasted for 40 days (between December 18, 1667 and January 26, 1668) and involved the participation of 25 missionaries (21 Jesuits, three Dominicans, and one Franciscan).[41] The difficulties in the implementation of the Church policy on the ground often gave rise to multiple doctrinal interpretations and was therefore a source of continued debate. The Chinese mission was not different in that sense. For this reason, the objective of the Canton Conference was to preserve the uniformity of preaching and action in the missions. One of the Jesuits, the Italian Prospero Intorcetta, SJ (1626–1696), explained the objective of the conference in a letter to the *Propaganda Fide* in 1672:

> In view of our uncertain future, the Canton exiles would certainly have the time to examine, to great benefit, the books, rites, customs, and practices of our Mission [...]. Mainly because of the desire of the fathers of St. Dominic, supported by all of us, the Father Vice-Provincial resolved to *celebrate a kind of synod* in which we would discuss all the controversies

38 For this episode, see Appendix 1, "Canton: Internment and flight", in Cummins, *The Travels*, 412–424.

39 See, among others, Raini, "Catechisti e capi", 97–156; Entenmann, "A Mission Without Missionaries", 31–54; Entenmann, "Catholic Clergy", 389–410.

40 The *Confucius Sinarum Philosophus sive scientia Sinensis latine exposita* (Paris, 1687) was the first complete translation of the Four Books into a European language. For an analysis of the book production, see Golver, "The Canton-Macau as a lieu de savoir", 214–233.

41 During the confinement two missionaries died, Inácio da Costa, SJ on May 11, 1666 and Michel Trigault, SJ in September of 1667. For an analysis of the nationalities, ages, education, and experience on the mission of those missionaries arrested in Guangzhou, including graphics, see Esquivel, *El confinamiento de los misioneros*, 230–244.

> between us and with the members of other religious orders, and the need of uniformity for the preaching of the Holy Gospel.[42]

Father Intorcetta described the conferences as "a kind of synod" which is symptomatic of the difficulties they encountered when trying to implement in these territories the more orthodox instruments used by the Church to regulate their praxis.[43] Spaces of negotiation were part of the Catholic tradition and the synod was one of them. From the point of view of canon law, a synod was "a gathering of church representatives to study daily problems of the spiritual life, give an impetus or restore ecclesiastical laws, promote divine worship and religious practice."[44] The Canton Conference directly responded to these special needs.[45] They founded a system to clarify the practice of the Church in China and reach their objective of providing a set of common rules for pastoral activity in the mission.

The missionaries established their own procedure for conducting the conference and defining the new rules for the mission: discussions would be resolved by vote under the presidency of Vice-Provincial Feliciano Pacheco, SJ (1622–1687) with the Italian Jesuit Giovanni Francesco Ferrari, SJ (1609–1671) acting as Secretary.[46] Navarrete would speak for the Dominicans and Antonio de Santa María Caballero, OFM for the Franciscans. Given the disparity in the number of missionaries of each order, Navarrete also claimed the right to speak for the three Jesuits living in Beijing and the five Dominicans that were hidden in the inland provinces. The Dominican wrote down this decision and highlighted his claims in his *Controversias* in this way:

> Based on what has been said, the Fathers of the Society [of Jesus] agreed to propose some points so that, once everyone has made their opinion felt, it could be decided by vote how to proceed. I became worried because we were only three, one belonging to the Franciscan order, and

42 Italics are mine. "Frà queste icertezze al nostro flato futturo, gli esiliati in Canton havemmo certo il tempo per esaminare, non senza gran fruto, i libri, i riti, gli usi, e conseutudine della nostra Missione [...] desiderandolo li Padri principalmente di S. Domenico, col parere di tutti li nostri si risolvè il Padre Vice Provinciale di fare un come Sinodo, nel quale trattassimo tutti insieme le cose controverse tra noi, e gli altri religiosi, e d'una uniformità necessaria per la predicatione del Santo Evangelio". Cicé, *Acta Cantoniensia*, part. I, 16–17.

43 Missionaries in their writings also refer to these conferences as *juntas*, *discusiones*, or *disputates*.

44 Vaquero, *Diccionario*, vol. 4, 2487.

45 See also Metzler, *Die Synoden*, 11–43.

46 Fernández de Navarrete, *Controversias*, Trat. IV, 190.

> 19 of their Fathers [Jesuits]. It was clear that their votes would always prevail, with which they could do what they wanted.[47]

This excerpt describes how they established the voting system, but it is also noteworthy that they were following the *disputatio* logic of late scholasticism in their procedure. This method consisted of announcing the question that would be discussed by the participants beforehand. Nevertheless, it was an open and pluralistic process. During the celebration of the conference, Chinese catechists who lived in the house were consulted when certain doubts on local uses arose during their discussions. Navarrete, in his *Controversias*, gives an example of their intervention when there was a disagreement between the participants about the presence of the soul in the funerary tablets:

> Refers particularly to the tablets of the deceased and Confucius. The author explains the two Chinese terms *I Xin* at will; and to speak with total security in this matter, I called Brother Antonio Fernandez [...], he told me it meant that the souls came to rest on the tablets [...]. The next day I asked the same question to Juan, the catechist, and he answered the same. During the afternoon I asked bachiller Marcos, he answered in the same way and he wrote it with his own hand.[48]

In total, three different Chinese brothers were consulted to clarify the question. In addition, further information was available to all members through some collections that had been brought to Guangzhou from the Macau college archives, including manuscript texts and print books both in Chinese and Western languages.[49] Furthermore, the missionaries also maintained continuous contact with the outside world and their exchange of letters was not interrupted.[50] The final resolutions of the Canton Conference were condensed into 42 articles in the form of an act. Several copies are preserved in archives around Europe, although most of these copies do not include the minutes of

---

47 Fernández de Navarrete, *Controversias*, Trat. IV, 190.

48 Fernández de Navarrete, *Controversias*, Trat. VII, 396.

49 Noël Golvers provides a list of the Western printed books in Golvers, "The Canton-Macau as a lieu de savoir", 228–232. See also 223, 225 fn. 35.

50 At the beginning of their detention, Chinese authorities conducted a rollcall and missionaries were tightly guarded. These measures were relaxed over time and from the summer of 1668 onwards they increasingly enjoyed freedom of movement. Cummins, *A Question of Rites*, 144–145. Golvers refers to a brief period of break in 1667 due to some discordances with magistrates. Golvers, "The Canton-Macau as a lieu de savoir", 226, 225 fn. 38.

the conference.[51] Its resolutions had the objective of providing a uniform regulation for the liturgical praxis and should have put an end to previous disagreements and rivalries within the mission. Most of them were devoted to the proper administration of the sacraments, but there were also articles focused on the regulation of the liturgical calendar, nocturnal gatherings, religious imagery, and the catechesis for children, among others.[52]

3.2 *The Customs of the Church or the Style of the Land: The Question of Head Coverings in the Canton Conference*

The topic of attending mass with or without head coverings played an important role in the Canton Conference. Eleven out of the 42 articles related to mass and three of them referred to clothing and bodily practices. The privilege conceded by Paolo V in 1615 to have one's head covered during mass was brought back to the table in 1667, though it is not clear who instigated this. The Franciscan Santa María in a letter dated November 14, 1668, indicated that it was both António Gouvea, SJ (1592–1677) and Father Feliciano Pacheco who made the request to celebrate mass without a hat, at least within the confines of the Guangzhou house and its chapel.[53] But the Italian Dominican Domenico Sarpetri, OP (1623–1683) accused Santa María of provoking this controversy himself. However, Jesuit Father Jean Valat, SJ (c. 1614–1696) defended him, stating that it was the Jesuit fathers who had made the proposal.[54]

Regardless of who began the discussion, the issue was debated in the conference. The *quaestiones disputatae* asked "If it is convenient for the priest to celebrate mass with his head uncovered, and for the Christians to attend in this manner and receive communion?"[55] Concerning this passionately contested issue, they finally reached the following rule:

---

51 They were printed in 1700 and known as the *Acta Cantoniensia Autentica*, part 2, fols. 19–42 by Luis-Armand Champion de Cicé, MEP (1648–1727). A German translation of the 42 resolutions can also be found in Metzler, *Die Synoden*, 24–28. To see on which documents the author based his translation see p. 28 n. 11. Navarrete included all the articles with his comments as part of his *Controversias*. Fernández de Navarrete, *Controversias*, Trat IV, 190. For this work, an autographed version preserved in the Roman Archives of the Jesuits (ARSI) with the reference Fondo Gesuitico 722/12 was also consulted.

52 For a general analysis of the content of all articles, see Esquivel, *El confinamiento de los misioneros*, 265–273.

53 *Sinica Fanciscana*, Vol. IX, 1026.

54 Copies of the testimonies of Jean Valat and Adrian Grelon supporting Santa María can be found in APSR, Ritos Chinos 35, Tom. 3, leg. 6, fol. 324r–324v.

55 Fernández de Navarrete, *Controversias*, Trat. IV, fol. 222r.

> In the presence of the Chinese no reverence can be made by removing the hat from the head, but instead embrace all kinds of signs of respect for a man of such high stature, the Chinese should be always covered: Christian mysteries require the greatest reverence, which must be demonstrated in the presence of the locals; neophytes who attend the Holy Sacrifice, who help the priest serving at mass, or who receive Holy Communion, should have their heads covered with a cap to honor the great mystery.[56]

As this text shows, first, they permitted that Christians attending mass should have their heads covered and, second, that the priest's assistants should also be covered. This was voted by a majority. However, the three French Jesuits Adrien Grelon, SJ (1618–1696), Jean Valat, and Humbert Augery, SJ (1610–1672), the Portuguese Jesuit Manuel Jorge, SJ (1621–1677), the Spanish Dominican Felipe Leonardo, OP (1627–1677), and the Spanish Franciscan Santa María voted against the ruling.[57]

Before sending the final resolutions to the superior general, some members of the conference decided to seek the approval of Luís da Gama, SJ (1610–1672), the Portuguese Jesuit Visitor of Japan and China residing in Macau. Father da Gama, after studying the matter over the summer, suggested that these two points agreed in the conferences should be changed because he considered that attending mass with head coverings went against the customs of the Church.[58] Instead, the visitor proposed modifying both articles so that

---

56 "Cum apud Sinas pileum e capite deponere nulla sit reverentia; quin immo omnis externa Veneratio tam homini, quam vero, aut putato Numini tecto capite semper à Sinis exhibeatur: Christiana autem mysteria summam exigant reverentiam, quae praesentibus etiam Ethnicis probetur: Neophyti sive sancto Sacrificio assistantes, sive sacerdoti sacris operanti in servientes, sive etiam ad Sacram Communionem accedentes ob tanti mysterii reverentiam caput pileo tectum gerant". BNCR, Fondo Gesuitico, ms. 1257.18, fol 163r; ARSI, Fondo Gesuitico, 722.12, fol. 3r.

57 Bontinck, *La Lutte Autour*, 123. Santa María argues that French Jesuit Jaques Le Faure, SJ (1613–1675) and Pietro Canevari, SJ (1596–1675) were in favor of head coverings during mass and he added: "el P. Juan Valat, llamáronle entonçes a confessor a un padre moribundo, el P. Manuel Jorge por no se opponer al voto del padre viceprovincial *latenter* se levantó y se fue a su retrete. Los demás padres que a mí me avian llamado para el intento del celebrar sin virete [Gouvea and Pacheco], se viraron [their votes] allí por acomodarse al parecer del padre vice provincial y padre ançiano Canavari lisiados *in capite*, y dexáronme a mí solo, y por esso quando dixe mi parecer, que sin virete, no faltó quien *submissa vocce*, que oy, çumbó de mí". Sinica Franciscana, vol. IX, 1026.

58 Bontinck, *La Lutte Autour*, 123–124; Cummins, *A Question of Rites*, 156–157; Cummins, *The Travels and Controversies*, 416.

Christians could be covered during mass, with two exceptions: acolytes in surplices should be bareheaded (art. 20) and Christians' heads should also be uncovered when receiving communion (art. 22). His new proposal is found in Table 9.1:

TABLE 9.1 Articles 20, 21, and 22 of the Canton Conference suggested by the Visitor da Gama

	Latin	English
Art. 20	*Qui Sacerdoti ad altare operanti inservit, (g) si sie superpelliceo indutus, inserviat capite discooperto; secùs si sine superpelliceo*	If the Mass servant (g) wears surplice, he should uncover his head; otherwise, he should be covered
Art. 21	*In Missae ministerio non abrogetur usus superpellicei*	The use of surplice during Mass is not abrogated
Art. 22	*Accedentes ad Sacram Comunionem Neophyti caput discooperiant: In Missa autem pileati assistant: Si quis autem propter inopiam pileo careret, non id illi exprobratur*	Neophytes should approach the Holy Table with their heads uncovered. If they attend Mass, they can cover their heads. If someone because of his poverty does not have headwear he should not worry.

SOURCE: CICÉ, *ACTA CANTHONIENSIA*, FOLS. 26R–27R; FERNÁNDEZ DE NAVARRETE, *CONTROVERSIAS*, TRAT. IV, FOLS 219R

Some of the conference members were surprised by this response. The suggestion of using the European tradition for the mass servants and during holy communion meant, for them, that the visitor was rejecting the significance attributed by the Chinese to head coverings. Most missionaries that were taking part in the conference tried to change his mind, and his decision gave rise to numerous memorials and letters, especially towards the end of 1668. In fact, the disagreements he provoked with his intervention led to the existence of the sources that give testimony to what was said about head coverings during the conferences. [59]

59 "Como en las resoluciones escritas hubo diversidad grande de pareceres, y demasiada oposición, es conveniente manifestar aquí lo principal de la dificultad, con lo que acerca de ella se dixo de una, y otra parte". Fernández de Navarrete, *Controversias*, Trat. 4, fol. 220r.

Thus, both the *Respuestas* and the *Dudas* appeared during this period. These manuscripts illustrate the arguments of the early stages of this controversy. The manuscript of the *Respuestas*, dated September 17, 1668, is signed by those who voted in the conference against the permission to be covered, with the addition of the Italian Jesuit Andrea-Giovanni Lubelli, SJ (1611–1685) while the *Dudas* manuscript was concluded by Navarrete on September 25, 1668.[60] Afterwards, on October 10, 1668, Father Giovanni Francesco Ferrari submitted a further statement in defense of the primitive articles that allowed the attending of mass while wearing a hat.[61] In response, da Gama ordered Adrien Grelon to write a short treatise exposing the conflicting view.[62] Father Santa María also submitted a treatise to the General of the Jesuits with his opinions on the question and several letters arrived at the Jesuits' Roman Curia complaining about the visitor's intervention in the matter.[63] Finally, on December 10, 1668, da Gama sent the act, together with a document, signed by 15 missionaries from the Chinese mission, that included the articles 20 and 22 from Table 9.1 in its original version but merged into one (Figure 9.2).[64]

The intervention of the Portuguese Jesuit Visitor da Gama was interpreted in different ways by the conference participants. For some of them, it was a way to provide greater backing to their decisions. However, for Navarrete, who had voted in favor of the permission, there was no need for such consultation.[65]

60 New additions were made some days later, on October 2, 1668. APSR, Ritos Chinos 35, Tom. 3, leg. 6, fols. 341r–342v.

61 "Apud sinas in signum reverentiae tegendum esse caput". BNCR, Ges. 1257.18, fols. 149r–154v. See also Bontinck, *La Lutte Autour*, 123, fn. 48. Ferrari wrote directly to the Superior General in October as did the French Jesuit François de Rougemont, SJ (1624–1676) and António Gouvea. Cummins, *A Question of Rites*, 156–157; Bontinck, *La Lutte Autour*, 124–125.

62 "An deceat et expediat Chistianos Sinas aperto capite Sacr interesse et Sacerdoti sacris operanti ministrare". BNCR, Ges. 1257.18, fols. 155r–161v.

63 The treatise by Santa María is called "Tratado sobre algunos puntos tocantes a esta missión de la gran China remitido desde esta ciudad de Cantón ar Mui Revdo. P. Luis de Gama de la Companía de Jesús, Visitador de las provincias eiusdem Societatis de Japón y China, residente en su Colegio de la ciudad de Macao. Por Fr. Antonio de Santa María, Prefecto Apostólico del Orden Seráphico de los Menores de la Regular Observancia en el sobre dicho reyno de la China". See *Sinica Franciscana*, vol. IX, 1019, fn. 3 and *Sinica Franciscana*, vol. II, 343.

64 They were sent along with the authenticated memorials by Ferrari and Grelon.

65 He openly complains about those who did not accept the resolution about the head coverings. And argues that there had been other issues during the conference in which he did not agree but accepted because it was the decision of the majority. Fernández de Navarrete, *Controversias*, Trat. IV, fol. 225r.

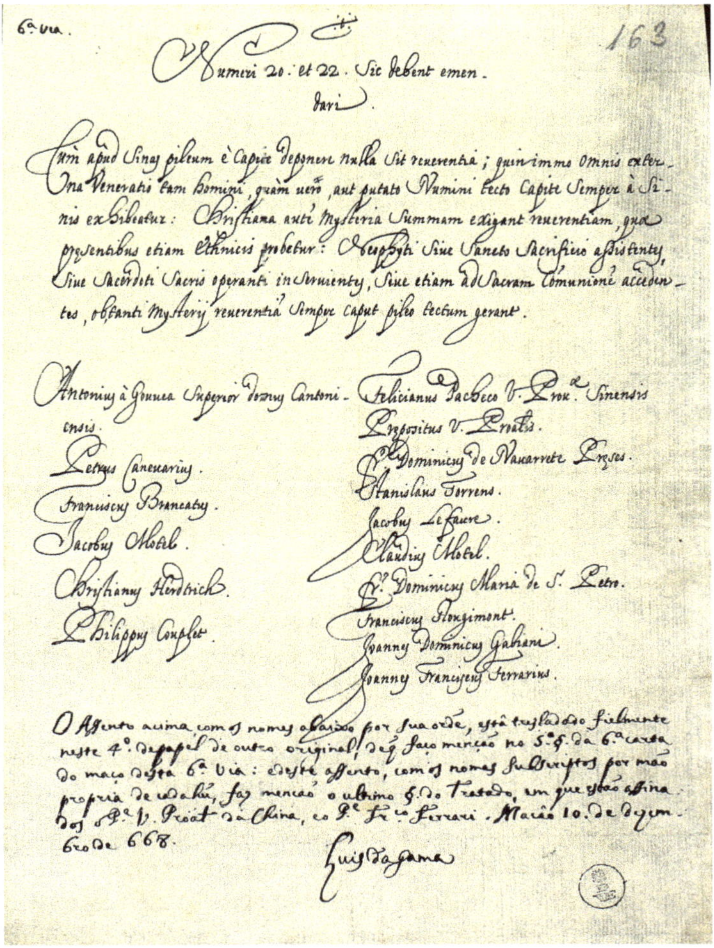

6a. via. 163

Numeri 20. et 22. Sic debent emendari.

Cum apud Sinas pileum è Capite deponere nulla sit reverentia; quin immo omnis externa veneratio tam homini, quàm vero, aut putato Numini tecto Capite semper à Sinis exhibeatur: Christiana autem Mysteria summam exigant reverentiam, quae praesentibus etiam Ethnicis probetur: Neophyti sive Sancto Sacrificio assistentes, sive Sacerdoti Sacris operanti inservientes, sive etiam ad Sacram Communionem accedentes, obstanti Mysterii reverentia semper caput pileo tectum gerant.

Antonius à Gouvea Superior domus Cantoniensis.
Petrus Canevarius.
Franciscus Brancatus.
Jacobus Motel.
Christianus Herdtrich.
Philippus Couplet.
Felicianus Pacheco V. Prov.ae Sinensis Praepositus V. Provincialis.
Fr. Dominicus de Navarrete Praeses.
Stanislaus Torrens.
Jacobus Le Faure.
Claudius Motel.
Fr. Dominicus Maria de S. Petro.
Franciscus Rougemont.
Joannes Dominicus Gabiani.
Joannes Franciscus Ferrarius.

O Assento acima com os nomes assinados por sua ordem, está trasladado fielmente neste 4º de papel de outro original, de que faço menção no 5º §. da 6ª carta do maço desta 6ª via: e deste assento, com os nomes subscriptos por mão propria de cada hu, faz menção o ultimo §. do Tratado, em que estão assinados os P.es V. Prov.al da China, e o P.e Fr.co Ferrari. Macao 10. de Dezembro de 668.

Luis da Gama

FIGURE 9.2 Agreement on the articles by fifteen missionaries at Canton and authentication by the Visitor Luís da Gama.
BNVE, GES. 1257.18, FOL. 163R

His acknowledgement that the decisions of the Canton conference did not necessarily require the approval of superiors reveals the missionaries' capacity to make norms for the mission in China. Each circumstance required a distinctive solution. In 1615, the Jesuits asked for a privilege when they found specific problems regarding head coverings in the performing of the Christian rituals in China. Decades later, in 1667, it was also the missionaries who decided to organize a conference that proved to be an effective instrument for regulating their praxis.

4 Two Positions, Multiple Authorities: Normative Claims in the Hat Controversy

The question of the head coverings reveals the multiple actors participating in the normative order as well as the different procedures for deciding how to deal with practical issues in the mission such as attending mass. What should have been an uncontroversial issue, due to the papal decree of Paolo V, became the object of a heated controversy that generated new normative knowledge that drew on different sources of authority. This section explores the different normative sources—from canon law and moral theology to practical experience—that were mobilized during the discussions. This analysis shows how norms were justified based on different sources of authority without the preeminence of a specific one. In order to defend their own position, each group drew upon different legal rationales, and their performing of this conflict reflects their distinctive juridical agency.

4.1 *Natural Law versus Positive Divine Law*

When discussing the issue of head coverings, both in the case of converts and priests themselves, there were commonplace factors that determined their opinions. Missionaries were embedded with their own theological and juridical background and, naturally, they applied this knowledge to their discourses in order to defend their positions in the debate. Navarrete and most of the participants in the conference understood the practice of head covering as part of the positive law, constituted *institutione hominum*. To complete his argumentation, the Dominican followed St. Thomas Aquinas' views on the morality of human action, which distinguished the interior acts that correspond to the individual dispositions that accompany the performance of the exterior acts that can be expressed through words, signs, and actions. Among the external acts there were those corresponding to God, which were common to all nations, such as sacrifices, temples, and altars, and those indifferent actions that included, for instance, genuflections, the tilting of the head, or the bowing of the knee. Following Aquinas' argumentation, Navarrete highlighted how those external actions depended both on the object and the intention, so if man be the object of the action, it would be considered by Aquinas as "observance".[66] This category characterized a type of worship within the doctrine of the Church and meant that there was no inconvenience to practicing

66 If God is the object of worship, it is called *latria* (theological term), if Church is the object, we refer to *perdulia*, if a saint is the object *dubia*, and if evil is the object *idolatría*. APSR, Ritos Chinos 35, Tom. 3, leg. 6, fol. 331r.

reverences to other men, because it was compatible with the worship of God, the Church, and the saints. Uncovering your head would not be *ex natura sua* but *ex hominum beneplacito et institutione*, thus it would belong to the laws of nations. And the different manners of showing respect not only between members of different classes, but also among Christians themselves, proved it:

> We see that the Jews and Turks worship the true God with their heads covered while we do it uncovered [...]. Among the Christians there are some religious people who kneel down and kiss the floor, others do not do that [...], some of us, Europeans, hear all mass on our knees while others sit [...], for a Dominican friar it would be dishonest to help while barefoot, while for a Recollect friar it would be if he wore shoes [...]. Even in the Church to worship God [...] sometimes they are depicted in Scripture on their knees [...], sometimes with their faces covered as in the case of the cherubs [...], sometimes 24 elders of Apocalypse are shown with the crown thrown at the foot of the Throne [...], sometimes standing or sitting.[67]

As can be seen, Navarrete beautifully enumerates dozens of examples to show the acceptance of variety in different traditions and faiths—*Yglesia non ita horret ceremonias gentilicas*. In his discourse, following St. Jerome, he also highlighted the many traditions in the Roman Catholic Church that could be traced back to pagan rites, including fasting, the use of candles, the burning of incenses, and the offering of flowers and bouquets. Therefore, he asserted, it was possible to conclude that such diversity was accepted by the Church and there were not better or worse ceremonies, since the best ceremonies for a kingdom—China, in this case—were those chosen by its inhabitants. Consequently, Navarrete considered that for the mission these would be Chinese rites, and not those of Europeans.[68]

Fathers Grelon, Santa María, Lubelli, Manuel Jorge, Augery, Leonardo, and Valat, in their *Respuestas*, recognized that the best ceremonies for a particular kingdom were those created *institutione hominum*. However, they also judged that the best set of ordinances for divine worship were those of canon law and not those derived from the law of nations. The Church was governed by the Holy Spirit, so not only did this mean that it had the capacity to select the most appropriate ceremony, but also that the Holy Spirit "enhances and elevates it

---

67 APSR, Ritos Chinos 35, Tom. 3, leg. 6, fols. 331v–332r.

68 "Dudas", APSR, Ritos Chinos 35, Tom. 3, leg. 6, fols. 332r–332v.

FIGURE 9.3
Figure of Madonna and child, c. 1690, Kangxi period, Qing dynasty.
COLLECTION OF THE ASIAN CIVILISATIONS MUSEUM, SINGAPORE

[the ceremony] to a different level, making it more excellent",[69] as happened with the woods and metals used to build a church's roof, which could thereafter never be reutilized for non-sacred purposes.

It appears that Navarrete could say little to the argument about the primacy of canon law, so the Dominican opted to refer in his answer to the case of women, which remained a case of high controversy in the Chinese mission. Chinese Christian women used to wear a veil at the time of confession, as can be seen in the statuette of the Madonna and child (Figure 9.3).[70]

---

69 "Respuestas", APSR, Ritos Chinos 35, Tom. 3, leg. 6, fol. 325v.

70 In fact, missionaries approved in article 19 the obligation to wear a veil or something similar between the priest and the penitent: *In mulierum confessionibus audiendis interponatur velum, seu aliquid aliud inter Sacerdote, et penitentem*. Cicé, *Acta Canthoniensia*, 26. See also Menegon, "Deliver us from Evil", 36.

This delicate porcelain, depicting a fine Christian veil worn over the traditional Buddhist curly hair of the Virgin, was probably used by the missionaries to strengthen the faith of the natives. However, Navarrete argued that Christian women in China attended mass uncovered, following their ordinary practice to pay respect to their superiors and Gods in this way. St. Paul the Apostle had given women the directive to pray with their heads covered (1Cor 11:3–9) so the Dominican asked, with a rhetorical flourish, why his opponents did not criticize that practice too. He posed the question directly: should the missionaries not be able to also introduce this regulation in China?[71]

Navarrete further argued that the custom of covering the head to show respect was, in fact, in accordance with Roman Church law because it was granted by the brief of Paolo V mentioned earlier. He considered it a reasonable petition by the old missionaries and that there would be no benefit in having it overturned. For him, it was good to maintain honest and virtuous habits and prevent conflicts. Otherwise, the missionaries ran the risk of hurting Chinese pride.[72] In addition, he believed that the Pope's decisions to uphold Chinese Christians' rites and to not seek uniformity should not be questioned.[73] Political conditions were also important because, at any time, the Chinese could wrest power from the Tartars and the status of the Christian missions could suddenly change.[74]

In response, the other group outlined that the need to ask the Pope for a privilege was precisely the most evident manifestation of the preeminence of the Church's regulation over the law of nations. They also suggested that the Pauline privilege did not exist and, even so, it would no longer reflect the Pope's will, since the circumstances had changed. From their point of view, the barriers that had made such a concession necessary in 1615 no longer existed in 1668. Thus, although they were in fact confined in Guangzhou, they thought that changing the hat regulation would not have any negative effects on Christianity from the Chinese authorities because they were convinced that it was not such a serious offense for the Chinese. For the group of the *Respuestas*, it was a privilege used without need. By contrast, they demanded the privilege be reserved for women because, in that case, there was still an evident difficulty in trying to introduce the European tradition. The missionaries ultimately had

71 Fernández de Navarrete, *Controversias*, Trat. IV, fol. 222r.

72 "Dudas", APSR, Ritos Chinos 35, Tom. 3, leg. 6, fols. 335r–335v.

73 "Dudas", APSR, Ritos Chinos 35, Tom. 3, leg. 6, fols. 325v, 336r.

74 "Dudas", APSR, Ritos Chinos 35, Tom. 3, leg. 6, fol. 335v.

the duty to incorporate Roman ceremonies whenever there was a chance, and therefore had to persist and lead by example, they argued.[75]

Though Navarrete agreed with this last point, he thought the right moment was yet to come:

> Although it is good and admirable to gradually introduce the customs of the Roman Church into the missions [...] it is necessary to wait for the right moment and for the Law of the Lord to have firm roots.[76]

The need to gain the favor of the natives was one of the main reasons for Navarrete's insistence on adapting Christian ceremonies to the Chinese tradition. Quoting Aquinas, Christ's actions, Cardinal Lugo, and the historian Henri de Sponde, among others, he explained the need to respect the Chinese traditions that went back thousands of years.[77] However, in their *Respuestas*, Grelon and the like denied rejecting local rites and ceremonies. On the contrary, they accepted the Chinese dress style, paid their visits following local etiquette, and sat in the Chinese way. Furthermore, in their opinion, their brothers were overreacting about the matter of the cap. From their point of view, Chinese Christians were aware that Catholicism, like other religions, had its own rules. It was even usual during evangelization that Chinese natives asked to learn the rules they had to follow before converting, meaning that the "right moment" had already arrived.

4.2 *Moral Theology in the Chinese Mission*

One of the most heated arguments occurred about the Chinese Christian practice of being bareheaded during confession, as was common for criminals in China when condemned for their crimes (Figure 9.4).[78] This practice was added by the Jesuit fathers of the early mission; the reasoning behind this was that penitents at confession took on the role of convicts and sinners. Otherwise, throughout mass and Eucharist they had permission to be covered again, following what was for them the Chinese manner too. During these acts, the faithful were in a state of grace before God and they acted as guests at Christ's table, accepted as friends, brothers, and disciples, but not as sinners.

---

75 "Respuestas", APSR, Ritos Chinos 35, Tom. 3, leg. 6, fols. 326r–326v.

76 "Aunque es bueno y loable el ir introduciendo en las misiones nuevas las costumbres de la iglesia romana [...] es necesario aguardar a tiempo oportuno y a que tenga raíces firmes la ley del señor". "Dudas", APSR, Ritos Chinos 35, Tom. 3, leg. 6, fols. 335v–336r.

77 "Dudas", APSR, Ritos Chinos 35, Tom. 3, leg. 6, fol. 334v.

78 For the rite of sacramental confession, see Menegon, "Deliver us from Evil", 34–46.

FIGURE 9.4 "Trial before the Court". Gouache by anonymous author. Canton, c. 1860. Real Colegio PP. Agustinos (Valladolid).
COURTESY OF THE MUSEO ORIENTAL DE VALLADOLID

In his *Dudas*, Navarrete defended the appropriateness of this old practice in the Chinese mission. From his point of view, Roman tradition perceived the confessional as a court of justice, the confessor as a judge, and the penitent as an offender (*reo*). And, in his opinion, getting the Chinese to remove their hats was the perfect act to make them feel as if they were in a court of justice. The Dominican elaborated:

> the cap is taken off in the way the habit is taken off a knight before slaughtering him, which is felt like death itself to him. The Chinese feels the same while removing his cap. For that reason, he is ordered to go uncovered to confess.[79]

The Franciscan Santa María and the ones who signed the *Respuestas* countered this position by stressing that Christians were permanent sinners and condemned under God's law, not only during confession. Thus, they should be bareheaded during mass, Eucharist, and confession.

As Figure 9.5 shows, they considered two different hypotheses, after having heard the reasoning of Navarrete and their opponents, to elaborate their argument. They first appealed to the role of the believer: Since they all agreed upon the condition of sinners as *reos* in confession (1a), Santa María

79 "Dudas", APSR, Ritos Chinos 35, Tom. 3, leg. 6, fol. 340r.

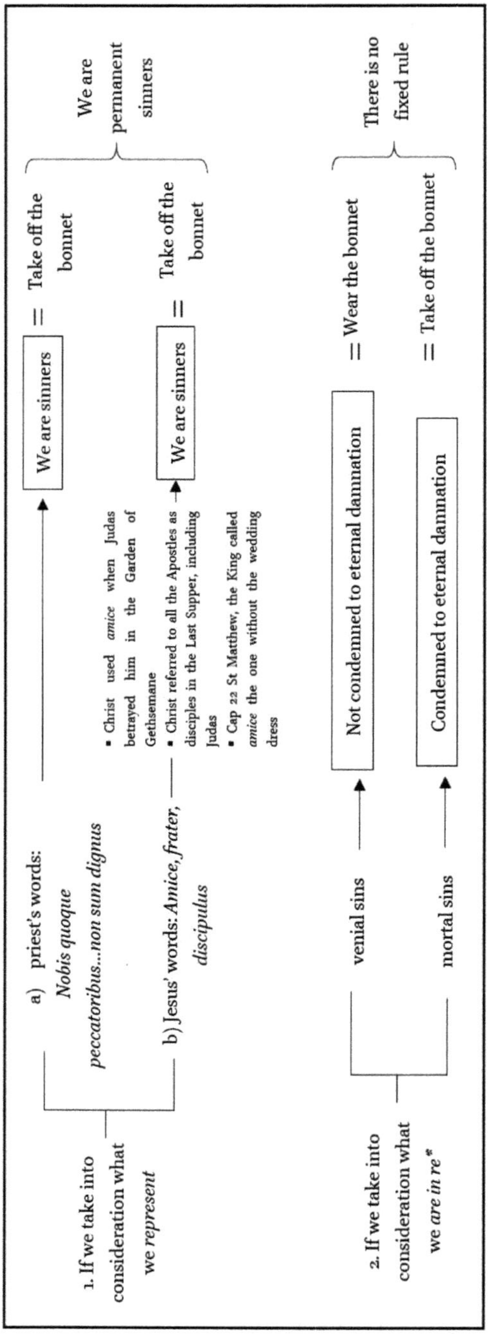

[a] *In re*, situation in which the holder of a right is

Source: Compilation based on "Respuestas". APSR, Ritos Chinos 035, Tom.3, leg. 6, fol. 327r-327v.

FIGURE 9.5 Moral theology applied in the mission.

used several biblical examples (mainly of Judas) to show that during mass and communion they were also *reos* (1b). Second, they introduced the categorization of sins according to categories of classic medieval theology and demonstrated that a Christian would not always be punished to eternal damnation and be considered a *reo* (2). The outcome would depend on the type of sin the penitent had committed. Following this reasoning there was no fixed rule to follow. Moreover, the sinner could also be in a state of sin not only during confession, but also during mass; and those in confession could have committed mortal or venial sins. If one extended this logic, Christians should be uncovered or covered regardless of the time of the ritual. At this point, it is of note that the supposedly most conservative group that wanted to implement the "European style" was in fact proposing a more adaptative stance than the ones who defended Chinese customs. In China, only those condemned to the death penalty appeared bareheaded. And, from the point of view of the authors of the *Respuestas*, Navarrete and his allies were demanding to follow Chinese judicial rules without realizing that during confession not all penitents were condemned to eternal damnation.

4.3 *Chinese Customs and Uses as Seen by the Missionaries*

The significance for the Chinese of the uncovered head was at the heart of the dispute. Thus, the missionaries' perception of the relevance of the hat is fundamental to understanding the different positions adopted by each group. In the discussion, both groups of missionaries affirmed their respect of Chinese etiquette and culture. In fact, what was put into question was the gravity of the rule concerning head coverings for the Chinese. The conflict arose because each group had different views regarding the importance of this rule for the Chinese. While Navarrete and those supporting him thought that being covered was a central expression of humility for the Chinese, the group of the *Respuestas* believed that this practice was not as important as their opponents judged and, consequently, Chinese Christians could be bareheaded, i.e., the custom could be changed.

There are two examples which illustrate that the missionaries' understanding of Chinese culture was a key element that influenced their positioning in the debate. The first one is the dynastic change in 1644. For the group of the *Respuestas*, which were in favor of changing the custom of being covered during Christian rituals, the regulation of hats was not considered a long-standing custom in China since it could be changed by dynastic precept. The 17th century saw a change in the imperial dynasty when the Manchu made their way to Beijing. As a result, new styles and customs were implemented, although characteristics of the Ming era were maintained during the Qing era. Santa María and his allies affirmed:

> We see that they are not tied to the enforcement of the rules except when it suits them not to use them. Rather, the Chinese show off their resemblance to the Tartars in being cruel, in removing their beards (something they valued greatly before), and this also affects the Chinese mandarins who sit on the ground without their bonnets and other such examples that are well-known.[80]

For Navarrete, by contrast, it was unquestionable that the Chinese custom was still in use despite the changes in the headwear that accompanied the change of dynasty. He thought his opponent's argumentation was invalid because they were referring to rural areas of China instead of observing the etiquette of the cities and in court. From his point of view, state rituals and worship to heaven and earth as well as to ancestors and other types of deities, such as *Ching Hoan* (城隍神 *Chenghuangshen*, City God) had been part of Chinese ritual life since ancient times and the Manchus accepted the Confucian canon as the foundation of their power. Inferior to superior, disciple to master, son to father—all showed their respect invariably with their heads covered. And the Dominican affirmed that the Qing emperors did not change these rites.[81] In his defense, he even considered that the native Christians' ceremonies were perhaps more civilized than those of Europeans. While hatless Europeans partially bowed the knee to show respect—sometimes to the ground—or the most zealous kneeled fully, the Chinese made their prostration with their head touching the ground three or four times—the so-called 叩頭 *koutou*.[82]

Navarrete further argued that civility in China was related to the use of a head covering. He based his arguments on his own experience and the reading of "their books", as the following paragraph shows:

> In one [book] it is said that the beginning and origin of reverence is the cap on the head. In another [book] it is said that man is not a man if the ceremony of putting the cap on his head is removed [...]. And so, a poor villager, broken and barefoot but with a cap, would make courtesy to his emperor without anyone noticing. However, if he would have footwear

80 "Respuestas", APSR, Ritos Chinos 35, Tom. 3, leg. 6, fol. 325r.
81 "Dudas", APSR, Ritos Chinos 35, Tom. 3, leg. 6, fols. 333r–333v.
82 "Dudas", APSR, Ritos Chinos 35, Tom. 3, leg. 6, fol. 338v.

and be well-dressed but without a cap, he would not dare show courtesy, and no one would forgive him for his rudeness.[83]

Both sides thus defended the need to respect Chinese tradition. The difficulty lay in understanding to what extent the enforcement of a rule on head coverings confronted a central value of Chinese tradition. The consequences of the dynastic change were interpreted differently by each side, resulting in new arguments that needed to be exposed.

One of the most powerful tools employed by theologians in the early modern period involved the use of analogy. To defend the imposition of a new rule for the Chinese natives and the priests in China, the authors of the *Respuestas* compared the case of the hats with the Muslim tradition of going barefoot into their mosques in China. This group claimed that this tradition was accepted in the Chinese empire without difficulty. And they included an excerpt (*traslado*) in their text bearing testimony to this special practice in the Chinese empire:

> According to the custom of the Moors in China [...] when they go to pai [拜 *bai*, worship] our Lord or a God (who they do not believe to be triune and only one being without dislocation of people), when entering the mosque called pai ly, where they have hung the letter ii [一 *yi*, one] [...] and silks, everyone takes off their shoes when entering in reverence etc. The numerous Moors of Nankin wear white bonnets in the streets, cut their mustaches following the style of their bad sect [...] and keep the rites and ceremonies of their law.[84]

The people known as Moors at the time appeared to have introduced their own practices on Chinese soil without difficulty and Grelon and his allies questioned why this was not possible for Catholicism. In his response, Navarrete reminded his confreres of Islam's deeper roots in China compared to Christianity's. In his counterarguments he also made a direct attack arguing that the permission for Muslims to go barefoot was simply because they had bribed the Chinese authorities. In a tongue-in-cheek tone, the friar even challenged his opponents to raise enough silver from New Spain and Tierra Firme to try a similar bribe. He ironically guaranteed them that by paying a lot of money to Chinese authorities being uncovered would become a new tradition in the Chinese mission. Moreover, he risked declaring that those converting to Islam were not in fact Chinese but relatives from the same Muslim family—in other

83 "Dudas", APSR, Ritos Chinos 35, Tom. 3, leg. 6, fol. 338r.
84 "Respuestas", APSR, Ritos Chinos 35, Tom. 3, leg. 6, fols. 329r–329v.

words, foreigners—or even those who were Chinese and who eventually apostatized, so would be classified by Navarrete as "not pure Chinese".[85]

Navarrete also did not waste the opportunity to criticize his counterpart's arguments. From his point of view, they were comparing two unrelated realities; instead, they should have compared the use of the hat in both traditions—Islamic and Chinese. In fact, Muslims allowed their converts to remain covered in their mosques because, Navarrete insisted, the most important manifestation of courteousness in China was related to the use of the hat and not with being barefoot.[86] This would mean that new customs that did not contradict long-standing traditions could be observed; new rules contra-consuetudo could not.

4.4 *The Importance of Experience in the Missionary Field*

Experience in the missionary field also played its part in the hat controversy. Each member that took part in the conference had worked in a different province, sometimes in more than one, and for a different amount of time, and all of them brought that experience to the debate. On the one hand, Father Adrien Grelon and his companions, who were in favor of changing the custom of being covered in the Christian mission, declared in his *Respuestas* that there were already several places in China in which Christians attended mass, took communion, and prayed bareheaded without any disturbance. They named the province of Shandong where both Santa María and Jean Valat had their residence.[87] The Beijing mission, led by Father Schall, was also used as an example. His authority made this case particularly valuable in supporting their position since he was publicly recognized as the most experienced person of the Chinese mission at that time.[88]

Grelon, Santa María, and the others who signed the *Respuestas* presented other significant examples to demonstrate that the Chinese were not as strict about hats as their brothers suggested. The missionaries went to the emperor's court years earlier and visited the 禮部 *Libu* (Board of Rites), the most

85 "Respuestas", APSR, Ritos Chinos 35, Tom. 3, leg. 6, fol. 330r.

86 "Dudas", APSR, Ritos Chinos 35, Tom. 3, leg. 6, fols. 337v–338r.

87 "Respuestas", APSR, Ritos Chinos 35, Tom. 3, leg. 6, fol. 325r. Grelon in other letter on June 1668 says: "E pera não dissimular nada, ainda que sempre houve e inda hoje há alguns christãos que ouvem a missa cubertos, com tudo a maior parte a ouvem descubertos, e com tudo ate agora nunca se vio que os Padres mandassem aos que estavão desscubertos que se cobrissem, se não por ventura em Ch'ang-shu aonde disem que o P. Rougemont o mandou a seus christãos que ate então tinhão sempre usado o contrario". Margiotti, *Alcuni problemi*, 32–33 fn. 113.

88 *Sinica Franciscana*, vol. IX, 1023.

important institution in the empire that oversaw all state and secular ceremonies, rituals, and sacrifices. To their surprise, officials were not wearing hats.[89]

Santa María also recalled the case of the Italian Prospero Intorcetta. The significance of this case for the group of the *Respuestas* came from the fact that Intorcetta was actually in favor of using the hat but later changed his mind, opting to follow "European style" despite his first inclination to follow "Chinese etiquette". He came to this conclusion because he had decided to solve the question of the hat in his mission by following his own method. According to Santa María's account, Intorcetta, having observed the lack of uniformity in his church, gave the parishioners the possibility to decide among themselves whether to use the hat or not. The believers opted not to wear the hat because they considered it the most honorable way to show their respect, so he too decided to follow their wishes.[90] In this case, we can clearly observe how Santa María and his group, by adding the example of Intorcetta, mobilized the customary law argument: Intorcetta was a newcomer and ignored Chinese etiquette when he first arrived in the mission so that Europeans also had to learn Chinese customs through their parishioners. In the words of Santa María, "they know much better, as Chinese natives, than us, foreigners, the political and religious reverence in this kingdom whatever it may be".[91] The vindication of this custom involved the recognition of Chinese agency. Santa María solidly affirmed that Chinese commoners and "mandarins" would have openly shown their disagreement in case of any objection and, therefore, it was not such a show of serious disrespect to appear bareheaded.[92]

In his response, Navarrete argued that neither Christians in Beijing nor Father Schall would ever dare to visit the imperial apartments without wearing the proper hat. Importantly, though it was true that imperial officials were bareheaded in the *Libu*, there were two situations when this was possible. First, it was commonplace that they took their hats off in the summer, but they always asked for permission before doing so. Second, removing one's hat was a clear sign of disrespect to and disregard for the missionaries as prisoners.[93] Navarrete additionally gave several examples of his experiences, including his visit to the 兵部 *Bingbu* (Board of War) and the missionaries' visit to the authorities of Guangzhou during their confinement. But, although he answered by referring to his own experiences, in Navarrete's opinion, the anecdote of the visit to

89 "Respuestas", APSR, Ritos Chinos 35, Tom. 3, leg. 6, fol. 324v.
90 "Respuestas", APSR, Ritos Chinos 35, Tom. 3, leg. 6, fol. 325r.
91 *Sinica Franciscana*, vol. IX, 1023.
92 "Respuestas", APSR, Ritos Chinos 35, Tom. 3, leg. 6, fol. 325r.
93 "Dudas", APSR, Ritos Chinos 35, Tom. 3, leg. 6, fols. 334r–334v.

the *Libu* and the few examples presented by the authors of the *Respuestas* were not valid as evidence since they did not provide a reliable representation of the traditions of such a vast empire.

As shown, the missionaries included several types of examples in their discourses. Their selection depended on different factors, mainly based on the degree of credibility of the referred person or group. Chinese Christians, as natives, provided authority, while Schall, working in the capital for the imperial court, also added value to the debate. In the discussions, there was also a minor tussle between the two groups regarding the authority of the old missionaries over the new generations. While Navarrete vindicated the importance of age for a more accurate opinion and educated judgment, his adversaries did not have the same opinion. They considered it was not necessary to have many years of experience in the mission, nor to be old, to have a proper perception of Chinese reality. In their response, they swiftly replied: "You should not state 'I did not see therefore it does not exist' [...]. There is no need of many years nor to be old to experience and verify what is happening [...]. It is neither a question of antiquity nor related to past".[94]

When the ages of the missionaries and their years of experience in the Chinese mission together with their votes are analyzed, however, one can reach two conclusions. First, regarding age, the average age of both groups was almost the same (52 for the authors of the *Respuestas* who voted for the implementation of the "European style" of being uncovered and 54 for the ones who favored the "Chinese style" of being covered). Thus, it does not seem that there were any significant differences relating to age that affected voting on the regulation of the hat. Second, the average years of experience was 14 for the *Respuestas* group and 23 for the others. Aside from Santa María, who was one of the oldest and most experienced men—he was 66 years old in 1668—the most experienced men in the mission were most in favor of letting the Chinese wear their hats during mass and maintaining the use of the papal privilege conceded to the Jesuits decades before.[95]

---

94 "No se signe no lo vi luego no lo ay, ni porque sean antiguos y viejos, porque para ver esto no son menester muchos años, ni es menester ser viejo porque es cosa presente que no es menester muchos años para experimentar y palpar en las manos, no es cosa antigua ni pasada". "Respuestas", APSR, Ritos Chinos 35, Tom. 3, leg. 6, fol. 330r.

95 Average age (in 1668) is based on the information of "Anexo" in Esquivel, *El confinamiento de los misioneros*, 367. Average years of experience (in 1666) in the mission is based on Esquivel, *El confinamiento de los misioneros*, 237; Dehergne, *Répertoire des Jésuites* and Busquets, "La formación y los recursos", 5.

5 Conclusions

In addition to their obvious religious role, historians have analyzed the part of missionaries in China as political agents, intellectuals, ethnographers, translators, and ambassadors. Yet little has been written about their role as lawmakers. In this chapter, the Canton exile has proven to be a unique moment in the history of Christianity in China that attests to the missionaries' active participation in the regulation of their own praxis and that of their parishioners.

The need for a coherent, standardized, and centralized set of rules in the mission resulted in an exceptional meeting in the history of the early Chinese mission. Missionaries from three different religious orders of six different nationalities and subjected to different jurisdictions held a conference to negotiate the rules for pastoral activity in the Chinese mission. They also set up the conditions for the meeting and reached their own resolutions for the conflict in the missionary field that would be later confirmed by their superiors. The *Acta Canthoniensia* was the outcome of this important event that decisively changed the practice in the missions over the subsequent decades.[96]

In their formulation of arguments, both groups searched a corpus of norms for authority to construct new rules. Sources reveal that practical conditions were an essential element that explained their position in the debate. Moreover, the creation of new norms also involved the need to observe Chinese customs alongside a process of learning about Chinese culture. Their knowledge about Chinese etiquette and its importance for Chinese natives also played a major role in the debate. Missionaries transformed into anthropologists, rendering accounts of their observations influenced by their readings and exchanges. And their accumulated knowledge was also influenced by their own experiences which became a source of authority in the debate. The missionaries' ability to argue effectively was also affected by their theological-juridical background imbued with Tridentine policy and their capacity to apply moral theology to the case of the hats.

Together, these aspects helped them produce a new discourse composed of a variety of elements that resulted in a new normative order. The missionaries regularly invoked the Fathers of the Church—St. Augustin and St. Jerome—as well as passages from the Bible, and the names of Aquinas, St. Paul, the Cardinal Lugo, and the theologian, philosopher, and jurist Francisco Súarez resonate throughout their discourses. But, simultaneously, their vision was embedded

96 See Standaert, *The Interweaving*, 118–121.

in the Chinese context. Not only did they consult Chinese classical books to be informed about the underlying meanings of Chinese rites and practices, but they also directly sought the opinion of Chinese converts to back up their arguments and counted on their own experience in the field to add legitimacy to their opinions.

Moreover, concerning the question of the hat, context is one fundamental element that runs through the debate; the conference was favored by the situation of Christianity at the time. Although the capital of Beijing fell in 1644 and the Ming dynasty collapsed that year, the definitive unification of China under the Manchus took almost another four decades. Chinese society faced important changes not only because of the dynastic change, but also in their economic and social system, and missionaries understood the uniqueness of this moment. However, each group had a different opinion about it. Some saw this moment as an opportunity to renegotiate old models and norms, while Navarrete and his companions claimed for the need to retain imperial favor and wait for stability in the future. The position of Catholics in China was that of subordination and the creation of new norms was inevitably influenced by the asymmetrical relationship between the European and Chinese; Europeans were foreigners on Chinese soil and the Chinese empire was respected and admired by many of them. In their arguments, Navarrete's side even defended the superiority of Chinese etiquette relating to administration, politics, and order. These clear facts led to more pragmatic argumentations that moved away from rigid orthodoxy. In their discourse, missionaries moved swiftly between what was tactically more advantageous to what was morally superior, and mobilized these different argumentations depending on their interest in defending one position or the other. And religious groups that were supposed to be allied—as in the case of members of the same religious orders—openly adopted different approaches regardless of their religious adscription.

The analysis of the sources has shown that the missionaries' discourses were not part of a simple debate based on the classical dichotomy of either adapting or not adapting to Chinese culture. Missionaries were not simply failed importers of Church law or successful practitioners of it. Although in the debate there were two different positions—incorporating the tradition of being bareheaded or keeping the custom of being covered as decided by the Jesuits in their arrival to the mission—their narratives represented their common effort to accommodate Church law. In this public representation, they made use of different elements to provide legitimacy that not only drew from the Roman tradition but from a large reservoir of norms that went far back in time and were tied to how missionaries reconstructed both the European and the Chinese past.

FIGURE 9.6 Painted ivory panel of St. Jerome praying before the crucified Christ. Southern China. 17th Century.
COLLECTION OF THE ASIAN CIVILISATIONS MUSEUM, SINGAPORE

In the missionary field a great decisional pluralism can be found, and the dynamic tension between the Tridentine Church and the Missional Church appears to converge on a complex reality. In this performance that takes place very far from the center of powers in Europe, subjects that are apparently passive agents in the process of law making become relevant agents capable of producing new normative outcomes.

The hat controversy exemplifies a case of norm-production in which all missionaries drew upon both Chinese and European traditions but also the different currents within them depending on their practical needs. The Canton Conference resulted in a hybrid reality in which the Chinese were permitted to be covered during mass, the priests continued using the 祭巾 *Jijin*, and the Roman Orthodoxy was also present. As can be seen in the painted ivory panel of St. Jerome praying before the crucified Christ (Figure 9.6), God Father is engraved in the image with the top of the head shaved following the Tartar style. Yet, he is not alone. The Tridentine Church makes its appearance, on the left, with the red hat representing the Roman Curia. As in this visual representation, Chinese and European traditions came together in the missionary field and gave shape to a new policy to guide missionaries and Chinese Christians in their path of evangelization over the next decades.

Acknowledgements

I would like to thank Isabel Murta Pina, Tomás A. Mantecón Movellán, Jorge Díaz Ceballos, Anna Busquets Alemany, Diego Sola, the editor of this book, and the two anonymous reviewers for their assistance with this contribution. I would also like to thank Ricardo Martínez Esquivel for delivering a copy of his doctoral thesis to me. This research is part of the project "Gobernanza, conflicto y construcción de cultura política en la Edad Moderna" (MICINN-FEDER/UE, PGC2018-093841-B-C32) and *RESISTANCE: Rebellion and Resistance in the Iberian Empire, 16th-19th centuries* (H2020-MSCA-RISE-2017 No.778076). Unless otherwise stated, all translations and errors are mine.

Bibliography

Manuscripts

Archives of the Santo Tomás Convent (APSR, Avila, Spain); "Respuestas a unas objeciones de las cortesías de los bonetes de China &ª firmado por varios PP. en la reclusión de Canton (incluido el VP. Fr. Antonio de Sta. María)". Sección Ritos Chinos 035. Tomo 3, Tratados misceláneos (1637, 1669, 1717), Carpeta 6, fols. 324v–330v.

Archives of the Santo Tomás Convent (APSR, Avila, Spain); "Dudase si en China es conveniente que asistan los cristianos a la misa cubierta la cabeza", Sección Ritos Chinos 035, Tomo 3, Tratados misceláneos (1637, 1669, 1717), Carpeta 6, fols. 331r–342v.

Archives of the Santo Tomás Convent (APSR, Avila, Spain); "Desmiéntese el P. Sarpetri con el testimonio de los PP. Balat y Grelon, de la Comp. De Jesus", Sección Ritos Chinos 035, Tomo 3, Tratados misceláneos (1637, 1669, 1717), Carpeta 6, fols. 324r–324v.

Roman Jesuit Archives (ARSI, Rome, Italy); "Praxes quadam a Missionariis Dominicains, Franciscan ac Societatis Iesu in Sinica Mission observandae: 1668", Fondo Gesuitico, 722–12, fols. 1r–4r.

Rome National Central Library (BNCR, Rome, Italy); "Apud sinas in signum reverentiae tegendum esse caput", Ges, 1257.18, fols. 149r–154v.

Rome National Central Library (BNCR, Rome, Italy); "An deceat et expediat Chistianos Sinas aperto capite Sacr interesse et Sacerdoti sacris operanti ministrare", Ges 1257.18, fols. 155r–161v.

Printed Sources

Cicé, Louis de, *Acta Cantoniensia authentica. In quibus praxis missionariorum Sinensium Societatis Jesu circa ritus Sinenses approbata est communi consensus partum Dominicanorum, & Jesuitarum, qui errant in China; atque illorum subscription firmata. Nunc primum prodeunt transmissa ex Archivio Romano Societatis Jesu, cum accessioni Epistolae*, Rome 1700: Gesuiti-Collegio Romano.

Collectanea S. Congregationis de Propaganda Fide Seu decreta instructiones rescripta pro apostolicis missionibus, 2 vols., Rome 1866: Ex Typographia Polyglota.

Fernández de Navarrete, Domingo, An *account of the empire of China; historical, political, moral and religious. A short description of that empire, and notable examples of its emperors and ministers. Also, an ample relation of many remarkable passages, and things worth observing in other kingdoms, and several voyages. There are added, the decrees of popes, and propositions defined at Rome for the mission of China; and a bull of ... Clement X., in favour of the missioners.* London 1732: H. Linton.

Fernández de Navarrete, Domingo, *Tratados Historicos, Politicos, Ethicos, y religiosos de la Monarchia de China. Descripcion breve de aquel imperio, y exemplos raros de emperadores y magistrados del. Con narración difusa de varios sucesos y cosas singulares de otros reynos, y diferentes navegaciones...*, Madrid 1670: Juan García Infançon.

Fernández de Navarrete, Domingo, *Controversias antiguas y modernas entre los Misionarios de la gran China. Repartidas en nueve tratados con lo que toca al culto y veneracion quel chino da a su maestro Confucio y a sus progenitores difuntos con respuesta á diversos tratados de los Pes. Dela Compañía de Jesus*, Madrid 1679.

Sínica Franciscana. Relationes et Epistolas Fratrum Minorum saeculi XVI et XVII collegit, ad fidem codicum redegit et anotavit P. Anastasius Van den Wyngaert OFM, Vol. II, Firenze 1942: Ad Claras Aquas.

Sinica Franciscana. Relationes et Epistolas Fratrum Minorum Fratum Minorum Hispanorum in Sinis qui annis 1697–98 missionem ingress sunt collegit, ad fidem codicum redegit et anotavit P. Fortunatus Margiotti, OFM, editionem autem prasentem praeparaverunt et correxerunt PP. Gaspar Han et Antolin Abad, OFM, Vol. IX, Madrid 1995: TECNOVIC Arte Gráfico.

Literature

Alberts, Tara, *Conflict and Conversion: Catholicism in Southeast Asia, 1500–1700*, Oxford 2013.

Aldea Vaquero, Quintín (dir.), *Diccionario de Historia Eclesiástica de España*, 5 vols., Madrid 1972–1987.

Alden, Daurin, *The Making of an Enterprise. The Society of Jesus in Portugal, Its Empire, and Beyond. 1540–1750*, Stanford 1996.

Anon., "Une pratique liturgique propre à la Chine: Le Tsikin ou Bonnet de messe", in *Bulletin Catholique de Pekin* 11 (1924): 376–377, 404–406.

Almster, Nadine, *Jesuits and Matriarchs: Domestic Worship in Early Modern China*, Seattle 2018.

Bastias Saavedra, Manuel, "Jurisdictional Autonomy and the Autonomy of Law: End of Empire and the Functional Differentiation of Law in 19th century Latin America", in *Rechtsgeschichte Legal History* 26 (2018): 325–337.

Bastias Saavedra, Manuel, "Diversity as Paradox: Legal History and the Blind Spots of Law", in *Max Planck Instituted for European Legal History Research Paper Series* No. 2020–05 (2018): 1–17.

Benton, Lauren, *Law and Colonial Cultures: Legal Regimes in World History, 1400–1900*, Cambridge 2001.

Benton, Lauren, Clulow, Adam and Attwood, Bain (ed.), *Protection and Empire. A Global History*, Cambridge 2018.

Bontnick, François, *La lutte autor de la liturgie chinoise aux XVIIe et XVIIIe siècles*, Louvain 1962.

Brockey, Liam Mathew, *Journey to the East: The Jesuit Mission in China, 1579–1724*, Cambridge (MA) 2007.

Brockey, Liam Mathew, *The Visitor: Andre Palmeiro and the Jesuits in Asia*, Cambridge (MA) 2014.

Brockey, Liam Mathew, "Authority, poverty, and vanity: Jesuit missionaries and the use of silk in early modern East Asia", in *Anais de História de Além-Mar* 17 (2016): 179–222.

Busquets, Anna, *Los tratados históricos, políticos, éticos y religiosos de la monarquía de china (1676) de Domingo Fernández de Navarrete: el texto y sus fuentes* (PhD Thesis), Barcelona 2008.

Busquets, Anna, "Más allá de la Querella de los Ritos: el testimonio sobre China de Fernández de Navarrete", in *Anuario de la Historia de la Iglesia* 24 (2015): 229–250.

Busquets, Anna, "La formación y los recursos intelectuales de los primeros dominicos en China", in Zhang, Xiping, Jingxiang, Wei and González, Inma (coord.), *Diego de Pantoja y China. Reflexiones sobre las relaciones históricas entre China y el mundo hispánico.* Beijing 2021, 534–564.

Cardim, Pedro et al. (eds.), *Polycentric Monarchies: How did Early Modern Spain and Portugal achieve and maintain a Global Economy?*, Portland 2012.

Castelnau-L'Estoile, Charlotte, "Une église aux dimensions du monde: expansion du catholicisme et ecclésiologie à l'époque moderne", in Arabeyre, Patrick and Brigitte Basdevant-Gaudemet (dir.), *Les clercs et les princes. Doctrines et pratiques de l'autorité ecclésiastique à l'époque moderne*, Paris 2013, 323–340.

Chan, Albert, "Late Ming Society and the Jesuit Missionaries", in Ronna, Charles E. and Bonnie B.C. Oh (eds.), *East Meets West: The Jesuits in China, 1582–1773*, Chicago 1988, 153–172.

Catto, Michela, "Monogamy in polygamy: An interpretation of Chinese marriage by the Society of Jesus", in *Ricerche di storia sociale e religiosa* 19:1–2 (2019): 7–22.

Collani, Claudia von, "Mission and Matrimony", in Ku Wei-ying 古偉瀛 (ed.), *Missionary approaches and linguistics in mainland China and Taiwan*, Leuven 2001, 11–32.

Collani, Claudia von, "The Jesuit Rites Controversy", in Županov, Ines G. (ed.), *The Oxford Handbook of the Jesuits*, New York 2019, 891–917.

Concilium Sinense, ed. Primum Concilium Sinense anno 1924 a die 14 maii ad diem 12 iunii in ecclesia S. Ignatii de Zi-Ka-Wei celebratum: acta, decretal et normaa, vota, etc., Shanghai 1929.

Cummins, John S. (ed.), *The Travels and Controversies of Friar Domingo Navarrete 1618–86*, 2 vols., Cambridge 1962.

Cummins, John S., *A Question of Rites. Friar Domingo Navarrete and the Jesuits in China*, Cambridge 1993.

Da Silva, Rômulo, "Casuística nos Trópicos: a pragmática teológico-moral de Francisco Rodrigues na Ásia portuguesa (séculos XVI e XVII)", in *Revista da Sociedade e da Cultural* 19 (2019): 399–318.

Dehergne, Joseph, *Répertoire des Jésuites de Chine de 1552 à 1800*, Rome 1973.

Dipippo Gregory, "The Chinese Sacrificial Hat, and Reflections on Inculturation in China", in *New Liturgical Movement. Sacred Liturgy & Liturgical Arts*, 2018. Online: https://www.newliturgicalmovement.org/2018/08/the-chinese-sacrificial-hat-and.html (last accessed 09.15.2021).

Dowd, Christopher, OP, *Rome in Australia: The Papacy and Conflict in the Australian Catholic Missions. 1834–1884*, Leiden 2008.

Dudink, Adrian, "The Holy Mass in Seventeenth- and Eighteenth-Century China: Introduction to and Annotated Translation of Yu Misa Goncheng (1721), Manual for Attending Mass", in Noël Golvers and Sara Lievens (eds.), *A Lifelong Dedication to the China Mission: Essays Presented in Honor of Father Jeroom Heyndrickx, CICM, on the occasion of his 75th birthday and the 25th anniversary of the F. Verbiest Institute*, Leuven 2007, 207–326.

Duve, Thomas, "European Legal History–Concepts, Methods, Challenges", in Duve, Thomas (ed.), *Entanglements in Legal History: Conceptual Approaches*, Frankfurt am Main 2014, 29–66.

Duve, Thomas, "Pragmatic Normative Literature and the Production of Normative Knowledge in the Early Modern Iberian Empires (16th–17th Centuries)", in Duve, Thomas and Danwerth, Otto (eds.), *Knowledge of the Pragmatici. Legal and Moral Theological Literature and the Formation of Early Modern Ibero-America*, Leiden 2020, 1–39.

Duve, Thomas, "What is global legal history?", in *Comparative Legal History* 8:2 (2020): 73–115.

Elliot, John, *The Count-Duke of Olivares: The Statesman in an Age of Decline*, New Heaven 1986.

Entenmann, Robert, "Catholic clergy and catechists in Eighteenth-Century Szechwan", in *Actes du Vie Colloque International de Sinologie, Chantilly, 1989: Images de la Chine, Le Contexte Occidental de la Sinologie Naissante*, Taipei 1995, 389–410.

Entenmann, Robert, "A Mission without missionaries: Chinese Catholic Clergy in Sichuan, 1746–1756", in Yangwen Zheng, *Sinicizing Christianity. Studies in Christian Mission* 49 (2017): 31–54.

Esquivel, Ricardo, *El confinamiento de los misioneros en Guangzhou (1666–1671): Entre las controversias de los ritos chinos y los anticristianismos en China* (PhD Thesis), Barcelona 2018.

Faria, Patricia Souza de, "Os concílios provincias de Goa: reflexões sobre o impacto da 'Reforma Tridentina' no centro do império asiático português (1567–1606)", in *Topoi Revista de História* 14:27 (2013). Online: https://doi.org/10.1590/2237-101X014027002 (last accessed 02.02.2021).

Friedrich, Markus, "Jesuit Organization and Legislation: Development and Implementation of a Normative Framework", in Županov, Ines G., *The Oxford Handbook of the Jesuits*, New York 2019, 23–43.

Gao Chunming 高春明, Zhongguo fushi mingwukao 中國服飾名物考 [Study of Chinese Dress and Personal Adornment], Shanghai 2001.

Golvers, Noël, "The Canton-Macau Area as a 'lieu de savoir': the Western Missionaries' Detention in the Canton Jesuit Residence (1665–1671) and their Written and Editorial Output", in Barreto, Luís Filipe and Wu Zhiliang, *International Colloquium Macau: Past and Present*, Lisbon 2015, 214–233.

Golvers, Noël, *François de Rougemont, SJ, missionary in Changshu (Jiangnan): A study of the 'Account Book' (1674–1676) and the 'Elogium'*, Leuven 1999.

Golvers, Noël, "New Jesuit testimonies from the far east on the comet of march 1668: The diary of visitor Luis da Gama (Macau) and a letter of Ferdinand Verbiest (Peking)", in *Almagest–An international interdisciplinary journal* 9:2 (2018): 89–99.

Gong Yingyan 龔纓晏 and Chen Xuejun 陈雪军, *Kangxi '1692 nian kuan rong chi ling' yu Zhejiang* 康熙'1692年宽容敕令'与浙江 [The Edict of Toleration of 1692 by the Emperor Kangxi with Zhejiang], in Huang Aiping 黄爱平 and Huang Xingtao 黄兴涛, *Xi xue yu Qing dai wen hua* 西学与清代文化 [Western Learning and Qing Dynasty culture], Beijing 2008, 178–182.

González, José María, *Historia de las misiones dominicanas de China 1700–1800*, 2 vols., Madrid 1964.

Hector, Valerie, "Chinese Bead Curtains, Past and Present", in *BEADS: Journal of the Society of Bead Researchers* 25 (2013): 40–71.

Hsia, Ronnie Po-chia, "From Buddhist Garb to Literati Silk: Costume and Identity of the Jesuit Missionary", in Paiva, José Pedro, *Religious Ceremonials and Images: Power and Social Meaning (1400–1750)*, Coimbra 2002, 143–154.

Jami, Catherine, "Revisiting the Calendar Case (1664–1669): Science, Religion, and Politics in Early Qing Beijing", in *Korean Journal of History of Science* 27:2 (2015): 459–477.

Ko, Dorothy, "The Body as Attire: The shifting meanings of footbinding in seventeenth–century China", in *Journal of Women's History* 8:4 (1997): 8–27.

Lach, Donald Friederick and Edwin J. Van Kley, *Asia in the Making of Europe*, vol. 3, Chicago 1993.

Lamalle, Edmond, "La propagande du P. Nicolas Trigault en faveur des missions de Chine (1616)", in *Archivum Historicum Societatis Iesu* 9 (1940): 49–120.

Lee, Keekok, *Warp and Weft. Chinese Language and Culture*, New York 2008.

Levy, Evonne, "Jesuit Identity, Identifiable Jesuits? Jesuit Dress in Theory and in Image", in Oy-Marra, Elisabeth, Remmert, Volker R. and Kristina Müller-Bongard (eds.), *Le monde es tune peinture: Jesuitische Identität und die Rolle der Bilder*, Berlin 2011, 127–152.

López Gay, Jesús, *La liturgia en la misión del Japón del siglo XVI*, Rome 1970.

Margiotti, Fortunatto, OFM, *Il cattolicesimo nello Shansi dalle origini al 1738*, Rome 1958.

Margiotti, Fortunatto, OFM, *Alcuni problemi pastorali nella Cina del '700*, Rome 1958.

Marcocci, Giuseppe, *A consciência de um império: Portugal e o seu mundo (sécs. XV–XVII)*, Coimbra 2013.

Martínez, Ricardo Eugenio, *El confinamiento de los misioneros en Guangzhou (1666–1671): Entre las controversias de los ritos chinos y los anticristianismos en China* (PhD Thesis), Barcelona 2018.

Menegon, Eugenio, "Deliver us from Evil: Confession and Salvation in Seventeenth- and Eighteenth-Century Chinese Catholicism", in Standaert, Nicolas and Ad Dudink (eds.), *Forgive Us Our Sins: Confession in Late Ming and Early Qing China*, Nettetal 2006, 9–101

Menegon, Eugenio, "European and Chinese Controversies over Rituals: A Seventeenth-Century Genealogy of Chinese Religion", in Boute, Bruno and Thomas Småberg (eds.), *Devising order. Socio-religious Models, Rituals, and the Performativity of Practise*, Leiden 2013, 193–222.

Menegon, Eugenio, "'The habit that hides the monk': Missionary fashion strategies in late imperial Chinese society and court culture", in Amsler, Nadine et al. (eds.), *Catholic Missionaries in Early Modern Asia. Patterns of Localization*, London 2020, 30–49.

Mensaert, George, "L'etablissement de la hiérarchie catholique en Chine de 1705–1785", *Archivum Franciscanum Historicum* 51 (1958): 369–466.

Metzler, Josef, "Mezzi e modi per l'evangelizzazione dei popoli secondo F.I.", in *Pontificia Universitas Urbaniana. Annales CCCLXI (1967–1968)*, 38–50.

Metzler, Josef, *Die Synoden in China, Japan und Korea 1570–1931*, Paderborn 1980.

Meynard, Thierry, "Could Chinese Vegetarians be Baptized? Part 1: The Canton Conference and Adrien Grelon SJ's Report of 1668", *Archivum Historicum Societatis Iesu* LXXXVII/173 (2018): 75–145.

Meynard, Thierry, "Could Chinese Vegetarians be Baptized? Part 2: The Canton Conference and Prospero Intorcetta SJ's Report of 1668", *Archivum Historicum Societatis Iesu* LXXXVIII/176 (2019): 285–341.

Minamiki, George, SJ, *The Chinese Rites controversy: From Its Beginning to Modern Times*, Chicago 1985.

Motoh, Helena, "Orphan(ed) Scroll: the Case of Contextualizing a Late Qing Object in a Slovenian Museum", in *Ming Qing Yanjiu* 24:1 (2020): 139–158.

Mungello, David, *Curious Land: Jesuit Accommodation and the Origins of Sinology*, Stuttgart 1985.

Noll, Ray R. (ed.), *100 Documents concerning the Chinese Rites Controversy (1645–1941)*, trans. St. Sure, Donald F., San Francisco 1992.

O'Neill, Charles E., S.I. and Joaquín M. Domínguez, S.I. (dirs.), *Diccionario Histórico de la Compañía de Jesús. Biográfico-Temático*, 4 vols., Madrid 2001.

Pavone, Sabina, "Riti cinesi", in Prosperi, Adriano, *Dizionario storico dell'Inquisizione*, vol. 3, Pisa 2010, 1324–1327.

Pavone, Sabina, “Spie, mandarini, bramini: i gesuiti e i loro travestimenti”, in *Il capitale culturale* 7 (2013): 227–247.

Pfister, Louis, *Notices biographiques et bibliographiques sur les jésuites de l'ancienne misión de Chine 1552–1773*, Shanghai 1932.

Philippi, Dieter, Philippi Collection, 2011. Online: https://philippi-collection.blogspot.com/2011/07/chinese-jijin-tsikin-tsikim-tsi-kim.html (last accessed 09.15.2021).

Pizzorusso, Giovanni, “Per servitio della Sacra Congregatione de Propaganda Fide: i nunzi apostoloci e le missioni tra centralità romana e Chiesa universale (1622–1660)”, in *Cheiron* 30 (1998): 201–227.

Pizzorusso, Giovanni, “Agli antipodi di Babele: Propaganda Fide tra imagine cosmopolita e orizzonti romani (XVII–XIX secolo)”, in Fiorani, Luigi and Adriano Prosperi (ed.), *Roma, la città del papa. Vita civile e religiosa dal giubileo di Bonifacio VIII al giubileo di papa Wojtyla*, Torino 2000, 477–518.

Pizzorusso, Giovanni, “La congrégation ‘de Propaganda Fide’ à Rome: centre d'accumulation et de production de ‘savoirs missionnaires’ (XVIIe-début XIXe siècle)”, in Castelnau-L'Estoile et al. (eds.), *Missions d'évangélisation et circulation des savoirs XVI–XVIII siècles*, Madrid 2011.

Pizzorusso, Giovanni, “La Sede apostolica tra Chiesa tridentina e Chiesa missionaria: circolazione delle conosenze e giurisdizione pontificia in una prospettiva globale durante l'età moderna”, in *Rechtsgeschichte Legal History* 20 (2012): 382–385.

Pizzorusso, Giovanni, “La congrégation de la Propagande: une instance centrale pour l'élaboration d'un statu juridique du clergé misionaire”, in Arabeyre, Patrick and Brigitte Basdevant-Gaudemet (dir.), *Les clercs et les princes. Doctrines et pratiques de l'autorité ecclésiastique à l'époque moderne*, Paris 2013, 47–60.

Prodi, Paolo, *Il paradigma tridentino. Un'epoca della storia della Chiesa*, Brescia 2019.

Prosperi, Adriano, “Il missionario”, in Villarci, Rosario (ed.), *L'uomo barocco*, Bari 1991, 179–218.,

Raini, Emanuele, “Catechisti e capi laici delle comunità nella storia della chiesa in Cina: prospetto stotico e documenti”, in *Urbaniana University journal* (2019): 97–156.

Rajamanickam, Savarimuthu, “The Goa Conference of 1619”, in *Indian Church History Review* 2:2 (1968): 81–96.

Sanfilippo, Matteo, “Travestimento o tradimento? I missionari cattolici in Cina nei secoli XVI e XVII”, in *Miscellanea di storia delle esplorazioni* 21 (1996): 113–123.

Sanfilippo, Matteo, “L'abito fa il missionario? Scelte di abbigliamento, strategie di adattamento e interventi romani nelle missioni ad haereticos e ad gentes tra XVI e XX secolo”, in *Mélanges de l'École française de Rome, Italie et Méditerranée* 109:2 (1997): 601–620.

Sanfilippo, Matteo, “Adattamento e travestimento: l'abito religioso nelle missioni”, in Rocca, Giancarlo (ed.), *La sostanza dell'effimero. Gli abiti degli ordini religiosi in Occidente*, Rome 2000, 113–118.

Seah, Audrey, "The 1670 Chinese Missal. A Struggle for Indigenization Amidst the Chinese Rites Controversy", in Clark, Anthony E. (ed.), *China's Christianity. From Missionary to Indigenous Church*, Leiden 2017, 86–120.

Schutte, Josef Franz, SJ, *Valignano's Mission Principles for Japan*, St. Louis 1980.

Standaert, Nicolas, "Jesuit Corporate Culture as Shaped by the Chinese", in O'Malley, John et al. (eds.), *The Jesuits. Cultures, Sciences, and the Arts 1540–1773*, Toronto 1999, 352–263.

Standaert, Nicolas (ed.), *Handbook of Christianity in China,* vol. 1, Leiden 2001.

Standaert, Nicolas, *An Illustrated Life of Christ Presented to the Chinese Emperor: The History of Jincheng shuxiang (1640)*, Sankt Augustin 2007.

Standaert, Nicolas, *The Interweaving of Rituals. Funerals in the cultural exchange between China and Europe*, Seattle 2008.

Struve, Lynn A. (ed.), *The Qing Formation in World-Historical Time*, Cambridge (MA) 2004.

Torres Trimállez, Marina, "Misionares franciscanos y redes locales en Oriente: visiones, identidades y estrategias de evangelización", in *Nuevo Mundo Mundos Nuevos* (2018). Online: https://journals.openedition.org/nuevomundo/73095 (last accessed 02.02.2021).

Vareschi, Severini, "Martino Martini S.I. e il decreto del Sant'Ufficio nella Questione dei riti cinesi (1655–56)", in *Archivum Historicum Societatis Iesu* 63 (1994): 209–260.

Wakeman, Frederic Jr., *The Great Enterprise: The Manchu Reconstruction of Imperial Order in Seventeenth-Century China*, 2 vols., Berkeley 1985.

Wilkinson, Endymion Porter, *Chinese History: A New Manual*, Cambridge (MA) 2013.

Zampol, Linda, "Purple Silk and Black Cotton: Francisco Cabral and the Negotiation of Jesuit Attire in Japan (1570–73)", in Maryks, Robert Alejsander, *Exploring Jesuit Distinctiveness: Interdisciplinary Perspectives on Ways of Proceeding Within the Society of Jesus*, Boston 2016, 137–155.

Zorkina, Mariana, "Taoist garments in Rituals and Monastic Life", in *The Silk Road. Papers from the International Conference organized by Confucius Institute in Sofia* (2011): 162–165.

Županov, Ines G. and Pierre-Antoine Fabre (eds.), *The Rites Controversies in the Early Modern World*, Leiden 2018.

CHAPTER 10

Time as Norm: The Ritual Dimension of the Calendar Book and the Translation of Multi-Temporality in Late Imperial China

Fupeng Li

1 Introduction

The Great Voyage not only triggered the geographical connectivity of the Iberian Peninsula to the world, but also brought about a global reconciliation of temporal order through the circulation of Western astronomical knowledge.[1] In the face of intercultural encounters between China and the Iberian empires, two types of normative knowledge were spread by missionaries, but with diametrically opposed outcomes in the Chinese context, thus forming a tale of two cities: Portuguese Macau and Beijing, concerning religion and science, respectively.[2] In contrast to the prohibition of Christianity due to the Rites Controversy over the religiosity of Confucianism,[3] the scientific knowledge of astronomy was incorporated into Chinese traditional ritual practices by the Jesuits serving at the imperial court, in the formulation of calendar books, after the German Jesuit Adam Schall von Bell (1591–1666) was appointed as director of the Imperial Observatory (欽天監) in 1644.

By focusing on the distinct ways of marking time in China and Christianity, this chapter, first, demonstrates the differences between the two genres of knowledge—Jesuit astronomy and traditional Chinese numerology—by revisiting the calendrical controversies during the late Ming and early Qing dynasties so as to redefine the Chinese calendar as a manual of rituals for guiding the actions and decision-making process of daily life. Second, the chapter

1 For a representative study on temporal order in late imperial China, see Struve (ed.), *Time, Temporality, and Imperial Transition*. For the overview of the exchange of scientific knowledge between China and the Jesuits, see Zhang, *Making the New World Their Own*; Deiwiks et al. (eds.), *Europe meets China, China meets Europe*. On studies of mathematics and cartography related to Jesuit astronomy, see Jami, *The Emperor's New Mathematics;* Smith, *Mapping China and Managing the World.*

2 Hsia, "Christianity and Empire", 213, 218.

3 For a comparative study on rites controversies from a global perspective, see Županov and Fabre (eds.), The Rites *Controversies in the Early Modern World.*

further discusses how the Chinese calendar constructs a synthesis of multiple orders—the natural order of unifying the universe/heaven and man, the imperial order of spatial integration, and the life order of ordinary people—by incorporating Chinese or Jesuit knowledge into ritual practice. Finally, in terms of the regime of temporality, this chapter goes on to explore how the encounter between China and the Iberian empires not only shaped the segregation, coexistence, and overlapping of multiple communities of time, depending on various ritual rhythms, but also opened up another perspective on approaching global legal history as a translation process of normative knowledge between multi-temporalities.

2 Between Time and Ritual: Revisiting Calendar Controversies

The Jesuit global mission to China coincided with the dramatic change of Chinese dynasties from the Ming to the Qing, established by the Manchus. Not only did the Jesuits contribute valuable historical records of this transition period from the external perspective, for instance, Martino Martini's *De Bello Tartarico Historia* (Antwerp, 1654), but, within the Chinese Empires, Jesuit astronomer Schall also took advantage of this shifting moment to serve the Imperial Observatory, thus approaching the Chinese imperial power through the making of calendar books.

By revisiting calendar controversies in which the Jesuits were deeply involved, including the calendar reform in the late Ming dynasty (2.1) and the calendar case in the early Qing dynasty (2.2), this section discusses the different genres of knowledge regarding heaven, among Portuguese Jesuits and Chinese literati, so as to provide insight into why the imperial calendar book could be considered part of a ritual manual of normative knowledge based on mantic techniques for guiding human behavior (2.3).

2.1 *Calendar Reform in the Late Ming Dynasty (1629–1644)*

The calendar has always been of supreme political and symbolic significance in traditional China. This was especially true for each newly established dynasty, which had to correct the first day of the lunar month (改正朔), typically by issuing a new calendar in the name of the founding emperor to mark the beginning of a new order after the chaos within the eternal cosmic cycle.[4] This appears to be why the reform of calendar, repeatedly

4 On the religious and political significance of calendars in the Chinese context, see Ge, *An Intellectual History of China*, 61. Jami, *The Emperor's New Mathematics*, 33.

proposed between 1596 and 1611 in the late Ming dynasty, became urgent due to the significant increase in inaccuracies of the Great Concordance Calendar (大統曆), based on the Muslim astronomical system, resulting in a growing discrepancy between the calculations of eclipses and actual observations, as well as the underlying crisis of symbolic legitimacy.[5] It was in the second year (1629) after the final Ming emperor's assumption of the throne that another significant error in predicting a solar eclipse occurred, prompting Emperor Chongzhen (1628–1644) to order the Vice-Minister of Rites, Chinese Christian scholar-official Paul Xu Guangqi (1562–1633), to open the Calendar Bureau (曆局) for a revision of the calendar.[6]

As one of the so-called 'Three Pillars of Chinese Catholicism', Xu invited Jesuits Johannes Schreck (1576–1630), Niccolò Longobardo (1565–1654), and, later, Giacomo Rho (1593–1638), along with Schall to be his European collaborators.[7] From 1629 to 1634, they translated and compiled the works of Nicolaus Copernicus, Johannes Kepler, and Galileo Galilei, etc., archiving a new epistemic body of celestial knowledge, well-known as The Calendrical Treatises of the Chongzhen Reign (崇禎曆書).[8] In this way, not only did the Jesuits complete a paradigm shift through the global circulation of Western astronomical knowledge, but they also formed an epistemic community primarily composed of missionaries and baptized Chinese scholar-officials within the Calendar Bureau, who actively engaged in the calendar reform.

In the face of fierce controversies over the different models based respectively on the official Great Concordance Calendar, the Muslim system, the new Western method, and Wei Wenkui's method, the Chongzhen Emperor insisted on "achieving uniformity" (務求劃一),[9] thereby leaving the absence of a new calendar until the collapse of the Ming dynasty. This impossible demand for synthesis, along with the emperor's extremely pronounced prudence, goes far beyond a purely technical discussion, shedding light on the specificity of knowledge concerning how to understand, systematize, and interpret the celestial phenomena in the Chinese context.

On the one hand, the political and religious facets of the Chinese calendar were repeatedly articulated in the imperial edicts of the Chongzhen Emperor. For instance, in an edict to Xu in 1629, the emphasis was placed on his role as

5 For the historical background of the calendar reform of the Ming dynasty, see Peterson, "Calendar Reform Prior to the Arrival of Missionaries at the Ming Court".

6 On Xu's role in the calendar reform, see Hashimoto, *Hsü Kuang-ch'i and Astronomical Reform*, 7–73; Hashimoto and Jami, "From the Elements to Calendar Reform".

7 For a background on Jesuit astronomers, see Collani, "Astronomy versus Astrology", 423–424.

8 For a media perspective of the Calendrical Treatises, see Chu, "Archiving Knowledge".

9 Xu, *Zhi Li Yuan Qi*, 1602.

a Sage King for his divine sensation of heaven by modeling a timing sequence reverently following the celestial order (朕惟授時欽若，王者所以格天).[10] On the other hand, and of more significant concern to legal historians, was the way in which the normative role of the calendar was treated by different epistemic communities. Chinese scholars generally categorized the Jesuit techniques of calculating, observing, and predicting the heavenly phenomena as a kind of practical learning (实学),[11] which addressed the tangible things of material life but failed to serve a pragmatic use of calendar crucial for the formation and the maintenance of normative orders in everyday life.[12]

However, Chinese Christian Li Tianjing (1579–1659), who succeeded Xu in charge of the Calendar Bureau in 1633, insisted on the Western method without compromise. This was, of course, partly due to the technical inconsistency between different models, but also disclosed a deliberately hidden religious intent,[13] which surfaced in the period of transition from the Ming to the Qing dynasty. In 1645, Schall presented the Calendrical Treatises of the Chongzhen Reign to the new rulers after renaming it the Calendrical Treatises in Accordance with the New Western Methods (西洋新法曆書). Through an archive reconstruction, Jesuits replaced China with the West, as well as old ways with new methods, in an attempt to establish a new orthodoxy beyond the technological dimension.[14] This, however, brought about the externalization and intensification of the calendar controversies which, in turn, led to the calendar case in the Kangxi reign in early Qing China explored below.

2.2 *The Calendar Case in the Early Qing Dynasty (1664–1669)*

In May 1644, Qing troops conquered the city of Beijing, prompting Schall to turn his missionary hopes over to the Qing court. He presented his astronomical predictions, based on the Ptolemaic system, to the Manchu prince and regent Dorgon (1612–1650), and was thus appointed to produce new astronomical instruments and a new calendar for the new rulers. From 1645 until the end of the 18th century, the Qing dynasty relied on the Jesuits,[15] along with

---

10 Xu, *Zhi Li Yuan Qi*, 1547, 1599.

11 On the concept of practical learning, Jami, *The Emperor's New Mathematics*, 31.

12 On the different uses of pragmatic literature and practical literature between legal history and history of science, see Duve, "Pragmatic Normative Literature and the Production of Normative Knowledge", 24–25.

13 The religious purpose of the Jesuits can be gleaned from their letters to the Jesuits in Rome. See Collani, "Astronomy versus Astrology", 446.

14 Chu, "Archiving Knowledge".

15 On the power struggle within the Imperial Observatory, especially with Muslim astronomers, see Huang, "Qingchu Qintianjian zhong ge Minzu Tianwenjia de Quanli Qifu"; Huang, "Qingchu Tianzhujiao yu Huijiao Tianwenjia de Douzheng".

the new Western methods, to produce the officially issued Temporal Model Calendar (時憲曆/書).[16] Its name was taken from the Confucian classic Shangshu, which stated that only the Sage King could model the heaven for marking time (惟聖時憲), highlighting the political intentions of the Manchu regime on reconstructing legitimacy for the vast majority of Han Chinese. During this long-lasting collaboration between Western technology and imperial symbols, there was only one brief interruption, the calendar case in the Kangxi reign (1664–1669),[17] which led to the resurgence of the Ming great concordance calendar (1666–1668) and the Muslim system (1669).[18] It was the most significant anti-Christian case in the early Qing dynasty, which not only attacked Jesuit astronomers, severely hindering the missionary enterprise in China, but also shed light on different types and uses of celestial knowledge.

Concerning the causes that led to this calendar case, scholars have proposed various interpretations, ranging from power struggles within the court to religious rivalries and private jealousies.[19] In any case, however, almost all relevant research must confront two core allegations against Schall. The first charge results from the phrase printed on the title page of the calendars: "Temporal Model Calendar printed by the Imperial Observatory according to the new Western method and promulgated throughout the empire" (欽天監依西洋新法印造時憲曆日頒行天下). The expression of the new Western method was seen by Yang Guangxian (1597–1669) as threatening the legitimacy of the new empire. However, another more serious, accusation by Yang directly blamed the Astronomical Bureau for prescribing an inauspicious time for the burial of Prince Rong, which led to potential misfortune for the imperial family. Emperor Shunzhi and Rong's mother also died of smallpox shortly afterwards.[20]

After a sudden earthquake in Beijing, believed to be a warning from heaven, Schall and three other Jesuits were released from their death sentences. Accordingly, those with a death sentence were committed to house-arrest in Beijing. Other missionaries, however, did not have such fortune. While five Christian

---

16 On the process of orthodoxizing the Western calendar system, see Huang, "Tang Ruowang yu Qingchu Xili zhi Zhengtonghua".

17 For a summary of the calendar case, see Dudink, "Opponents", 513–515.

18 Chunhua, "Lun Qingdai Banfa Hanwen Shixianshu Shimo", 170.

19 For a comprehensive review of this topic, see Jami, "Revisiting the Calendar Case". The use of the Manchu archives is particularly helpful for exploring the details of dynamics of power within the court. See Deiwiks, "The Secret Manchu Documents on the Trial of Jesuit Missionary Johann Adam Schall"; An, "Tang Ruowang An Shimo"; An, "Tang Ruowang zai Hua Chuanjiao zhi De yu Shi".

20 Huang, "Selection of Auspicious Dates and 'Calendar Lawsuit' in the K'ang-his Reign Period", 20–26; Menegon "Yang Guangxian's Opposition to Johann Adam Schall".

astronomers in service to the Imperial Observatory were executed previously, numerous Catholic missionaries residing in the provinces were repatriated to Macau.[21]

The core controversy in this case can be revisited and reinterpreted from a legal-historical perspective. There is a growing body of research that goes beyond the overemphasis on the universality of Western science within the history of science[22] or a focus on the morality in the field of the Christian mission,[23] focusing instead on the relationship between knowledge, rituals, social-political orders, and the techniques of imperial governance in the context of late imperial China. Focusing on hemerology and divination, for example, Huang argues that Schall and his confreres were in fact being judged for the policy of their Church by exerting authority over popular culture, which Chinese rulers saw as undermining the government rituals and popular values that were embodied in the making of calendars.[24] Similarly, Chu argues that the dispute "was perhaps less about who was in the proper position to organize knowledge than about who was in a proper position to organize the social order".[25] From a legal-historical perspective, the controversy was thus also less about conflicting visions about science and more about determining who had the authority to give the norms and values of everyday life.

There is also the potential for convergence between different types of knowledge. According to Catherine Jami's research, Ferdinand Verbiest's demonstration of his advanced astronomical skills in 1669 not only led to the rehabilitation of Jesuit astronomy, but also enabled the Jesuits to return to be the emperor's court, since the Kangxi Emperor was deeply aware that astronomical knowledge was a necessary technique of governance for achieving the integration of the multiple orders of the empire.[26] Therefore, the making and application of the Temporal Model Calendar is a case that should be revisited as it combines and entangles two kinds of pragmatic knowledge that were crucial for the governance of the Qing empire in the early modern world: the practical learning of Western science and the normative density of Chinese rituals.

---

21 Collani, "Astronomy versus Astrology", 452–453. Jami, "Revisiting the Calendar Case", 462.

22 Needham, *Science and Civilisation in China*, 449–450.

23 Dunne, *Generation of Giants*, 221–222, 260.

24 Huang, "Court divination and Christianity", 17–18.

25 Chu, "Scientific Dispute", 31.

26 On the Kangxi Emperor's emphasis on Western learning, see Jami, *The Emperor's New Mathematics*, 239–259.

2.3 *The Calendar as a Manual of Rituals*

The calendar controversies, not least the calendar case of Schall, thus underline the tension between two intellectual traditions performed by various epistemic communities—the doctrines of the Catholic Church for astrology or divination and the traditional numerology handed down by Chinese calendrical experts (疇人)—with regard to the means of constructing social and imperial orders, through the practice of everyday life, especially in the context of the empire formation in the Qing dynasty. Of course, both parties to the dispute had been striving to observe, understand, and, to some extent, adjust their own intellectual and political positions so as to distinguish or accommodate the knowledge of their counterparts, as manifested in the Chinese calendar book. It is therefore necessary to analyze the use of the two kinds of knowledge in the calendar carefully, as well as how they jointly structured the ritual orders within the Qing empire.

From the perspective of the Society of Jesus, Claudia von Collani summarizes this above-mentioned intellectual tension as "Astronomy versus Astrology". Not only do the challenges come from Chinese official scholars, but also from other Jesuits and the Catholic Church based on the established definition of superstition even after the Council of Trent. One of the most representative criticisms, fiercely represented by the treatise of the Portuguese Jesuit Gabriel de Magalhães (1610–1677), argued that Schall had departed from the Christian faith by virtue of the superstition and divination contained in the calendar book for which he was responsible.[27] While Schall absolves himself from blame by distinguishing between two different elements of calendar books, Verbiest attributes what is called superstition by Magalhães to certain kinds of folk customs originating in Chinese traditions, which serves to place the public welfare in harmony with the natural order, providing a template from which to select auspicious dates for important events of daily life, such as when to marry, conclude a contract, or carry out a ritual.[28] Similarly, when facing the Chinese official scholars, Schall and Verbiest, in their book Enlightening the Bewildered Regarding the Commentary in the Civil Calendar (民曆鋪註解惑), clarify that the annotations on the calendar about good fortune and bad luck were not based on the new Western calendar system, but were merely the preservation of Chinese customs that contributed to the moralization of the

27 Collani, "Astronomy versus Astrology", 431–432.

28 Collani, "Astronomy versus Astrology", 445–447. For Ferdinand Verbiest's criticisms of Chinese mantic arts, see Chu, "Against Prognostication".

people by gradually internalizing a grand imperial order in every state, in every family, and in the body of every subject (化天下為一國，化一國為一家，化一家為一身).[29]

By reframing the genealogy of Chouren, Chinese traditional astronomical experts in the Qing dynasty, Chu Pingyi refers to these two kinds of knowledge as "Numerology and Calendrical Learning". Although the epistemic community of Chouren were aware of Yang Guangxian's technical inferiority in astronomy compared to the Jesuits, they still insisted that the mantic function, based on Chinese numerological tradition, was more critical to the use of an almanac for daily decision-making.[30] Thus, in addition to the ongoing potential for technical competition, the Jesuits, in collaboration with their Chinese partners in the Imperial Observatory, produced a hybrid form of calendar by employing three major Chinese mantic arts: astrology, geomancy, and genethlialogy.[31]

Despite endorsing a way of making calendars that reconciled these two kinds of knowledge, imperial rulers were still apprehensive about the divergent views on the traditional mantic arts. In other words, having unified the method of calculating time, they also wanted to unify the way of marking time. Accordingly, with regard to Chinese numerology, the Qing court published three books as the official standard: the Almanac for Day Selection (選擇通書, 1683) and the Imperially Approved Investigations into Stars and the Calendar (欽定星曆考原, 1713) in the Kangxi reign and the Imperially Approved Treatise on Harmonizing the Times and Distinguishing the Directions (御制協紀辨方書, 1741) in the Qianlong reign.[32] In the preface to the last book, Emperor Qianlong explicitly stated that the key to good and bad fortune did not lie in the mantic technique, but rather existed between "respect and disrespect", thereby shaping a centralized authority of imperial governance through the use of calendars to arrange the daily lives of the people.

In short, the Jesuits, the Chinese Chouren, and the new rulers of the new empire all clearly perceived the conflict between these two types of knowledge and epistemic communities. However, whether for religious or political purposes, they all acknowledged, to some extent, the validity of each other's knowledge, especially by connecting Chinese mantic arts to normative concepts, such as custom, ritual, and order. It is in this sense that the calendar book could be conceived as a container of normative knowledge that not only served the spatial governance of an ever-expanding empire, but also

29 Schall von Bell, *Minli Puzhu Jiehuo*, 8.
30 Chu, "Numerology and Calendrical Learning", 483.
31 Chu, "Numerology and Calendrical Learning", 488.
32 Smith, "The Legacy of Daybooks in Late Imperial and Modern China", 337.

functioned as a pragmatic manual of rituals that instructed the ways different roles within the Qing empire were to be performed.

3 The Calendar and Its Multiple Orders

As a manual of rituals, the Qing calendar book acted as a hub of knowledge that oriented behaviors and decision-making. In every official almanac, Jesuit astronomy and traditional Chinese numerology were integrated into the Chinese rituals, creating multiple overlapping orders of different layers, ranging from imperial governance to daily life. The first layer was a cosmogony of unifying and harmonizing the universe/heaven and man (天人合一), symbolized primarily in the Diagram of the Position of the Sprits for the year (年神方位之图), which very distinctly shows the principles of how to arrange life in the coming year based on the operation of the natural order (3.1). The second layer was the secular order, "All under Heaven" (天下), simply understood as the imperial order, embodied mainly in a system of issuing the official calendar of 24 seasonal markers of time (节气) to the locals inside and outside the Qing empire, following Jesuit cartography and astronomy (3.2). Finally, there was a layer of life order, consisting of various individual or collective behaviors mainly in the form of daily predictions of good or bad fortune throughout the year (3.3).

3.1 *The Natural Order of Heaven and Man*

A quasi-religious relationship between the universe/heaven and human beings underpins the fundamental assumptions of Chinese self-conception. Briefly stated, both Confucian and Taoist Chinese philosophical thought generally holds that human beings share the same nature as the universe/heaven. Thus, the secular life should conform to the natural rhythm, a sexagenary cycle formed by the movement of heaven and earth, which serves as the ritual foundation for making a Chinese calendar.[33] This section focuses on the Diagram of the Position of the Spirits for the Year (年神方位之图) and other markers for recording significant dates typically attached before or after the death days of emperors and empresses, birthdays of the gods, and celestial signs for good or bad fortune.[34]

33 See Smith, "The Chinese Sexagenary Cycle and the Ritual Origins of the Calendar", especially 22–23, 25, 26.

34 For a material perspective on the relationship between text and image in Chinese calendars, see Arrault, "Les calendriers chinois: l'image du temps, le temps dans les images".

Due to the limitations of the subject matter, a comprehensive explanation of the details of this diagram of the year cannot be offered,[35] however it can be emphasized that it represents an earthly mirroring of celestial operations by placing the course of time into a certain kind of spatial guidance. For example, among the 24 directional units of the external circle, the four most prominent corners represent four directions of the sprits of the year, namely, Memorialist (奏書) standing for honor, Erudite (博士) for fair, Strongman (力士) for foul, and Silkworm (蠶室) for disaster. Therefore, according to the Chinese tradition shown in the calendar, if someone plans to lay a foundation or build a house, they should by all means choose an auspicious position or avoid an inauspicious direction. To this, the almanac provides more detailed guidance, but need not be mentioned further here.

Another group of guidelines for daily life are printed in red, either at the beginning of the book or attached to the diagram of the year. The content varies slightly depending on the version, but almost always includes three types, in order of dates of emperors' and empresses' deaths, birthdays of the gods, and celestial signs of good or bad fortune.[36] The combination of these three types of information is well worth discussing, not least for understanding how Qing rulers reinforced their legitimacy by incorporating themselves into a collective memorial system. First, the anniversary of the death of the supreme rulers was ritualized by making it a national day of commemoration, with a strict prohibition on pleasure seeking, celebrating weddings and assuming office. Second, the sacralization of the secular order was achieved through the juxtaposition of the imperial rulers with the birthdays of the gods, primarily consisting of the major Buddhist and Taoist festivals. Finally, both the death days and the birthdays are rationalized again by being integrated into the system of celestial signs. This placed the Qing emperors as communicators between heaven and their subjects, thereby securing a proper order.

3.2 *Representing a Unified Imperial Order*

With the use of Jesuit cartographic and astronomical knowledge, the Qing calendars included a timetable for sunrise and sunset composed of 24 seasonal markers pertaining to different localities, from the capital Beijing, local

---

35 For a more detailed explanation of this diagram, see Smith, "The Legacy of Daybooks in Late Imperial and Modern China", 349–351; Smith, *Chinese Almanacs*, 10–13.

36 According to the Qing calendars collected in Harvard-Yenching Institute, this juxtaposition had already begun during the Qianlong reign. But by the Guangxu reign in the late Qing, the calendars retained only the national jubilees, while leaving out the birthdays of the gods. See Harvard-Yenching Library Collection, T7190.8/6350 (1790, 1793, 1883).

provinces, and frontier regions to the tributary states, such as Korea and Ryukyu/Okinawa. This exemplifies how Western "practical learning" could be used in the service of Qing imperial governance. For instance, an imperial project of mapping the Atlas of the Chinese Empire (康熙皇輿全覽圖) from 1708 to 1718 was mainly carried out by French Jesuit Jean-Baptiste Régis (?–1738) and Joachim Bouvet (1656–1730), with the support of the Kangxi Emperor.[37] Moreover, through a system of issuing the official calendar that extended from the Forbidden City to the imperial peripheries and the tributary states, the Qing calendars have consistently translated Jesuit knowledge into ritual practices, thus presenting the ongoing process of integration of the multinational empire of Qing, the relationship between imperial center and peripheries, and even the evolution of the tributary system as the territory of the Qing empire continued to expand.

The gradual increase in the number of regions covered in the official calendars is consistent with the expansion of the Qing Empire, primarily taking place during the Kangxi and Qianlong reigns. The restitution of the Jesuit Verbiest as head of the Astronomical Bureau ended the calendar case (1664–1669) and marked the beginning of the Kangxi Emperor's personal rule over the empire. After settling the internal revolt of the three feudatories (1673–1681), the Kangxi Emperor succeeded in conquering the Mongols. Accordingly, by imperial decree, 24 new regions (mainly of the Khalkha Mongol of the north) were added to the timetable of the official calendar in 1692/1693. Another 15 new regions (mainly including the Dzungar Khanate of the west and Hami) were included in the calendar in 1713. In addition to continuing to consolidate the northwest, the Qianlong Emperor suppressed the Jinchuan Hill Peoples in the southwest, thus listing 13 new regions in 1777.[38]

Within the tribute system, Chosŏn/Korea was already listed in the Qing calendar of 1645; Annam/Vietnam and the Ryukyu were included in the official calendars in 1789 and 1809 respectively due to their request for the issuing of the official calendars. However, other vassal states like Siam, Burma, Sulu, and Lan Xang were never mentioned in the calendars. In short, interior provinces, newly conquered frontiers, and tribute states were all arranged according to their longitudes on the map from Shengjing downwards (各省序次盛京而下悉依地圖地之經度所列), Shengjing being the birthplace of the Manchu Qing, so as to construct the image of a unified imperial territorial order. Moreover,

37 See Ribeiro and O'Malley (eds.), *Jesuit Mapmaking in China*.

38 For the official record of the addition of regions in the Great Qing Collected Statutes (大清会典), as well as its representation in the calendars, see Chunhua, "Lun Qingdai Banxingli 'Shikebiao' nei de Diming Tedian", 449–457.

as shown in the official calendar of 1883,[39] Vietnam and the Guizhou province and Korea and the Jilin province were juxtaposed in the same space, in a way that blurred or dissolved the spatial distinction between the inside and the outside of the empire. It was intended to leave people with a general impression of all-under-heaven (天下), along with the widespread practice of rituals for issuing the official calendar within the empire.

Every year, on the first day of October, the ceremony of issuing the official calendar was solemnly conducted outside the Meridian Gate of the Forbidden City. Participants were limited to the emperor, princes, nobles, and high officials in the capital. The promulgated calendars were available in Manchu, Mongolian, and Chinese languages.[40] The officially issued calendars would then be distributed throughout the empire, reaching the counties as the lowest administrative bodies. Additionally, the Board for the Administration of Outlying Regions (理藩院) forwarded the calendars to the Mongolian feudatories while the Ministry of Rites (禮部) transmitted them to the tributary states.[41] For instance, according to the archives of the Nanbu county (南部縣) of Sichuan province, a county would be assigned 2,000 copies of the civil calendar, which would then be further handed out by the local official in charge of rites to local communities of practice in religious, social, and economic fields, such as monks, Taoists, yin-yang masters/geomancers, medical practitioners, clan associations (會總), and so on,[42] so as to guide ordinary people's behavior and decision-making in their daily lives.

3.3 *A Life Order of Shaping Individual and Collective Behavior*

As noted above, Jesuit astronomers explicitly denied that the daily annotations in the calendar were of their own making, instead ascribing them to traditional Chinese customs and rituals for the sake of public welfare—a soft form of governance that internalized the imperial order into individual behavior through daily decision-making. According to the Imperially Approved Treatise on Harmonizing the Times and Distinguishing the Directions, there were 67 items, 30 for imperial use and 37 for civilian use, basically covering all essential aspects of the daily life of the emperor or the ordinary person. These matters constituted a ritualized setting of daily life in a traditionally calculated manner concerning the motion of celestial bodies.

---

39 Harvard-Yenching Library Collection, T7190.8/6350 (1883).

40 Chunhua, "Lun Qingdai Banfa Hanwen Shixianshu Shimo", 171.

41 For a more detailed analysis of the relationship between calendars and the territory of the Qing dynasty, see Wang, "Calendar Books of the Qing Dynasty and the Formation of a Modern, Unified and Multinational China", 198–203.

42 Archives of Nanbu County, no. 17–00833–4.

As for the 37 civilian matters, they not only set out the critical affairs that every ordinary person may encounter during the year, but also formed a cycle of life, from ancestor-worship to burial, including the rituals for different stages of life (schooling, coming of age, and marriage), the care of one's body and security (bathing, healing, and traveling), the maintenance of real estate (laying foundations, construction, and renovation), and commercial and agricultural practices (contracting, trading, and planting). These and other rituals are illustrated in Table 10.1, below.[43] Similarly, the additional 30 matters for imperial use mainly focused on the requirements of being a good emperor. These included, for instance, internal selection and appointment (appointing ministers, recruiting the virtuous, and elevating the righteous), diligent governance and caring for the people (compassion for the weak, correcting injustices, and delaying punishment), and external military affairs (pacifying borders, selecting generals and training soldiers, and sending out troops).[44]

In this sense, the calendar transformed the year's life, either of the emperor or the ordinary person, into time-based rituals. Moreover, through a cyclical view of time and history, the practice/performance of major matters was strung together into a ritualized life for individuals. Of course, the rules in the calendar should not be rigidly applied to imagine people's daily behaviors, for the practice of living always reflects, to a great or lesser extent, discrepancies with norms. For instance, in a calendar of 1873 used by a village doctor, he clearly recorded going out to visit a patient on days when travel was not advisable. Of course, major country ceremonies still strictly followed specific dates, such as the ritual performance for sending away the god of plague. It is clear that ordinary people were always inclined to compare, control, and modify their behaviors in concrete settings and to pursue the favorable and avoid the unfavorable. Undoubtedly, traditional Chinese calendars, as a kind of ritual manual or index,[45] set up the most noteworthy aspects of this underlying scenario of Chinese life with several limiting premises.

4 Regimes of Temporality in Global Legal History

Based on the above analysis of the multiple orders embodied in the official Chinese calendars, this concluding section explores further how the calendar understood as a manual of rituals, shaped the communities of time during China's encounter with Christianity (4.1). In addition, through the lens of

43 *Yuzhi Xieji Bianfang Shu*, vol. 11, 2b–3b.
44 *Yuzhi Xieji Bianfang Shu*, vol. 11, 1b–2b.
45 Smith, *Chinese Almanacs*, 2.

TABLE 10.1 Thirty-seven Matters about Civil Life according to the Imperially Approved Treatise on Harmonizing the Times and Distinguishing the Directions

No.	English	Chinese
01	Offering sacrifices to gods/ancestors	祭祀
02	Presenting a memorial to gods/emperor	上表章
03	Taking up an official position	上官
04	Starting school	入学
05	Coming-of-age ceremony	冠带
06	Engagement	結婚姻
07	Visiting friends and relatives	會親友
08	Wedding	嫁娶
09	Increasing family members	進人口
10	Traveling	出行
11	Moving to a new house	遷徙
12	Installing a new bed	安牀
13	Bathing	沐浴
14	Barbering	剃頭
15	Healing	療病
16	Tailoring clothes	裁衣
17	Construction or laying foundations	修造動土
18	Installing pillars or beams	豎柱上梁
19	Installing the spinning machine	經絡
20	Opening for business	開市
21	Signing contracts	立券
22	Trading	交易
23	Receiving property	納財
24	Renovating the house	修置產室
25	Digging canals or wells	開渠穿井
26	Installing a stone mill	安碓磑
27	Cleaning the house	掃屋舍
28	Leveling roads	平治道途
29	Demolition of the house or fence	破屋壞垣
30	Lumbering	伐木
31	Exterminating pests	捕捉
32	Hunting	畋獵
33	Planting	栽種
34	Grazing and breeding	牧養

TABLE 10.1 Thirty-seven Matters about Civil Life according to the Imperially Approved Treatise on Harmonizing the Times and Distinguishing the Directions (*cont.*)

No.	English	Chinese
35	Building graves	破土
36	Burial	安葬
37	Reburial	啟攢

regimes of temporality, an alternative understanding of global legal history is proposed as a process of translating normative knowledge between multi-temporalities (4.2).

4.1 *Temporality, Normativity, and Community of Time*

As for the temporality embodied in the Chinese calendar, it is necessary to clarify primarily that the concept of time discussed here is understood as a "social construct",[46] resulting from the systematic marking, ordering, and sorting of different life moments by various agents in the religious, social, and economic spheres. It is in this sense that Richard Smith argues, with great insight, that Chinese "almanacs serve as a convenient index of Chinese hopes and fears, aesthetic preferences, ethical concerns, and forms of symbolic expression, as well as a measure of continuity and change".[47] As the most basic "liturgical texts" of the Chinese,[48] mantic arts that were so disputed and reproached by the missionaries can also be seen as the ordering instruments of the ritual cycle, guaranteeing the predictability of nature, imperial, and life orders, as well as harmonizing the multiple temporalities of past, present, and future.

In performing the ritual cycle, temporality endows rituals with normative qualities. Like the study of the relationship between law and time, the normativity of ritual could be formulated in two ways. The first is approaching "law as temporality",[49] in which time is interpreted as the cultural background or container of social actions. In other words, time provides rituals with a vast,

46 For a fundamental piece on social time, see Sorokin and Merton, "Social Time". For a study on the calendar from time's social dimension, see Rüpke, *The Roman Calendar from Numa to Constantine*, 1–5.

47 Smith, "The Educational Role of Chinese Almanacs", 16.

48 Menegon, "The 'Teachings of the Lord of Heaven' in Fujian", 184–185.

49 For more on this approach, see Mawani, "Law as Temporality" and Mawani, "The Times of Law".

but somewhat distant, conception of justice, through which social time is gradually materialized into a social structure.[50] The second approach is that of “law’s temporality”, which examines the “coproduction of law and temporal norms”.[51] As a normative procedural system, rituals seem to be better suited than the law to inquire into the normative production of time. Specifically, through temporal rhythms, each ritual has a fixed date, a particular program, and organizes the year as a ritual cycle with the other rituals. Moreover, when considering Chinese rituals as a form of temporal norms, pointing to everyday life, it appears that the Chinese calendars can be viewed as a pragmatic manual that, though undoubtedly different from the manuals of moral theology widely applied in colonial Spanish and Portuguese America,[52] can be seen as an important Chinese genre of pragmatic literature for understanding the ways in which Christianity was assimilated into different places during the process of Iberian imperial expansion.

The calendar functions as a medium of cultural synchronization that contributes to ordering the individual and the empire into a community of time. Such a medium is both technical and normative, providing an interface for achieving some degree of systemization, standardization, and modularity.[53] Jörg Rüpke’s study of the fasti, the ritual ordering of activities, festivities, and commemorations which followed the Roman calendar, argues that the political and judicial structure of time illustrates that religious practice was understood beyond the distinction of secularization and sacralization.[54] Similarly, the Chinese calendar, through the ritualization of daily actions, weaves individuals into different organizational bodies. This shaped multiple temporal communities, as well as temporal divisions, that could not subsume oversimplified categories of rationality or superstition, but should be taken seriously as normative knowledge.

4.2 *Global Legal History as Translation of Multi-Temporality*

In terms of the regime of temporality, the encounter between Chinese and Christian conceptions of time shaped the segregation, coexistence, and overlapping of multiple communities of times. By selecting, ordering, and sorting

50 For a study of justice in linear time, see Greenhouse, “Just in Time”.

51 For more on related research topics, see Beynon-Jones and Grabham (eds.), *Law and Time*, Introduction; Grabham et al., “Exploring Relationships Between Time, Law and Social Ordering”.

52 See Duve and Danweth (eds.), *Knowledge of the Pragmatici*, and especially Duve, “Pragmatic Normative Literature”, for a general overview of this research field.

53 Hoof, “Calendar”.

54 Rüpke, “Rationalizing Religious Practices”.

different temporalities; the ritual matters, however, both allow different religious communities to be kept apart as much as they present the possibility of such temporal overlapping, along with increasing encounters from local to global.

In using the term "regime", taken from François Hartog, we do not attempt to explore the more static "temporal structure of a certain culture",[55] but rather "a set of practices prescribed or adopted to regulate the rhythms of a society"[56] and, more importantly, how social constructs, such as identity, community, and order, are produced and reproduced through the making and marking of time.

On one hand, time was divided between local religious community practices and Chinese imperial precepts. Eugenio Menegon's detailed analysis of Christian community in Fuan, a remote locale of southern China, for example, vividly illustrates how Christians and people following traditional Confucian ethics positioned themselves in "two worlds" and "two times" in the 17th century, through the superposing of a new temporal rhythm according to the Roman liturgical calendar of celebrations, introduced by the Spanish Dominican friars, onto the Chinese lunisolar calendar. A similar pattern of temporal divisions was also apparent in the Muslim and Jewish communities in late imperial China.[57]

On the other hand, missionary activity helped harmonize time beyond local communities, both toward the Chinese imperial space as well as the global sphere of influence of the Iberian empires. The Jesuits in the service of the imperial court not only promoted the temporal unification of various regions within the Qing empire, structuring a hierarchy of time between the Qing empire and the surrounding tributary states, but also contributed to the formation of an underlying sense of global time, especially in the context of the global Iberian empires in the early modern period.

It is in this sense that the themes of global legal history, such as circulation, interaction, and connection, etc., have undoubtedly accelerated and exacerbated confrontations and reconfigurations of various communities of time, thus creating an asynchronous coexistence of multiple temporalities. In this way, global legal history could be perceived as a translation process of normative knowledge between multi-temporalities.

55 Hartog, *Régimes d'historicité*, 26.

56 Jordheim, "Multiple Times", 509. Please also see the special forum of "Multiple Temporalities" in the same issue.

57 Menegon, "The 'Teachings of the Lord of Heaven' in Fujia". Menegon also discusses a similar pattern of temporal divisions of the Muslim and Jewish communities in late imperial China.

Bibliography

Manuscripts

Nanbu Xian Dangan 南部縣檔案, no. 17–00833–4.

Printed Sources

Li, Guandi 李光地, *Qingding Xingli Kaoyuan* 欽定星曆考原, 1713.

Qintianjian 欽天監, *Da Qing Guangxu Jiu Nian Suici Guiwei Shixianshu* 大清光緒九年歲次癸未時憲書, Harvard-Yenching Library Collection, T7190.8/6350, 1883.

Qintianjian 欽天監, *Da Qing Qianlong Wushiba Nian Suici Guichou Shixianshu* 大清乾隆五十八年歲次癸丑時憲書, Cambridge 1793: Harvard-Yenching Library Collection.

Qintianjian 欽天監, *Da Qing Qianlong Wushiwu Nian Suici Gengxu Shixianshu* 大清乾隆五十五年歲次庚戌時憲書, Cambridge (MA) 1790: Harvard-Yenching Library Collection.

Qintianjian 欽天監, *Xuanze Tongshu* 選擇通書, 1683.

Schall von Bell, Johann Adam, *Minli Puzhu Jiehuo* 民曆鋪註解惑, 1662.

Yunlu 允祿, *Yuzhi Xieji Bianfang Shu* 御制協紀辨方書, 1741.

Literature

An Shuangcheng 安雙成, "Tang Ruowang An Shimo" 湯若望案始末, in Lishi, Dangan 歷史檔案 3 (1992): 79–87.

An Shuangcheng 安雙成, "Tang Ruowang zai Hua Chuanjiao zhi De yu Shi" 湯若望在華傳教之得與失, in Lishi, Dangan 歷史檔案 3 (1996): 72–82.

Arrault, Alain, "Les calendriers chinois: l'image du temps, le temps dans les images", in *Arts Asiatiques* 66 (2011): 11–32.

Beynon-Jones, Sian, and Emily Grabham (eds.), *Law and Time*, London 2018.

Chu, Pingyi, "Against Prognostication: Ferdinand Verbiest's Criticisms of Chinese Mantic Arts", in Lackner, Michael (ed.), *Coping with the Future*, Leiden 2017, 433–450.

Chu, Pingyi, "Archiving Knowledge: A Life History of the Calendrical Treatises of the Chongzhen Reign (Chongzhen lishu)", in *Extrême-Orient, Extrême-Occident* 6 (2007): 159–184.

Chu, Pingyi, "Numerology and Calendrical Learning: The Stories of Yang Guangxian and Liu Xiangkui", in *The Korean Journal of the History of Science* 37, no. 2 (2015): 479–497.

Chu, Pingyi, "Scientific Dispute in the Imperial Court: The 1664 Calendar Case", in *Chinese Science* 14 (1997): 7–34.

Chunhua 春花, "Lun Qingdai Banfa Hanwen Shixianshu Shimo" 论清代颁发汉文时宪书始末, in *Manxue Luncong* 满学论丛 6 (2016): 170–188.

Chunhua 春花, "Lun Qingdai Banxingli 'Shikebiao' nei de Diming Tedian" 论清代颁行历"时刻表"内的地名特点, in *Mingiqng Luncong* 明清论丛 15 (2015): 447–458.

Chunhua 春花, "Lun Qingdai Manwen Shixianshu Neirong Banben ji Banfa" 论清代满文时宪书内容版本及颁发, in *Journal of Jilin Normal University* (Humanities & Social Science Edition), 1 (2018): 72–77.

Collani, Claudia von. "Astronomy versus Astrology. Johann Adam Schall von Bell and his 'superstitious' Chinese Calendar", in *Archivum Historicum Societatis Iesu* 82, no. 164 (2013): 421–457.

Deiwiks, Shu-Jyuan, "The Secret Manchu Documents on the Trial of Jesuit Missionary Johann Adam Schall (1592–1666) before the Supreme Court of Beijing" in *Monumenta Serica* 51 (2003): 641–648.

Deiwiks, Shu-Jyuan, Bernhard Führer, Therese Geulen, and Alois Osterwalder (eds.), *Europe meets China, China meets Europe: The Beginnings of European-Chinese Scientific Exchange in the 17th Century*, Bonn 2014.

Dudink, Ad., "Opponents", in Standaert, Nicolas (ed.), *Handbook of Christianity in China*, vol. 1, Leiden 2001, 503–533.

Dunne, George, *Generation of Giants: The Story of the Jesuits in China in the Last Decades of the Ming Dynasty*, Notre Dame (USA) 1962.

Duve, Thomas, "Pragmatic Normative Literature and the Production of Normative Knowledge in the Early Modern Iberian Empires (16th–17th Centuries)", in Duve, Thomas and Otto Danwerth (eds.), *Knowledge of the Pragmatici. Legal and Moral Theological Literature and the Formation of Early Modern Ibero-America*, Frankfurt am Main 2020.

Duve, Thomas, Otto Danwerth (eds.), *Knowledge of the Pragmatici: Legal and Moral Theological Literature and the Formation of Early Modern Ibero-America*, Frankfurt am Main 2020.

Ge, Zhaoguang, *An Intellectual History of China, Knowledge, Thought, and Belief before the Seventh Century* CE, vol. 1, Leiden 2014.

Grabham, Emily, Emma Cunliffe, Stacy Douglas, Sarah Keenan, Renisa Mawani, and Amade M'charek, "Exploring Relationships Between Time, Law and Social Ordering: A Curated Conversation" in *feminists@law* 8:2 (2018).

Greenhouse, Carol J., "Just in Time: Temporality and the Cultural Legitimation of Law", in *The Yale Law Journal* 98, no. 8 (1989): 1631–1651.

Hartog, François, *Régimes d'historicité. Présentisme et expériences*, Paris 2014.

Hashimoto, Keizo and Catherine Jami, "From the Elements to Calendar Reform: Xu Guangqi's Shaping of Scientific Knowledge" in Jami, Catherine, Peter Engelfriet, and Gregory Blue (eds.), *Statecraft and Intellectual Renewal in Late Ming China: The Cross-Cultural Synthesis of Xu Guangqi (1562–1633)*, Leiden 2001, 263–278.

Hashimoto, Keizo, *Hsü Kuang-ch'i and Astronomical Reform: The Process of the Chinese Acceptance of Western Astronomy 1629–1639*, Osaka 1988.

Hoof, Florian, "Calendar", in Beyes, Timon, Robin Holt, and Claus Pias (eds.), *The Oxford Handbook of Media, Technology, and Organization Studies*, Oxford 2019, 54–67.

Hsia, R. Po-chia, "Christianity and Empire: The Catholic Mission in Late Imperial China", in *Studies in Church History* 54 (2018): 208–224.

Huang Yi-Long 黄一農, "Qingchu Qintianjian zhong ge Minzu Tianwenjia de Quanli Qifu" 清初欽天監中各民族天文家的權力起伏, in *Xin Shixue* 新史學 2, no. 2 (1991): 75–108.

Huang Yi-Long 黄一農, "Qingchu Tianzhujiao yu Huijiao Tianwenjia de Douzheng" 清初天主教與回教天文家的鬥爭, in *Jiuzhou Xuekan* 九州學刊 5.3 (1993): 47–69.

Huang Yi-Long 黄一農, "Kangxichao sheji 'Liyu' de Tianzhujiao Zhongwen Zhushu Kao" 康熙朝涉及"曆獄"的天主教中文著述考, in *Shumu Jikan* 書目季刊 25.1 (1991): 12–27.

Huang, Yi-Long, "Court Divination and Christianity in the K'ang-hsi Era", in *Chinese Science* 10 (1991): 1–20.

Huang Yi-Long 黄一農, "Tang Ruowang yu Qingchu Xili zhi Zhengtonghua" 湯若望與清初西曆之正統化, in Wu, Jiali 嘉丽吳 and Ye Fengsa 葉鴻灑 (eds.), Xinbian Zhongguo Kejishi 新編中國科技史, vol. 2, Taipei 1990, 465–490.

Huang Yi-Long 黄一農, "Selection of Auspicious Dates and 'Calendar Lawsuit' in the K'ang-his Reign Period" 擇日之爭與"康熙曆獄", in *Qinghua Xuebao* 清華學報 21, no. 2 (1991): 1–36.

Jami, Catherine, "Revisiting the Calendar Case (1664–1669): Science, Religion, and Politics in Early Qing Beijing", in *The Korean Journal of the History of Science* 37, no. 2 (2015): 459–477.

Jami, Catherine, *The Emperor's New Mathematics: Western Learning and Imperial Authority During the Kangxi Reign (1662–1722)*, Oxford 2012.

Jordheim, Helge, "Introduction: Multiple times and the work of synchronization", in *History and Theory* 53, no. 4 (2014): 498–518.

Mawani, Renisa, "Law as temporality: Colonial politics and Indian settlers", in *UC Irvine Law Review* 4 (2014): 65–95.

Mawani, Renisa, "The Times of Law", in *Law & Social Inquiry* 40, no. 1 (2015): 253–263.

Menegon, Eugenio, "The 'Teachings of the Lord of Heaven' in Fujian Between Two Worlds and Two Times", in Struve, Lynn A. (ed.), *Time, Temporality, and Imperial Transition: East Asia from Ming to Qing*, Honolulu 2005, 197–243.

Menegon, Eugenio, "Yang Guangxian's Opposition to Johann Adam Schall: Christianity and Western Science in His Work Budeyi", in Malek, Roman (ed.), *Western Learning and Christianity in China: The Contribution and Impact of Johann Adam Schall von Bell, SJ (1592–1666)*, 2 vols., Nettetal 1998, vol. 1, 311–338.

Needham, Joseph, *Science and Civilisation in China. Mathematics and the Sciences of the Heavens and the Earth,* vol. 3, Cambridge 1959.

Peterson, Willard J., "Calendar Reform Prior to the Arrival of Missionaries at the Ming Court", in *Ming Studies* 21, no. 1 (1986): 43–61.

Ribeiro, Roberto M., and John. W. O'Malley (eds.), *Jesuit Mapmaking in China: D'Anville's Nouvelle* [*sic*] *Atlas de la Chine (1737)*, Philadelphia 2014.

Rüpke, Jörg, "Rationalizing Religious Practices: The Pontifical Calendar and the Law", in Tellegen-Couperus, Olga (ed.), *Law and Religion in the Roman Republic*, Leiden 2012, 85–106.

Rüpke, Jörg, *The Roman Calendar from Numa to Constantine: Time, History, and the Fasti*, New Jersey 2011.

Smith, Adam, "The Chinese Sexagenary Cycle and the Ritual Origins of the Calendar", in Steele, John M. (ed.), *Calendars and Years II: Astronomy and Time in the Ancient and Medieval World*, Oxford 2010.

Smith, Richard J., "The Educational Role of Chinese Almanacs: Past, present, and future", ERIC Document Reproduction Service No. ED368603, 1992, 16–20.

Smith, Richard, "A Note on Qing Dynasty Calendars", in *Late Imperial China* 9, no. 1 (1988): 123–145.

Smith, Richard, "The Legacy of Daybooks in Late Imperial and Modern China", in Harper, Donald and Marc Kalinowski (eds.), *Books of Fate and Popular Culture in Early China*, Leiden 2017, 336–372.

Smith, Richard J., *Chinese Almanacs*, Oxford 1992.

Smith, Richard J., *Mapping China and Managing the World: Culture, Cartography and Cosmology in Late Imperial Times*, London 2013.

Sorokin, Pitirim A., Robert K. Merton, "Social Time: A Methodological and Functional Analysis", in *American Journal of Sociology* 42, no. 5 (1937): 615–629.

Struve, Lynn A. (ed.), *Time, Temporality, and Imperial Transition: East Asia from Ming to Qing*, Honolulu 2005.

Wang Yuanchong 王元崇, "Calendar Books of the Qing Dynasty and the Formation of a Modern, Unified and Multinational China" 时宪书与中国现代统一多民族国家的形成, in *Social Science in China* 中国社会科学 (5) 2018, 185–203.

Xu Guanqi 徐光启, *Zhi Li Yuan Qi* 治历缘起, Shanghai 2009.

Zhang, Qiong, *Making the New World Their Own: Chinese Encounters with Jesuit Science in the Age of Discovery*, Leiden 2015.

Županov, Ines G., Pierre Antoine Fabre (eds.), *The Rites Controversies in the Early Modern World*, Leiden 2018.

Index

www.ingramcontent.com/pod-product-compliance
Ingram Content Group UK Ltd.
Pitfield, Milton Keynes, MK11 3LW, UK
UKHW022208051026
15624UKWH00001B/64

9 789004 472822